THEATRE BLOGGING

Megan Vaughan is a writer and researcher, currently based in Colchester, Essex. Widely regarded as one of the most innovative and influential bloggers to have covered London theatre, her blog, *Synonyms For Churlish*, was active from 2008 until 2016. Now a PhD researcher at Royal Holloway, University of London, she is completing a thesis on amateur theatre criticism and the internet.

THEATRE BLOGGING

THE EMERGENCE OF A CRITICAL CULTURE

methuen | drama
LONDON · NEW YORK · OXFORD · NEW DELHI · SYDNEY

METHUEN DRAMA
Bloomsbury Publishing Plc
50 Bedford Square, London, WC1B 3DP, UK
1385 Broadway, New York, NY 10018, USA

BLOOMSBURY, METHUEN DRAMA and the Methuen Drama logo are trademarks of
Bloomsbury Publishing Plc

First published in Great Britain 2020

Copyright © Megan Vaughan, 2020

Megan Vaughan has asserted her right under the Copyright, Designs and Patents Act, 1988,
to be identified as author of this work.

For legal purposes the Acknowledgements on pp. 255–6 constitute an extension of this copyright page.

Cover design: Charlotte Daniels
Cover image: *Three Kingdoms* at the Lyric, Hammersmith (© Tristram Kenton)

All rights reserved. No part of this publication may be reproduced or transmitted in any form or by any means, electronic or mechanical, including photocopying, recording, or any information storage or retrieval system, without prior permission in writing from the publishers.

Bloomsbury Publishing Plc does not have any control over, or responsibility for, any third-party websites referred to or in this book. All internet addresses given in this book were correct at the time of going to press. The author and publisher regret any inconvenience caused if addresses have changed or sites have ceased to exist, but can accept no responsibility for any such changes.

A catalogue record for this book is available from the British Library.

Library of Congress Cataloging-in-Publication Data
Names: Vaughan, Megan, author.
Title: Theatre blogging : the emergence of a critical culture / Megan Vaughan.
Other titles: Theater blogging
Description: New York : Metheun Drama, 2019. | Includes bibliographical references and index. | Summary: "Megan Vaughan contextualises the key debates and writings of more than forty bloggers with current research, and brings past and present practitioners into conversation with one another. The work of prominent and influential early adopters such as Encore Theatre Magazine and Chris Goode in London; George Hunka and Isaac Butler in New York; Jill Dolan at Princeton University and Alison Croggon in Melbourne is featured and considered alongside those who followed them. Vaughan presents arguments that have impacted on both arts journalism and the theatre industry. The book also includes: activist bloggers writing about fringe working conditions and diverse casting, explorations of new dramaturgical practices that have been developed and piloted by bloggers a rigorous assessment of the institutional changes – in theatre, in academia, and for newspapers – which have been attributed to bloggers since their emergence. Vaughan concludes by posing two key questions: to what extent have theatre bloggers established a new critical culture? Has the potential of the form been realised"—Provided by publisher.
Identifiers: LCCN 2019012535 | ISBN 9781350068810 (paperback) |
ISBN 9781350068841 (pdf) | ISBN 9781350068834 (epub)
Subjects: LCSH: Theater—Blogs. | Dramatic criticism. | Theater and social media.
Classification: LCC PN1707 .V38 2019 | DDC 808.2/—dc23
LC record available at https://lccn.loc.gov/2019012535

ISBN:	HB:	978-1-3500-6882-7
	PB:	978-1-3500-6881-0
	ePDF:	978-1-3500-6884-1
	eBook:	978-1-3500-6883-4

Typeset by RefineCatch Limited, Bungay, Suffolk
Printed and bound in Great Britain

To find out more about our authors and books visit www.bloomsbury.com
and sign up for our newsletters.

CONTENTS

List of Illustrations	viii
Preface	ix

Part One History and Practice — 1

1 Introduction — 3
2 Theatre Blogging Since 2003 – a History — 14
3 Theatre Blogging in Practice – a WhatsApp Dialogue — 45
4 Theatre Blogging Under Threat — 71

Part Two Selected Posts — 79

5 **A Note on the Texts** — 81

6 **Theatremaking and Authorship**
  Laura Axelrod: The Fuzzy Factor — 85
  Mac Rogers: Director vs. Playwright – Intro — 86
  Mac Rogers: Director vs. Playwright Part 1 — 86
  Isaac Butler: Directors and Writers (perhaps part one) — 88
  Laura Axelrod: Would You Like Ketchup With Your Worms? — 90
  Deborah Pearson: Imagine people took me seriously — 92
  Chris Goode: What's It All About Albee? — 93
  Alison Croggon: The Writer, The Theatre, The Play — 101
  Adam Szymkowicz: a hammer — 105
  Matthew Freeman: Rules for the Writing of Plays — 105
  Chris Goode: Opening the house — 107
  Alex Swift: [. . . a short thing on work . . .] — 110

7 **Anger and Dissent**
  'Theatre Worker', *Encore*: Bye Bye Sir Trevor Nunn — 112
  'Theatre Worker', *Encore*: Don't Cry for Him — 113
  Frances d'Ath: It's All About The Money — 115
  Andy Field: Michael Billington Being Rather Silly — 116
  Matt Trueman: Fussing Over Foss — 117
  Corinne Furness: I could have screamed but instead I wrote this — 120
  Don Hall: Why Isherwood Should Just Blog Instead — 122
  Eve Allin: A Response, From a young and unpaid critic (or theatre blogger – up to you) — 123
  Ava Wong Davies: Thoughts on The Writer and this DANG INDUSTRY — 125

Contents

8 Reviews and Reviewing

Alison Croggon: Forumitis	129
Andy Field: Attempts on Her Life at the National	131
David Eldridge: A major event in our theatre	132
Andrew and Phil, *West End Whingers*: Review – Love Never Dies, Adelphi Theatre	134
Maddy Costa: how you do this is up to you	138
Andrew Haydon: Embedded	144
Daniel Bye: Embedded Criticism: some Arguments, an Offer and a Dare	150
Catherine Love: Translunar Paradise & Critical Distance	155
Dan Hutton: The Strange Undoing of Prudencia Hart	157
Jill Dolan: Criticism Redux Redux Redux	160
Maddy Costa: Got life, got music, got theatre	162
Gareth K Vile: Behaviour: Lippy and Western Society	164
Megan Vaughan: Application for review	165
Kate Wyver: Revolt. She Said. Revolt Again.	168
James Varney: revew: Walter Meierjohann – Uncle Vanya	171

9 Representation and Visibility

Jill Dolan: On Women Directors	175
Mike Lew: "a fiercely provocative, insightful mediation on race"	178
Jill Dolan: Wondering about The Fiddler On The Roof at Arena Stage	180
Vinay Patel: Why I Wrote True Brits	185
Erin Quill: In the Depths of British Theatrical Racism @the_printroom	188
Daniel York Loh: Feature: Scenes From A Yellowface Execution	195
Melissa Hillman: The "Playwright's Intent" and the Dangers of the "Purist"	196
Harry R McDonald: Road @ Royal Court: Somehow a Somehow	198

10 On *My Name Is Rachel Corrie*

Garrett Eisler: Censorship Comes To Downtown	202
Garrett Eisler: NYTW	202
Isaac Butler: It Just Gets Worse and Worse	204
Matthew Freeman: The saga of Rachel Corrie	205
Isaac Butler: Response to Walter Kabak	207
George Hunka: Infamous Words	209
Ben Ellis: Ideas and text, the body and Rachel Corrie	211

11 On *Three Kingdoms*

Andrew Haydon: Three Kingdoms – Lyric Hammersmith	219
Catherine Love: Three Kingdoms: New Ways of Seeing, Experiencing, Expressing	224
Dan Rebellato: Three Kingdoms	229
Matt Trueman: Review: Three Kingdoms, Lyric Hammersmith	233
Megan Vaughan: An incitement to smash some fucking shit up	237

Sarah Punshon: on walking out of Three Kingdoms	238
Maddy Costa: fanning the bonfire	240
Catherine Love: Revisiting Three Kingdoms	246

Biographies	253
Acknowledgements	255
References	257
Index	263

ILLUSTRATIONS

1 Screenshot from *Edinburgh Furinge Reviews* by Eve Nicol, *c.* 2013. Courtesy Eve Nicol. — 39
2 *Paint Never Dries* image created by Phil Whinger, *c.* 2010. Courtesy West End Whingers. — 137
3 *Behaviour* diagram created by Gareth K Vile, *c.* 2015. Courtesy Gareth K Vile. Internal images used: Western Society images (3 on the left-hand side) by David Baltzer, *c.* 2015. Courtesy David Baltzer/bildbuehne.de. Lippy image top-right (silhouette) by Jeremy Abrahams, *c.* 2014. Courtesy Jeremy Abrahams. Lippy images bottom-right (×2) by José Miguel Jiménez, *c.* 2014. Courtesy José Miguel Jiménez. — 164
4 'Review C' image adapted by Megan Vaughan from a photograph by Keith Pattison, *c.* 2015. Hugh Skinner, Kate O'Flynn, and Sian Thomas in rehearsal for The Trial. Original photograph courtesy Keith Pattison. — 168
5 Image showing Han Dynasty regions and warlords, shared on a Creative Commons licence by user Seasoninthesun, *c.* 2017. Image title removed from bottom right. Original: https://commons.wikimedia.org/wiki/File:End_of_Han_Dynasty_Warlords.png. — 190
6 Meme image created by Erin Quill, *c.* 2016. Courtesy Erin Quill. — 194

PREFACE

Hiya. I'm Meg. Thanks for picking up this book. I'm dead proud of it. 😊

I pitched the idea to Bloomsbury back in early 2017, shortly after I had started my PhD (on amateur theatre criticism) and was really beginning to worry about the legacy of the blogosphere. So many posts were gone, links broken, the contributions of key bloggers forgotten. This book is really for them, a way to celebrate their achievements and safeguard their ideas for the future.

The whole thing is a bit illogical though, isn't it? I mean compiling *online* writings into a *printed* book. I realize that's what it takes for certain parts of the academy and theatre industry to pay attention to what is happening online, but still, I am conscious of how counterintuitive it feels. For starters, the links aren't clickable, and none of the animated GIFs work. 💔

There's also something I find a little uncomfortable in having one person's interpretation of events given precedence over others'. One of the most wonderful things about the internet is the fact that so many feelings and opinions sit side by side, freely navigable by anyone with a phone or computer. It has made me extremely conscious of my own decision-making here, not just in the posts that I've chosen, but in my interpretation of the events that surround them. One piece of feedback I've consistently received in the writing process is that I have a tendency to undermine myself, often by being at pains to explain that mine is not the only perspective on these issues. Lots of those equivocations and ambiguities have been removed as I honed each successive draft, but it still feels crucial to use this opening statement – my welcome address to you all **royal wave** – as a place to acknowledge my position and recognize my own fallibility. While I've worked hard on this research for the best part of two years, the idea that the publication of a book elevates me to a singular position of authority on the subject feels kinda distasteful. Others may choose to preserve and celebrate entirely different writings, from entirely different theatre scenes, different countries, different languages. I have tried to counter the blind spots that emerge from my personal history and inherent privileges (white, cis, able-bodied, heterosexual, middle-class), but there's no doubt I developed this interest in the first place because I was already aligned with the most prominent voices within the theatre blogosphere, its contributors speaking to theatre cultures I am broadly familiar with, in a language I understand.

It might be useful for you to know that I was a theatre blogger too, starting on-and-off from about 2008, then winding down again from 2016. I used my blog as a platform to dissect the work I was seeing, argue about the structures in which it was made, and make grand plans for my future. In doing so, I joined a community of writers which both enriched my life – socially, creatively, intellectually – and changed the course of it. My relationship to my subject, therefore, is intimate and personal, emerging from real, lived experiences and reflecting close friendships. It might be that some of you feel a similar connection to the materials here (**cue secret blogger handshake**), but I hope it will be just as interesting to those who want to read about contemporary theatre more broadly. The issues and concerns you'll find discussed here are, I think, relevant to anyone navigating this dynamic, fast-moving, troubled and beloved industry.

Love,
Meg xxx

PART ONE
HISTORY AND PRACTICE

CHAPTER 1
INTRODUCTION

I'll probably be accused of hyperbole for this opener, but... fuck it.

deep breath

The theatre blogosphere has made a more significant and far-reaching contribution to theatre – its practices as well as its profile – than anything else in the twenty-first century.

I mean, it's probably not even that controversial a statement. Since its popular emergence in the late 1990s, the internet has revolutionized many industries. We order our groceries online, do business on our phones, and FaceTime our families on the other side of the world. We catch up with our friends in WhatsApp group chats and find new people to date on Tinder. We stream our telly now. Even my Dad, a man baffled by most technological developments since about 1982, lurks on the forums of his local fishing club, admiring photos of barbel and volunteering for riverbank clean-up sessions. Throughout the global north, we have integrated the digital realm into our meatspace lives, and theatre, even as an artform which depends upon presence, liveness and communion, has adjusted too.

Over the course of the last fifteen years, fuelled by technological change and inspired by writers covering music and politics amongst many other subjects, theatre bloggers have expanded and democratized the discourse around theatre more than any other group, professional or otherwise. Their interrogation of form, commitment to transparency and resistance to a paternalistic and parochial mainstream press has had a tangible impact on the way theatre is made and talked about today. Key industry issues – from the role of the playwright to the ethics of reviewing, from the nature of censorship to the politics of casting – have been debated and advanced by theatre bloggers, almost all of whom were writing without pay, simply because it mattered to them. For all its bruised egos and damaged reputations, theatre blogging is a fundamentally benevolent activity, undertaken through a genuine love and concern for this brilliant, exhausting art form.

But I am not here to proclaim blogging the saviour of theatre. With its high prices, limited audience capacities, and concentration in a handful of wealthy, Western cities, it is very possible that theatre cannot be saved. And any partial redemption will surely require a sea change in the way work is commissioned, funded and cast, plus mass resignations in its major venues and drama schools. The inherent exclusivity of theatre cannot be easily countered by the kind of large-scale digital reproduction and distribution which has altered other forms of art and media. While organizations like the UK's National Theatre or New York's Metropolitan Opera have additionally commodified their shows by broadcasting them live to cinemas, the essential irreproducibility of live performance prevents any real structural transformation. Theatre is fleeting, and it relies on physical proximity.

It does, however, have a chance of wider impact through the publicly disseminated recollections of its audiences and makers. But this means that every time – every *single* time – we hear or read about a show we didn't personally see, our understanding of it is mediated by the person who did. When we read a review in the *Guardian* or the *New York Times*, we are having our impressions steered by those writers. When we only learn about theatremaking processes in the classroom, or from the memoirs of old white men on their retirement, a traditional way of doing things, and a traditional *route into* doing those things, is reinforced. When those with the power to communicate what theatre is, how it is made, what it means, how it makes us *feel*, all look and sound the same, and all share the same educational background and life experiences, then theatre stagnates. It is starved of new ideas, its audiences either get bored or get old and die, and it sacrifices its relevance to the numerous other (cheaper) art forms and cultural activities that do actually reflect people's lives.

Many of the theatre bloggers celebrated in this book come from traditionally privileged racial and socio-economic backgrounds, but, increasingly, many do not. The emergence of the theatre blogosphere in 2003 established the conditions in which new voices and perspectives could be heard, outmoded practices could be questioned, and fresh ideas and initiatives championed. Its moments of greatest impact, which are chronicled in Chapter 2, demonstrated the potential of independent commentary to hold the theatre industry to account, often revealing the shortcomings of a declining mainstream press in the process.

Before we can start exploring that history however, it's important that we understand what we mean when we use the term 'blog'. It's a word that has been used to describe a huge variety of websites, posts and projects, and, as our online habits shift, its meaning requires constant reassessment. To define the blog requires an understanding of blogging's history, including the technological, economic, and ideological changes that have impacted its development; so that is where we begin.

The earliest blogosphere

Blogs were, of course, initially called 'weblogs'. This term was coined by one of the form's earliest practitioners, Jorn Barger, back in December 1997, a time when you still needed to know how to code in order to put anything online at all. The following year, another blogger, Jesse James Garrett, made a list of all the 'sites like his' he found as he surfed the burgeoning internet. There were twenty-three, and it reportedly took less than fifteen minutes to read all of them, every day (Garrett, n.d.). These first bloggers were all tech enthusiasts whose weblogs were link-driven; they pointed to the most interesting sites and webpages they found, supplemented with their own commentary and opinion.[1]

Garrett sent his list to another blogger, Cam Barrett, who, in turn, added it to his main homepage. He used a sidebar so it would remain visible and accessible to visitors even as he continued to post other content. Before long, this practice of sidebar blog recommendations (which would come to be called the 'blog roll') caught on; it was in Peter Merholz's sidebar list, in May 1999, that he playfully announced his decision to switch to a new abbreviation: 'For What It's Worth, I've decided to pronounce the word "weblog" as wee'-blog. Or "blog" for short' (Merholz 2002).

By autumn 1999 this term 'blog' was firmly established, initially thanks to its swift addition to *Jargon Scout*, a popular catalogue of emergent web terminology, but also because a new piece

---

[1] The first blogger is now generally recognized to be Justin Hall, who started updating his homepage back in 1994. It was even called *Links.net*.

Introduction

of online software adopted the term in its name. On 23 August 1999, Pyra Labs launched Blogger. It wasn't the first free tool created to help coding novices self-publish online (Pitas, Open Diary, and a handful of others preceded it), but it quickly became the most popular, and, thanks to the simplicity of its user interface, was soon credited with instigating a small but significant shift in the nature of blogging.

In September 2000, Rebecca Blood compared Blogger's back-end with that of *MetaFilter*, a community blog site which was launched only a month earlier. At the time, *MetaFilter* required users to complete three prescriptive fields in order to post an item to the feed there: URL, title and comment. It was built in the mould of those original link-driven weblogs, which were literally *filtering* the web for interesting things to share with readers.[2] Blogger, on the other hand, offered just one box for, well, everything, with each post automatically stamped with the time and date, and ordered chronologically, most recent first. These apparently minor technological choices on the part of Blogger's designers, explained Blood, meant that before long, 'increasing numbers of weblogs eschewed [the] focus on the web-at-large in favour of a sort of short-form journal' (Blood 2000). We started to use the internet as a place to publish details of our lives, relationships and where we positioned ourselves politically. The sharing of interesting links still took place, but were now just as likely to direct readers to the blogs of our friends, or the websites of our favourite bands, than to random sites we had stumbled upon. We revealed much more of ourselves and our personal lives, and as readership grew, new friendships and relationships were forged, and new creative projects born. Bloggers started to realize that their thoughts, opinions, and ideas – however commonplace – mattered to others.

The definition of a blog changed too. In January 1999, Cam Barrett (he who had posted the very first blog roll) had initially defined it as 'a small web site, usually maintained by one person that is updated on a regular basis and has a high concentration of repeat visitors' (Barrett 1999), but after Blogger's release, definitions of the form were all prioritizing reverse chronology.[3] By 2003, Jill Walker Rettberg considered subject-specific blogs to be significant enough to address in her definition, considering the blogosphere as a 'continuum from confessional, online diaries to logs tracking specific topics or activities' (Walker Rettberg, 2003). The era of the political blog was born, predominantly in the United States, where bloggers would analyse, fact-check and comment upon news reports on the Clinton Presidency, the September 11 attacks, and military actions in Afghanistan and Iraq. This was blogging as 'citizen journalism'. Meanwhile, 'MP3 blogs' such as *Said The Gramophone*, *Stereogum* or *Fluxblog*, shared new music, often from unsigned bands. This was blogging as advocacy, with its roots in local scenes or pre-existing fandoms.

By 2005, the blogosphere was booming, its original 23-strong list having expanded into multiple communities and niches. At the same time, analysis of the blogosphere had become entangled with debates on 'Web 2.0', the supposed second phase of the internet's development. Web 2.0 was almost synonymous with blogging to begin with; it was often used to describe the new technologies (like Blogger) which were enabling much larger numbers of people to contribute to the internet. More accurately though, it denoted a shift in the internet's relationship to commerce.

---

[2] It still does that today. I have a lot of love for *MetaFilter*.
[3] Notably Rebecca Blood's from 2000 and Jill Walker Rettberg's from 2003, both cited in this chapter.

Theatre Blogging

The web as platform

After a period of high investment in the digital economy at the end of the 1990s, the 'dotcom bubble' had burst in 2001, wiping millions of dollars in value from the earliest web-based businesses. In the years immediately following that crash, many technologists became preoccupied with analysing what had gone wrong. Before long, some started to attribute the failure to a change in the way people participated in online space.

The first computer networks, bulletin board systems and email newsgroups which had emerged in the mid-1980s had been both accessible (provided you had the required kit) and participatory (provided you knew how to use it). These 'virtual communities', to use a phrase coined by Howard Rheingold,[4] were largely built upon existing offline networks of media fans, amateur technologists and countercultural activists; it was their shared interests and exchange of knowledge which kept those networks buzzing. However, once Tim Berners-Lee's 'World Wide Web' (one of several systems now facilitated by the internet) began to expand, it became clear that a growing number of websites offered no meaningful interaction for users beyond reading and clicking the odd link. Lively forums and chat rooms existed, of course, but beyond those, the internet was becoming little but a collection of static reading materials. Web businesses were advertising their services online as if their sites were just virtual billboards, while software companies relied on users purchasing regular, expensive updates. The corporate world simply did not know how to monetize the web.

Web 2.0 offered a new way of conceptualizing the internet *as a platform*, prioritizing the exchange of ideas and information. It was no longer about browsers and software and banner ads, but about providing a place for people to congregate, engage and 'share'. Make no mistake, this was all still in the service of capitalist economics; the habits and preferences of the humble web user, as we searched for holiday recommendations, browsed Ebay or watched ~~porn~~ funny cat videos, became an asset in the race to cultivate a database of users which could themselves be monetized. Ultimately, it laid the foundations for corporations to exploit our private lives by targeting us with ads and selling our data, but for a time at least, it refocused corporate attention away from *stuff*, and onto the quality and depth of *user experience*.

The blogosphere was championed by Silicon Valley researchers as the quintessential Web 2.0 practice. When Tim O'Reilly detailed the emergent concept of the web as a platform in September 2005, he defined a blog somewhat flippantly – 'just a personal home page in diary format' (O'Reilly 2005) – but went on to acknowledge bloggers as, collectively, the most influential internet users of the new Web 2.0 era. Citing the importance of RSS technology (which automatically pushed new blog posts to subscribed readers) and the advent of the permalink (which allowed bloggers to reference and respond to their peers' specific posts),

---

[4] Technology journalist Howard Rheingold published the highly influential book *The Virtual Community* in 1993. In it, he used a schema from Marc Smith (then a research student at the University of California) to present the 'collective goods' of an online social community according to three categories: social network capital, knowledge capital and communion. Rheingold explained how these elements were found through the global WELL community: social network capital meant he knew people in cities he had never been to, knowledge capital helped him find quick and easy answers to questions, and communion equated to the kind of emotional support he gave and received when times were challenging (Rheingold 1994). In simpler terms, we might think of these categories as contacts, information, and friendship.

O'Reilly recognized that bloggers, in the years before search-engine optimization became its own parasitic industry, had 'a disproportionate role in the shaping of search engine results'. The links that bloggers were using to direct readers to the other blogs they rated (or didn't), and the things they liked (or hated), were literally reshaping and reordering the internet. The blogosphere had become a powerful amplifier.

A moving target

Through its constant repetition and analysis in the discourse concerning Web 2.0, the definition of a blog was slowly solidifying. By the mid-2000s, most scholars and commentators agreed that they could be identified by the frequency and chronology of posts, the informal style of writing, their use of links, and the bloggers' focus on their own lives and interests. Most people knew what a blog was – at the very least, they knew one when they saw one – and they had become ubiquitous enough that starting a new blog was certainly no guarantee that it would be read. Web technologies and practices were also moving *fast*. With the launch of YouTube in 2005, vloggers arrived, and when Twitter followed in 2006, so did the term 'micro-blog'. Media and scholarly attentions moved away from blogging and onto their new obsessions, 'transmedia' and 'social networking', and bloggers themselves began to get tired of constantly evaluating their own behaviours every five minutes.[5] Blogging was still huge, but the task of definition was no longer a real concern for academics or practitioners.

Contemporary definitions, therefore, are somewhat confused. The *Oxford English Dictionary* still retains the early focus on frequency, chronology and 'personal observations', while *Merriam-Webster* is broader, highlighting the multimedia nature of today's blogs but also adding a second, more problematic, classification: 'a regular feature appearing as part of an online publication that typically relates to a particular topic and consists of articles and personal commentary by one or more authors'. By responding to the practice of hosting a blog as a discrete section within a broader website, this definition collapses the previously fundamental distinction between the voice of the independent blogger and the editorial hierarchy of the mainstream press, which often chases the credibility of internet culture while ghettoizing certain voices and perspectives in the margins of their digital spaces.

Perhaps, then, the best thing to do is to forget trying to define the blog, and instead investigate the act of *blogging* as a set of practices. This is what Alexander Halavais advocates in his 2017 overview of blogging's impact on the web. By doing this, he suggests, we foreground the intentions and motivations of the blogger, positioning the blog itself as 'a *vehicle* for personal self-expression, for sharing ideas, but for doing so in a space that remains personalized' (Halavais 2013: 112, italics my own). Just as the commercial imperative behind Web 2.0 moved the internet from a collection of artefacts to a platform for engagement, to ask what blogging *can do*, rather than what a blog *is*, is to situate it as an extension of its author, in dialogue with

---

[5] In a 2006 paper from researcher danah boyd, she quotes from an interview with 'six-year veteran' Carl, who told her he had 'given up on definitional questions and gone for "... tautologies. Like blogging is what we do when we say, "We're blogging." ... It's a blog because a blogger's doing it. It's a blog because it's caught up in the practice of blogging. It's a blog because it's made on blog tools. It's a blog because it's made up out of blog parts. It's a blog because bloggers are engaged with it, and everyone points at it and says, "It's a blog!"' (boyd, d. 2006).

a community of people who might encounter it and act upon it in numerous different ways: reading, sharing, commenting, responding, raving about what they find or spitting on the floor. That necessarily moves it away from the mediated space of professional journalism, in which a commissioning policy and house style negate the autonomy of writers, even when they are nominally contributing to a 'blog'.

Attempting a working definition

What, then, of the *theatre* blog? How do we define that? *Can* we define that?

I'll be honest with you, few have bothered. The limited scholarship on the theatre blogosphere generally assumes readers understand what a blog is to begin with, despite the progressively muddied divisions between blogs, volunteer-run review sites and the professional publications which now situate themselves online. The closest thing we've got is probably the taxonomy of Australian theatre blog posts created by Neal Harvey, Helena Grehan and Joanne Tompkins in 2010. They hoped to provide a framework for other academics whose research would benefit from engaging with the theatre blogosphere, so analysed a selection of posts to try to determine what was being discussed there, and how. They categorized them either as reviews, discussions of the role of the blogger-as-critic, blogosphere round-ups, autobiographical industry perspectives, or 'extra-curricular' comment. While this was no doubt useful on publication, it quickly became outdated (when was the last time you saw a blogosphere round-up post?) and overlooked the multiple ways in which different categories of post merged and became tangled. The internet simply moves too quickly for lasting classification.

Nevertheless, I have attempted my own definition of the theatre blog. It feels important to offer my take on it at the start of this book, for no other reason than to help you understand where I'm coming from for the rest of it, even if it is an ultimately futile task. The internet is going to be different again in five minutes' time. But, in an attempt at longevity, I've ploughed on, basing my definition not on what a theatre blog *is*, but what it *isn't*. There are five factors here. The first two are primarily here to question prevalent understandings of the blog format, and as such should not be used to exclude any blog or blogger, but the final three I am much stricter about. These are my theatre blog dealbreakers.

1. It isn't necessarily frequent.
As is only natural for a book which presents a historical overview of a practice, I have ignored any traditional onus on frequent posts. Not only is this required frequency rarely quantified by those who suggest it is essential, I do not assign significance according to hours worked, and do not believe that a blog is retrospectively delegitimized once its author has stopped updating it. You will find the work of both the erratic and the erstwhile in these pages.

2. It isn't necessarily chronological.
I have also ignored any past stipulation for posts organized in a certain way. While the mechanisms of most major web publishing tools do still default to reverse-chronological order, the prevalence of tagging, which allows us to add searchable keywords to blog posts, increasingly facilitates browsing by theme and subject. Indeed, my own blog is now hosted on Medium, which – aside from a front page of ten recent posts – presents my work to users of that site according to popularity, not date of publication.

3. It doesn't rely on the acquiescence of gatekeepers.
For no other reason than a profound disappointment in mainstream arts journalism and an instinctive distaste for authority, I do not consider online writing that was commissioned, edited, or uploaded by another person with editorial responsibilities or admin rights to be part of the same geneology of self-publishing as the work of the autonomous bloggers who first began sharing their lives and favourite links with us in the earliest days of the internet. This does not rule out multi-authored sites, or those who ask others to proofread their work before posting, but it does exclude those contributors who are subject to a hierarchical system of content approval.

4. It isn't formal in style.
Theatre bloggers are not academics, or if they are, they are not writing like academics. Their posts are informal and personalized (even where anonymous) and offer readers an opportunity to get to know them over time. I'm sure many will disagree, but online writing which obfuscates the author's personality and politics in favour of a tradition of 'objective' formality is, in my opinion, not blogging.

5. It isn't a marketing tool.
While many theatre bloggers are also makers, and those who have achieved a certain profile with their blogging will certainly have sold a few more tickets as a result, the theatre bloggers I am interested in are not doing it in order to publicize their latest show or boost the profile of their company. They may be theorising their work or developing their creative manifestos, but they post in a personal capacity, not a professional one.

For the purposes of this book, therefore, we can define theatre bloggers as those who self-publish personal, informal posts, primarily about theatre, in an online space they control. While location and income have no bearing on this definition, theatre bloggers often live in or near major theatre cities, yet have the potential to reach a large and unknown public, and they are typically unpaid, although might attract small-scale advertisers and reader contributions.

This does leave some collateral damage. It excludes some highly-regarded magazine sites which have done much to democratize the discourse around theatre yet maintain commissioning processes and editorial controls. It excludes some excellent writing shared on the websites of venues and theatre companies in order to open up their practices and encourage new audiences to experience their work. And it excludes the work of prolific and dedicated theatre bloggers whenever they are commissioned for other publications. It is not my intention to undervalue the importance of theatre commentary which occupies these positions, simply that, here, in this book, I am interested in exploring the contribution of the unedited, the informal, the amateur and the autonomous.

Theatre bloggers as antagonists?

Over the last couple of years, I've come to think of theatre bloggers as part of a movement of 'outsider' criticism, something which would also include vloggers, podcasters and zinemakers, everything from *Hamilton* fan art to your mum's Facebook updates. The term 'outsider' has obvious connotations with outsider art – those works by self-taught artists who have few interactions with mainstream or commercial galleries – and while the multiplicitous ways in which we can now publish theatre criticism are often a little more fluid and entangled that a strict insider/outsider dichotomy would imply,[6] coverage of theatre bloggers' activities (in the press and in academia) has persistently presented them in terms of a binary opposition with mainstream arts journalism.[7]

In a 2007 article for the *Guardian*'s website, Michael Billington paid brief lip-service to bloggers before explaining why they were so much worse than professional journalists: blogs contained too much 'pre-emptive guesswork', had no 'definable structure', and were aligned with the 'relentless din' of PR and promotion (Billington 2007b). Mark Shenton, formerly of *The Stage* and *Sunday Express*, has repeatedly compared the blogosphere, where there is 'a lot of noise to filter', to the mainstream press, which has 'the authority of those actually appointed (rather than self-appointed)' (Shenton 2015). More recently, in an article for the technology-focused *Wired* magazine, Rowland Manthorpe presented a vision of theatre criticism in which impartiality has 'devolved' into 'crowdsourced comments', 'creative misreadings' and the 'toxic politics of "fandoms"' (Manthorpe 2018). These are just three of many, many protectionist thinkpieces which, over the last fifteen years or more, have painted bloggers as significantly less reliable and trustworthy than those who get paid and edited, regardless of how they secured those positions in the first place.

I want to take a couple of paragraphs to be really clear on where I stand on the impact of theatre bloggers on the livelihoods of mainstream critics and arts journalists. While articles like those from Billington, Shenton and Manthorpe can be self-fulfilling prophesies, causing significant anger and leading to counterattacks from the blogosphere, theatre criticism is *not* disappearing from the mainstream press because of bloggers. Theatre criticism is disappearing from the mainstream press because when the newspapers, who had initially put all their content online for free, could see clear and transparent data on which parts of their sites people were reading, they realized that their theatre coverage had never been all that appealing to begin with. Theatre is, after all, a niche interest with significant financial, geographic and cultural barriers to attendance.

Supplied with the knowledge that the majority of online readers aren't actually all that bothered about theatre, editors were only too happy to reduce the amount they spent on theatre coverage in favour of more popular content, where adjacent ad space was worth more, and so the critic redundancies began.[8] As time went on, and a larger and larger percentage of readers were visiting the papers' websites rather than buying their printed editions, the effect of this

---

[6] In journalism, many professional publications regularly recruit writers from the blogosphere, and many ex-critics are now writing blogs (the *New York Stage Review* site in New York was set up by a group of professional theatre critics who found their opportunities to get paid were disappearing, while Libby Purves' *Theatrecat* blog was established when she lost her job as lead critic for *The Times*). Meanwhile, when we think of the theatre industry, many bloggers might be more accurately considered *insiders* than outsiders, bringing creative expertise and knowledge of industry structures to their posts.

[7] The idea of a singular, dominant mainstream has been usefully problematized by academics researching subcultural capital, such as Sarah Thornton on clubbers and ravers in the early 1990s (Thornton 1995), and Mark Jancovich on cult movie fans a decade later (Jancovich 2002).

[8] Most recently, in May 2018, *Time Out Chicago* let Kris Vire go, just a few months after the *Chicago Sun-Times* had made Hedy Weiss redundant, leaving only one full-time print theatre critic covering that whole city (Chris Jones at the *Chicago Tribune*). By the time you read this, another handful will probably have gone.

was compounded, and it shows no sign of relenting, even as internet economics shift again. Paywalls and membership schemes can help shore up the less popular parts of a website, but they still rely on readers believing that newspaper journalism is worth their cash, and there have been times when even regular theatregoers have been left disappointed by newspaper criticism. In Andrew Haydon's whistlestop history of online theatre criticism in England, he suggested that theatre blogging attracted attention because, at the time of its emergence, 'the combined personal tastes of *all* the first stringers no longer represented a significant proportion of the theatre-going public' (Haydon 2016: 143).

The idea that theatre bloggers are constantly training their crosshairs on professional journalists has also been perpetuated in academic scholarship. In the previously-mentioned taxonomy developed by Harvey, Grehan and Tompkins, they highlighted moments of discord and division over harmony and consensus, giving the impression that the theatre blogosphere is driven by anger and abuse.[9] Meanwhile, in his historical overview of the critical reception of Shakespeare, Paul Prescott describes 'the remorseless march of the new model army of citizen critics engaged in an apparently asymmetrical civil war with the erstwhile aristocrats of print' (Prescott 2013: 175), which I think you'll agree is probably a bit much, even if he is being semi-ironic.

There are, of course, academics and researchers who have taken a more measured tone. Bud Coleman's history of musical theatre criticism acknowledges blogs and online review sites as fruitful alternatives to shrinking newspaper coverage (Coleman 2017), while Karen Fricker, who also works as a critic for the *Toronto Star*, has argued that bloggers are actually helping to mitigate the impact that a loss of professional criticism has had on theatre artists. She uses the language and theory of Marx to make it clear that the emergence of online criticism (in all its forms, not just on blogs as I have defined them) 'is a superstructural response to changes at the base level of the means of production in contemporary media. Those who write for free', she says, 'are responding to a changing media landscape, not causing that change ...' (Fricker 2015: 49). She goes on to explain that the resistance of some mainstream critics to blogging is simply 'because the rise of blogging is evidence that their power is not what it used to be' (ibid. 50).

The typical lead theatre critic at the turn of the twenty-first century was old, white, male and privately-educated. In the UK, most had studied English at either Oxford or Cambridge. In the US, most had graduated from prestigious Ivy League and liberal arts colleges. They were writing from a position of cultural dominance, where their tastes and opinions were assumed to be universal and objective. This assumption was supported by the fact that so much of the theatre produced in Western countries was being made, and watched, by those with similar levels of cultural privilege, but it was also perpetuated by historically dominant modes of art appreciation, in which dispassionate, 'distanced' judgement was prized above other modes of engagement and response. One of the key impacts of the theatre blogosphere has been the disruption of this critical distance, and with it, the gradual cutting of criticism's ties to its snobbish and patriarchal past. I'd suggest that if theatre bloggers can be accused of antagonism, it is towards these attitudes and approaches, not as some blanket attempt to punch up at the mainstream press for the sake of their own profile.

---

[9] Of the eight blog posts or conversations analysed for this paper, five constitute disagreement, conflict or harassment.

Theatre Blogging

The joy of oral text

Almost all of the scholarship on theatre blogging published since Harvey, Grehan and Tompkins' taxonomy has been primarily concerned with criticism. This is likely a result of several corresponding factors: the disproportionate reduction in reviews over news stories or interviews in the mainstream press; the series of high-profile critic redundancies; the relatively large number of blog review posts in comparison to those which take other forms; the central role still played by criticism in the visibility of theatre and the success of its makers; and the archival significance of the review to scholars of theatre. The landscape of theatre criticism has been changing at an unprecedented speed, sending numerous ripples out over much wider theatre communities, with several academics attempting to articulate and analyse these changes.

Using examples from immersive theatre and performative 'happenings' alongside work in traditional auditoriums, Eleanor Collins has explained how the impossibility of uniform, reproducible audience experience and the unpredictability of a person's response proves 'the essential incompatibility of the current model of professional reviewing with the multifaceted, necessarily subjective experience of performance' (Collins 2010: 330). Instead, she suggests that blogs can facilitate a shift towards 'forum-led theatrical reviewing', where responses to a show can be collected from multiple reviewers from diverse perspectives, each seeing separate performances and having different experiences.

Michelle MacArthur argued something similar in her overview of feminist theatre blogging practices. She found that while bloggers were not automatically challenging the hegemonic power of traditional criticism just by virtue of existing, they were doing so through the 'strategic use' of their platforms (MacArthur 2013). By this she meant two things. Firstly, the blogosphere could be used as a place for people who had been marginalized by mainstream discourse and practices to meet one another, arguably forming a stronger and larger community of feminist theatremakers and audiences than could reasonably organize away from online spaces. Secondly, the way feminist theatre bloggers navigated mainstream discourse, celebrating and critiquing as appropriate, challenged the way that the distribution of power in online spaces often replicated traditional inequalities. Through tactical negotiation of these spaces and systems, an online community of feminists could proactively amplify voices and perspectives which were rarely heard elsewhere, and 'contribute to diluting the power of the hegemonic critic'.

Perhaps the most interesting theorization of online criticism, however, comes from Duška Radosavljević, who uses the geographical metaphor of a *landscape* to think about its relationship to older forms of criticism. Online reviewing, she explains, shouldn't be analysed according to the same frameworks as printed media; it must be considered part of a separate paradigm of digital communication, a new form of 'rhetorical action' (Radosavljević 2016: 17). This situates the theatre blog within a history of orality over literacy, and aligns it not with the newspaper, nor even the academic journal, but with spoken dialogue.

The transmission of information through speech, rather than through the written word, requires fewer tools and less formal education; it is free, accessible and communal. Moreover, it facilitates the collective organization of people who forge shared cultural identities even when they have few resources and little power. When humans learned to read and write, and later developed printing technologies, the written word became an instrument of power. Those who could communicate in writing – and therefore across distances and with larger audiences – were able to trade overseas, set political agendas, and win wars. Speech wasn't superseded by these new skills however; we all still chatted to one another. Babies still learned to communicate by listening and mimicking, and conversation remained the principal mode of information exchange for the poor and those without formal education.

When radio and television appeared in the twentieth century, Walter Ong suggested that these mediums were heralding a new 'secondary orality', something which Radosavljević (and others, such as bloggers Zeynep Tufekci and An Xiao Mina) suggest continues in a contemporary digital sphere. Even though the internet requires literacy, and we largely communicate on it by writing, the strict rules we were taught to follow at school are very often ignored in online spaces. 'When it comes to writing,' Radosavljević explains, 'the hierarchies of the publishing world have demanded that we abide by certain orthographic standards ... However, with the removal of those editorial hierarchies in the digital world we have been freed to revert to more personal, more creative and more conversational means of expression' (ibid. 18).

The consequence of this for theatre bloggers is significant. As well as positioning online theatre criticism as 'distinctly emancipatory, community-oriented, performative and potentially non-literary' (ibid. 17), it frees theatre bloggers from the historical lineage of newspapers and magazines, where they are so easily framed as the rebellious teenage siblings of a haggard but honourable establishment, and repositions them as an evolution of the fan communities and countercultural movements which first used bulletin board systems and email newsgroups to communicate with one another back in the 1980s. This idea of the theatre blogosphere as a social space is one I will return to at several points in the following chapters, but it sits at the very front and centre of the next one, on theatre blogging's history since 2003. Here, we see how relationships and communities have both flourished and been tested by over fifteen years of *The Discourse*.

CHAPTER 2
THEATRE BLOGGING SINCE 2003 – A HISTORY

When the playwright David Eldridge reflected on his reasons for starting a blog back in October 2006, he told me about his wish to demythologize playwriting, and how, before artists started using social media to communicate the trivia of their lives, there was little opportunity to talk publicly about 'the ups and downs, the practical realities, the absurdities' of that career and lifestyle. If a playwright was written about in a newspaper (generally only when they were lucky enough to get something produced by a major London theatre), the journalist would search for a way to connect the personal history of the artist to their work, often forcing biographical contextualization into a false narrative. 'What I found a bit ridiculous', he said, 'was the element of it that was just completely ignorant speculation about why people had made the work they'd made, what sort of motives they had, *how* work was made. I wanted to correct that a bit, if I could.'

David's words have stuck with me as I've researched and written this chapter. Just like a journalist grasping for an 'angle', it is astonishingly easy to get carried away when writing a history of theatre blogging, of anything really. Earlier drafts had the first bloggers pretty much riding through Manhattan on white horses, ready to take back Broadway from commercial forces by duelling at high noon. I was doing exactly what I set out not to do: presenting the theatre blogosphere as part of some great imagined war between good and evil. And let's be honest, it is rarely that. As a series of small but swift interventions into public discourse, theatre blogging is *incredibly* mundane. We sit behind our computers, or thumbing our phones, and we write a bit of something that is on our mind, something that is pissing us off, something that happened the night before. The story of the theatre blogosphere is no great epic tale; it is just a bunch of people, with a shared interest, who have chosen to participate in a certain way.

However . . . (and there is always a 'however'), blogging about theatre is not a solo pursuit. It engenders dialogue, builds community and affects change on and off-stage. It is therefore just as irresponsible to present the blogosphere as a collection of lone wolves, their motivations contradictory and their conversations mere coincidences, as it is to present them as part of some great heroic struggle. Even in the international territory of the internet, theatre remains tied to time and place, and its commentators are similarly clustered within localized theatre cultures – primarily in New York, Melbourne and London. The history of theatre blogging is therefore a history of how those connected by geography, interest and taste have employed developing technologies in order to strive for common goals.

The fact that this practice has blossomed in wealthy Western cities can be attributed to multiple language and economic factors; factors which have also helped perpetuate the commercial success and academic attention given to theatre made in those cities. But the *really* uncomfortable truth is that those factors are themselves a direct result of a brutal history of colonialism and the systematic exploitation of people of colour and their land. Telling this story with integrity doesn't just mean accurately recording the major events of the theatre blogosphere, it also means acknowledging the structural inequalities that have caused it to develop the way it has, from the sidelining of women to the absence of Black voices. Chris Goode thinks of theatre blogging as 'a social situation within an industrial situation', something which brought 'a changing sense of who we could hope to think of as an ally'; a history of theatre blogging also needs to be about allyship, even where that is forged through dissent.

Foundations: America

The year 2003 is several hundred years ago in internet time. Several *millennia* even. People were still talking about how the internet was 'over' following the dot-com crash. The term 'Web 2.0' was yet to be invented. Mark Zuckerberg had only just turned up at Harvard, and none of us had even been rickrolled yet. But, as we learned in Chapter 1, blogging was booming. Playwright and actor Laura Axelrod had been writing hers, *Gasp!*, for over a year already, posting thoughts on her daily life and activities, comment on news and politics, and sharing insights into her professional life in theatre. *Gasp!* was hosted on the now-defunct blogging site JournalSpace,[1] and while the people she met there weren't otherwise connected to the New York theatre world, they were keenly interested in her life and the way that theatre was part of it. Then, sometime towards the end of 2003, two new bloggers got in touch with her. Isaac Butler, a director, and George Hunka, a playwright, had both recently started blogging, and were reaching out to others who were also blogging about theatre in New York. Isaac wrote *Parabasis*, George wrote *Superfluities* and, as well as Laura, they contacted Mac Rogers (*Slow Learner*), Dan Trujillo (*Venal Scene*), and Terry Teachout (*About Last Night*) who was also a theatre critic for the *Wall Street Journal*. Laura, Isaac, George, Mac and Dan (Terry was busy) all went out for Vietnamese food to chat about this blogging thing they were doing, and how difficult the life of a theatremaker could be.

Axelrod remembers 'how nice it was to be able to talk to people about theatre – people who knew. Before that I hadn't talked to a lot of theatre people, and, being a woman, it was difficult to get taken seriously.' Following that first meeting, she decided to reboot *Gasp!* and turn it into something more wholly focused on theatre. Butler and Rogers moved to new platforms at the same time. By linking to one another, and promoting each other on blogrolls, the conversation around theatre began to traverse their separate sites quickly. They were soon joined by others, including James Comtois (*Jamespeak*), Garrett Eisler (*The Playgoer*), Matthew Freeman (*On Theatre and Politics*), Jason Grote (*One Hundred Years of Jason Grote*) and Mark Armstrong (*Mr Excitement*). After Terry Teachout, other professional arts journalists started blogs too: David Cote (*Histriomatrix*), who was theatre critic for *Time Out New York*, and then-freelancer Rob Weinert-Kendt (*The Wicked Stage*), who is now the editor of *American Theatre*. Elsewhere in the US, Scott Walters (*Theatre and Ideas*) joined the conversation from North Carolina, as did Don Hall (*Angry White Guy from Chicago*) from, obviously, Chicago. Meanwhile, down in Austin, Jill Dolan began *The Feminist Spectator*, one of the first blogs dedicated to the practice of longform criticism.

Jill was a professor at the University of Texas, whose blog shared the same title as the influential academic treatise on feminist criticism that she had published seventeen years

---

[1] In 2009, all of JournalSpace's data, including every single blog post hosted on it, was deleted by a disgruntled employee (*Tech Crunch* 2009).

earlier (Dolan 1988). In that, feminist spectatorship is presented as an active practice of resistance to the white, male gaze of much theatre and film. In advance of launching *The Feminist Spectator* as a blog, she had talked to a couple of local papers in Austin about reviewing for them, but realized fairly quickly that she didn't want to work within those journalistic structures: 'I really didn't want to be assigned things. I wanted to be in control of my own destiny. I wanted to take whatever time I needed, or wanted, and use as many words as seemed appropriate to do the work that would give me pleasure and that also might speak to a certain kind of community.'

Foundations: Australia

Another early blogger with a history of mainstream publication, albeit slightly different from Jill's academic work, was Alison Croggon. Based in Melbourne, Alison was a poet and novelist but, perhaps most interestingly, in the early 1990s she had also been a fairly high-profile professional theatre critic at a weekly magazine called *The Bulletin*. There, she had found herself in the middle of a controversial battle with the artistic director of a company called Playbox Theatre, who, after she had reviewed their work negatively, had first tried to get her sacked, then ostentatiously banned her from their shows.[2] The whole situation built into something of a media shitstorm, with Alison having to appear on national television to explain the nature and purpose of theatre criticism, and defend her right to her professional opinion. While the editors of *The Bulletin* had supported Alison throughout this drama, it had understandably left a bit of a bad taste in her mouth, so when she realized she could earn more from her poetry and a single parents' pension, she resigned.

By 2004 though, Alison's itch to write about theatre had returned. She rang around a few theatres, let them know what she was planning, and launched *Theatre Notes* in June of that year. In her first post (Croggon 2004), she addressed those who remembered the Playbox controversy of thirteen years earlier: 'My work didn't need justifying then and it shouldn't need justifying now.' Within a year, Alison was joined by Jana Perkovic (*Mono No Aware*, later *Guerrilla Semiotics*), a Croatian-born critic recently relocated to Melbourne, and in 2006, by Chris Boyd (*The Morning After*), a professional reviewer of some twenty years.

Foundations: United Kingdom

While those first New York bloggers were meeting up for Vietnamese food, in London, playwright and academic Dan Rebellato was thinking about doing 'a kind of samizdat thing', photocopying newsletters and leaving them lying around theatre bookshops. That idea was quickly superseded by another though. 'A friend of mine emailed me one day – or maybe we spoke on the phone, god knows – and said "Blogs. Blogs are your samizdat publication."'

---

[2] Croggon reflected on these events when I spoke to her in June 2018: 'There was a campaign against me basically. I don't think it helped that I was young and female, that certainly fed into it. I was kind of like the bitch critic. It all dribbled out into embarrassment on their part but it was totally exhausting.'

A little different from the personal blogs being established elsewhere, *Encore Theatre Magazine* was a multi-authored site in which anonymous contributors, writing from within the theatre industry, could 'champion what is good and attack what is not'. This spirit, part advocacy and part watchdog, was inspired by the style and editorial policy of its namesake magazine, which had run from 1954 until 1965. The original *Encore* vigorously defended theatrical bravery and experimentation at an exciting time for the British stage,[3] but also asked difficult questions when that experimentation was deemed to fail. 'The name was very deliberate,' explained Rebellato. 'The first *Encore* was a great magazine; it had that aggression and certainty, and it was about new stuff. So I nicked the name and then thought . . . now what do I put in it?'

He contacted a few people he knew and put the word out. They were all going to write under the shared pseudonym 'Theatre Worker', a nod to industry solidarity but also a means of protecting *Encore*'s contributors from the professional risks of criticizing peers or the venues who might commission or employ them. As in New York, many were playwrights, such as David Greig and Duncan Macmillan, but before long, posts were being sent in by friends of friends of friends. To this day, there isn't one person who knows who all the 'Theatre Workers' were.

Those of you who have been paying attention will no doubt be asking why I'm even talking about *Encore*, when a magazine-style site which relies upon one person managing the submissions of others does not fall within my working definition of a theatre blog, even if it was initially hosted on Blogger. *Encore* is important, however, for a couple of reasons. Firstly, its launch in 2003 was still several years ahead of the other UK-based theatre blogs which would gain prominence later that decade; indeed, it counted many of those future bloggers within its readership. Secondly, its anonymity was unusual. While many internet users adopted pseudonyms for all sorts of purposes, including blogging, the theatre blogosphere was generally much more transparent, even from the very beginning. This had its benefits for some, as theatremakers who blogged forged new collaborations and raised the profile of their various projects, but that transparency also came with complications. Isaac Butler told me that he missed out on directing opportunities because of his profile as a blogger, which makes sense in some ways; if the rehearsal room is a sacred space, where artists are allowed to be vulnerable and make mistakes as a fundamental part of their process, having a blogger in the room risks disrupting that environment. It can foster mistrust. What *Encore* enabled through its use of a shared pseudonym was a way for theatremakers to participate more freely in a dialogue about their industry, even when their individual positions were still too precarious to allow them to speak up under their own names. This way, the site became a place where truth could be spoken to power. It criticized programming decisions at the National Theatre and Royal Court, campaigned for a better standard of criticism in newspapers, and made a measured and articulate argument against the Labour government's 2004 study into theatre's economic impact.

After a brief hiatus in 2005, *Encore* reappeared as a new site in 2006, away from Blogger, where it continued for another year or so. Much of these later posts were lost when the hosting

---

[3] This period is principally remembered for the rise of the 'Angry Young Men', a group of playwrights and novelists largely from working and lower middle class backgrounds, who wrote politicized narratives featuring characters disillusioned with the traditions of British society. Notable Angry Young Men included John Osborne, Alan Sillitoe and Harold Pinter.

lapsed, but by that point *Encore* was no longer a lone UK outpost of the theatre blogosphere. In 2005, playwrights Benjamin Yeoh (*Theatre and Writing*) and Stephen Sharkey (*O, Poor Robinson Crusoe!*) started new theatre blogs, while director Paul Miller (*My London Life*) decided to concentrate his personal, journal-style blog on theatre. They were joined by Ben Ellis (*Parachute of A Playwright*), an Australian playwright based in the UK at the time, and Andy Field (*The Arcades Project*), who was initially a student in Edinburgh but would move down to London within a year. In 2006 they were followed by theatremaker Chris Goode (*Thompson's Bank of Communicable Desire*), and David Eldridge (*One Writer and His Dog*), whose recollections began this chapter.

While those UK bloggers were all artists of one flavour or another, 2006 was also the year in which two audience members, Andrew and Phil, became so infuriated by the Old Vic's production of *Resurrection Blues* that they only went back after the interval because they had 'always wanted to boo at the end of a show' (*West End Whingers* 2006). While the booing was purportedly cathartic in some respects, it didn't quite relieve the pain of the experience for Andrew and Phil, who started their irreverent review blog, *West End Whingers*, just a couple of days later. A month after that, Natasha Tripney, a freshly graduated writer who had begun contributing to *The Stage* and music website *MusicOMH*, started her blog, *Interval Drinks*. The London theatre blogosphere was gradually catching up with New York and Melbourne, just as the New York bloggers were experiencing their first moment in the spotlight.

2006: *My Name Is Rachel Corrie*

Rachel Corrie was the young woman from Olympia, Washington, who, in 2003, was killed by a bulldozer in Gaza, where she was acting as a human shield in front of Palestinian homes. Following her death, the actor and director Alan Rickman and the newspaper editor Katherine Viner used Corrie's diaries and emails as material for a play, *My Name Is Rachel Corrie*, which told the story of how she had become involved in political activism. After two successful runs at the Royal Court in London, it had been due to transfer to the New York Theater Workshop (NYTW) in March 2006. Although the Theater Workshop had not yet formally announced the show in its season, tickets had been listed for sale online and arrangements were being made for Rickman, Viner and cast member Megan Dodds to travel to New York. On 28 February 2006 however, the New York Theater Workshop announced that the show was going to be 'delayed'.

According to an article in the *New York Times* (McKinley 2006a), artistic director James Nicola had spoken to members of the local Jewish community, and found that there were concerns about the timing of the production, given that it was critical of the Israeli government. At the time, there was great political uncertainty in the region. Prime Minister Ariel Sharon was critically ill in a coma, and the Palestinian military group Hamas had just received strong support in elections. Corrie's writings gave a pro-Palestinian perspective on the conflict, leading Nicola to say that 'the fantasy that we could present the work of this writer simply as a work of art without appearing to take a position was just that, a fantasy'. He withdrew the play from the theatre's season, apparently pending new dates, but the view from London was slightly different. Talking to the *Guardian* (Borger 2006), Alan Rickman was unequivocal: the run had been cancelled, and the New York Theater Workshop was practicing 'censorship born out of fear'. The implication was that the theatre's management were prioritizing the wishes of their donors above any artistic mission.

Theatre bloggers were some of the first to notice the story. Garrett Eisler shared the link to the story on his blog, *The Playgoer*, under the title 'Censorship comes to Downtown' (Eisler 2006a). Later that day, he would post again on the same subject (Eisler 2006b):

> ...keep in mind a mass rebellion of subscribers is not necessary to make a nonprofit company shiver. It takes just one big donor, one prominent board member to object. One wonders if the very idea of a woman denoucing [sic] Israeli militarism and supporting Palestinian statehood from the stage of NYTW would be enough to rub some v.i.p. the wrong way. Or, being that board is made up of nothing if not good businessmen, someone advised a little caution and 'risk management'.

Eisler was soon joined by other bloggers, all asking why Nicola had turned away from this political play. Was the cancellation a financial decision? Had donors threatened to cut the theatre off? Who were the members of the Jewish community that Nicola had consulted with, and why weren't equivalent Arab-American groups polled? The blogosphere erupted with opinion. Isaac Butler suggested that Nicola was 'using the buzzwords of audience outreach and responsible art making to justify what he's doing' (Butler 2006), George Hunka suggested that this was a sign that private institutions – not the state – were bringing a new, economically-driven censorship to America,[4] Jason Grote shared a petition to reverse the decision, while others called for comment from Tony Kushner, not only one of New York's theatre establishment, but someone who had encountered similar opposition around his work on the film *Munich*. The conversation on the blogs was so animated, and moved so quickly, that Matthew Freeman would even wonder if the controversy hadn't 'been latched onto and exploited by the blogosphere, to attack and cajole and shame producers' (Freeman 2006).

Eisler's blog, *The Playgoer*, became something of a hub for the story, with regular recaps and links to other web publications. 'It was something I learned from the political blogs. Bloggers could be a hub, a sort of one-stop shop so that you can go to one place and find out what's going on with that story, and also get commentary that is giving a context.' Between the news breaking on 28 February and the end of the following month, he would publish 101 posts about the *Corrie* controversy, reporting with greater depth and attention to detail than any other publication, even spending time searching Alan Rickman fansites (Eisler 2006c), turning up evidence that, contrary to their statements, NYTW had indeed begun to promote the show before it was pulled.

It was clear that this relatively small group of bloggers, many of whom were themselves theatremakers, were providing the kind of knowledge and expertise that could keep up pressure on the theatre. Eisler remembers how unconvincing the theatre's PR messages were: 'When Jim Nicola said things like "well, we couldn't do it because the set was too big to move into the theatre", we could call bullshit on that. It was enough to fool the layman, it was enough to fool the *Times*, but anyone with any experience working in a theatre would just see all these red flags. And we also knew how relations with the donors were.'

---

[4] This post is now lost, but is paraphrased by Butler (2006).

Theatre Blogging

Throughout March 2006, the *New York Times* largely remained happy to reprint the theatre's press releases and wait for the whole thing to go away. And they certainly weren't ready to acknowledge the importance of the debate happening on theatre blogs. In fact, when playwright Christopher Shinn spoke out against the cancellation in a comment on *The Playgoer* (in Eisler 2006), the *New York Times* couldn't even bring themselves to mention the b-word, instead explaining that Shinn had 'published a short essay online' (McKinley 2006b).

By the end of that month, a number of other artists, activists and commentators had joined the bloggers in speaking out about the cancellation. An open letter was published from twenty-one Jewish writers based in the UK, and a new website set up, *Rachel's Words*, to campaign for the US production to go ahead. The team behind this site (including representatives from Democracy Now and the Arab American Institute) presented a reading of the play in a Manhattan church. The New York Theater Workshop programmed a series of panel discussions to debate the Israeli-Palestinian politics and the issue of censorship, though these were heavily mediated by a PR firm, who insisted on pre-approving all audience questions. Meanwhile, as Rickman and Viner opened *My Name Is Rachel Corrie* at the Playhouse Theatre in London, the Minetta Lane Theater in Greenwich Village was hired by Dena Hammerstein of commercial producers James Hammerstein Productions; they, not NYTW, would present the first New York production in October that year.

The impact of the *Corrie* debate

For theatre bloggers in New York, the *Rachel Corrie* story had been galvanizing, bringing new readers but, more importantly, a newfound sense of possibility. *The Nation* had run an article on the controversy which included an interview with Eisler and celebrated the theatre blogosphere for championing artistic freedom and advocating greater transparency in the arts (Weiss 2006). Other theatres were also becoming aware of the importance of bloggers to the discourse around their own productions; that summer, Isaac Butler and Mark Armstrong would encourage a number of venues to host the first bloggers' nights in the city, supporting blog critics to attend shows which were unlikely to attract reviewers from the main papers. Bloggers were exploring other similar stories in light of the *My Name Is Rachel Corrie* conversation too; over in London, Ben Ellis reported on the Comédie-Française's decision to cancel a Peter Handke play after it emerged that he had links to Serbian war criminal Slobodan Milošević.[5]

But while many new bloggers were encouraged by the *Corrie* story to start writing, and others started to take their blogging practice more seriously, some were put off by the newfound attention being paid to the blogosphere. An element of competition had arrived, which brought individual egos into play. Laura Axelrod remembers this as the beginning of a period in which the New York blogosphere would become dominated by in-fighting, disillusionment and sexism:

> The Rachel Corrie thing, that had a huge effect on the whole community of us. It brought the media in, and once that happened, whatever was building changed. I backed off. I

---

[5] Ellis has since taken his blog down, so these posts are no longer online.

didn't feel any weirdness about being the only woman at first, but with more guys joining, and more women too, I noticed we were kinda becoming the auxiliary crew.

Isaac Butler felt similarly. He remembers previously close friendships breaking down over aggressively-worded blog posts. 'It's the same thing that happened in all sorts of online communities: a group of poisonous people ruined it by being assholes. It got to the point where it wasn't fun anymore, because debate became about trollery, bullying people and attacking them personally.'

Often, when an online community experiences its first significant profile boost, or sees one or two members achieve success, that can attract new, ambitious voices, and cause existing contributors to ask themselves whether or not it's still fun. For those who wished to use theatre blogging as a step towards a personal career goal, or as a way to accrue industry status, it can be a strategic decision to be disparaging or divisive. After all, posts which drag someone or something (or some *show*) are often the most widely read and shared, even if only because people disagree. In the case of the first wave of New York bloggers, it would be unfair to say that divisions within the community were *wholly* a result of the *My Name Is Rachel Corrie* debate, but it is certainly the case that increased attention made blogging about theatre more attractive to those who sought personal advancement over collective conversation, and made those already participating vulnerable to ego and power play more swiftly and suddenly than would have otherwise been the case. Over the following two or three years, the collegiality which existed between that first group of bloggers would dissipate; some stopped altogether, while those who remained were forced to grow much thicker skins.

By the end of 2006, the Australian theatre blogosphere experienced something similar, when one theatre blogger found themselves the target of coordinated bullying. In December, the actor and theatremaker Ming-Zhu Hii blogged about her experience of watching an early performance of a show which was to be featured in a festival of short plays. While Hii's work was also going to be presented as part of the Short + Sweet festival, she wrote on her blog *Mink Tails* that the work she saw was of such poor quality it had caused her to question her decision to take part. So far, so innocuous, but within a couple of days of her post being published, an anonymous emailer sent details of Hii's post to everyone participating in the festival, suggesting that the festival's trustees were considering its future as a result of her words, and calling for artists to 'visit her blog and let her know not everyone agrees'.[6] The claims made in the email were never corroborated, but nevertheless, Hii received over a hundred angry and abusive comments. Even after she removed her original post in an attempt to stop the torrent, other bloggers who defended her received similar hurtful comments on their blogs. This only stopped when Chris Boyd explained that he had taken a note of the commenters' IP addresses, so knew where the messages originated from.[7]

I don't want to make it sound like 2006 was a year of crisis for theatre bloggers, because these unpleasant incidents were rare, and part of a much broader narrative which also encompassed much goodwill and meaningful engagement. The blogosphere was growing, tackling issues of

---

[6] This email can be read in full on Chris Boyd's blog (Boyd, C. 2006).
[7] For more information on this dispute see Harvey, Grehan and Tompkins (2010). There is also a fantastic post from Alison Croggon (responding to thoughts from George Hunka) which addresses the controversy in the broader context of comment culture and libel law (Croggon 2006).

real significance for theatremakers and their audiences, and the instances when blogs were thrown into the spotlight were primarily exciting and invigorating for all involved. Existing hierarchies of power and popularity were establishing themselves online though, no doubt evidence that a truly benevolent and equitable internet had always been unrealistic. As with any part of our social and professional lives, theatre bloggers encounter opposition, learn to navigate hostility and determine their particular ethical and political positions through practice and experience, as the first big talking point for the UK theatre blogosphere would demonstrate.

2007: On writing for theatre

British theatre in 2007 was experiencing a series of dramatic changes, spearheaded by new, genre-bending forms. Immersive theatre, like that made by Punchdrunk, was effectively remaking the relationship between performer and audience for a whole new generation of audiences; *War Horse* made a huge hit out of a large-scale collaboration between directors Tom Morris and Marianne Elliot and the Handspring Puppet Company from South Africa, while Katie Mitchell was regularly re-interpreting classic texts with live onstage filmmaking. Reflecting the success of these new experimental forms and processes, Arts Council England (ACE) were re-evaluating their funding priorities, announcing significant cuts to over 200 regularly-funded organizations, many of them focused on the development of new plays. The Bush Theatre in West London, Orange Tree Theatre in Richmond and Northcott Theatre in Exeter all faced cuts to their core grants from ACE, while some of the most high-profile proponents of collaborative, devised and form-shifting theatre work (such as Punchdrunk, Artichoke, Shunt and Fuel) were either regularly funded for the first time, or had their grants increased.[8]

For these reasons, 2007 felt like a moment of regime change in British theatre, and while that was exciting for some, for others it was a time marked by fear and uncertainty. Different philosophies of taste and practice, coupled with the anxieties fostered by a competitive funding landscape, meant that the online community which had started to blossom within the London theatre scene was fracturing as nuances of contrasting approach were discussed and fought over at length. Was the playwright the primary creative force in theatre, the text its initiating document? Or was theatremaking a collaborative act, fundamentally live, for which the text can never be more than a partial or lifeless component?

In debating these ideas, a group of London theatre bloggers would influence, inspire (and provoke) the theatre community in that city to think harder and more deeply about the work they made and watched, while subsequently fuelling the fears of mainstream critics who were beginning to see economic cracks appearing in their own industry. (That Michael Billington article about the 'pre-emptive guesswork' of bloggers that I mentioned in Chapter 1? That was 2007.)

---

[8] After an outcry from high-profile actors and a vote of no confidence in the Arts Council, some of the planned cuts were reduced and a new report into playwriting in Britain was commissioned, but the process encouraged ACE to re-evaluate and repurpose its system of regular funding. By 2011, a new system of 'National Portfolio Organisations' was introduced, with all regularly funded companies having to formally re-apply through an open application process which is now repeated every three to four years.

The contributions made by two bloggers in particular – themselves respected theatre artists – have come to epitomize the contrasting perspectives on playwriting and processes of theatremaking that occupied the UK blogosphere in 2007. David Eldridge was an established playwright who had had his first work produced during the second half of the 1990s and was known for his quietly beautiful evocations of working class life, as well as much grander Ibsen adaptations. His blog was full of words of support for his peers, championing playwrights for their heart and invention and arguing for their working conditions within a brutal commissioning system. Chris Goode, in contrast, was an experimental performance maker whose works were largely concerned with intimacy, and which, even though he was also a playwright, were most often made through a collaborative devising process. Goode had been the artistic director of Camden People's Theatre from 2001 to 2004, a role which saw him provide a platform for a new generation of unusual and small-scale theatre works, often with more in common with histories of performance art or cabaret than with plays. Neither could be said to have initiated the conversation about form and process – that, of course, was a response to broader industry conditions, with *Encore* making reference to a perceived rift between 'literalists and metaphysicalists' in November of the previous year (*Encore* 2006) – but both Eldridge and Goode put forward their arguments with commitment and fervour, whether on their own blogs or in the comments elsewhere.

The two had chatted in a comment thread on Goode's blog at the very start of 2007 (Goode 2007a), each presenting their wish for a broad and inclusive theatre culture fairly amicably, albeit inevitably falling back on certain assumptions implicit in their different practices, but it was at the end of February 2007 when the conversation was re-ignited. In an interview with *LA Weekly* (Morris 2007), the playwright Edward Albee had argued that actors and directors who impeded the writer's vision were 'the forces of darkness', but he didn't stop there. In a widely-shared quote, he also said:

> The big problem is the assumption that writing a play is a collaborative act. It isn't. It's a creative act, and then other people come in. The interpretation should be for the accuracy of what the playwright wrote. Playwrights are expected to have their text changed by actors they never wanted. Directors seem to feel they are as creative as the playwright.

The US blogosphere had responded, mainly to argue against his perpetuation of unnecessary divisions between artists, but it was once the piece had its signal boosted by an article on the *Guardian*'s website (Caines 2007) that Chris Goode responded to Albee's words, using the comments made by Eldridge on his earlier post as a way to reference and paraphrase the argument of those who considered playwriting to be the central creative act in theatremaking (Goode 2007b). (The positions taken in this argument have been historically referred to as the 'text-based' versus the 'devised', but these are fairly superficial and unnuanced terms, so I've avoided them here.) Goode supposed that the disagreements which accompanied these ideas (also presented by *Encore* and, in the United States, George Hunka) emerged from a series of imbalances. Firstly, of simple 'cordiality', but also imbalances of a structural nature: the fact that the majority of theatre in the UK was still made according to traditional processes of playwriting and direction, but the majority of criticism and media coverage focused on formal innovation; the pedagogical shift which meant undergraduate theatre courses were encouraging young makers to move away from traditionally defined roles and skills; and the differences in programming structures that meant conventional plays generally had much longer runs than experimental performance. Finally, Goode presented the key differences between what he saw as *writing a play* and *writing for theatre*: the first is *closed* and needs to be 'broken' in order to be made into a live work; the second is *open* 'in a way that allows for, and ideally fosters and enjoys, liveness and contingency and unpredictability and ephemerality and, above all, the turbulence of the travel between stage and audience'.

It sounds beautiful, doesn't it? As I write this section I am trying exceedingly hard to remain impassionate and not take sides, but reading Chris's post now makes me want to ride into battle with him. *Of course* theatre should be about openness, *of course* it should be about collaboration, *of course* it should foster new ways of working over the old and inflexible. The thing is though, playwriting *also does that*. If it didn't, nobody would ever bother reviving anything. Directing would be as simple as assembling furniture. There would be no rehearsal room edits or rewrites. And there would be no recontextualization for changing times or changing politics. It makes me think of watching the twentieth anniversary production of Mark Ravenhill's *Shopping and Fucking* at the Lyric Hammersmith in 2016; Ravenhill had rewritten the ending of the play, completely shifting its central proposition from one about ideological defeat and nihilism to one in which we are all crushingly and inescapably wedded to the very grand narratives the original production sought to demolish.

British commentators would often refer to exponents of this kind of editing and re-interpretation of a text – a common practice in many parts of mainland Europe – as 'auteurs', a term which demonstrates their desire to identify the one chief artist in every process, the *boss* of every show. Regularly used to describe Katie Mitchell, whose experiments with film and hyper-naturalism challenged conventional British expectations of theatre, 'auteur' could also be used sneeringly, even as a sexist dog whistle, where it could imply a domineering woman with ideas above her station. Indeed, one of Mitchell's works would be the next big event to feed into the conversation about writing, as, less than a fortnight after Albee's comments, her visionary production of *Attempts On Her Life* by Martin Crimp opened at the National Theatre.

2007: *Attempts On Her Life*

In this interpretation, Crimp's episodic text was presented as a series of disjointed vignettes, each created live on stage but filmed by roving cameras which would project individual scenes of intimacy and spectacle onto the screens above. These images were often fast-moving and aesthetically contrasting: a post-punk rock band, an intense police procedural, an executive car advert, an Abba pastiche, all working together to create a sense of a life almost entirely mediated by the contemporary media landscape.

While the production was met with either boredom or hostility by most newspaper critics,[9] and cries of pretentiousness and wankery from contributors to the *What's On Stage* messageboard, London's theatre blogosphere was united in admiration, even while some

---

[9] A few gave polite three-star equivocations, but some of the Sunday critics were particularly brutal. In the *Sunday Telegraph*'s magazine, Tim Walker called it a 'wretched thing'; in the *Mail on Sunday*, Georgina Brown called it 'the worst play I've ever seen'; and in the *Sunday Express*, Mark Shenton reported that, during its two hours, he was 'seriously contemplating making an attempt on [his] own life' (Walker 2007; Brown 2007, Shenton 2007).

admitted to finding the pace and form of the piece difficult to absorb. Perhaps surprisingly, given his belief in the integrity of the playwright's text, David Eldridge was one of the most effusive, heralding the show as 'a major event in our theatre'. While he did not explicitly refer to the differing approaches to theatremaking which had been on everyone's minds, he took care to explain that it was precisely the play's recontextualization within contemporary society and politics which provided its power and relevance: 'Post 9/11 terror and in a truly post-Soviet age of rampant consumerism, eastern European sex trafficking and of 'Big Brother' and Blair this play has found it's [sic] place in our culture.'[10]

Others were equally enraptured, and keen to make the connection between *Attempts On Her Life* and the preceding conversation about writing. In one of his three posts about the show (Field 2007a), Andy Field made explicit reference to Goode's idea of *writing for theatre* in terms of the relationship between Mitchell's conceptual direction and Crimp's elusive, fragmented text: 'Crimp is clearly writing *for* theatre. . . . Plays such as Crimps [sic] are only complete when their creativity is accompanied, supplemented and realised by the creative weight of the full apparatus of theatre.' Elsewhere, the anonymous blogger behind the *Notional Theatre* would suggest that this interpretation 'seemed conscious of its status as not the only ever production' (*Notional Theatre* 2007), a suggestion that this kind of radical, visual staging can sit perfectly well alongside more conventional interpretations in the production history of a single play. By the end of 2007, however, the rift that *Attempts On Her Life* had appeared to briefly heal was re-opening, and it was about to move to a much more prominent platform.

2007: Comment thread disputes

After reading Michael Billington's recently published book, *State of The Nation*, which asserted the playwright's central position in British theatremaking, David Eldridge cheered his approval. In a post from 12 November, he restated his position on the primacy of playwriting, italicizing his closing words for impact: '. . . it is *the playwrights and writers who finally move the form forwards. . . . And we should never forget it either.*'[11]

But it was on a *Guardian* post by Andy Field in December 2007 in which the comments got ugly. (By this time the *Guardian*'s 'theatre blog' section, which had begun commissioning artists and bloggers to write about their experiences of the sector in October 2006, had become a fruitful site for discussion, in the comment threads especially. It was considered by some – probably somewhat snobbishly – to be the thinking person's alternative to the more gossip-driven *What's On Stage* forums.[12]) Field's article moved things on from Goode's idea that a published play needs to be 'broken' to come alive, instead presenting the playtext as 'a memorial to performances past' (Field 2007b). Eldridge was one of the first to make his disagreement known. While he was at pains to point out that his comments should not be taken as a dismissal of different methods, he argued, over ten blistering paragraphs, that Field's argument was a 'sly

---

[10] This post is no longer online, but has been reproduced in section 8, on Reviews and Reviewing.
[11] No longer publicly available.
[12] The discontinuation of the *Guardian*'s 'theatre blog' section in 2017 was ostensibly a cost-saving measure, but it was no doubt also a reflection of the fact that, as so much mainstream newspaper content was now only published online, cursory distinctions between main content and 'blog' content had all but collapsed.

attack', 'laughable rubbish' and 'naff, undergraduate grand-standing', before accusing Chris Goode of 'peddling' similar sentiments 'at every opportunity', and finishing with a call for the 'auteur-types' to 'Just shut up, leave us alone and get on with making the work you believe in.'

The thread that followed was alternately illuminating, funny and bruising, as commenters gathered to respond both to Field's article and Eldridge's reply, bringing examples from Peter Brook, European ensemble work, the Arts Council's proposed funding cuts, the nature of rehearsal, neoliberalism, the educational dominance of English Literature, and Gothic imagery, as well as various frank assessments of the unsavoury tribalism which was becoming entrenched in certain quarters of the theatre community. In the midst of all this, Eldridge offered an apology for his 'un-seasonal blog-rage', but his ire had attracted new commenters to his own blog, where the conversation continued. There, Eldridge argued passionately with his readers, even resorting to deleting anonymous or angry comments which threatened to derail the otherwise respectful dialogue taking place.

This might be where I fall down in my attempt to tell this story without creating any sensationalist false narratives that are going to piss David Eldridge off. I obviously don't want to paint a picture of him and Chris Goode in opposite corners of a boxing ring – the discourse of the blogosphere was so much more careful and nuanced than that – but at the same time I do think that the impact these arguments had on the theatre community in the UK can be at least partly attributed to the sense of drama fostered by such an aggressive and passionate mode of writing. While these *battles* were being *fought*, the *generals* at the head of each *army* were providing an education to those following them, or, should I say, reading their *despatches from the front line*. Andrew Haydon, who started his own blog, *Postcards From The Gods*, right in the midst of all the 2007 arguments about authorship, would say as much in his reflections on the period:

> Here were some of the brightest minds making and/or writing about theatre offering new, live debate on a subject that they chose and cared about. I learnt more from following that one discussion and the comment threads under the blogs it generated, than I had in several years of reading mainstream newspaper theatre coverage, because it wasn't neatly packaged as a single article. It was an ongoing negotiation.
>
> *Haydon 2016: 141*

As part of that negotiation, there was a profound sense that everyone was listening to one another. Yes, it would occasionally break down into flippancy or frustration, but on the whole, it was an exemplary example of the kind of ongoing rational-critical discourse that Jürgen Habermas posited as an important step towards political democracy.[13] What was once

---

[13] Habermas argued that the culture of debate which flourished in eighteenth-century Europe, facilitated by gentleman's clubs, coffee-houses and new types of periodicals such as *The Tatler* (1709–11) and *The Spectator* (1711–14), contributed to the emergence of a new *public sphere*, both a social realm distinct from the private domestic space of the family, and a source of authority independent from church or state. The establishment of this public sphere, he argued, was fundamental to the ability of the emergent middle-classes to assert and represent themselves within a larger political system (Habermas 1989). Habermas' theory has since been problematized for its focus on the bourgeois patriarch over other demographic groups, including women, the working classes, people of colour and the queer community, who, frequently excluded from public life, often adopt strategies other than debate to seek and protect their collective representation.

happening in the coffee-houses and early periodicals of eighteenth-century London was now happening on blogs and comment threads, and the real practices of those making theatre were being re-imagined and remade as a result.

More than a decade on, these particular battle lines have broken down considerably. The generation of theatremakers who were emerging in 2007 are now running companies and venues, and making work on some of the largest and most significant stages in the country, often combining the strengths and possibilities of both approaches. Today's new playwrights are more open to directorial and design-led interpretation than ever before, while much of the more esoteric and experiential performance work on the fringes is (stop me if I'm over-reaching here, but I don't think I am) paying much closer attention to narrative and structure than in the heady days of the mid-2000s, when *immersive* and *interactive* were our favourite buzzwords.

Goode and Eldridge have since reflected on their past disagreements on Goode's excellent podcast, *Thompson's Live* (Goode with Eldridge 2018). Speaking in May 2018, they conversed with a kind of angsty good-humour, caught between acute embarrassment at the obstinance of their younger selves and a visceral recollection of just how *important* it all was. They also placed their theatrical factionalism in an economic context in a way which wasn't possible at the time. 'In recent years,' explained Eldridge, 'when there's been even less money because of austerity, a lot of that antagonism within various different bits of the theatre family seems to have fallen away. We've *all* felt a bit like … *oh shit*.' What we know now, that we didn't then, is that the economic crash of 2008 and the election of a Tory-led coalition government in 2010 would bring a new series of swingeing cuts to the arts in England, making the changes proposed in 2007 seem pretty minor overall. My enemy's enemy is my friend, after all.

2007: Yep, there's still more from 2007

The conversation about playwriting, devising and *Attempts On Her Life* wasn't the only thing that happened in the UK theatre blogosphere in 2007. In May, Nicholas Hytner, then the artistic director of the National Theatre, accused the collective body of first-string newspaper critics of the sexist treatment of female directors. In his interview with *The Times,* Hytner cited negative critical responses to Emma Rice's production of *A Matter of Life and Death* and misogynistic reviews received by Katie Mitchell. It was his choice turn of phrase which really got the juices flowing though; he explained that 'too many of the theatre critics are dead white men' (Hoyle 2007). This was noteworthy not just because it implied mainstream theatre criticism was tired and outmoded (that came as no surprise to anyone), but because it suggested a redistribution of power was already underway. Gone were the days of a handful of newspaper critics making or breaking a show; here was the artistic director of arguably the most important theatre in the country telling the mainstream critics that they needed to get their shit together. That he did so only a couple of months after the theatre blogosphere had offered a collective counter-argument to negative newspaper reviews of *Attempts On Her Life* is not insignificant; that show had proved that theatres no longer had to rely solely on this small group of ageing men for the critical reception of their works.

Hytner's words precipitated a good bit of huffing and puffing from the oldest (and arguably deadest) of the white men with lead critic positions. Nicholas de Jongh, Charles Spencer and

Theatre Blogging

Michael Billington each responded with varying combinations of outrage and counter-accusation (de Jongh 2007; Spencer 2007; Billington 2007a), which bloggers fell upon with delight,[14] but few focused on the most significant implication of Hytner's words: that there was an astounding lack of diversity within theatre criticism. The West End Whingers probably came closest to addressing the problem in their post of 20 May, moving the conversation on from ageism in order to ask specific questions about the racial diversity of both the newspaper critics and the bloggers (*West End Whingers* 2007), but it is striking how few commentators – wherever they published – were interested in taking a stand over this, perhaps the most glaring power imbalance of all.

A level playing field?

When we look back at the popular emergence of the internet, and of blogging, one of the principle narratives presented to us is that of the *levelled playing field*, the internet as an egalitarian space in which anyone can publish anything, thus bypassing the gatekeepers of established media. And that is true, in some ways, provided you have the requisite skills and technology, plus the time and energy to devote to largely unpaid activities. In practice though, at least for the first decade or so of theatre blogging, that simply wasn't the case. The majority of theatre bloggers were still white men with university educations, and in the UK, they were often already known to each other, either through professional networks or from friendships made at the long-running National Student Drama Festival (NSDF), which had its own criticism magazine, *Noises Off*, and a popular, if short-lived, web forum. Some of the personal links between bloggers were international too; despite living on opposite sides of the globe, Alison Croggon and Chris Goode had known each other for years through the poetry scene. With such a small pool of theatre bloggers achieving prominence, there were clearly still cultural barriers standing in the way of diversification.

I can identify a few reasons why this might have been. Existing friendships and professional relationships undoubtedly encouraged those in some social groups to start blogging much more readily than others, and these same friendships and relationships influenced which blogs were being read and linked to. The wider theatre industry had its own major problems of access and representation which meant that those developing a serious interest in the form were more likely to be white and middle-class. From October 2007 though, a number of theatre bloggers found their work filtered into the mainstream via the *Guardian*'s weekly blog round-up column (also called *Noises Off*, just like the NSDF mag). Reporting on conversations from the theatre blogosphere each week, *Noises Off* had four different writers in the six years before its discontinuation (Kelly Nestruck, Chris Wilkinson, Andrew Haydon and Matt Trueman), each of whom became something akin to a blogosphere gatekeeper. Their interests, preferences and attentiveness dictated which bloggers were featured each week, while the column's focus on argument and opinion over show reviews meant that bloggers who were quietly developing a critical practice – rather than making wild proclamations about *the state of things* – were generally overlooked. Most noticeably, this put women at a disadvantage, as frequent and

---

[14] Notable responses include Andy Field's, which is reproduced in section 7, on Anger and Dissent.

committed bloggers such as Jill Dolan, Natasha Tripney, Stacey 'RevStan' Meadwell, Webcowgirl, Linda Buchwald of *Pataphysical Science*, Laura Motta and Aileen McKenna of *The Craptacular*, Jana Perkovic of *Guerilla Semiotics*, and Jane Howard of *No Plain Jane*, all focused primarily on reviewing. It was particularly telling that when Jill Dolan won the 2010–11 George Jean Nathan Award for Dramatic Criticism, the only blogger to have been awarded that prestigious prize, she had still never been featured in *Noises Off*.

When social media platforms grew in popularity (especially Twitter, which was founded in 2006 but really boomed in 2008 and 2009, and crucially permitted non-reciprocal follows rather than the mutual friending required by Facebook), both the profile of female theatre bloggers and the connections between them really grew. Women who were blogging as audience members, often without any pre-existing connections in the theatre industry, could find one another easily for the first time, while those who were using these platforms to share their posts were demonstrating to others that you didn't need to be a white guy with an axe to grind to say something worth reading. Nicole Serratore was one of several bloggers who told me how social media introduced her to the possibilities of theatre blogging: 'I was really miserable at my day job and had started spending a lot of time on Twitter, but then I realized that I didn't have enough space to talk about everything I wanted to talk about, and people there were really encouraging me to talk more, so I decided to expand. I was like, oh, okay, blogs, is that what people do? Okay, I'll do that.'

Similarly, it was Twitter which first connected me to the theatre community in the UK. At a time when I had moved a lot closer to London, and my cultural tastes were becoming more adventurous, I discovered a whole world of alternative and experimental performance work just by searching 'theatre' and following all the interesting people who came up. Those I connected with on that site in 2009 became the first and biggest champions of my blog, when I still had a readership of about five (on a good day) and was largely unaware of the extent of the theatre blogosphere in the UK.

Later, Twitter would come to help bloggers network and coordinate their activities,[15] but its signal-boosting effect was nothing compared to the audience achieved in 2010 by two of theatre blogging's biggest stars.

2010: 'Paint Never Dries'

Andrew and Phil of the *West End Whingers* had been writing their irreverent and gloriously bitchy review blog since 2006, even hosting a series of parties to encourage London theatre bloggers to emerge from behind their laptops, but it wasn't until their review of Andrew Lloyd Webber's *Love Never Dies*, in March 2010 (*West End Whingers* 2010a), that they came to the attention of the media. Having been to a preview performance of the show, a sequel to *Phantom of The Opera*, they reviewed it in a series of 'for' and 'against' paragraphs (except the *fors* also sounded a lot like *againsts*). The review was an absolute panning, and included an alternative

---

[15] The London Theatre Bloggers initiative, started in 2014 by Rebecca Felgate, encouraged its community to use the #ldntheatrebloggers hashtag to arrange meet-ups, share press tickets and publicize posts. For more information, see: https://www.officialtheatre.com/ldntheatrebloggers/.

poster image which took a tiny, almost throwaway, line from their post and made it into the new show title: Paint Never Dries. That phrase – a neat, rhyming summary of the boredom and frustration Andrew and Phil had experienced while watching *Love Never Dies* – became a recurring reference point in what was very quickly an international news story: that the sequel to *Phantom* was crap.

Shared widely amongst '*phans*', who mostly agreed with Andrew and Phil and were engaged in their own online war against the show,[16] the impact of the Paint Never Dries review started to snowball when it was mentioned on BBC lunchtime news on the day of its official opening. Phil was working at his kitchen table with the TV on in the background, and heard the announcer introducing the segment. 'It came up that it was, you know, "Andrew Lloyd Webber's long-awaited sequel to blah blah blah is opening tonight, and it's already been dubbed Paint Never Dries . . ." My head shot up. And then the phone started going. It was on all the news bulletins that day. We were interviewed by Sky News that evening.'

While the media enquiries kept coming in, and the Whingers wrote on their blog of feeling 'decidedly puffed up' by the whole thing (West End Whingers 2010b), Lloyd Webber told reporters that 'all this stuff on the net' was 'a very worrying situation for anybody who's opening any kind of play or musical' (Thorpe 2010). In reality, the fan backlash, combined with the equally unenthusiastic reviews from mainstream critics that followed, was more than likely enough to damage the show's commercial prospects, but having such a headline-worthy epithet to lead with undoubtedly increased the mainstream coverage of such a significant flop. It also gave Andrew and Phil a brief but exciting moment in the spotlight. After the Sky News interview, they did a second for ITN's *News at Ten*, both, somewhat hilariously, while wearing Phantom masks (they still decline to give last names for the sake of their privacy). Later that year, a trip to New York saw them appear on the PBS show *TheaterTalk* after the Broadway transfer of *Love Never Dies* was postponed (it was later cancelled completely).

In terms of reach, the Paint Never Dries phenomenon is probably still the most significant moment in theatre blogging history. While conversations around censorship and theatremaking had been lengthier, with a greater number of blogger contributions, Andrew and Phil's killer put-down had propelled theatre blogging into public consciousness, connecting with a much larger fan movement to quite seriously affect the prospects of the latest megamusical from one of the world's richest and most successful theatremakers. And, just as in 2006 after *My Name Is Rachel Corrie*, the Whingers' impact and visibility in 2010 proved inspirational for a whole new generation of theatre bloggers. Many new voices would join the conversation after discovering their site, while others who had been idly blogging about shows alongside other topics (I count myself in this category) would begin to focus their attention on theatre as a central subject.

There is one more crucial element of this that I haven't yet mentioned though, one which would grow into a significant concern for the UK blogosphere over the following year. Andrew and Phil's review of *Love Never Dies* was posted in advance of its opening night. They had seen a preview, about a week into the run, and so their review was one of the first to be published, before any newspaper critics had been in. A similar thing would happen in the case of

---

[16] The *What's On Stage* messageboard, then owned by Lloyd Webber's Really Useful Group, had become a key site of fan protest. There were sixty-two pages of angry comments on the thread about *Love Never Dies* by opening night, apparently boosting the site's hits by 70,000 (Hoyle 2010).

Spiderman: Turn Off The Dark, a new musical with large-scale aerial stunts which began previews on Broadway in November 2010 but didn't officially open to critics until the following summer, after delays incurred by injuries and changes to the creative team.

By this point in our history of theatre blogging, most bloggers were dedicated to criticism, with many of the earliest theatremaker bloggers posting rarely, if at all. As a result, the theatre blogosphere was becoming a testing ground for new practices, and a lively forum for exploring the ethics and practicalities of reviewing. The issue of reviewing previews was to be one of its recurring concerns. On the one hand, previews are a key component of the theatremaking process, and many changes are still being made as a show meets its first audiences; to review a preview is to review the unfinished. On the other hand, the theatre industry sells preview tickets to audiences just like any other performance, and for big commercial shows on Broadway and in the West End these are still extremely expensive. When theatre bloggers have bought their ticket and will not be getting paid to write their review, they have no obligation to uphold the conventions of professional journalism.

2011: Ethical questions and 'cynical practices'

It was a debate which engaged bloggers and mainstream journalists alike. While bloggers Sans Taste and Webcowgirl received angry messages from performers who felt they had been unfairly reviewed before opening night (*Sans Taste* 2010), some professional critics in New York decided to ignore the embargo imposed by *Spiderman* producers and publish early.[17] But it was – once again – an article in the *Guardian* which really ignited the discussion amongst the UK blogosphere. In a piece from February 2011, Matt Trueman suggested that reviewing previews was a 'cynical practice', implying that if bloggers wanted to be taken seriously, they needed to commit to the same structures and processes as mainstream journalism. His article even passive-aggressively linked to one blogger who had reviewed an early preview of *Frankenstein* at the National Theatre (Trueman 2011).

Trueman's argument was celebrated by some artists who were feeling understandably vulnerable in this new era of audience feedback, but much of the theatre blogosphere (especially those who weren't also makers) were frustrated by his assumptions. Ian Foster of *Ought To Be Clowns* disputed Trueman's implication that every blogger is seeking a career as a newspaper critic – 'I have a job thank you very much' (Foster 2011) – while Corinne Furness of *Distant Aggravation* found the accusation that bloggers were reviewing previews purely in order to boost their hits pretty laughable: 'If I were really after hits I wouldn't be writing about theatre. I'd write about Justin Bieber EVERY DAY' (Furness 2011). In a delicious counter-accusation, Sans Taste noted that publication on the website of a major newspaper hardly exempts writers from chasing hits: 'you think I'm behaving badly in a cynical attempt to chase hits? Pot kettle, Matt' (*Sans Taste* 2011).

In reality, each blogger's individual position on the issue was influenced by a complex entanglement of factors, from price and diary management to personal ambitions and professional relationships. It was true, of course, that posting a review before the newspapers

---

[17] This included Ben Brantley from the *New York Times*, who decided to stick to a date previously identified by producers as the show's official opening night, despite its further postponement (Brantley 2011).

had posted theirs could increase traffic to a blog post, but considering most bloggers didn't even title or tag their posts in a way that search engine crawlers could easily recognize, hits-chasing was rarely a priority. In my experience, the rewards of early reviewing came from the dialogue that would emerge in the days afterwards, following the mainstream reviews too. Being part of a conversation with other critics, bloggers and audience members made me feel more connected to industry trends, more informed about contemporary practices and more aware of my own developing tastes. Crucially, each exchange was time-dependent; theatre is a fast-moving industry, especially in a city like London, and online discourse even more so. Deciding to review a preview wasn't some Machiavellian attempt to scoop the papers, it just meant we could take advantage of cheaper tickets while still participating fully in the public debate that followed a new opening. After all, if theatre blogging wasn't an inherently social activity, we'd all just stick to writing our diaries.

Understandably, anger and upset rippled through the blogosphere in the days after Trueman's article was published. Many felt misrepresented, the resentment no doubt exacerbated by the fact that, despite his professional assignments, Matt Trueman was a blogger himself, and a highly-regarded one at that. His criticism was intelligent, perceptive and often beautifully articulated. At a time when anti-blogging sentiments were rife in newspapers,[18] and bloggers were being lazily presented as some kind of amorphous body of amoral saboteurs, receiving such harsh criticism from one of your peers was particularly upsetting.

In hindsight, this argument over previews was a significant moment of fracture for the UK theatre blogosphere, wherein a small group of bloggers favoured by venues and theatremakers – often because they adhered to press embargoes or had been taught a certain type of critical thinking on arts and humanities university courses – worked hard to distinguish themselves from those who treated their blogs as theatre diaries, or who chose gentle reflection over polemic certainty. Indeed, in Andrew Haydon's broad defence of Trueman's position, he used links to the same passive-aggressive ends: celebrating one blogger for being 'well-written, reliable, entertaining and insightful' while attacking another for posting 'any old badly-written drivel' (Haydon 2011).

Divisions were also appearing across the world in Sydney. Teacher and performer Jane Simmons started her theatre blog, *Shit On Your Play*, in June 2011, citing disappointment both in the shows being made in the city at that time, and the response from professional critics, who she felt 'often reward the attempt and not the actual production' (Simmons 2011a). Initially written anonymously, *Shit On Your Play* gave Simmons a platform to speak her mind about the failures she perceived in the Sydney theatre scene, with contemporary interpretations of classics by rising stars Benedict Andrews and Simon Stone becoming early targets. Andrews' version of *The Seagull* was a 'heartbreaking misinterpretation' which made her 'internal organs atrophy' (Simmons 2011b), while she found 'the stink of desperation' seeping through Stone's re-imagining of Brecht's *Baal*: 'Remember those terribly pretentious things you wrote or staged

---

[18] There are too many examples of this to list them all here, but previously cited pieces by Michael Billington (2007) and Vanessa Thorpe (2010) are representative of the 'concerned parent' tone adopted by many journalists when they considered the idea of a democratised critical culture. And in a more extreme example, Laura Axelrod told me that when she joined the staff of a regional newspaper in the US, staff there were openly hostile to her for being a blogger: 'There was a lot of animosity in the newsroom about it. Like, people were yelling at me sometimes. "You're taking our jobs!" y'know. "You're not trained!" I was there for a year as an editorial assistant, but I was working with about eight editors, so I had to be really careful about my blog.'

at university when you felt that you & maybe a select few of your generation were the only people who really understood the world & then years later you realized you were full of shit? Welcome to STC's production of Baal' (Simmons 2011c).

After Simmons was interviewed about her blog for a freshly launched news website, the *Global Mail*, as an example of bloggers who were 'more tough-minded' than newspaper reviewers (Crittenden 2012), criticism from elsewhere in the Australian blogosphere quickly started to appear. Alison Croggon was characteristically diplomatic about Simmons' right to say whatever she liked on her blog, but explained that 'blogging is much more interesting, diverse, porous (and long-lived)' than was represented in the *Global Mail* feature (Croggon 2012). Jana Perkovic felt similarly, writing that Simmons was 'a singularly *poor* model of theatre blogging' (Perkovic 2012), and Augusta Supple made connections between online anonymity and antagonism: 'I will ask those who delight in the style of writing that empowers the anonymous and aggressive – if this is the tone and style of the artistic conversations we should be having? Is this the best we can do for each other?' (Supple 2012). Simmons would later adjust the title of her blog from *Shit On Your Play* to *SOYP: The People's Theatre Advisor* (eventually handing it over to a new writer, Manan Luthra, after a long hiatus), but the brief flurry of opinion that it had precipitated, alongside the debate about previews which had been happening concurrently in New York and London, had demonstrated that theatre bloggers were increasingly examining the ethics of their practices and relationships.

2011–12: Embedding

We have seen how ethical questions had the potential to divide the blogosphere, but there were other experiments taking place which brought bloggers and theatremakers much closer together. One fascinating case study for scholars of the theatre blog, and of criticism more generally, is Maddy Costa.

Having won the Harold Hobson Drama Critic Award at the National Student Drama Festival in 1997, Costa joined the arts desk at the *Guardian* in 2000, rising to Deputy Arts Editor two years later, and regularly writing reviews, interviews and features for the music and theatre sections, as well as commissioning others. In April 2011, while still working at that publication alongside raising two small children, she started her blog, *States of Deliquescence* (later just *Deliq.*), initially in order to help counter the negative critical response to Kneehigh's production of *The Umbrellas of Cherbourg*, a show which she had seen and loved (Costa 2011). She recounted her emotional reaction to 'the overwhelming, heart-wrenching loveliness and pain and purity of the story' and how much she regretted that the show was going to close early. Then, in some of the final words of the post, she cheered the bloggers who had felt what she had, and explained how *The Umbrellas of Cherbourg* had given her the impetus to join them: 'I know writing about it here won't make the blindest difference. But it did remind me how much I adore the theatre. And that if you want something, there's no point in waiting for other people's permission to get it. Or, as Mme Emery so sagely shrieks, on peut toujour ecrire,[19] no matter what.'

Costa was emerging from a period in which she had mostly felt dissatisfied and disillusioned by theatre, but within a couple of weeks of posting on *States of Deliquescence*, she had started

---

[19] 'On peut toujours ecrire' translates as 'we can always write'.

an email dialogue with Chris Goode, whose own blogging practice had inspired him to think differently about how his experiences as a theatremaker were mediated by writing. Goode was starting a new company, and in an email to Costa (Costa 2016), explained that he was looking for someone to join him in narrating their activities: 'A cross between a dramaturg, an archivist, a documentary artist, an outreach officer, a brand manager and Jiminy Cricket.... Not just an outside eye (and ear) but also a memory, a conscience, a nagging voice. A heart.' As a long-time admirer of Goode's work, and someone who had reviewed it on several occasions, Costa was the ideal person for this experimental, collaborative and as yet unnamed role.

Fast forward almost a year, and fellow theatre blogger Andrew Haydon was travelling around Kurdistan with the Actors' Touring Company, preparing to write a feature for *The Stage* on their experiences of performing Roland Schimmelpfennig's *Golden Dragon* to audiences in the region. The recent history of the area (it was only six months since the last US troops had left Iraq, and a no-fly zone had been in place over Kurdistan since the end of the first Gulf War in 1991) led the company to jokingly refer to Haydon as an 'embedded' journalist, a more theatrically inclined version of those reporters and photographers who travelled with military regiments from the earliest days of the US invasion of Iraq in 2003. Here, simply by way of eating and travelling with them over the course of a week, Haydon found himself thinking differently about the company of artists and performers he was there to write about. In a blog post published on his return (Haydon 2012a), he wrote: 'Apart from anything else, it humanises them. It strikes me that in the usual run of things, theatre criticism sometimes kind of requires you to forget the humanity of those about whom you're writing.'

By virtue of Haydon choosing to title his post 'Embedded', theatre bloggers began to imagine the potential (and potential limitations) of this 'embedded criticism', a term which could be fruitfully applied to a whole spectrum of practices, everything from simple features by writers who had been granted access to rehearsals, right up to the dialogic collaborations of Costa and Goode, which would often expand beyond the internet.

For the *Riot Act* Open House week in 2015 and Goode's contemporary adaptation of Derek Jarman's *Jubilee* in 2017, Costa created physical fanzines, a gesture to punk aesthetics, but also a conscious attempt to create a more representative narrative through collective authorship, joining her own voice with others'. In another collaboration, the *Dialogue* project (with Jake Orr, founder of *A Younger Theatre*, which provided a platform for reviewers aged under twenty-six),[20] Costa would convene 'theatre clubs', bringing audience members together for discussion about shows in-person, and without the presence of any member of the creative team or venue staff. Here, the emphasis is on the equality of participants, who interpret the show they've seen through discussion, rather than the traditionally top-down structure of a post-show Q&A with writer or director. Costa would come to conceptualize her rejection of these hierarchies as indicative of the 'critical horizontalism' advocated by writer and producer Andy Horwitz,[21]

---

[20] Costa and Orr had met at the UK's annual *Devoted and Disgruntled* event in January 2012, an 'Open Space' forum for conversation between artists, audiences and theatre workers which is run by Improbable. There, Costa had proposed a session on the changing artist–critic relationship (Costa 2012a).

[21] Horwitz approaches criticism as a combination of dramaturgy, advocacy and engagement, arguing that the position of the critic should be reframed '*within* the institution or *within* the artist's creative process rather than on the outside passing judgement' (Horwitz 2012). These ideas were explored on *Culturebot*, the site he founded in 2003 as a blog for New York venue Performance Space 122, before it grew into an independent organization in 2007.

but we can just as easily see her pioneering work as an 'embedded' critic, and her ongoing commitment to welcome multiple voices into the public dialogue about theatremaking, as a vindication of the kind of democratization that had been slowly extending throughout the discourse on theatre since the first theatre blogs emerged.

Just as the very first bloggers at the end of the 1990s had provided a model that would drive the philosophy and technologies of Web 2.0 for another decade or more, so the growth of theatre blogs – and, crucially, the gradual diversification of those writing publicly about the shows they were seeing – had sown the seeds for a re-imagining of what theatre criticism could be. The era in which a handful of privileged voices would present some kind of fixed, definitive, notionally 'correct' judgement of a show was waning, and we were starting to see the fruition of ideas and initiatives that could only have emerged in a world which gave a voice – and, crucially, the respect and attention of an interested community – to more participants than ever before.

2012: *Three Kingdoms*

The next chapter of this story is probably the most documented, a moment in which several plotlines from this theatre blogging story converged in something of a narrative climax. It had been five years since 2007, when *Attempts On Her Life* had shown that bloggers could rival newspaper critics, and Chris Goode and David Eldridge had locked antlers about writing for theatre. In that time, the London theatre community had become increasingly connected through social media, while Andrew Haydon, one of the most well-known theatre bloggers in the UK, had dedicated a significant amount of his coverage to the theatre being made in Europe, travelling to festivals in cities such as Prague, Helsinki, Wiesbaden and Berlin, to record and evaluate for an anglophone readership. Haydon's posts fuelled the imaginations of a new generation of theatremakers and audiences who had been developing a taste for the post-dramatic, a term which described the way stories could be broken apart and rebuilt, often with injections of contemporary imagery, pop music, and striking design statements. Here, the writer's text was a plaything – just one part of storytelling, rather than the whole deal – and it was to be epitomized for many in London by a new international collaboration: *Three Kingdoms*.

Three Kingdoms was a truly international show. Its partners spanned three countries (Munich Kammerspiele in Germany, Teater NO99 in Estonia and the Lyric Hammersmith in the UK); there was a British writer (Simon Stephens), German director (Sebastian Nübling) and Estonian designer (Ene-Liis Semper); the acting company had members from the Kammerspiele and NO99 ensembles, plus three British performers; and the show also toured to each country, opening in Tallinn in September 2011, before playing in Munich a month later, and finally arriving in London in May 2012. The story traversed each country too. After the decapitated head of a sex worker, Vera Petrova, is found in a rucksack washed up in the Thames, two detectives follow the trail of the investigation first to Germany, and then Estonia. Each act could be read as a subtle sending-up of the theatrical traditions of that country, beginning with a darkly comic police interrogation set in Hammersmith nick frequently described as 'Pinteresque', moving into a second act in a German brothel where we witnessed a series of sex acts performed with strap-on dildos, squirty cream and, at one point, a baseball bat, and then onto Estonia, where we met a violent, hyper-masculine gang who demonstrated their physical strength by pounding the walls with boxing gloves. By that point though, what was real had become much less certain; the lead detective, Ignatius, initially frustrated by the language barrier (the production was appropriately multi-lingual, and unpredictably surtitled for the audience), had become progressively disconnected from time and space. His partner had disappeared somewhere along the way, his German girlfriend was on the phone from the past, and there was a chance he might have been framed. By the end, the production (which had always been surprising, its walls breaking open unexpectedly, performers suddenly falling into one corner of the stage as if gravity had tipped, and a silent overseer appearing in a white suit to sing karaoke) became *really* wild. I remember two women dancing with hobby horses, a man with a bale of hay on his head, and everyone singing PJ Harvey's *Last Living Rose* as Ignatius went through some kind of bizarre sacrificial ritual. It was almost impossible to follow, but it was *brilliant*.

For those audience members, like me, who had never experienced a theatrical culture outside their own before, *Three Kingdoms* felt like having scales plucked from our eyes. Even now, over six years on, during which time I've travelled to Germany purely to watch theatre on numerous occasions, I can still say with some confidence that I've never had a viewing experience quite like it. The combination of sudden and unexpected imagery, unstable language, the constant threat of violence and a rising sense of madness could make you feel like you were freewheeling through the show just like Ignatius was. For a certain community of UK theatre bloggers, many of whom had become seriously invested in conversations around dialogic and collaborative forms of criticism only a couple of weeks beforehand, *Three Kingdoms* blew the doors off everything all over again.

Many of us wrote about having to sacrifice a part of ourselves to the sensory and cerebral overload. Catherine Love left the theatre 'in a state of confusion, disorientation and uncertainty' (Love 2012a), Matt Trueman explained that watching *Three Kingdoms* was like 'a joyride' for which you 'need to jump in the back seat' (Trueman 2012a), while Andrew Haydon likened the experience to 'giving your synapses an electric shock' (Haydon 2012b). When I attempted to distil my impressions of the show into a blog post, the only way I managed to share the excitement and disorientation of the show was by running parts of my posts through Google Translate, obscuring my English recollections with German and Estonian text (Vaughan 2012).

We had clearly taken significant delight in being thrown far outside our comfort zone as audience members; where British theatre had traditionally celebrated the clear articulation of a thematic argument – a socio-political thesis over two hours of naturalism – *Three Kingdoms* asked us to stop worrying about making sense of things and start thinking by *feeling*. And oh boy, we did *some serious feeling*. Matt Trueman probably said it best (Trueman 2012a) when he wrote: 'Let's blame the adrenaline flooding my bloodstream. Let's blame the breathlessness and the dizziness; the disbelief and the sheer fucking thrill. I was putty. I was windswept. I was in love.'

The exhilaration of it didn't dissipate on leaving the auditorium either. The experience of writing about that show, and witnessing the way it invigorated a whole community of bloggers and theatremakers, was a powerful thing to be part of. When I talked to Catherine Love about that time, she remembers being back in her old bedroom at her parents' house, furiously refreshing Twitter for all the latest posts, and the responses to them. 'I know a lot of it is that dopamine hit, people liking something you've written, but I think it was more than simply vanity; it was like, *oh, I'm part of a dialogue with all these other exciting, interesting, clever people*.'

Over the course of around ten days, a small group of theatre bloggers (ably joined by the new magazine site *Exeunt*, which had been founded the previous year) collectively wrote somewhere approaching 60,000 words about *Three Kingdoms*. While we attempted to communicate details of its storytelling and direction, learning about ensemble theatremaking, new theatre cultures, and investigating differing notions of globalization and misogyny, we were also relishing the opportunity to rebalance some of the negative criticism the show had received from mainstream newspapers and websites. When we read Quentin Letts describe our beloved as 'magnificently bad, laughably awful, a real honking turkey' in the *Daily Mail* (Letts 2012) and Michael Coveney accuse anyone who liked it of being 'debauched beyond redemption' on *What's On Stage* (Coveney 2012), we became united in opposition to all those critics who were unable – whether due to individual competence or journalistic convention – to approach *Three Kingdoms* the way it deserved: with curiosity, imagination and a willingness to look beyond one's own cultural expectations. That generosity, combined with the growing reach and influence of theatre blogs as they worked in tandem with social media discourse, meant that by the end of the show's two-week run, what had started as mostly empty houses were soon almost full, packed with young theatremakers who wanted to see Nübling's iconoclastic direction for themselves, and adventurous audiences intrigued by the sheer strength of opinion on both sides of the critical divide.

The fervour didn't mean that the bloggers were not rigorous in their criticism however. One place this was demonstrated with greatest depth and care was in the discussion about *Three Kingdoms*' treatment of women. That the play largely silenced its female characters was indeed problematic, and the effect of that was exacerbated (several times over) by the physical and emotional horrors that are inflicted on women within the story. It is certainly worth noting that parts of the UK theatre blogosphere that celebrated *Three Kingdoms* for the potency of its narrative and the energy of its production have been criticized by feminist scholars for failing to properly interrogate perceived misogyny at the heart of the play. Melissa Poll has suggested that the show's biggest blog champions uphold damaging tenets of post-feminism by focusing on an overarching allegory for globalization over the horrors of trading in women (Poll 2016).

On reflection, it is true that some of the blog reviews failed to pay proper attention to the brutality of the gender inequality on display, and I include my own contribution in that assessment. Indeed, I have recently wondered how the show would be received today, when one consequence of the 2017–18 #MeToo movement achieving long-overdue justice in high-profile cases of sexual abuse and harassment has been that women all over the world have been forced to repeatedly revisit their own traumatic experiences when simply watching the news or scrolling their feeds. The steps we have collectively taken to address abuses of power across a number of industries – both historic and recent – have been brave and vital, but they have also been emotionally exhausting, demanding that we reassess many of our previous experiences with art as much as with the people in our lives. I'm not just talking about those works which have been made by abusers, but in acknowledgement of how draining it can be to traverse a cultural landscape in which so many works of art and performance present women in demeaning and subjugated roles. Re-reading reviews of *Three Kingdoms* as research for this book, I find I now flinch at mere written descriptions of certain scenes in the play, when watching the action up close in 2012 shocked me only in a superficial, almost tantalizing way, something akin to watching a horror film over the experience of genuine fear. That said, I think it is incorrect to suggest that the theatre blogosphere of 2012 failed to address the topic of misogyny in their consideration of *Three Kingdoms*. A close examination of its treatment of women took place across blog posts by Catherine Love, Maddy Costa, Sarah Punshon, Andrew Haydon and Hannah Silva, and there was a lengthy round-table dialogue on the subject published on *Exeunt* (Love 2012b; Costa 2012b; Punshon 2012; Haydon 2012c; Silva 2012; Tripney et al. 2012). After the initial wave of joyful exuberance, the conversation had settled into a thorough and detailed debate on gendered violence and the theatre's duty of care.

In some ways, *Three Kingdoms* was simply a useful crucible for a series of industry debates, but while it may be true that change was a-coming anyway, those changes were facilitated by the theatre bloggers who championed *Three Kingdoms* in the face of significant hostility from members of the mainstream press. Over the coming years, some of the larger theatres in London became much more welcoming of non-linear narratives, non-naturalistic performances, and postmodern, post-dramatic direction and design. Shows like *Adler and Gibb* at the Royal Court and *Pomona* at the Orange Tree showed that mainstream British theatre's historic attachment to naturalism was waning; directors like Robert Icke, Ellen McDougall and Jude Christian increasingly used ideas and techniques from European theatremakers; and Belgian director Ivo van Hove became the darling of London and New York. And at the Lyric Hammersmith, the theatre which had presented *Three Kingdoms*, artistic director Sean Holmes launched the *Secret Theatre* project, forming an experimental ensemble which would operate throughout the building's refurbishment between 2013 and 2015.

In his opening speech, Holmes explained how the internationalism of *Three Kingdoms* had revealed how the 'things we thought of as rules were merely assumptions, and assumptions that had become so ingrained we didn't even notice them anymore' (Holmes 2013). These included the precarious working conditions which actors and theatre artists are forced into in the UK, and the way that time and economic constraints hold back inventive interpretations of texts, but it also extended into the coverage and criticism of theatre by newspaper reviewers, whose five-star reviews had received 'exaggerated respect'. Holmes also opened up *Secret Theatre* to bloggers, with several spending time in rehearsals with the ensemble, further exploring the possibilities of embedded criticism. Alternative approaches to criticism which had been championed by bloggers were now being embraced by major London venues.

Experiment, professionalism and experimenting with professionalism

While theatre bloggers had always been ready to innovate with language,[22] by 2013 we had started to do it with other media too. Eve Nicol, a blogger and theatremaker based in Scotland, created *Edinburgh Furinge Reviews* in August that year, using triptychs of cat pictures to reflect her experience of theatre shows at the Edinburgh Fringe. Each one charted her journey through the work chronologically, presenting an embodied response using the imagery and language of digital culture, where cats had been employed by memes and reaction GIFs since some of the

---

[22] I'm thinking here of the West End Whingers reviewing the National Theatre's 2009 production of Wole Soyinka's *Death and the King's Horseman* in the form of a scam email, or Dan Hutton reviewing David Greig's *The Strange Undoing of Prudencia Hart* (see section 8) in the form of a border ballad, but there are many other examples too.

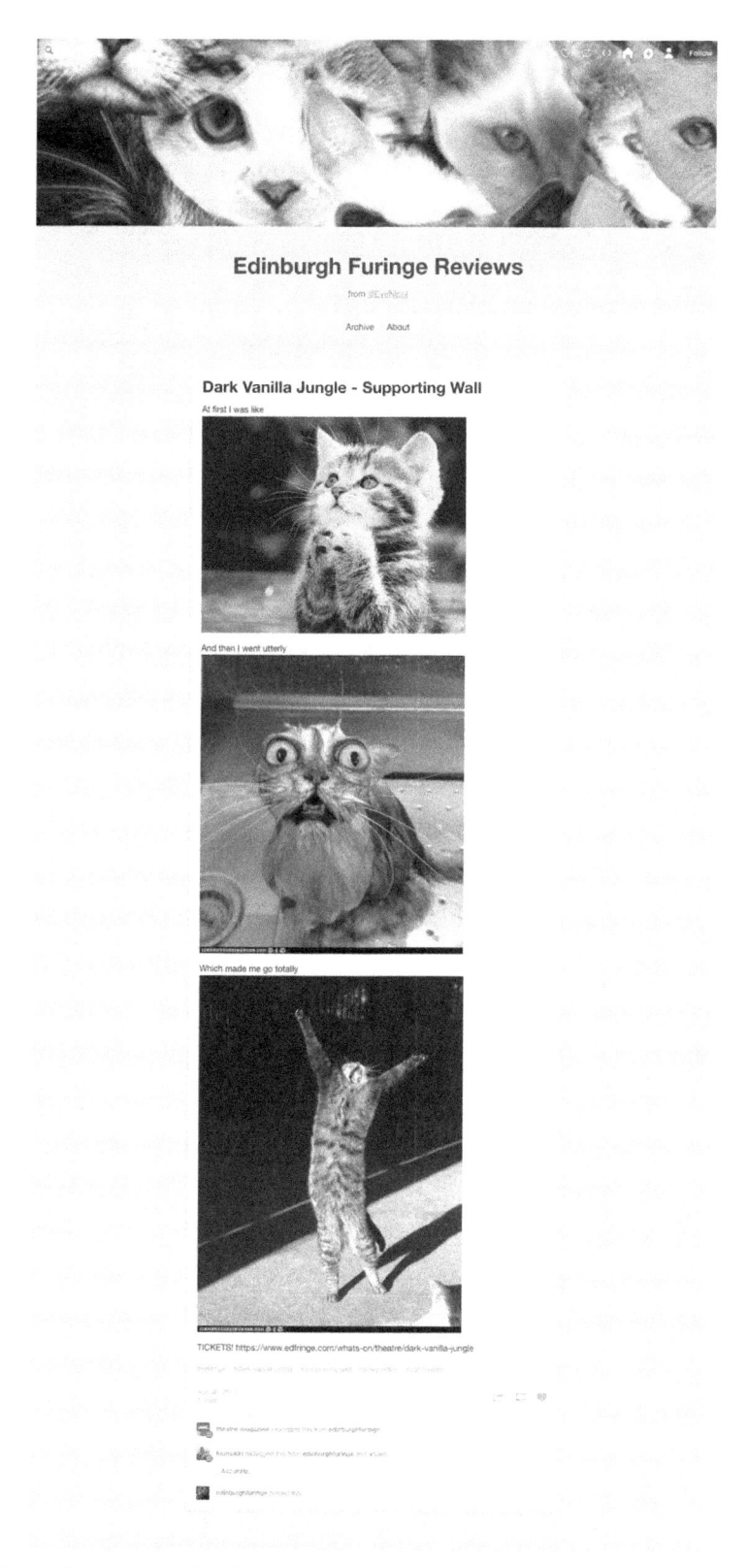

Figure 1 Screenshot from *Edinburgh Furinge Reviews* by Eve Nicol, c. 2013. Courtesy Eve Nicol.

earliest web forums. The text on each *Furinge* post was minimal: just a few words, always following a similar formula ('At first I was all', 'Then I went a bit', 'And at the end I was all' is one example), and with a ticket link at the end. It was an immediate hit on Twitter – we, ahem, *lapped it up* – with Nicol quickly inundated with more ticket offers and review requests than she could keep up with. Andrew Haydon even posted a pastiche on his blog, using the same deadpan image of a fish – under the title 'Postcards From the *Cods*' – to review works he had disliked or been ambivalent towards (Haydon 2013).

I felt like Nicol's *Furinge* reviews tapped into thoughts and feelings I'd been having regularly in the year and a bit since *Three Kingdoms*: how do we, as theatre bloggers, more accurately and powerfully communicate the physical, visceral and emotional experience of watching a live work of theatre? In a culture of theatre criticism which foregrounds the articulate, cerebral response, and celebrates those who can superficially remove themselves from their dispassionate analysis of a show's theme or politics, where does the excitement, confusion, desire, boredom, fear, joy and exhilaration get recorded? It seemed to me like it was all there on *Edinburgh Furinge Reviews*, plus a whole lot of Nicol's wit and passion, but was so rare elsewhere.

In the years 2013 to 2016, I and a number of other UK bloggers embraced the critical possibilities of the digital space, often using the theme or form of a show to inspire a post which recreated our experience for readers. I posted screenshots of a WhatsApp emoji dialogue to review *Teh Internet is Serious Business* at the Royal Court, made readers complete a bureaucratic online form to access reviews of *The Trial* at the Young Vic, and created a 'choose your own adventure' style navigable review of Jamal Harewood's *The Privileged* using open source Twine software (Vaughan 2014, 2015a, 2015b). Tim Bano's review of *Teh Internet* was in the style of Buzzfeed clickbait, then, for *Exeunt*'s Pursued By A Bear podcast, he matched the headphone format of Complicité's *The Encounter* by creating a metatextual audio review in which he conversed with his past self (Bano 2014, 2015). Meanwhile, Nicol followed her *Edinburgh Furinge* success by taking her criticism to Snapchat, where that app's emphasis on ephemerality meant her posts would disappear after a designated number of seconds. Her responses to shows – expressed as drawings or decorated selfies – therefore vanished just as her residual elation, confusion or disappointment did.

While these formal innovations made up only a tiny percentage of the overall theatre blogosphere, they were indicative of the creative freedoms enabled by digital space but rarely permitted by more traditionally journalistic publications. By redefining what theatre criticism could be, whether through embedding, creative response or means of dissemination, bloggers were forging a new culture of critique – alongside artists and readers – that was participatory in a way that the newspapers could never have facilitated, even on their correspondence pages. More people were engaged in a public discourse around theatre than ever before, and the shape and content of that discourse was broader too. But while some bloggers worked on remaking theatre criticism for a digital space, moving further and further away from the form and style found in traditional publications, others made moves to professionalize. Leonard Jacobs, who had been an editor for trade paper *Back Stage* when he started the *Clyde Fitch Report* in 2006, repositioned his blog as an editorial website with a team of contributors within three years. Alison Croggon, who had originally left print criticism back in the 1990s, was approached by the *Australian* to make a return to professional reviewing in 2007, where she made sure her contract allowed her to continue blogging alongside that work. Matt Trueman left his job at an acting agency to become a full-time professional theatre critic in 2011; his blog soon became a place to catalogue writing published elsewhere. Many other bloggers found ad hoc freelance work with newspapers and paying websites, or began to host 'guest posts' from other writers as a first step towards expansion.

There were other experiments in professionalizing theatre blogging too. The New York-based Independent Theater Bloggers Association (ITBA), formed in 2009, had grown its membership to over 100, even initiating an awards scheme, but this network had become much less active by 2013.[23] Then, in 2015, *My Theatre Mates* was launched by Mark Shenton, critic at *The Stage,* and Terri Paddock, the founding editor of *What's On Stage*, as a portal which would bring posts from multiple theatre bloggers together on one site. Those registered as 'Mates' could access a larger readership and be part of a supportive peer network, but membership was reliant on reciprocal promotion of both the *My Theatre Mates* site *and* its advertisers, and interested bloggers had to provide references from artists, venues or PRs in order for their inclusion to be vetted. These requirements were eventually relaxed, but still, the initiative demonstrated a return to gatekeeping rather than a freedom from it.

More equitably, in 2016 bloggers Laura Kressly (*The Play's The Thing UK*) and Katharine Kavanagh (*The Circus Diaries*) joined forces to launch the Network of Independent Critics, ostensibly to help bloggers cover shows at the Edinburgh Fringe that August. By raising money through a crowdfunding campaign and organizing shared accommodation, they were able to significantly reduce the costs of living for theatre bloggers travelling to the festival, and ensure that priority was given to those who were focused on reviewing small-scale shows and under-recognized artists (such as student companies, or Black and LGBTQ+ performers). Through affiliation with the network, the bloggers taking part were also in a better position to request press tickets and artist interviews.

While these initiatives varied in their approach (and level of selflessness), they were combining with the career moves of a few high-profile writers to shift industry perception away from the tired image of bloggers as renegade egotists with no ethical code, and towards an appreciation of their contribution to the theatre sector. There was still a long way to go though, as one theatre blogger discovered in 2017.

2017: Payment, protectionism and the ATCA

In 2017, Philadelphia theatre blogger Jess Foley applied for membership of the American Theater Critics Association (ATCA). She had started reviewing as an intern at a local newspaper, *City Paper*, but that had been sold and shuttered in 2015, so since then she had been working multiple jobs, publishing occasional freelance articles, and, of course, maintaining her own blog, *Foley Got Comped*. She knew that even though paid opportunities in arts journalism were disappearing in her city, membership of ATCA would give her access to international conferences, workshops, and the support and mentorship of a peer network to help sustain her practice while she searched for new paid opportunities.

---

[23] Many US bloggers celebrate the ITBA for bringing their community together and helping to raise the profile of review blogs especially, but others expressed concern to me that the network was cynically employed by some of its coordinators to furnish the shows they produced with positive coverage.

Not only was the rejection letter she received from ATCA that October exceedingly unkind, it showed how out of touch with current practice that organization had become:

> Some of your work's off-putting features include: multiple instances of profanity (from 'Swallow' – 'turn my phone the f*** off'), making pointless comparisons between the play and today's political climate, making editorial statements about your personal political views, and discussing almost everything under the sun (from the set design to the playwright's background) in the first few sentences. These things do not encourage readers to have an understanding of what the play is about or what the playwright was trying to convey. Some of your work was focused more on YOU than the play.

When I first read the rejection, posted in full on Foley's blog (Foley 2017a), I thought it was satire. I assumed that she had written it herself, as a comment on an out of touch organization, but no, the whole thing was real. She had chosen to publish it 'as like a "Going Out of Business" sign' (Foley 2017b) to the Philadelphia venues and companies she had reviewed since 2012. Foley was able to see the humour in the situation, but she was also exhausted. Membership of ATCA was supposed to boost her morale, keep her motivated when paid opportunities were scarce, but this rejection did the opposite, and she stopped writing her blog for almost a year afterwards. 'If you create a situation that's unsustainable, where you have to work for free', she told me over Skype, 'sometimes you have to stop working.'

It was the same thing that had happened to so many theatre bloggers: life kicks up a gear, maybe you start a family or have to take a second job, and the time and energy you once had for blogging begins to dry up. Natasha Tripney told me how, as her journalism career took off, her blog became an aggregator for things she was publishing elsewhere, 'which wasn't what I wanted it to be, but I just couldn't do it and do it well'. Garrett Eisler told a similar story of juggling blogging and academia. There had been a time when he hoped a bigger publication would take on his blog, and host it on their platform, 'but people were only interested in doing that as long as there was no cost to them. No-one wanted to pay. No-one wants to have more full-time employees with benefits.' Meanwhile, the cost of living in the world's major theatre cities is rising; for Nicole Serratore, theatre blogging 'is a tremendous amount of side-hustle in a world where everyone's got a main job and a side-hustle *for money*. It's harder and harder to make these things work.'

There are crowdfunding sites like Patreon, and payment tools like Paypal and GoCardless, which allow theatre bloggers to accept regular donations from their readers, but while some have had minor success with those, it's never quite enough to allow theatre bloggers to drop other work commitments. At the same time, as newspaper critics find their word counts reduced and contracts left unrenewed, some begin self-publishing online as a way to sustain both a critical practice and a public profile. Consequently, the boundaries between 'professional' and 'amateur' are more porous than ever before. This was precisely Jessica Foley's argument when she answered her ATCA rejection. 'My response to them was to ask, "when the newspapers are falling down around us, how do you define professional experience?" The fact that I'm not able to support myself by writing about theatre is not a reflection of my ability.'

Following a mini-outcry from others who had been appalled by the way their letter had been worded, ATCA reviewed their membership guidelines, removing the requirements that critics must be paid and working under the supervision of an editor. The word 'professionally' was also removed from their criteria; membership is now 'open to any writer who regularly publishes substantive pieces reviewing or otherwise critically covering theater' (ATCA 2017). We could probably quibble over what 'substantive' means in this context, but still, progress is progress. And it remains significantly more open and democratic than the UK's Critic's Circle, which has no published application criteria, relying instead on an archaic system of nominations from existing members. The truth is that organizations founded to represent the interests of journalists still largely see bloggers as a threat, and rarely embrace the conscious subjectivity and non-traditional language of much blog writing.

A sustainable future

Many people now consider that the health of the theatre blogosphere – of theatre discourse in its entirety – is dependent on its financial sustainability. Certainly, something as essential to our industry as impartial reporting and representative criticism is worth paying for, wherever it is published. But we must also protect theatre bloggers from becoming entangled in yet another competitive and demoralizing aspect of late capitalism. After I set up a Patreon profile in 2015 in order to collect monthly donations from my blog readers, I was shocked by how quickly blogging stopped being a pleasure and became a chore. Even though I hadn't changed anything other than my income, and I knew my patrons wanted to support my practice out of generosity rather than commercial expectation, the newfound weight of responsibility I felt to those people was almost overwhelming. The idea that getting paid for something means that you must somehow do it 'properly' – in my case, worrying about not posting often enough, or not giving enough attention to theatre outside London – is deeply ingrained in us by the expectations of a labour market. I wasn't able to reconceptualize my relationship with money successfully enough to receive donations without my blog becoming just another workplace. After a year, I turned off my Patreon donations and announced that my blog would be taking a hiatus.

I now think about the sustainability of the theatre blogosphere in terms of wellbeing. This includes, of course, the wellbeing of individual contributors, from financial security to mental health, but it also refers to the wellbeing of the discourse itself. For the theatre blogosphere to flourish, it requires multiple posts from a broad spectrum of identities and perspectives, with active blogging communities in theatre cultures all over the world. It must uphold the distinction between blogger dialogue and industry marketing, rejecting the infiltration of corporate interests. That may reduce the earning potential of individual bloggers, but it means the blogosphere can truly support and enhance the work of theatremakers, encourage their experiments, explore their ideas, and critique flawed institutions and structures as much as individual shows.

It is by challenging the injustices and inequalities of theatre (and there are many) that bloggers make their most vital contribution. When Notting Hill theatre The Printroom cast a new production of Howard Barker's *In The Depths of Dead Love* – a play set in ancient China – with exclusively white actors in 2016, it was through blogs that the protest movement could articulate its concerns, direct from actors with East Asian heritage, such as Erin Quill, Vera Chok and Daniel York Loh (Quill 2016; Chok 2016, 2017; York Loh 2016). Annually since 2016, blogger Victoria Sadler has surveyed the programmes of London's major producing theatres in order to highlight their commitment (or lack of) to women playwrights (Sadler 2016, 2017, 2018). From 2015 to 2017, the anonymous blogger running *Hawks In The Wings*[24] used public financial records to look beyond cheerful press releases and to analyse the precarious economic practices of companies and venues such as English National Opera, Portsmouth's New Theatre Royal, and Summerhall in Edinburgh. And the Critics of Colour Collective – founded by Bridget Minamore, Sabrina Mahfouz and Georgia Dodds after the white critics who reviewed Arinzé Kene's *Misty* at the Bush Theatre in 2018 seemingly failed to understand much of the play's content and references – address that imbalance by showcasing critical perspectives by writers of colour.

Stepping away from existing formulas of *either* personal blogs *or* edited magazine sites, the first iteration of the *Critics of Colour* site[25] didn't operate any formal commissioning processes, instead making press tickets available on Twitter to any writers of colour who want to have a go at reviewing. They also pledged to publish critical responses without edits and in whatever form the writers prefer, while still providing personalized feedback to contributors. As a result, the initiative simultaneously developed new talent, facilitated a broader and more representative critical landscape, and opened up access to the traditionally closed industry territory of the press night comp list, all without replicating the unnecessary gatekeeping or editorial hierarchies of mainstream journalism.

The personal wellbeing of writers is also protected by being part of a collective. There is less pressure to maintain a certain frequency or consistency of output, or to spend hours on self-promotion, and those who are most often harassed and discriminated against are better able to protect themselves. Online, just as in other parts of life, there is strength in numbers.

Of course, not all collectives are formally articulated or share a platform like *Critics of Colour* do. Sometimes the mutual support and encouragement of peers is established organically, through shared practices and tastes, and social interaction. Throughout this history of the theatre blogosphere, these support networks emerge and decline periodically: the earliest bloggers sharing their experiences of the New York fringe theatre scene over Vietnamese food; the bloggers who rallied around Ming-Zhu Hii when her comments were the site of a coordinated attack; the Network of Independent Critics fundraising together and pooling resources to help broaden coverage in Edinburgh; the countless hours I've spent just chatting with my peers in the pub or foyer bar. To imagine an online space where there are no divisions and no conflict is naïve, but friendships and affinities can blossom within that. What I hope for is that theatre bloggers continue to seek one another out, offering mutual support and encouragement while working in dialogue to implore the theatre industry to, please, just *be better*.

---

[24] See http://www.hawksinthewings.com/.

[25] In December 2018, Minamore, Mahfouz and Dodds announced that they would be undergoing a period of reflection and research before extending the collective's work to achieve new goals (Minamore et al. 2018). In Summer 2019, shortly before this book went to press, they announced the first of these new initiatives: a criticism summer school at the Roundhouse, London, with bursaries available to those unable to afford the £15 sign-up fee.

CHAPTER 3
THEATRE BLOGGING IN PRACTICE – A WHATSAPP DIALOGUE

From the moment that the idea for this book was born, I knew that it had to give voice to those who are at the coalface of the theatre blogosphere. It's all very well pontificating about the history and culture of the form, but if you don't also look at the day-to-day experiences of a range of practitioners, you're really just creating another dusty textbook for public burial in the library stacks, or worse, a hundred thousand word thinkpiece. So, back in July 2018 I invited thirteen theatre bloggers – students, journalists, lecturers, actors and theatremakers, as well as those with no relationship to the sector beyond blogging – to join me in a conversation about what they do and why they do it.

In reflection of our eight different cities and five different time zones, but also in acknowledgement of how internet usage is increasingly mobile, we congregated in a WhatsApp groupchat, each dipping in and out over the course of a working week. I came with some questions about motivations, style and money, but the honest, generous and intelligent contributions took us into other territories too: those of friendships, etiquette, collectivity, fatigue, duties of care and conflicts of interest. These bloggers take their responsibilities to the theatre sector really seriously, even if that relationship can become fraught with stress and insecurity.

What follows is an edited version of what was initially over *thirty-seven thousand words* of chat. Sadly, for reasons of potential litigation as much as brevity, I have had to cut discussions of casting politics, critical flops, institutional awards schemes and sexual harassment scandals, but I hope these remaining highlights give some impression of the breadth and variety of theatre blogging practices, and the realities of our diverse experiences.

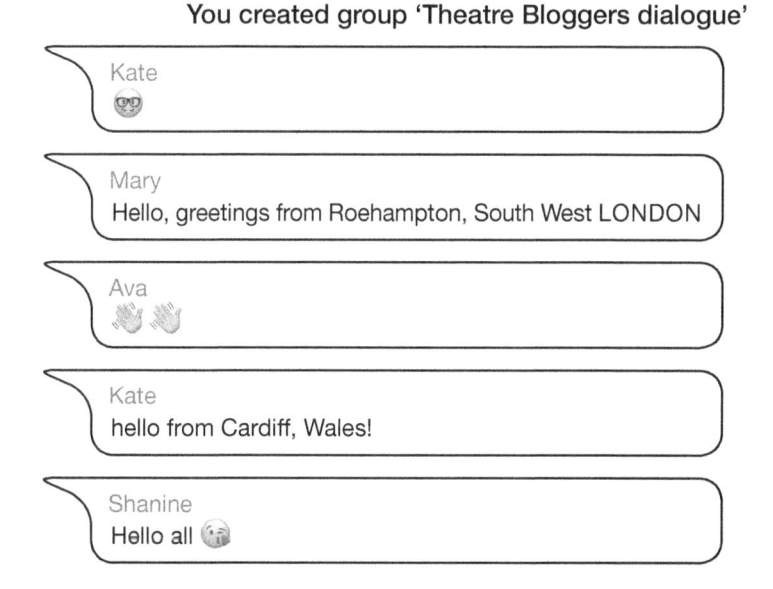

> You created group 'Theatre Bloggers dialogue'

> **Kate**
> 😁

> **Mary**
> Hello, greetings from Roehampton, South West LONDON

> **Ava**
> 👋 👋

> **Kate**
> hello from Cardiff, Wales!

> **Shanine**
> Hello all 🙈

Theatre Blogging

> **James**
> Hello from Manchester!

> **Kevin**
> Hello from Sydney

> **Jan**
> Hello from NYC

> **Daniella**
> 🙌🙌🙌

> **Anne-Marie**
> Hello from Melbourne

> **Ian**
> *waves from a train to Manchester*

> **Bob**
> Hello, all!

> **Meg**
> Hi everyone! Hope you're all ready to kick off a brilliant, fruitful conversation over the next few days. 😀

> **Mary**
> I'm ready! 🙋

> **Meg**
> I'm going to start us off by asking about blogging motivations. I'm interested in why you started and what keeps you going. So, over to you . . . why blog?

> **Mary**
> My motivation is mostly to give another opinion or reflection of a show's production. I have no academic background in theatre or opera. I'm a Londoner with parents from SE Asia. I'm a woman. I feel that my opinion counts because I can speak for many people who aren't represented and want to know about theatre and opera without the technical jargon. Knowing that I'm opening up the genres to different people/audiences who can enjoy the arts is gratifying to me.

Theatre Blogging in Practice – a WhatsApp Dialogue

Shanine
It is a nice talking point and I get free tickets but primarily it keeps me involved in a scene I would be interested in but not necessarily take much notice of day to day. I like seeing new faces, actors I love and crucially having the opportunity to hear about productions I wouldn't otherwise know about

Shanine
I've also met some really nice other bloggers who I see at press nights and other events.

Mary
Totally agree with you on the blogging friendships part :) It's nice to know we are not alone.

Anne-Marie
I still can't believe it's been so long (2006). I'd been working in arts management/programming/marketing for a long time and I'd hit the wall. I had to do something different and was accepted into a writing and editing course. I also wasn't getting work-related invites to shows any more, and being a student mean a less income, so I needed a way to keep seeing shows. I started on a website and moved to the blog a couple years later when I realised that they didn't really get read on the site.

Ian
I first turned to blogging as a post-break-up project and as way to meet the West End Whingers! It was also a way of chronicling my theatregoing – collecting programmes is well and good but I soon ran out of room, I kept losing ticket stubs, and so the blog serves as the one place that records all my theatre trips.

Stacey
I started blogging to keep a record, like Ian, but also because my journalist day job was moving towards editing rather than writing so blogging serviced my love of writing. I've since discovered a great community and made some great friends – and meet new people all the time.

Meg
Everything that you say about friendships helping to motivate and sustain blogging totally rings true for me too.

Theatre Blogging

> **Kevin**
> I graduated as an actor, worked as a Director, and a Teacher of Acting at a major Drama school in Australia for nearly 48 years. One of my ex-students encouraged me to write a blog so as to give 'an acting class' for former students to read. I also felt that the performing arts in Australia were ill-served. Reviews were typically advertising propaganda. As a practitioner in the field I thought I could write longer and more incisively about the work I saw.

> **Ava**
> i only started my blog a year ago and it was out of a desire to respond to theatre in a way that mainstream criticism doesn't (and literally can't), as mary says. i wanted to be able to write longform and expressively about theatre i'd seen, in a way that was just as formally inventive as the shows i'd see all the time.

> **Ava**
> i also felt an urge to respond emotionally to pieces of work – emotion in criticism is seen as being a bit weird, particularly in mainstream criticism, but to me it feels completely bizarre to negate our cultural biases in favour of writing a 'neutral' review.

> **Jan**
> I've been blogging since 2007. I'm a longtime journalist and as disruption began to hit the industry hard, I wanted an outlet that would distract me. I've been a theater lover since my grade school days and decided to write about it after reading about a food blogger. I treat the blog as a regular column. I do it all because I love theater and because, as a black woman, I feel it important to add a different voice.

> **Jan**
> I also think the lines between 'professional' and 'amateur' critics are disappearing. Publications here in the U.S. are cutting back on arts criticism and the people who used to hold those jobs (even some who used to diss bloggers) have set up blogs.

Theatre Blogging in Practice – a WhatsApp Dialogue

Anne-Marie
Yes, I had a paid gig as a reviewer with a daily, but that disappeared when that paper was slashed, then slashed even more. Many freelance friends lost their work, not only in arts. But I've kept going. I think of quitting – I've been very quiet recently – but I'm still seeing shows. I've been seeing and hanging with other writers 2–3 times a week for years; I don't know what else to do!

Kate
My start was a combination of two major factors: I needed to move away from performing/producing after my house/bus/theatre was burnt down in 2012, and had always enjoyed (and felt pretty good at) writing; I was massively frustrated that, after discovering the breadth and richness of circus-based performance whilst touring with a circus show, it was virtually impossible to find any info about this work online.

Kate
When circus work was reviewed in the mainstream press, they never talked about the shows in terms that meant anything to those who were familiar with circus in any way. They were all 'outsider impressions'. I wanted to fill the gap by addressing concerns of the circus sector.

Stacey
I've increasingly lost interest in mainstream criticism for similar reasons to those already mentioned. It doesn't seem to represent me, it's predominantly white middle-aged men – why would I care what they think?

Mary
I used to write for a couple of online outlets but I stopped 2–3 years ago. I felt the pressure of having to have my review figured out and ready for publication within a space of 12 hours. It wasn't enough time. I really needed to think about what I hated, enjoyed and loved about a show. Blogging gets rid of all of that pressure.

Theatre Blogging

Bob
Yeah I also used to write for the City of Chicago on culture. It was a steady gig. But I hated writing the same crappy listicles about whatever trendy nonsense. I went back to blogging for the opportunity to write what I wanted.

James
I got offered a free ticket to review a show when I was at university and I think that was the first review I wrote. Then I kept writing a few more (maybe five or so) while I was there, in exchange for tickets. Then I moved back to Derby, went to the theatre less often (cos it's expensive) but kept writing about shows with the goal I'd maybe get free tickets again one day. I work as a maker too so it was helping me solidify and articulate my thoughts about work as I was reviewing.

James
I think what I get out of blogging is being able to respond on my own terms to a show, without pressure to appraise it by any sort of metric. And it feeds massively into my work as a dramaturg and maker. And I wouldn't be able to afford to see theatre if I didn't get free tickets.

Ava
^^ i second everything james said about being a maker as well

Daniella
I started blogging in the summer after first year of uni because I was bored in my hometown. I didn't know much about the theatre blogging 'scene' at all and just kinda talked about stuff I'd already seen. Then, I guess because of twitter, I started getting invited to stuff and I felt well fancy and like I'd #MADEIT and my mum thought I was gonna meet the queen or something because she doesn't really get how the internet works lol.

Daniella
Then about a year ago I started reading a lot of smaller bloggers who blogged about stuff they enjoyed rather than press obligations, and they had a different form and writing style, and I guess I realised that I wanted to write how I wanted. I sort of had an internal crisis about whether my reviews really *meant* anything if they were written in the same style as everyone else . . .??

Theatre Blogging in Practice – a WhatsApp Dialogue

Mary
that's a good point Daniella. I get tons of invites and i don't say yes to all of them. i used to be a yes person, but i stopped. reason 1) because i don't have time, 2) i don't feel like I'd be the right person to review some shows I'm invited to

Anne-Marie
I could write a long time about this. I've worked in marketing/publicity – I get it. But if all you want is a star rating and an adjective – what's the point? If you want critical conversation . . . that is where bloggers really come in.

Anne-Marie
But I also never promise a review any more. There are many reasons we chose not to write. Time, illness, nothing more to add to the response. And often, especially with new work, because kicking a show in the guts does nothing for anyone.

Ava
i feel like i've kinda run out of juice – the point of the blog initially was to write about the stuff i loved and had a visceral reaction to, but since i've been reviewing more everything feels a little more watered down and less exciting.

Meg
I also recognise that, so much. 💔

James
It's so rare to have an unambiguously fun time at the theatre

Ava
yes omg i literally just want to have a good time

Ava
and sometimes a good time is crying the whole way through

James
I want to start going to wrestling instead

Theatre Blogging

> **Meg**
> I felt that burn-out over the last couple of years. I stopped blogging so much, stopped going to the theatre so much, and stopped putting so much pressure on myself. Now I go less often and write even less often than that, but some of my recent trips have been SO AMAZING. It's made me feel so rejuvenated, almost young again 😊

> **Ava**
> i've noticed recently that i've shifted away from responses to work that i loved and it's become more unpacking stuff i didn't like or that really frustrated me. which is good in a way, but i also kinda miss being positive lol

> **Stacey**
> The writing is part of the process and enjoyment for me. Sometimes it's not until I start writing that I really unearth what I think about a piece of theatre. Or the writing helps me work through my thoughts.

> **Stacey**
> If I realise I feel under pressure to write I take a step back, don't beat myself up if I don't review absolutely everything.

> **Kevin**
> I sometimes think of stopping but am encouraged to keep at it.

> **Kevin**
> I will write sometimes a week after seeing a production just to research and cogitate.

> **Mary**
> Well, this is how I see it. We have this great community of bloggers out there. Even if I have seen a show and had no time to write about it I know that there are people who will have written up a review, etc.

> **James**
> Yeah that's really lovely abt the sharing of the blogspace, Mary. We're not making individual pieces, we're contributing to a larger thing

Theatre Blogging in Practice – a WhatsApp Dialogue

Mary
Let's face it. The newspapers, even the Stage, Variety, NY Times, . . . they don't cover everything. Combined, we all do.

Mary
We are like the Avengers for theatre reviewing

Kevin
Blogs are becoming an increasingly important as the mainstream gets less and less space. Essentially, in a small pond like Sydney, the blogger's voice is important both for box office and art/craft definition. In Australia we are only 25 million people (nearly) so the pool is small and the arts are considered less important than, say, sport, which is why theatregoers have sought out the bloggers.

Bob
Chicago has around 200+ theatre groups at any given time. The goal of my blog has been to give a voice and representation to companies that might otherwise be passed by simply due to the volume of content, which our resource-strapped critical community can't hardly cover.

Meg
I had no idea Chicago was such a theatre city. From an outsider's point of view, it seems so eclipsed by NY.

Bob
Chicago is actually more of a theatre city than NY imho. A lot of it is the storefront scene. Broadway just has the brand and star power.

Kevin
There is a vibrant small co-op theatre scene in Sydney (theatres with seat capacity of 150 or less) that have become artistic rivals to the big companies. The word of mouth of bloggers has become essential to these companies.

Ava
i would be interested to know how many people here consider themselves makers as well as critics?

Theatre Blogging

> **Bob**
> I'm interested to know how you can critique as well as make. I've friends that did both and had to give up one because of conflict of interests. You inevitably have to review a friend and future colleague.

> **Ava**
> i feel ok reviewing ppl i know because i trust myself to write as empathetically as possible and my blogs are never really like flat out judgements on a piece, more explorations

> **James**
> Yeah same 🤷

> **James**
> I think it's about writing honestly and reflectively. There's a different quality to responding openly to a piece and 'reviewing' it. I joke a lot that my reviews are more 'this show reminded me of a book I read when I was 15', rather than appraising a show's worth

> **Shanine**
> I am intrigued by those that also work in theatre (either as press/marketing or as creators) as well as blogging because it can feel quite claustrophobic and demanding

> **Kate**
> The lack of critical engagement in the circus world is, I think, partly because of the incestuous nature of circus work – it's a VERY small world, and most people don't want to rock any boats. The inclusive spirit seems to be one of the key defining factors that distinguishes circus arts communities from theatre/dance/sport, and there is a tradition of secrecy and hyperbolic rhetoric in circus that a critical eye cuts through.

> **Kate**
> I am a natural born equivocator. Value judgements don't come easy to me, which means I'm not really 'reviewing' in the traditionally consumer-focused way.

Theatre Blogging in Practice – a WhatsApp Dialogue

Shanine
With no offence to actors here, I think it is a horrible, competitive job. I think they increasingly rely on bloggers to get good reviews, which may lead to good agents and a great career.

James
Honestly I think it's a shame to see criticism as just a way to support the way the industry already works. I hope that my writing encourages critical thought around the systemic structures that force the industry (and actors etc) to work in the way it does

Ava
i've been told to not openly criticise big theatres bcos it'll jeopardise my future career but they're so fucking flawed. reviewing institutions HAS to be a part of arts criticism imho

Ava
these shows don't exist in vacuums, the places they're being shown have manifestos and aims and they need to be analysed as closely as the shows inside them

Molly
I can actually pinpoint the exact moment I realized this was something I wanted to do, if you want to hear that story.

Kate
yes! story!

Molly
It was the day Carousel officially opened on Broadway. Carousel as a musical is my greatest enemy. And as the reviews starting coming in, I realized something fun. I realized that you could almost guess the content of the review based on the name of the reviewer.

Molly
David would think it was perfect, Sarah would think it was definitely timed inappropriately.

Theatre Blogging

> **Molly**
> And I realized that there's a lack of non-old straight white males in theatre saying what they think and feel.

> **Molly**
> So I got together some friends of different backgrounds, orientations, races and religions, and we got to work.

> **Meg**
> Yes! ✊

> **Molly**
> I tried to make it really diverse and even have a male perspective but I couldn't find one so we just have a lot of vaginas running around.

> **Meg**
> There's still an overall shortage of vaginas running around

> **Meg**
> Would you say it feels like the Theatrical Board is pushing for change?

> **Molly**
> I would say we're pushing back. I would say that it's been pushed on all of us to be quiet little women and to let the men speak and that our opinions aren't as valid because we aren't old enough – I don't like DEH very much either and my mom was talking to a woman who had seen it and mentioned her daughter didn't like it and the woman said 'Oh, how old is your daughter?' And my mom said '20'. And the woman said 'Oh, maybe she's just not old enough to understand.'

> **Molly**
> So we're pushing back against the prevailing idea that we're too young or too female or too poor or just not smart enough to get it.

> **Meg**
> Yes! I am so on board with this!

Theatre Blogging in Practice – a WhatsApp Dialogue

Meg
What's DEH btw?

Molly
Sorry, shorthand for Dear Evan Hansen, a musical about the teenage experience that you apparently have to be over the age of 20 to understand.

Jan
One of the things that's really impressed me about this conversation is the number of women in their 20s who are participating in it. It totally belies the argument that young people aren't interested in theater and it's proof that they have smart things to say about it.

Shanine
I do hope my race and gender amongst things give my reviews/comments some gravitas and understanding to why I think how I think.

Ava
like critics of colour

Ava
it is great in that it plays on the white liberal guilt of the majority of british theatres, they desperately want to give press tickets to CoC

Jan
I suppose I'm more interested in why people make the choices they do. I'd be curious if a director or company consistently chose plays that excluded people of color. I think it's often laziness. And I think it's perfectly OK to call people out for it.

Ian
I'd love the conversation that is happening around Critics of Colour to also happen around disability too. Diversity comes in all sorts of different ways yet it rarely feels acknowledged

Ava
👌 yes pls

Theatre Blogging

> **Kate**
> Get The Chance,[1] based out of the Sherman Theatre in Cardiff, seems to do a pretty good job of encouraging disabled reviewers to contribute

> **Mary**
> oh nice!

> **Ian**
> Interesting about the Welsh company, though access does remain a big issue. What happens if a reviewer were dependent on captioned performances, they're entirely at the mercy of the schedule and wouldn't be able to attend press nights

> **Ian**
> And that's before we even start on representation of disabled people on stage and opportunities in general for disabled actors

> **Meg**
> Yeah, so much to be done about venues and just simply getting there, before you even start thinking about shows

> **Kate**
> The more I think about disabled access to, well anything, not just the arts, the huger the problem seems.

> **Kate**
> I'm about to start making audio recordings of all my blog content. Likewise, all my YouTube videos will have to have their captions edited properly cos, if you're gonna do accessibility, don't do it by halves!

---

[1] *Get The Chance* is a multi-artform review site for and by people in Wales. It grew out of a Young Critics scheme that was initiated in 2010 by National Theatre Wales and Bridgend Council but is now run independently. *Get The Chance* have published audio reviews from contributors with visual impairments and video reviews from deaf contributors who use British Sign Language. http://getthechance.wales/

Theatre Blogging in Practice – a WhatsApp Dialogue

Jan
Maybe it's because I see theater criticism as a conversation but right now I'm most excited about podcasts. I contribute to two and really enjoy the chance to talk – often with theatermakers – about what contemporary theater is trying to say and should be saying.

Stacey
I've been thinking about non-wordy stuff like video. I've been doing Instagram stories and getting better engagement than in other social media.

Ava
i do feel like podcasts are such a better way to explore the inconsistencies in the industry and particular shows without being tethered to word count/specific styles

Meg
How would you describe your writing/blogging style? Does it vary?

Jan
My style was a bit more informal when I started (I used to talk about where and what I'd eaten after seeing a show) but I'm more straight ahead now. It may be my journalism background but I know that a lot of work goes into even the smallest show, so I try to give them the respect I think they deserve.

Mary
I change it up depending on my mood. Sometimes I'm very enthusiastic/fangirly; others, dry and straight to the point. Nevertheless, one thing i try to keep consistent is my voice – a personal 'mary' voice. i know i dont have an academic certificate on reviewing, but i feel seeing over 500 productions says a lot.

Theatre Blogging

> **Ava**
> i really write from the gut and always have – pretty much everything i write is rooted in my emotional state during the show. so that's helpful if i'm writing for myself and want to unpick my joy or my frustration. in terms of style, i like to keep it really informal and i like to follow the white pube's[2] method of using abbreviations and text speak in my reviews – i think it's quietly radical, and also democratising.

> **Ian**
> I'd love to be more experimental but the truth is there usually isn't the time to reinvent the form as well as formulating a decent response to a piece. I just spent a week agonising over just how personal to make a recent review (about a subject that really struck home)

> **Kate**
> When I write, I try as much as possible to translate my experience of being at the event into words, so I often find my reviews are very different styles from each other, because the range of show styles varies so much.

> **Kate**
> sometimes the form of my response appears unbidden in my mind and then I feel I can't really do anything else. Doesn't happen too often though. But, unless that kind of demand strikes I don't really *try* to come up with a particular formal conceit.

> **Shanine**
> View from the Cheap Seat is home for various bloggers, not just me. The only rule I have is don't exceed 600 words, I think that we are writing blogs not university essays. And there is always some imagery. I think pictures (though not rehearsal pics) are very important to get a sense of the production.

---

[2] *The White Pube* is an art review site and digital residency platform from Gabrielle de la Puente and Zarina Muhammad. Both trained as visual artists but they ignore any distinctions between high and low culture, reviewing theme parks and reality television as well as exhibitions. As Ava says, their chatty, informal writing style has emerged from practices of texting and internet discourse. They are *brilliant*. http://www.thewhitepube.co.uk/

Theatre Blogging in Practice – a WhatsApp Dialogue

> **Mary**
> I don't hold myself back on word count. It is usually 400–600 words but I've gone far beyond 1,000 before, just because I felt the need to ramble on about the origins of the story.

> **Anne-Marie**
> Style: I used to use the blog to experiment with voice and style. (And it showed me how 'critic' voice is boring and blah.) And I'm pretty comfy with my natural voice now. I do fall into a formal style when I'm tired, but I'm also ok with that. We do the best we can with the energy we have.

> **Bob**
> my style has shifted pretty heavily in the 13 years I've been steadily blogging. I used to have an informal, gossipy tone that I thought was cute. It wasn't. Now I strive for conversational informed gay best friend.

> **Daniella**
> I have no clue what I'm doing at the moment. Used to be quite formal and I guess that's why I kept getting press tickets? But recently because of nsdf[3] and reading stuff like the white pube (♥) I do wanna try and experiment with form and style, last year I tried to write in different ways, which was fine for seeing stuff off my own back, but when I get invited to stuff I always retreat and feel like I have to write in a formal style you'd expect to see in bigger publications.

> **Daniella**
> A review with an interesting form seems to take as much time as the show itself to make, rather than a furious typing of ***opinions***

> **Daniella**
> Like the care in writing

> **James**
> Yeah care is the word

---

[3] The National Student Drama Festival.

Theatre Blogging

Ava
i think when you know you have care in your review that's when you know you can defend it against ppl who didn't like it

James
It's a sign you're at least reflecting on your position and role as a 'critic'

Meg
What form does care take in a blog post? Is it content or process?

James
Both. It has to be integral

Ava
i wrote a review a while back that another critic absolutely hated – she said i needed to just say that i didn't like it if i didn't like it and stop pussyfooting around. which i was doing, tbf – it was a play about a young muslim woman in london and for me it didn't work and it was clunky and shallow but for the majority muslim audience it seemed to really resonate. so i didn't want to negate that – i may have gone too far in the other direction tho. but i resent being told that i needed to just make a decision bcos it's like – it's deeper than that. this is more important than just saying 'it was bad'

Daniella
I think it's the association between taking care in how you write a negative review. Carefully structuring the review or how to word the response in a way which maybe cares for the artist/show/company, rather than seeming like an angry/nasty/hasty review.

Ava
yeah i was talking to someone the other day and mentioned i was going to be reviewing at the fringe in edinburgh and she just said completely matter of factly 'oh well have fun being screamed at in public'

Daniella
Like I don't wanna mollycoddle people like I wanna be honest, just not be a prick about it

Theatre Blogging in Practice – a WhatsApp Dialogue

James
Maybe this is a reach but perhaps its partly taking time to define the show you're writing about 'positively'. So talking about and responding to what a show is, rather than what it isn't and where it lacks

Daniella
I get u

Ava
yeah i wanna judge the show on how it defines itself

James
Yeah reviewing what a show is literally doing, and not coming from the position of the perfect show that it wasn't

Meg
Do you all get free tickets for the shows you see?

Mary
I always note in a review whether or not I paid for a ticket or I was given a press ticket, to ensure that the reader knows there are no hidden agendas.

Ian
Do you think it makes a difference though, the provenance of the ticket? I pay for a few shows, get comps for a few others, even see some as the guest of someone who actually was invited to the press night – it's all much of a muchness to me, they all get the same treatment.

Mary
Ah, it doesn't change how I write the review, the quality is the same whether or not I bought the ticket. But I suppose the experience is slightly different. One I paid for might be with a mate, and the other one I could be alone with my serious face on.

Mary
Here's another question: does anyone write a review before the official press night? Bearing in mind, you bought the ticket . . .?

63

Theatre Blogging

> **Meg**
> I always happily review previews. I never take free tickets so have never had to worry about keeping in with anyone. Makes me kinda mad that some people try to hold bloggers to unfair and pointless standards.

> **Meg**
> That is a big ethical question though. Possibly one of the biggest.

> **Ian**
> *runs screaming from the preview debate*

> **Shanine**
> Ha! I have reviewed previews on Twitter, whether it be an odd comment or a full on 'WHAT THE FUCK IS THIS?' thread

> **Mary**
> I got into this masssssssssive twitter battle when I blogged about a dress rehearsal. They told me I shouldn't have done it. 1) Because I was reviewer for other online outlets at the time 2) it hadn't had an official press night. – I bought the ticket to see the show and it was a dress rehearsal that was absolutely epic. Some even said you shouldn't be allowed to even tweet about the show, even if it is a preview . . . I don't agree

> **James**
> If I've paid for a ticket I'm very rarely going to write about a show. Writing revews feels like work to me so if I don't feel any obligation I won't write about a show unless I really feel I need to get something out

> **James**
> If you're paying for your ticket then there's no contract with the theatre other than being a consumer I guess. I don't see why you shouldn't do what you like

> **Ava**
> yes, like i understand if it was a tiny fringe show in preview but i kinda think the big theatres are fair game if u bought ur ticket

Theatre Blogging in Practice – a WhatsApp Dialogue

Ian
I think there's an element of being willing to play the game though. I happily reviewed National Theatre previews way back when (and without fail got the highest hit and comment count), then moved to a position of holding the reviews until press night, and I don't doubt that that is one of the reasons I eventually ended up on their press list

Kate
The preview thing doesn't really apply to me, although I am aware that some shows change massively over the course of a run, so I try to talk about the stage the show is at sometimes – has it just opened? Just been recast? Come around for the 15th year? Contextualising like :)

Kevin
I do not often blog on previews. Occasionally I might because it is my only opportunity to see the production, but I do indicate that it is preview I am writing about. And if it is mess I won't write about it to be respectful to the artists.

Jan
I tend to honor the press embargoes and wait until a show has opened, even when I've bought my own ticket. I also try to see shows as close to opening night as I can so that the performance I'm reviewing is close to 'frozen'.

Ava
i think it's fine if you say it's a preview

Ava
but also i'm of the opinion that no one gives a shit about my blog so i'm like well how exactly am i going to harm this production at the national theatre yaknow

Meg
What kind of work/life balance are you all getting? Does blogging earn any money, or help you get other paid opportunities?

Theatre Blogging

Ava
i'm v lucky in that i'm a student and therefore have a student loan so i can blog and write for free more than the average person . . .

Shanine
Blogging is a hobby that has got out of hand. I have a full time job but it is seasonal in terms of being busy so it gives me plenty of time to write, arrange for other bloggers to attend shows etc. If it got to the point where I couldn't afford to do it anymore I would just stop.

Shanine
I do need to look more at monetization through ads etc but speaking to other bloggers I don't think any of them were managing to make any money.

Kate
I'm so with you Shanine on 'a hobby that got out of hand'! I toyed with the idea of advertising, but don't want to advertise shows because of perceived conflict of interest, and there is little else around that fits my niche audience. I haven't ruled out the possibility of big corporates that are entirely unconnected but might align their brand values-wise with circus, but I would need to take that very seriously and haven't had the time to put in. I did start a Patreon a couple of years ago, and had a pretty good initial uptake, but haven't actively promoted it since and people have dropped off. I keep meaning to do a big campaign boost but, again, time . . .

Shanine
I have a Patreon set up but I was terrible at communicating that the intention was to cover travel expenses etc and not just for me to buy new shoes!

Meg
I've done the Patreon thing in the past. The idea had been that I'd try to earn enough to help me go part-time at work and blog more, but I stopped it when it just added to the pressure. I was making a nice extra bonus each month, but that wasn't enough to drop even one day at the office, so it just meant I felt like I had 2 jobs. It definitely affected my enjoyment of blogging.

Theatre Blogging in Practice – a WhatsApp Dialogue

Ian
I did google ads for a bit but got about 59p, then I used a different one that played videos which worked out at about £30 a month but they've stopped operating now. And I don't think I'd ever go down the ticket affiliate route, I'd feel bad about endorsing a ticket buying service I'd never use myself.

Jan
Ah, money. I tried Google ads too. Made about enough to pay my subway fare to and from the theater for a couple of nights. I turned down ticketing agencies that offered to pay for ad space (and others that asked for free plugs). I know I'm lucky because I don't have to depend on theater writing for my living expenses but I do worry how the inability to make a living doing this will affect who continues to do it over the long haul.

Kevin
I have never sought monetary gain from my blog. It's purely an altruistic offer.

Molly
I have so many people on my team that this is really just a passion project for all of us – most of us will probably never see a dime, but it's important to me to stay independent from shows and theatres and producers so that way we aren't beholden to write nice things about things we don't believe are nice.

Kate
My blog has led to other writing work, workshop leading, lecturing, Arts Council funding and, starting this autumn, a funded path towards a PhD, as well as the branch back towards 'making' in the form of audio description. Cheesy as it sounds, I followed my passion and forged a place for myself to be paid to continue exploring what I love.

Kate
Of course I'm giving all the positives, because I see it as work that has paid off. My boyfriend, on the other hand, thinks I put way too much pressure on myself and stress myself out over completing 'work' that I am choosing to do rather than having any formal obligation.

Ian
I do find it useful to separate blogging from work. But then, I also never entertained any notion that this would be more than a hobby (god, I hate that word!)

Mary
I agree with Ian's point on compartmentalising. I have a full-time job away from theatre and writing and I think that is best for me. I used to work for a media company which really took the piss and made me work overtime for nothing. My friends used to say to me that they thought I had retired from blogging and that made me upset because I hadn't quit. Now, I work somewhere totally different which is GREAT, and lately the office has been quiet so I've been taking advantage of this free time.

Meg
It matters so much the kind of work you do around blogging I think. Some jobs take the wrong kind of headspace if you know what I mean

James
I suppose I blog really infrequently because I consider it part of my practice as a theatre maker, so don't prioritise it. But I do write about almost every show I see, I just don't see them as often as some of you seem to! I think going to the theatre feels like I'm at work if I don't really enjoy a show, so I just go to see stuff I think I might enjoy

Mary
Okay, random question: does anyone use Google analytics to check how their blog is doing from a data perspective (views, which types of articles are popular, where ppl find your blog, best times to post your reviews . . . etc . . .?)

Ian
It's funny, when I started, hit count was so important. But soon I realised that a) people are shallow (my most popular posts have always been the end of the year hottest men posts I used to do), b) some people are sick (the hits I got after reviewing a show called Reclining Nude with Stockings still make me shiver), and c) so many people just aren't interested (some of the writing I'm proudest of, and the shows I've loved the most, are some of the least read reviews – you can't make people have good taste, sadly)

Theatre Blogging in Practice – a WhatsApp Dialogue

> **Ian**
> So I don't look at stats at all now unless someone (like a PR agency) asks me for them

> **Kate**
> I do look at my stats once in a while, but I have no sense of perspective over what good hit rates etc are, so couldn't tell if it means I'm doing 'well' or not in the grand scheme of things

> **Ava**
> i only check stats if i need to ask a theatre to be on their press list lol

> **James**
> It never occurred to me that people would be bothered about hits, I've always assumed they'd care more about if the writing and thoughts were good (which probably isn't true)

> **Meg**
> What about SEO? Do any of you make any special efforts re google rankings?

> **James**
> What is SEO?

> **James**
> 😶

> **Meg**
> Search engine optimisation

> **Meg**
> Basically, trying to make sure you're on the first page of google

> **Meg**
> This question is dedicated to the other Megan Vaughan who's an anthropology professor at UCL (damn her and her incredible research profile)

> **Ava**
> oh that's so intense

69

Theatre Blogging

> **Ava**
> no pls

> **James**
> I put keywords in the little box for tags when I'm inputting a post. Is that related?

> **Meg**
> I think so . . .

> **Ian**
> I tag voraciously (for my own nerdish nature) and use heading text in the intro paragraph (which I was told to do for SEO). Don't know if it makes any difference though . . .

> **Meg**
> The internet is so dog-eat-dog these days. I suppose if we were really worried about stats and rankings then we'd blog about something a little more populist . . .

> **Meg**
> Right then folks, I'll sign off now, but before I do, I just want to say, honestly and truly, how much I've appreciated everything you've posted in this groupchat over the last few days. THANK YOU!!! 😘

> **Shanine**
> Thank you! I've really enjoyed taking part/gossiping.

> **Kate**
> yeah, it's been fun, thanks Meg!

> **Jan**
> Thanks for doing this and for inviting me to be part of it.

> **Mary**
> xxx

You left the group 'Theatre Bloggers dialogue'

CHAPTER 4
THEATRE BLOGGING UNDER THREAT

In an article for *The Stage* in December 2016, Matt Trueman suggested that theatre blogging was done for. 'A scene that seemed so vibrant a few years ago', he wrote, 'seems to have all but curled up and keeled over.'[1] Trueman questioned the ability (or, indeed, inclination) of review blogs to strike out against theatre's status quo, and worried that the success of magazine-style sites had created colleagues, not competitors, leading to 'fewer debates, fewer disagreements, and fewer interpretations'. His implication was that a collegiate working environment is detrimental to the discourse, and ultimately to theatre as an art form.

Others who were key to the development of the theatre blogosphere have also perceived a 'decline'. When I spoke to Isaac Butler over Skype in May 2018, he said that 'in America at least, the theatre blog is dead. It just isn't a thing anymore.' I heard something similar from George Hunka, who thinks of theatre blogging as 'old news'. Chris Goode, meanwhile, is surprised at how *Three Kingdoms* is still considered by many as the start of a new era in criticism when, in his eyes, 'it was probably a last gasp'.

In a way, I can see where they're coming from. As with any industry or practice, there are areas in ascendance and others in decline, practitioners emerging as others retire. Almost all of the writers who first established the theatre blogosphere as a place for contextualization, longform criticism and informed opinion on key industry matters have now moved on to other things. Often they are academics, professional journalists, or else they inch closer and closer to career success as playwrights or directors. Sometimes they have caring responsibilities which limit the time available both for going to the theatre and for dicking around online. Depending on where you're standing, generational shift can be positive or negative.

Many people also consider the democratization of journalism and growth in social media to have reduced the quality of public discourse to the point of real political danger; a global shift to the right (most easily exemplified by the British vote for Brexit and the election of Donald Trump in 2016) has been attributed by some to the proliferation of deceitful political memes designed to stir up hatred, primarily towards immigrants and people of colour. Any celebration of a participatory digital culture has to contend with this problem, even if the theatre blogosphere does remain primarily open-minded and liberal. If we acknowledge that the practice and culture of critique that emerged during the Enlightenment (and was sustained by a thriving press) was reliant on some voices having more clout than others, then it follows that any redistribution of power (such as has been enabled by the internet) will trigger cultural, political and epistemological instability.

I guess what I'm saying is that I appreciate how the internet can sometimes look like a failed experiment, and the theatre blogosphere, as it moves away from boisterous longform debates and towards a pick'n'mix of subjective recollections, like a rudderless ship. I too mourn the loss

---

[1] Eve Allin's post in section 7, 'A Response, From a young and unpaid critic (or theatre blogger – up to you)', responds to Trueman's article.

of great bloggers who are no longer active, especially those whose tastes and politics aligned with my own. However, my experiences online have also taught me to question the way that hierarchies emerge on the internet, just as they do everywhere else in life. When we bemoan the deterioration of 'critical debate', or give disproportional respect to aggressive, argumentative writing, we end up encouraging sensationalist, performative takes and can further exclude those already widely shat upon for not looking or sounding like the historically powerful.

So, as I consider the threats faced by the theatre blogosphere over the rest of this chapter (there are eight in total – I decided against just writing 'CAPITALISM' in all caps before going to the pub), I don't worry too much about individual retirements, the threat of social media, or any perceived loss of bite. I embrace the evolution of theatre blogging, whether that's in terms of style, approach or the diversification of contributors. Indeed, both magazine-style sites and email newsletters can be considered forces for good; many are keenly focused on democratizing and diversifying the conversation around theatre. That I acknowledge them as threats is purely in recognition of their potential effects upon access and autonomy.

Several of the threats I perceive are practical, rooted in economic concerns. Bloggers must decide how to approach their subject, how to manage their sites, who to collaborate with, who to take money from. I want to discourage approaches which force theatre bloggers to conform to traditional labour relationships ('hobby' is not a slur), but we must still find ways to look after ourselves while navigating both the theatre industry and the digital space.

Finally, in the last of these eight threats, I look at something a little broader, exploring the new linguistics of online conversation, and arguing against regressive judgements of quality that are at odds with much contemporary digital discourse. Sometimes I think that the key to everything lies in changing attitudes to different modes of communication; we could surely solve so much if we could just convince people that *different* doesn't mean *worse*.

Eight threats to the future of theatre blogging

1. The popularity of magazine-style sites
Just like theatre blogs, magazine-style sites are a mixed bag. They have vastly different objectives, concerns and house styles, so it is foolish to proclaim them all problematic. My favourite of these outlets (including *Exeunt* in the UK and New York, *The Theatrical Board* and *HowlRound* in the US, and *Witness* in Australia[2]) all proactively seek out and amplify under-represented voices, and give space to innovative review formats and conversational writing styles. That said, they do this at the discretion of their editors, and many other online review sites continue to lazily reproduce the most disheartening elements of mainstream criticism, imposing formulaic style and content guides, perpetuating the damaging consumerist implications of star ratings, and even refusing or delaying publication if writers review key advertisers negatively. Because these sites are generally volunteer-run and employ similar design features as blogs, many readers confuse the two, the troublesome practices of some adversely affecting the reputation of many others.

---

[2] *Witness* was established in 2018 by Alison Croggon and Robert Reid, six years after the former ceased updating her much-loved blog *Theatre Notes*.

I can understand the attraction of writing for these publications, of course.[3] For inexperienced or unconfident reviewers, the presence of an editor can be reassuring, while those who can only write about theatre sporadically are able to access a larger readership than they might build on their own. There is also much greater likelihood of accessing free press tickets to shows, often the only way that some writers are able to go to the theatre at all. All this comes at a price though: content is filtered through a small handful of editors, and there is a growing imbalance of power and profile between magazine sites and individual bloggers as the former adopt commercial fundraising strategies in a bid for financial self-sufficiency. Crucially, writers who might have once started their own blogs, developing independent critical voices, are working for others instead.

2. The 'turn' to newsletters

The practice of sending personal newsletters directly to a list of contacts is certainly not new, but its digital popularity has increased significantly in recent years. This can be attributed to a couple of different technological developments: Firstly, in 2011, the start-up newsletter platform TinyLetter was bought by MailChimp, who, until then, had primarily provided mass emailing tools for commercial clients. Their branding of the TinyLetter division, on the other hand, targeted individual creators who wanted to distribute artistic and journalistic content, such as short fiction or cultural recommendations. Then, in 2013, citing declining use, Google closed their widely-adopted RSS feed aggregator, Google Reader. What had been, at one time, a central driving force behind the global popularity of blogs, allowing users to subscribe to all their favourites and never miss a post, had been replaced by social media feeds which provided new content to our devices twenty-four hours a day, seven days a week. Bloggers could no longer guarantee that their posts would be read, but distributing an email newsletter direct to the inboxes of subscribers would at least make sure they were *delivered*.

Theatre newsletters now occupy a space somewhere between public blog post and private correspondence. The control that authors retain over who receives them (unwanted subscribers can be easily removed, and letters sent to only a small segment of a larger contact list if required), means they reduce some of the vulnerability that comes from publicly sharing your opinions; some of my favourite newsletters now come from feminists, people of colour, and others who are at greater risk of online abuse.

The theatre community, always a little slow in adopting new technologies, is also beginning to create great newsletters: director Tom Hughes combines music recommendations with honest and candid rehearsal room reflections in *Little Achievements*, playwright Vinay Patel offers thoughts on writing and advice to those taking their first steps in the field in his self-titled mailouts, Maddy Costa and Andy Field record heartfelt memories of their favourite theatre artists in *Criticism & Love*,[4] and, in a reflection of the early blogosphere practice of

---

[3] In 2018, Margherita Laera of the University of Kent and Diana Damian Martin of the Royal Central School of Speech and Drama conducted a survey designed to map the current ecology of theatre criticism in the UK. At the time of writing, that data was still being analysed and interpreted, but Laera and Damian Martin commented to me that it appears more people now write theatre criticism for multi-authored online-only publications than for any other type of outlet, with 67 per cent of surveyed critics indicating that they published on these platforms. This rose to 79 per cent when including those sites which publish periodically, as 'curated editions'. In contrast, 51 per cent of respondents reported that they published reviews on a personal blog, and a total of 30 per cent in national and local newspapers (Laera and Damian Martin, forthcoming).

[4] *Criticism & Love* ceased publication in 2019, after Costa and Field's posts were so popular that they attracted the attention of Oberon Books, who are to publish them as a collected volume.

signal-boosting the links of others, throughout 2018 Brian Herrera's dubiously-named-but-actually-very-good *TheatreClique* round-ups shared interesting theatre writing from across the internet.

But newsletters aren't an entirely utopian prospect for theatre discourse. To all intents and purposes, they are private, closed communications which can only be accessed if you have enough social capital and cultural nous to know where to look in the first place. They are also regularly stymied by over-zealous email spam filters, arguably making their dissemination no less of a gamble than posting a link on a fast-moving Twitter feed. If you subscribe to the idea that free, open, inclusive and democratic public debate is essential to ensuring the same for the theatre on our stages (and I do), then the efficacy of newsletters is surely limited.

3. Middle-class white people living in big cities
Don't you just hate them?

I am being wilfully provocative for laughs, obviously, but there is an important truth at the heart of my bad joke. The geographic clustering of theatre bloggers means that even when we survey the entirety of the theatre blogosphere as one collective entity, its weighting towards major theatre cities means it still only provides a partial account of the world's theatre. And despite the fact that theatre blogging has removed most of the barriers to publication that remain in place around mainstream publications, significantly diversifying the wider critical landscape, the economics of blogging still exclude those who don't come from traditionally privileged demographic groups.

It's a dilemma to which we currently have no workable solution. When the pleasure and freedom one finds in a beloved activity is adversely affected by an injection of capital (as I discovered during my short-lived Patreon campaign), and even those who seek payment for their efforts struggle to find it, then the pool of contributors to the blogosphere will be limited to those who enjoy financial comfort, or to successive cohorts of emergent cultural workers who are prepared to sacrifice time, money and sleep in order to make their contribution before they burn out completely.

Which brings me to . . .

4. Exhaustion (of mind, body and bank account)
It remains an overwhelming, overpowering truth that the pressure to monetize our every activity, and the way we are taught to evaluate success according to wealth and profit, encourages bloggers to exhaust themselves in pursuit of paid opportunities which rarely materialize. In doing so, the pleasure in writing, in expressing oneself and making connections, can all but evaporate. Now, I would much rather remake society to allow people meaningful, fulfilling and generative leisure time than embark on a fruitless search for ways to monetize and professionalize blogging, but that said, when a whole community of practitioners are hanging on by a thread, sacrificing their health, their relationships and getting into debt, all in order to chronicle a brutal and expensive theatre scene, we're in trouble.

Funders in the UK have started to pay attention to this problem only very recently: Arts Council England have demonstrated a willingness to support bloggers who want to make their sites and content more accessible to readers with disabilities,[5] and, in recognition of the central

---

[5] Katharine Kavanagh, who was part of the WhatsApp dialogue in Chapter 3, has been funded to ensure the posts on her blog, *The Circus Diaries*, are audio described for visually impaired visitors.

role played by theatre bloggers in championing global performance practices, the British Council have recently embarked upon a programme of international travel bursaries for bloggers. Those opportunities are limited and competitive though, and only exist where they align with a funding body's broader mission. So far, none of the major arts funders in the UK have been convinced that an individual blogger's core practice – meaning their time, of course, but also hosting overheads, local travel and ticket costs – is worth their grant money, despite the significant contribution made by bloggers to a theatre sector with dwindling opportunity to secure coverage in the mainstream press.

5. Sponsored posts and affiliate ticket links
One way that some theatre bloggers have managed to earn some money from their blogs is by writing sponsored posts and hosting ticket sales links, a practice which has also proliferated across the mainstream media. I don't want to be too judgemental here, because surely life's hard enough without looking all those gift horses in their mouths, but when it significantly alters the content of our theatre discourse, it becomes a huge concern. The most valuable thing that a theatre blogger has is the trust of their readers, and when the credibility of their opinion is called into question, following a few too many dodgy recommendations, a hard sell where none was required, or, further down the line, a willingness to give a pass to a company's unfair prices or racially insensitive casting choices because they throw some cash on the table every now and then, then theatre blogging becomes neutered, just another part of a parasitic PR process.

So, of course, by all means take the money if it's something you were going to write anyway, host that paid link if you *really were* going to finish by telling your readers to immediately drop everything and book themselves a ticket. But were you? Really? . . . *Really?*

6. The exploitation of embedding
The practice of embedded criticism, as developed and popularized by Maddy Costa in her work with Chris Goode and Company, is one of theatre blogging's greatest legacies, an example of the kind of equitable creative relationship which can emerge when we look beyond the rigid parameters of established roles and hierarchies. That said, the term 'embedded' has also been music to the ears of marketing departments, who can now dress up their publicity strategies in the language of collaboration.

Over the last few years I've heard of festivals which require daily website content from 'embedded' critics, and others who explain that fees are dependent upon bloggers successfully pitching their writing to more high-profile publications. For those who are keen to explore the possibilities of embedded criticism but cannot afford to be present in rehearsals for the requisite time without payment, it can be difficult to say no to some of these opportunities. Nevertheless, if we continue to allow this term to be abused, letting it slide from the description of a process or relationship to the term for a certain outcome or type of employment contract, we risk jeopardizing both the practice of embedded criticism and the perception of theatre blogging more widely.

7. The end of net neutrality
When the internet operates according to the principle of net neutrality, it means that all the data which travels through it is treated equally by internet service providers (ISPs). Without

this in place, specific users, sites or apps might be given preference or discriminated against, meaning that the internet cannot be truly open or accessible. Net neutrality has already been disrupted in numerous small-scale instances, often used as a measure to discourage sites which facilitate illegal activities (such as the infringement of copyright that takes place on many file-sharing platforms). However, it is larger potential abuses by ISPs (and those who pay them) which are most concerning. Imagine an internet on which the richest global news corporations can pay for their stories to load quicker than those of their rivals, where state governments can throttle the communications of political activists, and where religious leaders have the power to take away your porn. These are extreme examples, sure, but a worst-case scenario for theatre bloggers might be that our sites can't be seen by readers, either because they can't afford to pay for priority bandwidth, or we can't, or because there are media companies out there prepared to pay to ensure their independent competitors are running on fumes.

The protection of net neutrality lies in legislation, but due to the speed of change in these areas, and a lack of digital expertise in many legal and governmental departments, so far this has proven extremely difficult to get right. EU law prevents ISPs from blocking or slowing traffic to any apps, sites or services other than for operational reasons (such as to ease congestion and ensure the integrity of a wider network), something which is likely to be enshrined into UK law during the Brexit process, but at the time of writing, there is currently no legislative protection for net neutrality in the US. The Federal Communications Commission (FCC) had previously implemented rules for ISPs which supposedly covered it, but a legal challenge made by Verizon overturned them in 2014. New legislation was put in place the following year, with input from a wide range of communications experts, including hundreds of thousands of comments from internet users made via non-profit think tank the Electronic Frontier Foundation (EFF), but that in turn was repealed by incoming FCC Chairperson, Ajit Pai, who argued that it was their responsibility to maintain the internet as 'the greatest free market success story in history' (Pai 2017).

Thankfully, in April 2019, after much campaigning by grassroots activists, an important step forward was made; the new Save The Internet bill, preserving net neutrality, was passed in the House of Representatives by 232 votes to 190. But this draft bill must now pass in the Senate, where it will be debated and voted upon after this book has gone to print. Meanwhile, the governments of many other countries, including Australia, are looking to the US for a legislative model that can be adopted in their territories, so, for the time being at least, net neutrality remains at risk across much of the world.

8. Tired judgements of 'quality'

Often, when people talk about '*quality* criticism' or '*quality* journalism', what they really mean is that something reads like an article in a Sunday broadsheet, with standard spelling, grammar and punctuation, and an authorial voice which implies objectivity (even when there is none). In blog writing however, where the personal perspective is central, the communication of our identity and personality through our written 'voice' helps to demonstrate our relationship to our subject, but also indicates much bigger things, like who we are and what we stand for. Judging a blogger harshly for not conforming to preconceived expectations of 'good writing' can be a way to shut down alternative viewpoints and delegitimize the opinions of those with different tastes, priorities and life experiences.

When I think about everything the theatre blogosphere has achieved since the start of this century – demanding transparency after the cancellation of *My Name Is Rachel Corrie*, examining the rifts between playwrights and practitioners who devise, championing the internationalism of *Three Kingdoms* when other critics only opposed it – it is its freedom of expression and broadening of participation that I wish to celebrate above everything else. Duška Radosavljević introduced us to the idea of theatre blogging as 'rhetorical action', but internet users today are taking this even further, increasingly using non-literary forms of communication to express themselves. This includes knowingly 'incorrect' spellings, atypical capitalization and punctuation, and visual tools like emoji and GIFs. We have even seen from Eve Nicol that sometimes a cat pic is worth a thousand words.

When blogs are still seen by many as second-rate 'amateur' platforms, however, the deviation from formal modes of writing can give sceptics yet another reason to diss them. There is a pervasive belief that writing which employs internetspeak, emoji, even humour or swearing, cannot also demonstrate a deep intellectual engagement with a subject. You don't have to look very far to see how unfounded that is. A matter of days after I submitted the first draft of this book, Ava Wong Davies published a post which reflected on her position as both an artist and critic with a searing combination of fury, sadness and great emotional intelligence (Wong Davies 2018). In it, she used non-traditional spellings and punctuation for emphasis ('rhetorical action' writ large) but addressed fundamental questions about how our tastes emerge from our embodied experiences. She argued that objectivity is more than just irrelevant; it is a complete myth, and a harmful one at that: 'Objectivity *is* a fuckin lie. Of course it is. You are informed by ur surroundings n ur upbringing n ur skin colour n ur sexuality n whether or not ur queer coded or straight coded, white passing or not, etc etc etc. Why even bother 2 pretend that it exists?'

The implication of this is something which theatre bloggers have been collectively demonstrating, with passion and personality, ever since 2003: that there is no one 'proper' way to engage with this industry or evaluate its works, and no single route to knowledge or proficiency. This is an issue on the agenda of many other bloggers too, from Mary and Ian and Molly in Chapter 3, to Bridget, Sabrina and Georgia of the Critics of Colour Collective, to Maddy Costa, whose writing work is so often done in collaboration with theatremakers. In fact, in an interview that she recently did with the *Essential Drama* site (2018), Costa offered the perfect words of advice with which to end this section. Seriously, get this copied out in your best handwriting and stuck on the fridge asap: 'The only expertise that you need to bring to theatre to be able to understand it is expertise in being a human being, in being alive, that's it.'

PART TWO
SELECTED POSTS

CHAPTER 5
A NOTE ON THE TEXTS

The curation and compilation of these posts has been one of the most enriching and frustrating tasks I've ever undertaken. Enriching, because it has sent me down fascinating link wormholes, introduced me to some truly incredible writers and thinkers, and brought me into contact with ideas that have stimulated my imagination and energized my mind; frustrating, because, to someone much more at home in the wild west of social media than the contractual smallprint of a major publisher, the processes involved in getting something ready for print publication are – *oh my god* – just. so. fucking. tiresome.

I want to give a huge shout out to my editor, Anna, at this point. She's advised and counselled me through a whole host of little niggly problems and questions as I selected the texts, negotiated contributor agreements, dealt with long delays and attempted to navigate the gulf that opened at times between what I wanted as an author and what is considered to be acceptable by a publishing house. And if that didn't make her brilliant enough, she also gave me permission to write a new bit of the book – this bit – in order to talk about the difficulty of that process, and the exasperation felt when encountering the seemingly nebulous guidelines and practices around defamation and libel.

I'll cut to the chase here. *Basically*, section 3 of the Defamation Act 2013 is all about 'honest opinion': a statement cannot legally be defamatory if it is clearly framed as opinion, provided that opinion is justified by the facts available to you when you make it. When I compiled my initial selection of posts for this book, I read through everything with this legal advice at the forefront of my mind. Did all my contributors adhere to the law? Was everything said justified by the facts available at the time of writing? Would republication in a book risk getting anyone in trouble? The answers to those questions were, thankfully, yes, yes and no, respectively. I would never present anything in this collection that wasn't both legally and ethically sound, or anything which made my contributors vulnerable to retaliation. But the shift in context – from a personal blog to a book from a major academic publisher – is not insignificant. While it's possible to argue that anything appearing on a personal blog is inherently framed as opinion, that context shifts as the internet professionalizes, and a book is a different story altogether. Some of the things that can be said on the internet, with ease and without repercussion, can bring a commercial publisher out in a cold sweat. In some cases, material that I firmly believe to be a writer's 'honest opinion' stated with clear justification, has sat uncomfortably with the publishing company because of the nature of that opinion, or the force with which it has been articulated.

As a result, three of the posts featured here have had some of their text removed or obscured. In two cases, these appear as block redactions (I wanted to be really transparent wherever changes were made) and in a third the contributor preferred to use a simple ellipsis. All three posts now begin with a line which explains that an edit has been made 'at the request of the publisher', serving as examples of where the medium that is the subject of this book is, at times, incompatible with the processes and concerns of mainstream print publication.

You might think these minor edits are no big deal, not worth getting worked up over, but even though these changes are ultimately driven by economics – a fear of litigation rather than a wish to censor – as long as that fear remains, our defamation laws will disproportionately hinder angry or activist writing. I can deal with the inconvenience of extra correspondence and rounds of edits, but the imbalance of power at the heart of this system has made me sad, and (not gonna lie) sometimes angry.

Enough about that serious shit for now though. I was supposed to be using these pages to whet your appetite for Part 2.

The blog posts republished here have been ordered according to four key concerns for theatre bloggers – *theatremaking and authorship, anger and dissent, reviews and reviewing,* and *representation and visibility* – followed by two further sections collecting posts about the events which have energized and mobilized the theatre blogging community above any others: the New York Theater Workshop's cancellation of *My Name Is Rachel Corrie* in 2006, and *Three Kingdoms,* which played at the Lyric Hammersmith in 2012.

Determined by the interests and careers of its earliest practitioners, theatremaking was the first major talking point for the theatre blogosphere, but the *theatremaking and authorship* section will be of interest to anyone with more than a passing interest in this artform. Laura Axelrod, Mac Rogers and Isaac Butler explore the relationship between writers and directors, Deborah Pearson asks questions of the way characters are formed (and training is undertaken), Chris Goode presents the joy of rehearsal, and Alex Swift expresses concerns about the financial and emotional insecurity endured by theatre artists.

The *anger and dissent* section reflects a long and fertile tradition of the theatre bloggers responding to mainstream media, from commenting on news stories and disputing the perspectives found there, to proactively critiquing the established practices of newspaper journalism. Even as I have made a special effort to counter the assiduous argument that bloggers and critics are engaged in perpetual online warfare, this section shows how the blog has become a vital platform for protest in the theatre industry, from *Encore* reflecting on Trevor Nunn's tenure at the National Theatre, to Ava Wong Davies identifying disparities between the politics on display on and off stage.

The *reviews and reviewing* section could have filled this entire book, no problem at all. Criticism is the primary concern of most theatre bloggers now, and without the blogosphere, many theatremakers and producers would have little chance at any coverage at all, especially on the fringe. As well as documenting and communicating response to shows and experiences which would otherwise be fleeting and forgotten, it records the profound and complex relationships that are formed between artists and their audiences, extending them beyond auditoriums or rehearsal rooms and into the hearts and minds of readers. (You can tell I get a bit smushy about criticism because I just said 'hearts and minds' and meant it earnestly.)

I highlight those reviews which break new ground in terms of form, such as Gareth K Vile's Venn diagram critique and my own bureaucratic response to a new adaptation of Kafka's *The Trial*; those which offer a counterpoint to the narrative emerging in the papers, such as Andy Field and David Eldridge on Katie Mitchell's interpretation of *Attempts On Her Life*; and those which demonstrate new practices of critical collaboration, such as Maddy Costa's examination of the work of Chris Goode and Company. And of course, no collection of blog reviews could ever be complete without the West End Whingers' take on *Love Never Dies*.

Amongst these posts sit bloggers' thoughts on their shifting and developing practices, from Alison Croggon's early soul-searching to Jill Dolan's reflections on 'critical generosity', and including fascinating thoughts on embedded criticism from Andrew Haydon, Daniel Bye and Catherine Love. Lastly, in James Varney's post, we see the contemporary application of misspellings and internetspeak really blossom, throwing off typo-shame and instead embracing a register which, as he has written elsewhere, 'removes the shield of objectivity ... puts more of your self in ur writin' (Varney 2015).

The *representation and visibility* section profiles those bloggers who seek a fairer and more inclusive theatre culture. While it serves nobody to deny the fact that this community was initially somewhat monocultural, the internet remains a place where those who have historically been marginalized – by the press, by theatre institutions and by society – can find a platform. Here we find performers protesting industry injustices, such as Daniel York Loh and Erin Quill on 'yellowface' casting (it broke my heart to lose Quill's incredible reaction GIFs); artists and academics calling out systemic failings, such as Mike Lew on overly-simplistic plays about race written by 'white dudes'; and celebrations of the shows that get representation right, such as Harry McDonald on the northerners of Jim Cartwright's *Road*. And, while Jill Dolan's practice of feminist spectatorship runs throughout every post on her blog, it feels particularly appropriate to republish her work on the lack of recognition for women directors, and its reiteration of her 'life-long mission that's not over, yet'.

Interestingly, my research for this section uncovered very few writings on disability from the theatre blogosphere, and very little from writers of colour on what is surely the biggest theatrical phenomenon of the last decade, *Hamilton*. While there are fantastic examples of both on professional magazine sites and funded arts platforms, and *Hamilton* is the focus of a large and dedicated fan community who have generated hundreds of funny and inventive memes, the relative absence of either of these subjects indicates that a blog post may not always be the most accessible or appropriate format for certain communities, or when dealing with certain issues.

In choosing posts for the *My Name Is Rachel Corrie* section, I've tried to keep as full a timeline as possible, beginning with Garrett Eisler first noticing the 'postponement' story in the *New York Times*, continuing via Isaac Butler's perceptive questioning and Matthew Freeman's diplomatic criticisms, and featuring a rare example of George Hunka's sharp deliberations from his now-deleted blog. Then, concluding with something slightly different, the final post in this section is a dialogue experiment from playwright Ben Ellis. Following his experience of modern art at the Pompidou Centre in Paris, Ellis explores the concept of the 'disillusioned body', editing real text from web forums where Corrie's death was discussed in order to create 'a fugue for 5 voices'. I must give content warnings for this work – it includes sexual violence, racism and Islamophobia – but it is included here as a fascinating example of blogs being used both as an R&D lab for playwrights, and as a space to respond creatively to contemporary political and religious conflict.

I hope the final section on *Three Kingdoms* gives you a chance to experience the delight, disgust and sublime disorientation of that show, even if you didn't see it at the time. The criticism here still feels so evocative – it was clearly written with such urgency – while still giving adequate space to interpretation and discussion of the show's sexual politics. I only wish I could have collated *literally everything*. Matt Trueman's further reflections on form and structure (Trueman 2012b) are worth seeking out, as are assessments of potential misogyny by

Hannah Silva (Silva 2012) and Andrew Haydon (Haydon 2012c). In this instance it also feels particularly difficult – even detrimental – to exclude *Exeunt* from my definition of the theatre blog; Daniel B. Yates' review for that site (Yates 2012) is a spectacular piece of writing, and their 'Critical Girl-on-Girl Action' dialogue (Tripney et al. 2012) was a key part of the online conversation around *Three Kingdoms*. If only I had more pages to play with, I would have happily broken all my own rules to include those texts too.

Across all of these curated sections, we also find another subject emerging, one which could easily have warranted its own collection of posts: bloggers on blogging. Don Hall, Andy Field, Frances d'Ath, Corinne Furness, Eve Allin, Catherine Love, Dan Rebellato and Ava Wong Davies (plus others besides) all give insights into their concerns and priorities for their blogs, from shifting motivations to assessments of how their practice differs from conventional modes of writing. It would have been equally possible to organize these texts according to that theme.

As you read the blog posts compiled here, it is important to bear in mind that the materials cover a period of fifteen years; please do read them in the understanding that they are of their time and circumstances. Opinions change, problems get addressed by those in positions of responsibility, and positive changes are made. It is not our intention to condemn specific individuals or institutions, but to reflect the changing landscape of theatre and its online discourse both honestly and robustly.

As well as the handful of edits mentioned at the start of this section, a few other smaller tweaks have also been made. One or two contributors asked for their spelling or punctuation to be tidied up, and I fixed incorrect spellings in the names of shows or people, mainly so you have an easier time googling them, should you wish to. In a couple of cases we altered names and pronouns in order to more accurately reflect the gender identity of those cited or mentioned, and in one instance removed the identifying handle of someone whose tweets have been quoted, for the sake of their privacy. Sadly, due to a combination of space, cost and copyright law, most images (and all animated GIFs) have had to be sacrificed. I've focused instead on ensuring that those images which are fundamental to a post's integrity can be reproduced for you here.

Embedded links have been another challenge. Links are a brilliantly non-hierarchical referencing system which add detail, context and humour to online texts, but replacing them with a system which works in print can lead to many unnecessary distractions. Here, I have used footnotes where links are essential to comprehension (for example, when a blogger indicates that there is something to click on, or more to learn) but omit them where that is not the case, thus avoiding the temptation to over-explain references to theatres, artists, shows, festivals, critics, publishers, novelists, pop stars, politicians and cricket commentators.

Otherwise, all the posts reproduced here have been retained exactly as they were when published online, including any original errors. I've also included the current URL for all posts which can still be viewed online; I encourage you to type them into your phones or laptops, and fully explore the writings of these bloggers, their commenters and the glorious web designs of yore.

CHAPTER 6
THEATREMAKING AND AUTHORSHIP

> **The Fuzzy Factor**
> Laura Axelrod, *Gasp!*
> 20 May 2004
> No longer online

You'd be surprised how many people call you when they hear you have no voice. What is the purpose of that?

Anyway, I didn't want to let another day go by without writing, lest you people think I died or something. Conspiracy theorists have been asking me why I keep getting sick. It's in the stars I suppose. Or maybe the NYC air. Mom thinks that it has something to do with 9/11 ... Oh, if the explanation were that simple ... And you wonder why I collect Black Helicopter stories for a hobby.

But we won't talk about that, or the possible remedies for my illness, okay?) Not here, not in public. I do know that some relaxation is in order and I'm guessing that it will come in the form of Coney Island or Central Park this weekend. Rollarblading or sunbathing. Nothing that will require any thought, that's what I think.

Since I didn't acknowledge it yesterday or the day before, I do want to mention Tony Randall's death. The Odd Couple was one of the reasons I moved to NYC the first time. The other reasons? All in the Family and Barney Miller. Randall started a National Actor's Theater here in New York City, back in 1992. I never got to see them onstage, though I was able to pick up a National Actor's Theater mug before moving away. Anything for the cause, right?

Although his intentions were honest, I have a problem with "acting companies". First off, acting companies are dedicated to actors and directors and do little to further theatre. Theater needs playwrights, and I know they hate to admit that. Too many theater companies are doing the "classics", or Broadway retreads. I have usually found "acting companies" to be very selfish ventures that simply involve actors and directors wishing to gratify themselves without giving anything back to the theater.

I also believe strongly that directors aren't taught to have relationships with playwrights. College theater programs tell directors to lock playwrights out of the rehearsal process. How do I know that? Because I took a directing class where we were all taught that playwrights must never attend rehearsals. As well, many directors only know how to deal with dead playwrights. They don't know what to do with the live ones, and they present all sorts of power challenges to the director. Who's play is it anyway? What role does the playwright serve in the production process?

I'm still fuzzy and I'm not prepared for a theater rant right now.

Theatre Blogging

So to wrap up, I'm still sick though I'm getting better. I can speak, but I can't think. It might have something to do with a virus going around, however, blaming black helicopters and the state of the world makes me feel important.

Director vs. Playwright – Intro

Mac Rogers, *SlowLearner*
1 June 2004
http://slowlearner.typepad.com/weblog/2004/06/director_vs_pla.html

---

Laura wrote last week:

> I also believe strongly that directors aren't taught to have relationships with playwrights. College theater programs tell directors to lock playwrights out of the rehearsal process. How do I know that? Because I took a directing class where we were all taught that playwrights must never attend rehearsals. As well, many directors only know how to deal with dead playwrights. They don't know what to do with the live ones, and they present all sorts of power challenges to the director. Who's play is it anyway? What role does the playwright serve in the production process?

Canned worms, still wrigglin', dollar a dozen!

Probably playwrights can't help feeling – if not a permanent low-grade resentment – then at least a reflexive suspicion of directors. We all hear the play in our heads when we write it, we all see the characters moving about, and the directors are the ones who come along and make the play not sound or look like we were imagining.

I'm going to dedicate this week to thoughts on the relationship between the playwright and the director. Since it looks like I'll be a bit busier at work than usual, I'm going to parcel it out in installments. Here's what I'm roughly thinking:

> Wednesday – Development: The Director As Dramaturg
> Thursday – Rehearsal: My Words!
> Friday – The Director's Theatre

Let's get rowdy!

Director vs. Playwright Part 1

Mac Rogers, *SlowLearner*
18 June 2004
http://slowlearner.typepad.com/weblog/2004/06/director_vs_pla_1.html

---

The only reason I'm calling this "Director vs. Playwright" is to attract people with a sensationalist headline. And also 'cause Alien vs. Predator looks boss.

So instead of presenting this essay in the neatly planned-out format I projected weeks ago, I'm just going to post it in ragged bits as I finish them.

First of all, two things in regards to Anthony's comments[1]: 1) I've never had an experience like Laura was describing where a director excluded me or simply didn't know how to deal with me. Her comments just made me think about the inherent tension of the director-playwright relationship. 2) I've never had a professional production of any of my plays, so I can't speak to the playwright's role in that process. My discussion will be based on the no-money Off-Off Broadway model, the only model many playwrights will ever know. Under this model I've been through thirteen productions and worked with ten different directors.

So how do you pick a director? Well, everything depends on your position to the project itself. I've been paired with directors through three different processes:

1. I instigated the project as a producer (with coproducers) and we approached a director or directors we wanted.

2. I submitted the play to a festival, it was accepted, and was then assigned to a director.

3. A director read a play of mine and approached me about directing it.

Option 2 is the most worrying because it offers the playwright the least control. You won't have even had a conversation with the person before they're directing your play.

With options 1 or 3, there's a chance you know the director, know their work. Great. You can make at least an educated guess as to whether they're right for your play or not. But if you don't know their work, all you have is the interview and heresay.

And the interview is largely – though not entirely – useless.

A couple years ago my coproducers and I needed a director for a full-length play of mine that I was also producing. I met with a candidate recommended through a colleague. He was smart, personable, and insightful about the script.

For a variety of reasons I wasn't able to attend many of the early rehearsals. I began getting troubling reports from actors about the slow progress of the project. We were less than two weeks away from opening and not one jot of blocking had been done. All the rehearsal time had been spent on discussion and sensory exercises. I spoke privately with every member of the cast, and then my coproducers and I met privately. We decided we had allowed the director ample latitude and now we needed to protect the project.

The director was replaced. The whole business was stressful and unpleasant.

The point is that the interview can only tell you one thing: whether or not the director-candidate is pleasant to be around (which, to be sure, counts for something in a rehearsal process). You can't tell if they're competent. A person can often manifest an intelligence and insight in a conversation that they can't deployed in action.

It's worth pointing out that this is as much a problem for directors as it is for the people selecting them. What can a director bring to the table – the literal table, the interview table?

---

[1] Mac links to his 'Director vs. Playwright – Intro' post, where the first commenter had suggested that Laura's comments were 'so far from the way things actually operate in the professional theater world today that they are hardly worth discussing'.

Theatre Blogging

An actor can audition, a designer can hand over a portfolio, and a playwright can present a script. A director can give you a videotape or two (from which you'll glean nothing useful), a resume, and some recommendations, but they can't actually manifest their talent for you right in that room.

So the best they can do is just direct a whole bunch of plays, anywhere they can and as often as they can, and try to build up a reputation. This is where you come in, Off-Off Broadway playwrights.

You're going to need talented directors, and you'll need them to work for free or for next to no money. The only way you're going to find them is by going to plays. Off-Off Broadway plays. No doubt you have friends in shows. Probably you get half a dozen email invites a week. Go see some of them. It'll be a huge time/funds drain. Do it anyway.

When you see a well-directed play, hang out afterwards. Get the person you know in the show to introduce you to the director and members of the production company. Don't talk yourself up – ask about them. Theatre-folks aren't reticent, and they'll remember you positively if you show interest in them.

Get on their mailing list. Every time you do this you'll up the number of invites in your in-box. Do it anyway. You need those invites. They're your windows into what everybody's up to, and after you've looked in enough of these windows for a certain period of time, you start to see names recur and you come to realize that Off-Off is a more comprehensible ecosystem than it seems at first glance.

Go see more plays. Watch for directorial quality, sure, but more specifically, watch for obsessions that align with your own. A director you can't pay will be most powerfully lured by shared obsession.

Chat with the directors. Tell jokes. Network. I'm not kidding. Nobody will give your script a quality read unless they know you a little bit and have reason to believe you're not an idiot or a psychopath.

Even with all this time and effort put in, there's still a trial and error element. You're going to have to have some unhappy experiences with directors before you can know for sure what kind of working relationships you want. Everybody's different. Maybe a rehearsal process involving two solid weeks of discussion and sensory exercises sounds good to you, while for my coproducers and I it was a firing offense. You have to have some unsatisfactory experiences to be sure.

Next up – once you've got a director, you'll often find the li'l buggers want REWRITES. That's next . . .

Directors and Writers (perhaps part one)
Isaac Butler, *Parabasis*
20 June 2004
http://parabasis.typepad.com/blog/2004/06/directors_and_w.html

Mac Rogers details a great guide on how to pick a director to approach for your next play. He has said nothing I disagree with and, as a director, I can only say that his approach (seeing as much theater as possible and approaching as many people as you can after shows you like) works for directors looking for writers/actors/designers/etc. too.

Mac was responding to was Laura Axelrod's posting about how directors actively work against writers in an effort to get their "vision" across. All I can say to Laura is I'm sorry you've been working with such bad directors. That's all it is, plain and simple, bad directing (and bad directing teachers) who teach and believe that the director's job is to put their ego on the stage. It's not. The director is the one person in the rehearsal process whose responsibility is to the audience. The dramaturg is the advocate for the text (if the playwright isn't around), the actors advocate for themselves and their characters, the designers for the look of the show etc. etc. and so forth. The director's job is to shape the audience's experience of the play, and thus they become ultimately responsible for everything about a production.

A bad director freaks out and thinks that the only way to fulfill this responsibility is auteurism. The problem with this is that the good auteurs (the really non-collaborative, comes completely from them kind of directors) can be counted on the fingers of one hand. This is similar to the actor who freaks out and thinks the only way to get to their character is to go so deep within themselves, they lose everyone else on stage. You have a much better shot at fulfilling your responsibilities to the audience and the production if you think of yourself as constantly giving – you are giving to the actors, the designers, the audience, the text.

The pitfall with this is when you think of giving as a fundamentally submissive act. It's not, or rather, it's not always. Sometimes being giving means deferring to other people. Challenging someone, however is also way of being giving. Directness is a way of being giving. Telling a writer a scene doesn't work is a way of being giving to the text, as long as you really are searching for a solution, and not trying to rewrite the play for the writer. The thing to me is this: locking anyone out of a rehearsal process (either literally or figuratively) is denying yourself and opportunity to learn more. The more learned you are, the better chance you have of succeeding in building a successful production.

Remember: your job isn't to be giving to the people, it's to be giving to the show. That's everyone's job.

Let me be more concrete: I remember being made fun of in the rehearsal room of **First You're Born** because the designers and I would always talk about what "it" wants to be. Conversations would happen like this: "and I think it wants to have lots of props on the shelves." Sounds a little ridiculous but we established this as a way of talking about the play so that we could try to be open to what the production's needs were (aka being giving) instead of what we wanted (aka exercising our egos). Because we (the designers and I) were always able to keep focusing on the fact that the only thing all of us wanted was to make the best show possible, using the skills and backgrounds we all brought to the table, we were able to have a really constructive design process and make what was easily the best looking show I've ever done.

Writers and actors and directors and designers all need to learn ways of creating this kind of process in their conversations. Writers trying to protect their vision of a play need to take a deep breath, think about the show as a whole, and find ways of talking about the play that lead to collaboration and solution, instead of darkness and disarray. This also means abandoning the idea of getting what you want a little bit. Writers (and I don't mean Laura, whom I've never worked with, I just mean "writers" as a conceptual entity): if you don't want anyone else to be able to act on their view of the play, you should write one person shows that you direct and star in. Otherwise, you need to learn to start giving. In the collaborative process of theater, everyone's going to have views and takes and choices and opinions, and it is the director's job to synthesize these into a coherent whole, filtering out the ones that don't work along the way. Yes, some directors make bad choices, and you are going to go up against them time and time again. There are a lot of bad directors out there, or at least poorly trained ones. The important thing is that you approach a project with trust. If you don't trust a director, you have no business working with them, and your acting on that lack of trust will get you shut out of the process. Theater is not a democracy, it's a collaboration within a hierarchy and (in the rehearsal room at least) the director is at the top. Remember: no matter how scary something is that happens in the rehearsal room, the beautiful thing about rehearsal is that it can always be taken back, altered, adjusted. If you think a director is taking the play in the wrong direction you have an obligation to approach them and discuss it constructively.

I'm discussing mostly rehearsal room politics right now, and hopefully after Mac writes his post about "rewrites" we'll talk a little bit about the more private natures of the director-writer relationship. I will say this though: bad directors try to get a playwright to write the play in the director's head, good directors try to get the playwright to write the best version of the play in the writer's head. Not always an easy distinction to map out.

Would You Like Ketchup With Your Worms?
Laura Axelrod, *Gasp!*
21 June 2004
No longer online

Thanks to everyone for clarifying about clarifications. As I mentioned in the comment section below, the topic of the director/writer relationship is volatile. I think most of us have our defenses up when approaching this topic and that's also why I backed out of discussing it further when I accidentally brought it up. I'm glad that both Mac and Isaac have taken it on. Both entries are a very educational and worthy read for anyone – not just those who are involved in theater.

But I do have a number of thoughts about all this . . .

I've wondered if my experience as a female playwright is different from those of my male counterparts. The New York Times had a great article[2] back in December, spelling out the issues of sexism in theater with regards to female playwrights. It's something that most of us have secretly nodded to each other about, but have rarely discussed openly. I've felt this issue

---

[2] Laura links to: https://www.nytimes.com/2003/12/21/theater/theater-the-season-of-the-female-playwright.html.

hit home in two areas: in the realm of critiques and expectations of my work, and my relationships with directors.

When I've worked with male directors, I have often felt the inherent tension between us as a male and female. It colors our relationship and how we approach the material. At times, these dynamics can be quite subtle and other times, quite obvious. It can include such things as the cast thinking that the director and I are having a romantic relationship, a director asking me to run errands for him as if I was his personal secretary, all the way through to interpretation of material. "What did you mean by this – what did YOU as a WOMAN mean by this . . ."

Again, I will state this disclaimer: I haven't had 50 productions. What I discovered through and since that December Times article is that other female playwrights ranging in experience have had similar challenges.

About two years ago, I posted an ad on the Playbill website to actively recruit female directors. I was quite curious as to what it would be like to work with a female director. That project never got off the ground, but eventually I did have a production directed by a woman. Our style of communication was very similar. It was the first time I found myself feeling a true artistic partnership based on equality.

This kind of partnership is something that most male playwrights and male directors take for granted. Yet, it's the reason why women and people of color have had to create their own organizations.

And now, to move on, a quote from that same New York Times article:

"About 10 years ago, the playwright Theresa Rebeck was having drinks with a well-known male director when he made the kind of blunt comment you hardly ever hear in polite society. As Ms. Rebeck remembers it: '"Women don't write good plays,"' he said, adding, '"Look at history: they write good novels, but as for plays, they just don't have the knack for it."'

This is something I've also personally experienced. There is an expectation that as a female playwright I will only cover certain topics. One of the most stinging critiques I've ever received wasn't from a New York theater agent who yelled at me for writing what was, in that person's words, a "scandalous play". Instead, it was a comment by another theater professional – another well-known director – who upon reading my work said, "You always seemed like such a happy girl, why would you write a play like that?"

The comment wasn't personal. It was made in a professional setting in front of others. Despite my lack of experience at that point, I knew it was completely inappropriate. The rest of the critique was spent, not on the material, but on me as a person.

Some of you have read my work but honestly, I've chosen which ones to parcel out to you. Underlings took so long to write because I was working against my own grain – trying desperately to not upset people. Earlier drafts were very different. I've often envied people who were able to write crowd-pleasing plays. My earlier work was extremely violent. I've had audience members cry and/or yell at me after seeing one of my plays. From what I understand, an artistic director of a well-known West Coast theater has said after one production that "that play should never be seen onstage" because the subject matter was too difficult.

Theatre Blogging

People I've worked with and who have produced my work like the controversial responses. I don't. It frightens me. There's a balance between who I am on a personal basis and who I am as a writer. As shy and quiet as I can be, I'm a bit of a provocateur on the page. And once I state my truth, I'm often rubbed raw by the reaction.

My goal, as a writer, has been to eradicate this kind of thing from my work. I thought that maybe, if I grew as a person it would leave. Meanwhile, I wrote plenty of bad plays where, most people said, I was holding myself back.

Some of the response is, again, due to the idea that as a woman I shouldn't be writing what I am. The violence aspect used to give me an inroad to deal with my male playwright friends, but there was also a "who do you think you are" aspect to it. Or, as someone once told me, I didn't have to choose the subjects I was writing about since "after all, you could always write a meaningful story about a prom queen".

It's a challenge to have the sensitivities to create the material and then have the ability to buffer the reaction to that material. My reaction to our discussion about directors was a bit of a post-traumatic stress flashback to what I've just mentioned. As well, I'm terrified about my newest play project, which is controversial. I'm writing it because I'm extremely passionate about the subject. Yet, I'm scared because I don't want to get kicked in the teeth again.

I don't have an answer to any of this. But it feels good talking about it.

Imagine people took me seriously

Deborah Pearson, *Confessions of a Playwright*
16 February 2007
http://confessionsofaplaywright.blogspot.co.uk/2007/02/imagine-people-took-me-seriously.html

---

So the other day at school, I contradicted a teacher, whose name I will not here mention because he is probably more important than me and is friends with people who are definitely more important that me, depending on what you think the word "important" could possibly mean.

We were discussing "building character" in an exercise of his, hot seating characters in a play that takes place in 1932 Germany, and I asked one woman, who is a lovely Jewish girl, but was playing an anti-semitic Prussian woman, what her character thought of the fact that anti-semites would be despised in the future. That she was on the wrong side of history. Lloyd stopped the question in its tracks. (Shoot. I mentioned his name. Oh well. Apologies.) He said that asking a character about the future is not relevant to their present.

Now I guess I think differently, fair enough, but I am of the opinion that character building can begin from any point. An actor's decision about whether their character's mother died, or if they ate eggs in the morning is as relevant as what that character dreams about or how that character chooses to use their imagination. When I act, or invent a character, I try to step into that character's world, and that world will be populated by their hopes, dreams, and history.

Don't we all live in the present, past and future all the time anyway? And doesn't our vision of the future change on a daily basis? Isn't our vision of the future a barometer for what we want, for what we expect from ourselves, and for what keeps us going? Surely this should be important to a character. Integral to their motivation.

The way that I write characters is very much in keeping with the story of the Scorpion and the Frog, as told by Forest Whitaker with an Irish accent at the beginning of "The Crying Game".

A Scorpion walks up to a frog at the bank of the river and asks it for a ride across. The frog says, "Get away from me, Scorpion jerk."

The Scorpion says, "Look, think about this reasonably, Mr. Frog. Yes, under normal circumstances I may feel inclined to sting you. But if I stung you while you were taking me across the river, you'd stop swimming, sink, and then I'd drown, and then we'd both die. It just doesn't make any sense."

So the frog thought about it for a moment and conceded. "Hop on." He said, begrudgingly.

And sure enough half way across the river the Scorpion got this crazy look in his beedy little scorpion eyes, pulled out his taiser tail, and stung the frog.

While they were both sinking the Frog, with his last froggy breath, said, "Now why in the hell did you do that."

The scorpion apologized, and drowning wildly, the frog could make out the words: "Because it was in my nature."

Now I am of the opinion that people act according to their natures all the time. The way that someone opens a door, or rushes to work, or dreams about water, their character, and the flesh and bone of their character, their understanding of character should be ingrained in any of these activities.

Yeah, but the prof didn't like it. Or wasn't in the mood to let me push boundaries. And who am I anyway? Maybe one day when I'm famous he'll tell that story to his class and give it a chuckle. But for now I've fallen out of favour, meaning that if I ever do get famous, it may be with no help from him at all.

But now I'm just complaining to my blog, ain't I?

Apologies. It's in my nature.

(Wakka Wakka!)

What's It All About Albee?

Chris Goode, *Thompson's Bank of Communicable Desire*
4 March 2007
http://beescope.blogspot.co.uk/2007/03/whats-it-all-about-albee.html

An edit has been made to this post at the request of the publisher.

Theatre Blogging

I'm going to have to start by writing about the second most exciting theatre event of the past week, because the most exciting was self-evidently the opening of Gisèle Vienne and Dennis Cooper's *Kindertotenlieder* at the *Antipodes Festival des Arts Indisciplinaires* at Le Quartz in Brest, where I absolutely wasn't. It's coming to the Tramway in May, but I'll be at the very other end of the country – or, rather, the very other end of the country below – doing *Speed Death of the Radiant Child* in Plymouth, so I'll have to wait till it arrives in Nottingham in the autumn. In the meantime, take a look at the photos on Dennis's blog[3], and the commentary passim, and consider the prospect of the Stephen O'Malley & Peter Rehberg soundscore, and then look me in the eye and tell me you don't want to book right now. – With his usual gift for uncanny interventions, Dennis also posted a bunch of great River Phoenix-related stuff this week, just as I was disinterring my own RiP archive for feeding into the making of *Speed Death*. (His is the *Death* of the title, and he's sort of the *Radiant Child* too, though also that's a Keith Haring thing, or more importantly a reference to Rene Ricard's brilliant and infuriating Artforum essay on Haring and Basquiat. And yes I know it wasn't speed that did for River, it was a speedball [and cough syrup] death if you want to be finicky, but *Speedball Death* . . . is a much clunkier title and anyway I was thinking as much about, you know, hurtling . . . Anyway, you don't want to be finicky, do you? The sun's out, the sky's blue, and the Tate has bought back Turner's *The Blue Rigi*, it's a beautiful day. No finicking. Go play on the tyre swing.)

Phew. Where were we? Oh yes, the second most exciting theatre thing of the week. Well, my vote's going to Michael Sheen's spankingly good reading of Kenneth Tynan's theatre criticism, in the *Book of the Week* slot on Radio 4, tying in with the recent publication of Dominic Shellard's edition of Tynan's *Theatre Writings*. I haven't got the book yet, I didn't have a very formed impression of Tynan (at least of the particular character of his criticism), beyond sketches from other sources and a vague sense of ferocious intelligence gradually undermined by distractedness (mostly libidinal) and decline. As ever, what's missing from the caricature outline is the hard precision of the thinking. (No wonder the equally driven but essentially stupid and largely revolting Peter Hall couldn't abide the notion of keeping Tynan on when he took over the National.) Anyway, the readings were gripping, immobilizing; Sheen read superbly, a tricky task given the movement of ideas and tone in the writing. (We're so used now, not least in arts criticism, to irony being used to smudge and subdue, not to penetrate.) As of right now, all five programmes can be replayed at the BBC web site but will expire and be replaced seven days after broadcast. If you care about theatre at all and you didn't hear these readings, and particularly if your knowledge of Tynan is, like mine, diffuse and fourth-hand, I would really urge you to spend an hour and a quarter getting properly turned on by this unusually sexy intellect.

(It was a good week for this kind of 15-minute spoken word slot, which more often than not brings out the worst in programme-makers and readers alike. Over on BBC7 they were repeating a selection of Alan Coren's *Times* columns, read by the author. I know Coren's a bluff reactionary type . . . – But he's also, almost indisputably I should think, the best

---

[3] This post is now lost. When Dennis Cooper's blog, *The Weaklings*, was taken down in 2016 after an apparent violation of Google's terms of service a decade earlier, his lawyers had to fight to regain control of his data. While much of the deleted posts have now been restored at a new domain (https://denniscooperblog.com/), the earliest currently available are from 2010.

mainstream prose stylist this country's produced since G.K. Chesterton. Even when the attitudes it encapsulates are rotten, the writing is scintillatingly clever and musical. Talk about a guilty pleasure . . . Again, you've got seven days to 'listen again', as they perplexingly call it – I wonder how many people use the facility to listen to a programme a second time?)

Tynan's criticism wasn't, however, the only controversial theatrical discourse being aired this week. As the Guardian arts blog notes, Edward Albee has been telling the LA Weekly that directors and actors are "the forces of darkness"; a little bit of his outburst is worth reproducing here:

> "The big problem is the assumption that writing a play is a collaborative act. It isn't. It's a creative act, and then other people come in. The interpretation should be for the accuracy of what the playwright wrote. Playwrights are expected to have their text changed by actors they never wanted. Directors seem to feel they are as creative as the playwright."

Responses, according to the Guardian blog, have been various (though not at that blog itself, where the three comments so far left are uniformly pretty witless, even that of the normally reliably engaged and interesting George Hunka); personally it was, I had better admit, rather pleasing to see Alison Croggon quoting my remark[4] from a while back about how there are playwrights and then there are writers for theatre, which still sums up how I feel about Albee's ilk. But perhaps this needs a little amplification in the light of a recent post at Encore Theatre Magazine,[5] of whom I generally approve (even though they describe me as "affable", the *shits*): wherein, commenting on the new NT season – at first glance literally *nothing* I'm remotely interested in seeing, by the way, which is a shame; maybe the honeymoon's finally over and we're back to a National Theatre that's turned completely in on itself – they report on "a slight sense . . . that the tide of fashion is turning against playwriting. Not from audiences, but from theatremakers." Encore goes on to describe this turn as "rather peculiar and strangely moralistic".

Not surprisingly, a few folks show up to tilt at this big fat Celebrity Pork Windmill, including a furious Jon Spooner and an emollient and largely sensical Notional Theatre (who incidentally has also recently turned in a smart development of my earlier discussion of Robert Wilson's architectonic procedures[6]). But I think Encore may be right. I share the sense – which Albee obviously has, and which even an avowed big-tent centrist like David Eldridge seems to have been expressing in his recent comments here – that conventional playwrights (by which I mean, those who produce scripted plays which are to all intents 'complete' before rehearsals begin, though of course they may then be modified by the influence of the staging process) currently feel under attack. I can see why they would feel that, even though nobody ever really seems to attack them *as such*, which means that the ferocity of (what they consider to be) their counterattack can be surprising – though not, I think, inexplicable, for reasons I hope I can unravel.

---

[4] Chris links to: http://theatrenotes.blogspot.co.uk/2007/03/playwright-as-king.html.
[5] Chris links to a post now accessible via the Internet Archive's *Wayback Machine*: https://web.archive.org/web/20070310140029/http://www.encoretheatremagazine.co.uk:80/?p=9.
[6] Chris links to: https://notionaltheatre.wordpress.com/2007/02/16/shapes/.

Encore rejects the label "text-based" for this kind of theatre; George Hunka, defending Albee, doesn't appear to: "in scripted theatre, [writing is] the primary, originating act". Both are describing the same thing, though, and so, it seems to me, is Eldridge; their position glosses, roughly, like this. We who are playwrights, or support and approve of the work of playwrights, are the first to acknowledge that many elements go into the staging of plays – acting, direction, design, music, perhaps choreography, etc. – along with the script; and we furthermore acknowledge, with cheerful magnanimity, that theatre is nowadays made in multifarious ways, quite a bit of it privileging these other elements above the specialist craft of the writer. We accept that, and we accept that it sometimes works, and we try hard to say so. [I exempt Albee from this characterisation, obviously.] But (they would continue) the reciprocity between the "text-based" wing and the "devised" / "physical" / "visual" wing seems lopsided. Why won't they say that what we do as playwrights, with our primary originating acts of script-writing, is also legitimate and valuable in the ecosystem of the big tent? (As professional writers they wouldn't stoop to countenance such metaphor-mixing; I hope they'll forgive me for this misrepresentation, at least.)

I've come to see that it is this imbalance of cordiality, as it were, that so infuriates the playwrights: so a slow-burn of resentment builds up, as in any off-kilter relationship, until one quiet evening you only have to ask what's for dinner and you get a fork in the eye.

So, what is this imbalance? What's actually happening?

I don't suppose that what I'm about to describe are the only two indicators that such an imbalance is real, and is wider in nature and in influence than simply its pertinence to the broad-church courtesies of variously inclined practitioners in a large and jostling communion: but they're among the most significant.

Firstly – I don't know, are there any statistics on this? – my guess is that around 80 or 85 per cent of theatre produced in Britain [using the word 'theatre' in its generally accepted sense(s)] is still created along conventional lines, with a director responsible for realising a script that exists more-or-less complete prior to the rehearsal process; some considerable proportion of that textual work may have been 'workshopped' or 'scratched' or whatever but the text even so retains its primacy and its discrete originality. In this light, it would certainly be accurate to say that a disproportionate amount of what you might call secondary cultural attention – by which I mean media reportage and criticism, and, to a lesser extent, discussion within and around the creative industries as a whole – is bestowed on the non-traditional: the 'devised', the hybrid, the non-'text-based'. (Forgive all these scare quotes, I can't bear to do without them.)

Partly of course this is something to do with the eye-catching qualities of innovation – or, more accurately, both in respect of media and commercial interests and often the ideation of the work itself, the eye-catching qualities of novelty. Site-specific theatre, which is hardly ever pre-scripted by an individual before production work begins, is the obvious case in point: there's always an angle for the papers – not just newness but urgency. The attachment to novelty (for its own sake) is, wherever it occurs, despicable, and my own feeling is that even innovation is in itself value-neutral. But the urgency also arises from the rapid come-and-go of these projects, particularly the 'go': they're not just unusual, they're news, and if you don't catch them while they're hot, you've missed an experience you can't have any other way. Like I keep not getting around to seeing Punchdrunk's ecstatically-received *Faust*, but I've got to get my act together and go: and that sense I have of 'got to' is not just from wanting to see something that lots of people think is great, but also that it's all or nothing: be there or miss it forever. Whereas let's say I'm not too bothered about not having seen *The History Boys* at the NT, because it was clear from the start it would tour, it would probably wind up in the West End, there would be a film version, a radio version, probably a book on tape, maybe eventually a tea-towel, and above all, there'll always be a published play text, so not only can I read *The History Boys* on the tube, I can also mount my own production some other time, or wait for a student company to take it to Edinburgh. This I know to be true: that most of the people howling "No, no, that's not the same thing at all!" at this lackadaisical attitude are precisely the ones who want to argue that the play text is "the primary originating act".

What I'm getting at, and this is not an accusation but simply a description of one element in the imbalance I'm trying to explore, is that a play text is *not* a piece of theatre, not yet, not ever. It can become part of a piece of theatre, but it will never itself be theatrical unless it behaves as do the other elements in a theatrical production (including the other elements in its own production), and disappears. Almost everyone, not least the most literary and conventional playwrights, will speak out in favour of the 'liveness' of theatre, will agree that this here-and-now ephemerality is one of the medium's special and distinguishing characteristics. So those productions that emphasize this complex of signs and conditions that we refer to as 'liveness' will inevitably commend themselves more immediately to audiences and secondary commentators alike. A play which hits the bookshelves at the same time as it hits the stage has already forfeited its claim to those attentions.

Secondly – and again I apologise that I can't back this up with statistics but I'm certain it's true and I'm certain most industry folks would agree – the way that theatre is taught, to some degree in schools but particularly in universities and on many courses in specialist theatre training institutions, has changed rapidly and radically in the past few years. Broadly speaking there are two reasons for this: one, the generation who started going to the theatre in the late 80s and grew up with the non-traditional theatre models of Complicite or Forced Entertainment are now of the age where they're not just delivering but actually designing these degree courses; two, work in these areas of theatre tends more often to arise out of an exploratory, questioning attitude, one that rejects or is anxious about orthodoxies – and it therefore comes with a sort of built-in availability to strong educational and pedagogical processes. As the phrase "well-made play" implies, form for playwrights is secondary to content, in other words it's there to serve the content and set it up to its best advantage; this is precisely how it comes about that it's possible to tip the content of *The History Boys* into different containers and, though some modification is of course required, the essence of the piece remains the same, its qualities, its 'message' (if it will own up to having one, or many). In the work that the university theatre departments now favour, the medium *is* once again the message, and the question of what the theatre experience is, or can or could be, takes precedence over the surface detail of who says what to whom on what topic. (What's galling for the old guard playwrights is that this work is not simply the province of the academy; lay audiences flock to Lepage, to Shunt, to Stan Won't Dance, and find there a rich variety of pleasures and challenges.)

Theatre Blogging

It seems to me, from the direct experience that I've had, that maybe half of all graduate and post-graduate theatre-makers coming about now into the industry take the methodologies and critical underpinnings of non-traditional theatre as read. It would no more occur to them to accept the Albee model of theatrical creation than it would to light their stuff with oil lamps or cast Beerbohm Tree in it. (Actually, the oil lamps they might quite fancy.) In a strict sense, some of this is worrying – I suspect 'devising' is now too often an eight-week module with its own gradually ossifying orthodoxies, and we might be needing to clear that mess up in fifteen years time. But what it means *now* is a substantial shift in the expectations of younger audiences; it may not be a permanent shift in the culture, but it's permanent in those people, and they're going to be around for a while yet.

So: these two things, the disproportionate cultural saliency of non-traditional work, and the emphasis on that work in the encounters that younger audiences and emerging artists have with theatre as a whole, tend to unbalance perceptions on both sides of the fence. And of course both of these trends feed back into commissioning rounds and the operations of support and advocacy networks within and between institutions.

This is as fair and balanced (to borrow a phrase) as I think I can be about the cause of the "slight sense" of perturbation in the Encore ranks and the unappealing distemper of Albee, who, to be fair, has worked hard to develop and refine his own craft and become a playwright of some distinction – by which I mean, it's a long road from *Zoo Story* to *The Goat* but you can usually tell it's him. (I'll take *Zoo Story*, thanks, and actually, that's it.) But he makes plays: not theatre, which is something completely else, and which he apparently cannot comprehend.

But I should be a bit more careful to say exactly what I'm getting at. I don't particularly mind what playwrights do, how and where and when they work; if they believe they get good results by writing alone, for 'characters' in their imaginations rather than for people they already know and talk to, then that's fine. I prefer to work among people, actors in particular, and to draw on what they have to offer: I'd rather have my writing emerge out of a conversation between many voices, partly because I think richer and more complex work emerges that way and I think those things, richness and complexity, are themselves distinctively theatrical qualities. But then I'm always writing for theatre, not writing a play. I also prefer to work in collaborative ways and in collective settings because I spend so much of my life in those sorts of working environments – theatre is to me as Second Life has become to some other poor saps – and if I get to help invent the terms and conditions of those working and living environments then I'd prefer them to resemble the sort of society I'd rather be living in, rather than making them in the image of the society I want to use theatre to examine and critique. But that's a personal commitment, and good results can certainly come through other set-ups.

It's easy for me to say because I generally direct my own writing, but the fundamental point is this: that at the moment that the playwright (I mean very specifically the writer of *plays*) hands over his play text to the director, he is handing it over to be broken. A good director will understand that this is traumatic and will behave accordingly, soothingly and reassuringly like a good mohel or a decent undertaker. But the play *has* to be broken in order to become available for theatre use, because the play is *closed* and theatre (properly) is *open*.

What do I mean by closed and open here? The actual connotations of 'play' within the word 'play' as in 'play-text' have become a bit invisible, but they're there. A play is a little cell of fiction, secluded and complete (for all that it might treat of topical themes). As such it is a game, an ironic procedure, unable to sustain consequences outside of itself: the dead of the piece get up and bow, and even if on some self-consciously *avant garde* whim they carry on playing dead, we know it is still in play, because it's still in *a* play. For the play to be made into theatre, that closure has somehow to be breached. Some playwrights know this instinctively and will try to do it themselves, but very often will make the mistake of trying to do it at the level of content, by 'sharpening' it: use spiky realism or jagged sensationalism to skewer the bubble; but the bubble is a formal one, and to try to break it with content is like trying to untie a knot by swearing at it – it makes you feel better but it doesn't get the job done.

The formal problem, on the other hand, can be solved only when the play is configured so that its form is compatible with the terms and conditions of theatre: when those *distinctive* qualities that we associate with theatre are allowed, if not to occupy, then at least to touch, at one point or along one surface, the secluded area of the play. The best – the least traumatising – solution is to write for theatre in the first place, to write from the get-go in a way that allows for, and ideally fosters and enjoys, liveness and contingency and unpredictability and ephemerality and, above all, the turbulence of the travel between stage and audience. You can still write articulately, beautifully, rigorously, with all the craft and attention to detail that your literary talent encompasses; none of that is prohibited. If you're determined to be the sole author of what is spoken in the room, so be it. (I'm about to do that with *Speed Death*, for a change; there is neither disgrace nor dishonour in it, necessarily.) All of that is possible in writing for theatre. It's just that what you end up with then probably won't be publishable in a perfect-bound Nick Hern paperback for sale at the usual outlets. The way some of my texts have ended up over the years, loose-leaf nightmares of scraps and diagrams and lists and images and smudgy xeroxed journal entries, would remind anyone of what Wittgenstein said about how if animals could talk we wouldn't understand what they were saying.

If that's too frightening – why should it be?, but if it is – then here are the *only* other options. Carry on writing plays, give them to directors whose approach you find congenial, and consent wholeheartedly to the necessary breakage. Carry on writing plays, and publish them without them being produced; this is not much different to writing novels, admittedly, but then, that's the contract you're offering. Or carry on writing plays and direct them yourself. You'll either fail to let go of the writing function, and create wretched stillborn non-theatre; or you'll break everything left right and centre, and conceivably have a ball doing it. Whatever route you take (and we can be sure that Albee will take none of them), one thing remains true. The director's fidelity is to the demands of theatre, not to the demands of the playwright; indeed, once the director has the text in her hands, there is no playwright. There is only theatre. The playwright in the rehearsal room is utterly and irretrievably fallacious. – Or I suppose, there is one final option, the Albee-friendly option: continue to insist on whatever confused and superstitious model of theatre it is that's got you this far, the self-burning effigy that keeps on winning you those Pulitzers. Fret not, dear fellow, there's still plenty more of you than there are of us, and apparently we're already facing the backlash, as announced by Encore.

...The vitally important epilogue to this, though, is to remind everybody that there is as much untheatrical work on 'my' side of the fence as there is on Albee's. Devisors and, Lord knows, physical theatre practitioners can be just as self-deluding in their insistence on total control, repeatability, predictability, and so on. On this side, for 'play' read 'performance'. At least the deception is less complicated in physical theatre, as it doesn't depend on the *further* idiocy that most plays do – the dismally unexamined notion that language is merely a window through which 'characters' may be viewed going about their business: with perhaps some overlay of 'style' by which the playwright's own voice may be identified and hailed in the service of the Individual Genius industry.

So don't imagine that the work that is routinely called (or calls itself) 'experimental theatre' is immune to such hidebound and defeatist anti-theatrical behaviours; don't for a second believe the apparent 'conservative vs. radical' faultlines. Only this week, Tim Etchells was apparently in town (at the second of the Siobhan Davies events I was talking about last time[7]), describing his and Forced Entertainment's continued devotion to the idea of failure, and the amount of work and time and attention that goes in to making FE's on-stage "performance" of "failure" precise and repeatable and predictable. This is particularly exasperating because it's so close to being useful. For nearly ten years now I've been droning on about the vital importance of failure in theatre; but FE and its attendant failure fans, Adrian Heathfield and Matthew Goulish [both excellent persons, btw] and the like, make exactly the same reactionary category error as Albee. The creative fertility of failure inheres in the *medium* of theatre, the noise that distorts and displaces the signal and opens out the theatre experience by a thousand times, the failure that at once falls short of and exceeds the frames of performance and virtuosity. This is something fundamentally different to Etchells's project. Making work that is *about* these failures (while covertly trying to minimise them) is an abject dereliction of the possibilities for actual consequentiality in work that admits and discloses and is shaped by failure, theatre's perpetually breaking heart. FE's fetishistic mimicry of failure is the equal and opposite stigma of the BAC Scratch format's totemic simulation of risk. Forced Entertainment are brilliant and have been important (and Etchells in particular is, or was, one of the best theatre-writers of the past two decades): but if theatre now had its Guy Fawkes, I would want to send him not into the vicious nullity of the West End or the brooding grey conundrums of the big subsidised houses, but up the M1 to Sheffield, where, if I'm allowed to colour in this fantasy in a bit more detail, Forced Ents would be rehearsing for a revival of *Showtime*, and in would come Mr Fawkes with a *real* bomb strapped to his chest. I don't wish any of them any bodily harm, I just would like them to have to talk him out of it.

And before anybody asks, yes, I have just seen Tim Crouch's utterly brilliant *An Oak Tree* for the first time, and yes, it does (sort of appear to) say everything I've just said but in a third of the time and with five times the eloquence; fantastically good *writing for theatre* – ... and yes, I did buy a copy of the very nicely formatted Oberon play text.

OK, rant over. Partly I'm warming up for Tuesday, when I (finally) get to give the paper to the graduate seminar at Central that I should have done in November and missed due to an appalling administrative failure here at Thompson Towers. I can't quite remember now what

---

[7] Chris refers to a post from 25 February 2007: http://beescope.blogspot.co.uk/2007/02/three-threes-from-thursday.html.

I intended to say before, but anyway this time out it's basically the above rant threaded around some ideas about the misuse of 'liminality' as a word and concept in performance studies. Except last night (sorry, this is the Jimmy Stewart thing all over again) I dreamt I turned up to Central and the graduate seminar turned out actually to be a hairdressing demonstration.

Which further reminds me, as a p.s. to my previous post:

Becoming Jane, cert. PG. "Contains mild sex references and scenes of boxing."[8]

All together now: if I want that, I can get it at home.

Right-o, it's past my bedtime. But as the 38th Governor of California taught us to say: Albee back.

The Writer, The Theatre, The Play

Alison Croggon, *Theatre Notes*
5 March 2007
http://theatrenotes.blogspot.co.uk/2007/03/writer-theatre-play.html

---

The conversation on playwrights v. writers for theatre sparked by **Edward Albee** and continued in various blogospherical spaces is getting progessively more fascinating. I'm enough of a writer to be well versed in the arts of procrastination, and so temporarily abandoned my own very untheatrical writing to catch up on George Hunka's argument with Chris Goode's post on Albee, and Chris's response to that. Not to mention some comments here[9] by playwright Jodi Gallagher and others. Here I'm going to try to summarise the argument without traducing it too much (though you should really read the posts, which is worth the time): this will be long, I expect, so get a cup of tea. Or, if you're not interested, wander off elsewhere.

At issue is the vexed question of what a writer is in the theatre. Part of Chris's first post addressed why he thought conventional playwrights felt at siege in contemporary theatrical culture:

> Conventional playwrights (by which I mean, those who produce scripted plays which are to all intents 'complete' before rehearsals begin, though of course they may then be modified by the influence of the staging process) currently feel under attack. I can see why they would feel that, even though nobody ever really seems to attack them *as such*, which means that the ferocity of (what they consider to be) their counterattack can be surprising – though not, I think, inexplicable . . .
>
> Their position glosses, roughly, like this. We who are playwrights, or support and approve of the work of playwrights, are the first to acknowledge that many elements

---

[8] See that same 25 February post.
[9] Alison links to: http://theatrenotes.blogspot.co.uk/2007/03/playwright-as-king.html#comment-390279972891605696.

go into the staging of plays – acting, direction, design, music, perhaps choreography, etc. – along with the script; and we furthermore acknowledge, with cheerful magnanimity, that theatre is nowadays made in multifarious ways, quite a bit of it privileging these other elements above the specialist craft of the writer. We accept that, and we accept that it sometimes works, and we try hard to say so. . . . But (they would continue) the reciprocity between the "text-based" wing and the "devised" / "physical" / "visual" wing seems lopsided. Why won't they say that what we do as playwrights, with our primary originating acts of script-writing, is also legitimate and valuable in the ecosystem of the big tent? . . .

I've come to see that it is this imbalance of cordiality, as it were, that so infuriates the playwrights: so a slow-burn of resentment builds up, as in any off-kilter relationship, until one quiet evening you only have to ask what's for dinner and you get a fork in the eye.

He traces some of the changes in theatre practice which might be responsible for this sense (and that Jodi also alludes to). Chris then makes the obvious, if perhaps tendentious, point that a play text is not theatre. "Not yet, not ever. It can become part of a piece of theatre, but it will never itself be theatrical unless it behaves as do the other elements in a theatrical production (including the other elements in its own production), and disappears." In order for this to happen, Chris argues, the text has to be "broken": "A play is a little cell of fiction, secluded and complete (for all that it might treat of topical themes). As such it is a game, an ironic procedure, unable to sustain consequences outside of itself . . . For the play to be made into theatre, that closure has somehow to be breached." Chris posits this as a formal problem, a question of breaking the formal closure that inheres in a completed and autonomous text to permit the necessary "liveness" of theatre.

The formal problem . . . can be solved only when the play is configured so that its form is compatible with the terms and conditions of theatre: when those *distinctive* qualities that we associate with theatre are allowed, if not to occupy, then at least to touch, at one point or along one surface, the secluded area of the play. The best – the least traumatising – solution is to write for theatre in the first place, to write from the get-go in a way that allows for, and ideally fosters and enjoys, liveness and contingency and unpredictability and ephemerality and, above all, the turbulence of the travel between stage and audience. You can still write articulately, beautifully, rigorously, with all the craft and attention to detail that your literary talent encompasses.

This is where George comes in, with a post pugnaciously objecting to the idea of a play text being "broken":

It's not as if theatricality itself is inherently good or bad, and that a text must necessarily be sacrificed to whatever the hell this vague "theatre" is that they're talking about, any more than performers and conductors "break" a musical score in the service of some ideal of musicality. (I know there will be quibbles that theatre is not music, but both are performing arts, and there is more in common between them than not, as both a theoretical and a practical matter: both revolve around a collaboration between a composer/playwright and the disciplined live performer, and precision is basic to both.)

I am personally a bit chary of comparisons between music and writing, tempting though they are: words are very different phenomena to sound or musical notes. There's the pesky question of "meaning" for a start, which, however you define it, exists in words in a way it just doesn't in music. Chris answers here,[10] pointing out that he and George might have more in common than their differences seem to imply, citing Beckett as, in his view, an exemplary theatre writer.

I think that Chris is quite correct to identify a necessary act of violence in the transition from page to stage. I should make clear that I do not believe that Chris is speaking of the necessity to rip a text to pieces or to ignore its imperatives entirely or even to change the words: I think that he is suggesting something rather more subtle.

The way I see it, in the transition to theatre, something that heretofore exists only as a text is translated into another medium altogether, a medium with very different demands and imperatives: it moves from the past tense of writing into the present tense of theatre. (Before anyone quibbles, I think – from my own experience of writing – that writing is always past tense). This is the case, *no matter what theatricalities a writer may embed into his or her text.*

There is nothing that makes an event more untheatrical than reverence for the text. (Oh, ok, reverences of other kinds can be equally deadening, but for the meantime, let's talk about writing.) In my few forays into theatrical writing, I have sometimes been waylaid by this kind of reverence (also by its complete and distressing opposite, but that's a different story): it can be very difficult to get people to treat a text they consider "poetic" and "beautiful" with disrespect. Directors talk about wanting to preserve the beauty of the language, and actors begin to speak very clearly and in low voices, to fully enunciate the full, sensuous gorgeousness of the words ... This, my friends, is death for a text. Suddenly, rather than being an invisible but palpable part of the theatrical experience, it hovers above it: intact, inviolate, and excruciatingly dead.

Or, to speak less personally, think of a reverent production of Shakespeare you might have seen, in which everyone is crouched beneath the text, pointing upwards to the inimitable greatness of the Bard's language, and then think how bored you were.

Where I think Chris is being consciously provocative (and, to be fair, he undermines his own hard line at the end of his post) is where he claims that "productions that emphasize this complex of signs and conditions that we refer to as 'liveness' will inevitably commend themselves more immediately to audiences and secondary commentators alike. A play which hits the bookshelves at the same time as it hits the stage has already forfeited its claim to those attentions."

> As the phrase 'well-made play' implies, form for playwrights is secondary to content, in other words it's there to serve the content and set it up to its best advantage; this is precisely how it comes about that it's possible to tip the content of *The History Boys* into different containers and, though some modification is of course required, the essence

---

[10] Alison links to: http://beescope.blogspot.co.uk/2007/03/to-george-hunka.html.

of the piece remains the same, its qualities, its 'message' (if it will own up to having one, or many). In the work that the university theatre departments now favour, the medium is once again the message, and the question of what the theatre experience is, or can or could be, takes precedence over the surface detail of who says what to whom on what topic.

Of course, I recognise instantly the kind of plays Chris is referring to – or at least I think I do: those plays in which a form is taken as given, most usually a variation on naturalistic norms, and content or "issues" are then poured into the glass. David Williamson is the archetypal local example of that kind of writing. But at the same time, it seems to me that many people who would think of themselves as basically "conventional" playwrights also approach writing a play as, above all, a formal proposition.

I know it's too easy to refer to **Daniel Keene**,[11] but he's to hand and at the moment too far away to object, and he's a real Playwright; also a Playwright whose work often appears in book form, sometimes before it appears on stage. And I can say confidently, based on years of conversations, that he always approaches writing a play as a formal problem, to the point where the writing of the play is impossible until the problem becomes clear. He is most certainly a playwright who often (but not always) writes plays in the traditional way, grumbling in his study as he attempts to produce a "finished" text which exists luminously in its own right. With such a play – although, again, not in all his collaborations – he expects the actors to speak the words he has written, unless he agrees to change them.

Yet he hasn't a lot of time for the Albee position, which he equates with the "academic" playwrights in France whom French directors are always complaining about; and although he enjoys going to rehearsals, he doesn't believe he has a place there as a writer, except maybe during an inital reading. (He is not a bad director, and sometimes offers suggestions from that capacity). And nothing makes him more frustrated than overly respectful practitioners, or people who think he knows, from his privileged position as the writer, what the play is supposed to be *about*. How the hell, he demands, is *he* supposed to know? That's what other people are supposed to find out. For Daniel, meaning is something that is discovered in performance before an audience. Yet he would cheerfully (and honestly) consider himself a conventional playwright.

More interestingly, perhaps, he regards the text as an autonomous object which, when subjected to the pressures and travails of other players in the process, becomes something else. Perhaps this might be illustrated clearly by his recent insistence that the English publication of **The Nightwatchman** (by Currency Press for the upcoming Sydney production) preserved the original French character names (it was a French commission), although in the Australian production, the names have been Anglicised. The play *as written* is one thing; the play *as performed* is entirely another.

At this point, we might seem to be splitting hairs, and simply redefining "playwrights" as "theatre writers". But I'm not so sure: it does seem to me that the idea of the "dramatist" who "sits with the gods" (as I think Mrs O'Neill said of her husband) still has a bit of life in it.

---

[11] Keene is Croggon's partner.

Theatremaking and Authorship

a hammer

Adam Szymkowicz
7 March 2007
http://aszym.blogspot.co.uk/2007/03/hammer.html

I've been sort of freaking out lately. The normal stuff – what am I doing with my life?, how long can I stand being an administrative assistant?, should I continue to live in New York? etc. But also the fatigue is setting in. I've been working so hard – writing like it's going out of style (which it may be) – but also working so hard on getting my stuff out there, getting it read by strangers. I'm just really tired right now. Tired of all the work it takes to be a playwright. Tired of not seeing anything resembling a way to playwright for a living. And the other voice in my head is saying, "Really?" "Did you really think there was a way to make a living doing what you love?"

All this makes me want to quit, bow out, stop running the race. I'm in the middle of writing a new play. Literally at the intermission and I know I will finish it. Because that's what I do. And behind it I can visualize all the other plays I'm hoping to write in varying stages of clarity. And there is a novel there too, supposedly. And supposedly I'm going to go back to that novel after this play is written. Even though I hear other plays calling.

Even though I am so so tired. Of running on this track. And yet this track is also the only thing that keeps me sane some days. Try to talk to me sometime after I've gone a week without writing. It will not be a pleasant experience for you. You see, I need it to keep me sane but it's also slowly driving me mad. So I'm not so sure what to do about that. And I keep beating my head against the wall and chips of the wall tumble down but this wall ... how thick is this wall? Two feet? Three feet thick? And I need a fucking hammer, OK. My head is found to be insufficient.

But really I just want to stop, move to the country, somewhere where there are trees and I won't be able to see plays every night. Because it's not good for me anymore to see the amount of theatre I see. Theatre has taken my life away and I'm not fighting hard enough to get it back. But I love it too. I love the theatre and can't understand why everyone else doesn't love it too.

But this life isn't working right now. I got to take a break. I got to ... I got to finish this play. Dude, I am fucked.

Rules for the Writing of Plays

Matthew Freeman, *On Theatre and Politics*
16 November 2007
http://matthewfreeman.blogspot.co.uk/2007/11/rules-for-writing-of-plays.html

I have decided that this blog needs more substantive posts about the process of writing plays (playwriting, in the vernacular). Hence, I shall use the authority bestowed upon me by having free time, to write these important rules for playwriting. These rules, without a doubt, will exist for generations to come, who will Google the term "Rules for Playwriting".

RULES FOR THE WRITING OF PLAYS

1. Do not write "Chapter 1" at the top of a scene. Instead write "Scene 1".
2. When writing a play, remember that the operative word is "play". Have fun. For example, Samuel Beckett wrote a play called "Play". That play is a hoot. Enjoy yourself.
3. All the characters are "you", just as everyone in a dream is "you". Even if you are 19 years old and currently attending college in Connecticut, when you describe a character as "a 59 year old housewife with a mournful eye on her past as an alcoholic"; "she" is "you".
4. When you write "The End" or "Blackout" at the end of the play, remember that your work is not yet done. Soon, the vipers will descend, teeth full of venom.
5. Choose whether or not you will write a Drama or a Comedy before you decide if anyone in the play has cancer.
6. That joke you heard over coffee that seemed so darn great when your friend explained it in detail, his eyebrows going up and down while he did all the funny voices? Do not use that joke. It is not as good as you think.
7. Tell the truth. Except when caught. Then lie.
8. Your precious God will not help you. Prayer will only lead to revision. Avoid revision. Your first draft is your "vision". Revisioning your vision is also known as compromise. Do not compromise. Even for your precious "God".
9. If you are a playwright that is also a woman you are a "lady writer" and therefore must write about Abortion. If you do not, you are missing the whole point.
10. Tell long stories about drinking, but do not drink. Then you will have the edge in this poker game we call "The American Theater".
11. All of your best play ideas will come from the Utne Reader.
12. Dialogue is a cloud, whispy and soft. You can tell the way the wind is blowing by looking at this cloud. The higher the cloud, the further from the earth it is. The further from the earth, the less like fog. Fog is not dialogue; fog is a monologue.
13. Aristotle doesn't really "get" you. He's never played a single game on the Xbox and didn't have to pay student loans. F*ck him.
14. Write plays about issues. These issues include: war, sexism, racism and "those idiots in the Bible Belt".
15. You'll be told to write what you know. Think about it, though . . . do you really *know* anything? Does that mean you shouldn't write anything? I mean, seriously, we're all completely blind. So write about being blind. Try taking a tie and wrapping it around your eyes and wandering around for a day, trying to remember where all the light switches are and how many steps there are to get up to your room. Write about that.
16. There are dogs in the streets, howling. Heed them, oh Playwright.
17. Microsoft Word really helps the Dada in you. Cut and Paste, baby. Cut and Paste.
18. All plays have a beginning, middle and an end. Should the end come in the middle, and the middle after that, you've screwed up.
19. Keep a chart of the irony.
20. When you feel, deep in your heart, that you have completed the finest work of which you are capable . . . quit. Immediately. Who needs that next play, and the feeling of being over-the-hill. Trust your instincts. It won't get better.

Opening the house

Chris Goode, *Thompson's Bank of Communicable Desire*
11 June 2011
http://beescope.blogspot.co.uk/2011/06/opening-house.html

The best work I do is in rehearsal rooms.

Here we are, two-thirds of the way through the inadvertent but hugely satisfying trilogy of back-to-back ensemble processes that are making this spring such a pleasure. Tomorrow I get on a train to Leeds to spend the week in *Open House* at WYP. I don't think I've ever known so little about a project that's about to loom pretty large: we'll be immersed in it twelve hours a day (at least) and I feel like I might just about be able to predict, though with not much certainty, how it goes for the first half hour. Maybe 45 minutes. After that: there's just no way of knowing.

I explained *Open House* in my previous post[12] (and of course you can read about it on the WYP web site[13]) so I won't talk you through the ins and outs again, but for a bit more context you might want to have a look at this lovely piece[14] by Maddy Costa, whom I invited a few weeks ago to come along for the ride through these three wildly different landscapes. (Though for my part I might not want you to have a look at the accompanying photograph – I mean good grief I know I'm not an oil painting at the best of times but, wow, nothing prepared me for the bracing thwack of humiliation that went along with that little doozy.) Apparently the Radio 4 *Today* programme might come and sit with us at some point in the week: which is, er, a peculiar thought, but not a completely unappealing one.

Is *Open House* really newsworthy? We're so accustomed to thinking of what we do as something that carries so little weight in the broader culture (let alone in the ADHD cacophony of broadcast media) that it's almost impossible to conceive of it registering at all, let alone conveying any of the force and impetus that, at its best, it has for us on the inside. But thinking about the proposition that *Open House* makes – to its audiences, to WYP, to other artists, to those who hear about it at whatever remove – there's something very interesting in allowing oneself to reimagine it, albeit in an obviously ludicrous and self-indulgent daydream, as news.

The trouble is, the headline doesn't sound like it's earning its keep. "The best work I do is in rehearsal rooms." Why should that matter to anybody? – So here is the news, in case anyone puts a mic in front of my face at some point in the next week and asks me what we're up to.

---

[12] Chris links to: http://beescope.blogspot.co.uk/2011/05/tolstoy-in-rear-view-mirror.html, where he explains the open rehearsal concept: 'So anyone who wants to, whether they have any experience of theatre making or not, is welcome to rock up at any time... and they'll be admitted to the rehearsal room: where they're invited to engage however they please.'
[13] These posts are no longer online.
[14] Chris links to: https://www.theguardian.com/stage/2011/jun/07/open-house-christopher-goode.

Theatre Blogging

The best work I do is in rehearsal rooms. I'm very proud of the shows and pieces I make but I wish more and more that audiences could see inside the rehearsal room. That's where theatre is most like itself: a liquid thing, restless, full of spontaneities and unexpected shifts. The room I like being in is calm and careful but alive with attentiveness, with smart people trying to speak each other's languages, tune in to each other's invitations, respond to each other's desires. Negotiating in a spirit of curious enquiry and the delight that comes from being kind together. At its best it's a room where everybody falls a little bit in love, impelled by the knowledge that in a matter of weeks, days, hours, the time in which that love is immediately possible will end, its space will close down.

I loved the room we made together on the Cendrars project. Talking together, reading, dancing, pottering. Lots of pottering. Sketching each other, taking photos, making notes. Watching, watching. Someone taking a little nap after lunch one day while the rest of us watched an old episode of *Buck Rogers*. That was my favourite. It made me think back to the times I've slept in a rehearsal room. Times I've laid on the floor and laughed till I cried. Times I just cried. Times we all cried together. Times things fell into place after a long period of confusion and doubt. Times of sitting quietly on a window-ledge and looking out over the city. Times of hearing written texts spoken aloud for the first time. Times I've been touched, held, embraced, coaxed, tickled; times I've been able to do those things for other people. Times I've seen shyness: people singing songs without confidence, struggling to express themselves, standing up and trying something that was never going to work and then trying it again. Times of great gifts: seeing old friends in new ways; hearing a piece of music that changes everything; watching people I hardly know taking off their clothes and letting themselves be seen. Times I've been seen myself. Really, really seen. The relief of being really seen, and really heard.

Being in a rehearsal room – as I have the past four weeks, and am about to for another week – still feels like a treat, though if you laid those special periods of my life end to end they'd stretch for years now I suppose. A rehearsal room that's really working, where the things I've just described are possible, and easily possible, nearly inevitable: that's my favourite place to live. Maybe it's the only place I *really* live. And sometimes I must admit, though the pieces we make together in those rooms are always suffused with the atmosphere in which they've been made, sometimes I'm aware that when I'm talking about what important and transformative things theatre can do, I'm often not talking about the bit that most people only have access to, the bit that happens for an hour and a half in the evenings. I'm talking about the hopeful and loving way in which we did our best to get there.

Open House is an attempt to invite people in to the work so they can see what it's like, because I think there's such misunderstanding about how we make what we make, and why we make it. I think the thought and the care that go into the making, and not least the making of the room where the making will happen, might surprise some of those people who fulminate below the line on the theatre blogs – and several of those who get paid to fulminate above the line too. Perhaps they might find their cynicism a little bit dispelled. Their fear, too. Their uninformed trigger-happy assumptions about pretentiousness and self-indulgence.

This might be a useful end in itself but it's also a more significant beginning. I want a theatre that behaves more like the best, the most inclusive, the most supportive, rehearsal room, precisely because of what happens there, the things I've described here. Because those instances of very special, very heightened, or very calm but deeply engaged action, happen in a zone with no fictional frame around it. A little slippery liminality, perhaps: but you see people, not characters, you see actors and creative teams, you see real lives being lived, but also being crafted as they are lived, in the moment of their living.

I've often described theatre as a place where we figure out how to live together better; I realise for most people, even when they're watching pedagogic political plays or participating in supposedly interactive immersive walkabouts, that would be an almost inexplicable statement, because actually I'm talking about the processes that happen in the best rehearsal, the lives we lead there, where all our commitments are held and honoured but every detail of their activation is open to question and negotiation. Theatre performances that have somehow retained some sense of that promise are pretty rare and they almost never take place in the larger established buildings.

I think more and more about theatre as a place to know. We're quite attracted to the opposite: saying that there's something interesting – and so there is – in theatre practices and encounters that are about not-knowing, about doubt, about sitting with uncertainty and wondering. Certainly most rehearsal processes have a lot of that going on in them. But sometimes the doubt is so present in our minds that we don't see the knowing. We don't see what an act of knowing it is to come to this space in the first place. Not just for us makers but for an audience too. It's an act of knowing, and of wanting, maybe even of needing. Just as we've become so seduced by the rhetoric of unfocused 'risk' and the well-intended idea of "a safe space to fail" that we've become distracted from the exhilarating prospect of coming together in order to succeed, to succeed brilliantly in getting something done: so likewise we've overemphasized the permission to not know, when actually, sometimes, we *know*. Audiences too. Sometimes, it's true, we know things that audiences don't know, we have insights to impart, we have skills we can use to make beautiful things happen; but our insights as artists arise not because we're cleverer, smarter, than our audiences, but because we practise giving ourselves space in which those insights can live – and not only live, but live an examined life.

Everybody should have the space to know what they know, to feel what it's like to know it. To feel the fear and the distress that comes with knowing what they know, given the space to really feel it. And everybody should have the space to begin to do something with that knowledge. To begin to move, to change. Everybody needs a place of liquidity, of restlessness and shifting, of speculation and slipperiness; a place in which it's possible – encouraged! – to be thoughtful and kind and attentive. A place to do shy singing, to take off your clothes, to have a little nap in the company of strangers who'll make sure you're safe. A place in which we can start to negotiate the next place. Not a secluded, insulated, escapist place, but a temporary shelter. A room without walls. An open house.

It's funny: almost everybody, right?, at some point or another in their lives, has written a poem. A teenage 'nobody understands me' poem or a funny little 'roses are red' poem in a Valentine's card or whatever. Almost everybody does a bit of making, whether it's cooking or gardening or knitting or DIY or whatever – and it's not just target-driven activity, it's not just about needing a cake or a scarf, it's about having something to do that makes you feel like a participant in a wider project of being a civilised and creative individual in a society that overwhelmingly wants you to see yourself only as a consumer. But how many people will ever make a bit of theatre? Lord knows I've done enough gigs in people's kitchens and living rooms to know how possible it is to have a few friends round and tell them a story or show them something familiar that they've never really seen before. I believe more and more resolutely in the civic value of designated theatre buildings but I don't think they should have the monopoly on theatre any more than all the world's fish are in aquariums.

I was thinking in a sleepless spell last night about that cliché of *carpe diem* egging-on: life isn't a rehearsal, you know! Well, no, it isn't, and so we might all plausibly want to make the most of whatever time we have at our disposal. We might want to live in a way that's rich and expansive and detailed and careful and joyous and tender and hopeful and attentive. We might want to live in a way that feels so multitudinous, so teeming with possibility, that it begins to seem almost equal to the enormity and complexity of Life with a capital L. Were that so, we could hardly make a better start than to imagine a life that is, at least, *like* a rehearsal. Because it's too important to think of it merely as a show with a limited run.

In other words, the real problem with *Open House* is that we only get to be there twelve hours a day.

And now back to you in the studio, John.

xx

[. . .a short thing on work. . .]
Alex Swift
17 December 2013
http://www.swiftalex.co.uk/a-short-thing-on-work/

this is a short response to the 43000 blog posts i've read recently in which artists have justified themselves making a living in part by claiming never to work less than 29 hours a day and to have only once been on holiday in the last 14 years, and that was actually just a walk to the aldi at the end of the road to buy toilet paper.

Yeah, you know, fine. Whatever.

But also, here's a thing: work is not a moral good.

In fact when you start to talk as though it is, to justify yourself on the basis of how much work you do, even just to yourself, you've already implicitly bought in to the pernicious, inhuman ideology from which a strivers vs skivers narrative springs in order to justify attacks on the weakest and most vulnerable members of society. The value of a human being does not lie in how much supposedly productive activity can be extracted from them before they break. And it doesn't even make you good at hard-nosed business-savvy take-no-prisoners capitalism either.

Here's what Bill Gates says about lazy people:

I choose a lazy person to do a hard job, because a lazy person will find an easy way to do it.

Which is to say that even for the techno-capitalists' techno-capitalist, laziness can be a productive force, promoting invention and efficiency.

Any boss of any kind who mistakes getting people to work hard for getting people to work well is a shit boss. And that still holds if you're your own boss, as many artists are. christ – it still holds if you're a programmer trying to get something out of a computer – the brute force alogrithm is the least elegant, the least sophisticated, the least intelligent and the least efficient.

Here are some things that i've done, without which i would be unable to make some of the work i'm making now:

sat and looked at the sea
got a little bit drunk with some old anarchists in Bradford and listened to their stories of organising creative demonstrations against the national front
cycled up a mountain
stared blankly into space
got really drunk with some actors
listened to Bjork
set up a radical performance reading group
sang my daughter to sleep

All of these things have proved to be necessary for me as an artist and it is necessary for me to make space to do things like this in order for me to be an artist. But they are clearly not work in any sense of the word that anyone who's ever had to, you know, go to work would recognise. And it would be disastrous for me to start thinking of them as work, because that would instrumentalise them, fetishise them, and alienate me from the experiences and actions themselves, and consequently from what they would produce in me as well.

Now, maybe you deserve to earn a living as an artist. Personally i think all people deserve a living (whatever that is) even if through a combination of circumstances they are unable to work productively (whatever that is) but that's just because i'm a human being who thinks that human beings should be treated like human beings. But anyway, if there's value in your art, it's in your art, yeah? Not in your doing 78 hour weeks.

ps – i know there's a general line of attack that people like to make which portrays artists as scroungers who can't make their way, whose work is invalidated if it is publicly funded and doesn't appeal to all people ever and who are somehow morally lacking if they are not supported entirely through their engagement with the market. this line of attack is ideologically motivated and is concerned with trying to devalue all activity which isn't directly economically productive, even if it might have many indirect economic (and non-economic) benefits, and to confuse democracy with the untrammeled operation of the market. explaining to people who make this argument how hard you work won't make the tiniest difference. reject the premise and deconstruct the ideology behind the argument people.

CHAPTER 7
ANGER AND DISSENT

> **Bye Bye Sir Trevor Nunn**
> 'Theatre Worker', *Encore Magazine*
> May 2003
> http://encoretheatremagazine.blogspot.co.uk/Polemics.html#Nunn

Trevor Nunn's time at the helm of the National Theatre has been controversial. He has been accused of a safe repertoire, excessive reliance on musicals, of failing to provide this flagship theatre with a vision. His directorial choices have sometimes been tame, his handling of the material flabby, his tone complacent.

And all of this is true. It has taken only a matter of weeks with Nick Hytner in the chair to realise what a shabby regime has just been replaced. At his valedictory platform at the National, Sir Trevor pointed out that under his stewardship, the National produced six musicals and sixty new plays. He suggested, justifiably, that to read the press one would think those figures were the other way around. But let's examine that claim.

The first thing to note is that these are not the only numbers to quote; let's weigh the aggregated budgets of those new plays against the aggregated budgets of the musicals. I'm sure the difference would not be so stark. We might also remember that something like twenty of those new plays were premiered in his final year, during the bold Loft experiment. This season seemed to have thrown together in some haste, admirable though much of it was. It also played to very small audiences, for very brief runs, so take your pick: do we weigh budgets? numbers of performances? auditorium sizes?

And finally, although there were some excellent new plays produced with Sir Trevor's presumed support (Blue/Orange, Copenhagen, Mother Clap's Molly House), there were many disasters: and that's alright, the right to fail does not need to be argued for any longer. But works like Mutabilitie, or Battle Royal, or Remember This, or The Villain's Opera look like the work of a theatre that has lost any sense of what it wants to do. They were ill-matched to their theatres, underdeveloped, did not appear to have emerged from any sharpening dialogue with the theatre. The Lyttleton has developed an admirable reputation as a new-play-killer, a demerit to add to its many architectural liabilities. But at Sir Trevor's National Theatre there seemed to be no real policy for new writing. Jack Bradley is a good man but he has evidently struggled with a artistic directorship with no instinctive sympathy for the new play.

Sir Trevor's directorial abilities are undoubted. Indeed, his production of Gorky's Summerfolk will surely stand as one of the towering moments of the National Theatre's artistic history. But all those years in musical theatre appear to have given him a hallucinatory ability to detect 'numbers' where there aren't any. His production of The Relapse was marred by a sword fight that could have come from MGM's The Pirate; it blunted the bitterness and cleansing horror of the play's engagement with our sexual obligations. And in the second part of Stoppard's trilogy, The Coast of Utopia, the failed revolutions of 1848 were performed like a grotesque tribute to Les Misérables, as if the historical imagination of the play's director had been fly-blown by the flashily vacuous tableaux of the musical stage.

And as for those musicals themselves: there is no doubt that Oklahoma! is one of the three or four most important works in the history of the musical. It is entirely right that the National Theatre should revive it, excavate it, test its strength, and explore its contours. South Pacific, too, benefitted from its careful, toughened reworking. But My Fair Lady? Anything Goes? Singing in the Rain? These are entertaining enough, but on a West End stage they would have opened like a flower in spring; there was nothing for the National Theatre to do here, and they did nothing. Efficient shows, half-heartedly cast and sung, with, here and there, shameful pieces of miscasting.

Nick Hytner has chosen to bring in and develop Jerry Springer – The Opera. It is plainly a signature piece of programming, a slate-wiping production. The show is unbelievably vulgar; the lyrics are crude and awkward; the music is often repetitive and uncertain in register; the production is wooden; the second act is overblown; and yet the whole thing is wonderful. You sit in that drafty old theatre feeling that something remarkable, unprecedented is happening. It genuinely mixes high art with the popular; it has a vigour and dirt about it that suggests its creators are really exploring something new. It is caustic and hilarious. It is a show the like of which we have never seen in the National before. One thing is obvious: the show would have got nowhere when Sir Trevor was running the place.

At that goodbye platform, Sir Trevor was facing an entirely uncritical audience. At the end he received a standing ovation. Fair enough, anything else would have seemed an insult. But the only other time the audience applauded him was when he announced that he had kept the National Theatre in the black. There was a mild outbreak of clapping.

Is that it? Is that really Trevor Nunn's legacy to the National theatre? That he never got in debt? No one wants to applaud an artistic director who ruins a theatre's finances, but doesn't this tell us something about the safety-first priorities of this man? His was a wasted time, a conservative and complacent era in the National's history. Encore wishes him luck wherever he goes but we're glad he's no longer running what has the potential to be one of our most exciting theatres.

Don't Cry for Him

'Theatre Worker', *Encore Magazine*
4 August 2006
http://encoretheatremagazine.blogspot.co.uk/2006/08/dont-cry-for-him.html

---

Most people develop opinions because the world presents them with options. Lord Lloyd Webber seems to have opinions only when he's got a new show on. His latest off-the-peg rant is about the state of the West End. Yes, you heard me right, the state of the West End. The man whose horrible shows squatted a sizeable portion of it for the last twenty years and still owns seven theatres (including Drury Lane, The Palace, and the Palladium) thinks it's all up the spout.

First, he says in an interview in the Radio Times to publicise his naff and slightly fraudulent reality TV show, that only Billy Elliot, The Lion King and Phantom of the Opera are making money. First, as is well known, The Lion King probably isn't making money: its presence as a stage show is a loss leader designed to encourage us to buy other Disney™ products. Second, surely there are other shows that are making money. What's the point of Mamma Mia! if it's not making money? What about Les Mis? And, ahem, Andrew, haven't you just opened Evita?

The problem, says Lord Webber, is the lack of innovative new shows. What like Evita? Or The Sound of Music? He wants shows with a feelgood factor. Presumably he hankers after the old days of the musical when it was referred to as musical comedy with the emphasis on comedy. There are too many shows that pass almost the entire evening without a good joke, relying on ponderous adaptations of old novels, the score filled with unhummable pastiches of Puccini to show that you're a 'serious' composer. Woman in White anyone?

But then he gets to the nub of the matter. The West End is not commercially viable. Why? Because many of them are listed buildings. The Theatre Royal, Drury Lane, which he owns, needs air conditioning as part of an extensive renovation. Because it is a Grade I listed building, it will cost £20 million. 'If it wasn't listed we could do that for £1 million. No commercial person can find that sort of money and the theatre could never generate it, so what's the future?'

Listing a building is intended to preserve that building for all of us. So all of us are entitled to wonder why you bought the Theatre Royal if you were unprepared to maintain it. Last year, when he was in the process of selling four of his theatres, he insisted that

> I have always been keenly aware of the responsibility that comes with ownership of such valuable national assets, and throughout this process, have taken great pains to persuade my partner, Bridgepoint Capital, that we must sell only to someone who understands the particular nature of theatre and who will protect and preserve these very special buildings.

What's the point of the private sector running theatres – and boring us endlessly with the rigours of the box office – if it's going to bleat on and on about how expensive the whole business is. You basically want the buildings delisted and probably some kind of grant from Westminster council or the Historical Buildings and Monument Commission. In other words, the private sector, as always, wants the laws changed and a handout – so you can make more money. Because in fact how far have you 'protected and preserved these very special buildings'? The Palace got a nice refit, but Drury Lane and The Palladium are a shambles. What you did to the Adelphi was hardly about protection or preservation. The Duchess, The Apollo, the Lyric and Garrick hardly flourished under your care did they?

Any in any case, why should we bail you out? May we remind you, Lord Webber, that you're a very very rich man. According to the Sunday Times Rich List 2006, you are the 87= richest person in Britain. You are apparently worth £700 million. If you love these theatres so much, put your hand in your bloody pocket.

> ## It's All About The Money
> Frances d'Ath, *Supernaut*
> 19 December 2006
> https://supernaut.info/2006/12/its-all-about-the-money

Slagging match of the week goes to Melbourne Festival vs. The Media, wherein Robin Usher tries to sound a rhetorical question and get us all wondering, "Hey, yeah, maybe the Melbourne festival *has* lost its touch."[1]

Is this shifty journalism trying to find an angle to cut down contemporary arts in Melbourne and put the big companies – Oz Ballet, Opera, and Melbourne Symphony – back in their rightful place as the upholders of culture? I'm not a great fan of Kristy Edmunds, the current Melbourne Festival director who, it was announced last week has been given and "unprecedented fourth year". She does go for contemporary work, but I feel in the manner of a shopper, contemporary as commodity, and she isn't really exerting herself in finding anything outside the safe avant garde. That is to say, if the rest of the world wasn't raving about Socìetas Raffaello Sanzio, and they hadn't already been at Australian festivals this millennium, I'm not sure how probable it is Southbank would have been graced by the sound of falling truncheons.

It's programming based on prior box office, support of the contemporary by relying on publicists' copy rather than finding stuff on your own and be willing to say, "I think this is good art, even if no one else knows what I am talking about, and I'm willing to look like an idiot and take a beating in the press in my support of it".

Though contra this, the international apprehension of a nation's art is based on the commodification from within of a body of culture as representative of that nation, so from Taiwan we always see Cloudgate, even though within Taiwan there was a surprisingly low opinion of the company, and thus for an outsider to find interesting stuff not on the menu, and for there to be the funding and support to get this stuff to festival . . . it's usually easier to go with Cloudgate.

Comparing Edmunds' efforts with the execrable neo-colonial antics of Jonathon Mills, she at least is looking outside the cultural snobbery that often comes with festivals. Both though, and this is a general annoyance for me for Melbourne Festival seem to think art comes from Europe and its descendants, is of a certain size and weight (i.e. medium to large companies), and there is a striking lack of engagement with Asia, by which I mean everything east of

---

[1] Frances links to: https://www.theage.com.au/news/opinion/the-melbourne-festival-has-lost-touch/2006/12/13/1165685749982.html.

Pakistan, south of Mongolia and north of Antarctica. The inclusion of plenty of Japan stuff, coming on the end of two interminable years of Australia-Japan-Art-Freundschaft in my mind doesn't count, for the same reason touring Cloudgate from Taiwan doesn't.

But Robin Usher's extra-suss controversy-mongering and reductionist bottom-line dollar-dollar-bill-y'all art-as-finance in *The Age* is disingenuous.

A few days ago also, dance reviewer Hillary Crampton remarked, "Ideally such debates should take place in the mainstream media, but sadly they do not, owing to the lack of commitment by publishers to cultural debate". The context of this, within a commentary on critics vs. artists becomes another mediocre 'old vs. new media' trope or 'blogs vs. newspapers'. When the critical and intellectual position of the arts in mainstream Australia is represented by people like Robin Usher and Andrew Bolt, why should such debates take place where these pseudo-critics get a paycheck for intellectually feeble drooling?

More importantly though is the assumption that such debates find a natural home in traditional media. It's been a long time since I have paid more than cursory attention to the arts columns in old media. Even *RealTime*, which is by far the best arts periodical in Australia suffers from press-release-plus-advertisement-as-journalism. It is impossible to engage with old media without the suspicion of being on the receiving end of manipulated publicity, and there is a singular untrustworthiness in mainstream media that precludes exactly this presence of integrity.

Or to regard it from the perspective of a debate, old media is bereft of dialogue in any meaningful respect. A review, opinion piece, column, whatever, is a statement in which response is not part of the deal. Does the inclusion of a 'have your say' pretend-blog comments box at the bottom of these constitute debate? More particularly, where is the community? Blogs as an ecosystem of communities have this as one of their primary attributes; the comments on blogs as diverse as Peking Duck to Theatre Notes all have regular commentators or guest writers whose erudition and passion for their interests make for inspired reading.

In this world, the writing of Usher et al is clearly seen for what it is: weasel words, comment spam and trolling.

Michael Billington Being Rather Silly

Andy Field, *The Arcades Project*
24 May 2007
http://thearcadesproject.blogspot.co.uk/2007/05/michael-billington-being-rather-silly.html

---

Just off to bed but happened to notice a train wreck of an article by Michael Billington on the Guardian Blog which I can only imagine was written by the animated paper-clip on microsoft word while he tottered off for the evening to read some extracts from Kenneth Tynan.

On a purely pragmatic level, Hytner's argument is absurd. It's like suggesting that papers should change their political editors every time a new government is elected or that sports writers should be swapped around whenever our national soccer or cricket teams change coaches.

No Michael, I'm afraid it's not at all like that. Both the examples you cite represent a transfer of personnel within a field that by no means changes the notions or conventions that govern that environment. Or, in other words, it doesn't matter how many England managers you go through football is still a game played by 11 men under a strict code of laws in which the goals (no pun intended) have remained the same since time immemorial. Now if one young scallyway was to one day pick up the ball and run with it, that might require a 'critic' who at least acknowledged (and maybe even supported) this transformation; or who at the very least was able to admit that any time this happened it wasn't simply cheating.

He then goes on to unfurl a banner proclaiming the importance of the indi ... I mean his individual voice. Though I thought the problem in the first place was that his voice isn't sounding that individual these days. In fact, it's sounding remarkably similar to those of all the other daily critics for, though they may have different tastes and prose styles, they all share a fundamentally limited notion of what theatre can or should be – a notion that sees Billington dismiss Katie Mitchell's the waves as a 'sterile piece of theatre about theatre' that is nothing but a 'celebration of technical ingenuity' in much the same way as Nicholas de Jongh calls her work 'a dreadful form of directorial embellisment' and Spencer states that all devised theatre is becoming 'more like an acrobatic display than a piece of real drama'.

And yet Billington has the gall to defend himself by arguing that 'much of the finest postwar criticism has run counter to prevailing views'.

Well yes. it has.

Fussing Over Foss

Matt Trueman, *Carousel of Fantasies*
11 October 2009
Now available from http://matttrueman.co.uk/2009/10/fussing-over-foss.html

Last Friday, The Stage printed what is, quite frankly, an inexcusable and indefensible dismissal of interactive theatre[2] by critic Roger Foss. Mercifully, this week the industry paper is giving over a similar space for the artistic directors of the BAC, Davids Jubb and Micklem, to respond. While I am looking forward to read their perspective on the importance and vitality of such work, I wanted to get in there first and tear Foss's argument (of sorts) apart.

Now I don't lay claim to strictly syllogistic thought processes in my ramblings, but Foss's argument (of sorts) makes such leaps of logic that it is utterly impossible to spot a route

---

[2] Matt links to: https://www.thestage.co.uk/features/2009/its-play-time-how-much-interactivity-can-one-take/.

through, let alone follow it. Foss displays a total lack of understanding or, even worse, a positive misunderstanding of the work under discussion. For the most part this results from his tangled confusion over the vocabulary used. More damaging, however, is his stubborn refusal to accept the work on its own terms. No – in fact it's worse than that. From the start, Foss denies such work the right to even exist. He knows what theatre is and what it does because he's seen it. It does what it's always done. End of. Game over. Now, shit off, I'm trying to suspend my disbelief.

Alright, so maybe that's a little too facetious (if not downright obnoxious), but Foss certainly makes his position obvious from the start. He does not arrive at it through the course of an argument. Instead, he starts out with a definition (of sorts) that rules out anything that doesn't match a very stringent model.

Foss's first (and foremost) mistake is to view interactive theatre from the outside: "try and work your thoughts to imagine a theatre where there are no actors and no stage . . .". By asking us to visualise such a theatre, Foss manages to define an audience as those who watch. To do so is to miss the point of interactive theatre, that it is about doing not watching. Admittedly, there is little to be gained from watching someone take part in, say, Rotozaza's *Wondermart*. It would consist in following a 'shopper' wearing headphones and an unusual expression of bemused enjoyment as they stalk the aisles of a supermarket. However, *Wondermart* is not designed to be watched. It exists to be experienced, to be undergone, to be interacted with.

In fact, compare it to the same company's *Etiquette*. Here, the jigsaw might well piece together into something concrete or readable, even a narrative of sorts. It functions both from the inside and from the outside, when experienced and when viewed. It is designed in such a way that its being experienced translates into something worth watching. Crucially, however, the two modes of receipt bring about very different understandings of the piece. Almost to the point whereby one could even go so far as to separate experiencing and watching *Etiquette* entirely.

Having initially pitched himself outside of the work, Foss mistakenly continues with this notion when he comes to examine the experiential aspects. When he writes about what it is to undergo or to take part in interactive theatre, Foss does so in terms associated with making theatre or performing a play. He writes as if there is a distinct, external audience to whom we are performing when we participate. Hence, his use of phrases such as *"audience members will play all the roles"* or *"anyone can become living art"* and his subscription to the moniker *"citizen-actors"*.

The fact is that we are not citizen-actors or performers, but participants. We are not living-art, we are taking part in art. The game, the concept, the structures are the art. The taking part is the experience of it – just as looking at a painting is not itself a work of art – and this experience is itself a product of the art. Suddenly the flaw in Foss's logic becomes obvious when he writes, *"who needs artists or sculptors when you've got citizen-statues?"* Without the artist, there would be no work. We are merely materials, particularly in the curious choice of example Foss uses: Gormley's fourth plinth project, *One & Other*.

Secondly, when we are taking part we do not act, we do. At the heart of both actions is the notion of choice, but the difference them is the nature of those choices. An actor's choices are governed by aesthetics and a participant's by ethics. By this I do not mean to infer that performance cannot have ethical motivations nor that everyday actions cannot stem from aesthetic concerns, but that the primary impulse in each case is different. The actor addresses ethics at one remove – choosing how to present ethics aesthetically. The participant must decide how to act in the moment. Of course, this may be governed by aesthetic principles, but even in such events the choice is, first and foremost, an ethical one.

The very best interactive work places the participant in starkly ethical encounters, dilemmas even. On the wheelchair rickshaw that is *You, Me, Bum Bum Train*, I was genuinely shocked by my own impulsive actions. In the speed of the moment, acting solely on impulse, I threw a punch in a boxing ring and uttered some attempt at Swahili (of which, unsurprisingly, I know nothing) when asked to translate in a press conference situation. In retrospect, both actions are somewhat embarrassing.

But Foss refuses to allow a distinction between good and bad interactive work. When he writes, *"whether it's amazingly brilliant or utterly pointless, non-narrative theatre ticks all those artistically correct boxes for Arts Council England funding wonks"*, you feel as though he's writing not about individual works, but about the genre as a whole. (Of course, his repeated confusion of terms severely undermines his position as mere temerity. The differences between performerless, interactive, automated and non-narrative theatre are too many to name. However, anyone who can write, *"the trouble is that there's no instant label for actor-less theatre. Site-specific? Instalation? Stunt? Happening?"* should not be given a platform to call for its abolition. Anyway . . .)

For Foss the whole form is dismissed as inconsequential play. *"I can see some attraction in becoming a kidult and playing with a doll's house in a romper room for a couple of hours."* The point is that, at its best, interactive theatre is not just a game, but reaches beyond the rules imposed and into life. It remains real. It remains connected with the real world. Unlike Monopoly, for example, game-based theatre is not about winning, but about how you play. It's looking at both who you choose to be (as defined by your chosen actions) and also who you are. If it's play, it's play at its most serious.

Foss's conclusion stems from fear that interactive theatre will supplant more traditional forms. (You know, stories, stalls and sweets in the interval.) To deny that interactive work has the value of traditional forms is blind and obnoxious. To do so thus, as Foss does, is moronic:

"Don't let's kid ourselves that vogue-ish theatrical interactivity is anything more profound than a chance to grab a slice of live, edgy action in a bland, broadband world. Otherwise, we'll devalue the traditional playwright with a view on life and downgrade the link between author, actor and audience that makes theatre a unique, lived experience."

Firstly, the two are in no way mutually exclusive. The truth is that we can want both without contradiction and both can happily co-exist. In fact, they need to feed off one another if each is to improve. Secondly, interactive work is arguably more of a "lived experience" than more traditional theatre.

Finally, and most damagingly of all, the world we live in today is dominated by the mediatised and the virtual. The everyday revolves around these forms. We sit in front of screens and absorb more than ever before. So, what's wrong with a form of theatre that provides something else, something as necessary as traditional theatre was/is to the societies out of which it emerged. Theatre is made for man as social animal, not vice versa. To quote from Alan Read's *Theatre, Intimacy & Engagement*, what's wrong with thinking of theatre as *"a more prosaic evolutionary adaptation for circumstance: to the gradual increase in the appetite for affect in the screen-world of virtuality, the nostalgia for agency and the consequent retolling for action over reaction, the rediscovery of the potential for pleasure and increased states of excitation . . ."* In short, if interactive theatre fulfils a function in today's flatscreen society, how can you dismiss it in its entirety?

I could have screamed but instead I wrote this

Corinne Furness, *Distant Aggravation*
10 February 2011
http://distantaggravation.blogspot.com/2011/02/i-could-have-screamed-but-instead-i.html

---

Let me throw something out there before I write my response to Matt Trueman's post on the Guardian Theatre Blog.[3] Trueman's someone who, as a theatre critic (and indeed the owner of a blog), I respect. I enjoy reading his long-form criticism (criticism which his blog allows the space for). I think he writes intelligently and articulately about theatre, something I rate quite highly. And the note on his blog does say that his views should be shouted down. So this is me doing just that.

I've no desire to get into the critic vs blogger debate (seriously, I can't believe that we're still here), though it's difficult not to smell the whiff of the 'superiority' of that debate in some of Trueman's post. What I want to talk about is the blog post itself. The sentence that got me? "Equally, bloggers must stop the cynical practice of reviewing previews". If the "must" in that sentence didn't compel me to throw something at my computer screen (where was I when Matt Trueman was voted commander-in-chief of theatre bloggers?) then the "cynical" did. I am cynical about many things (including but not limited to TFL, possible British success in any sport that doesn't involve sitting down, anything that comes out of Nick Clegg's mouth, the fashion trend of leggings and haggis). Theatre and blogging would make the top ten list of things I am least cynical about. They both involve far too much personal effort to be otherwise.

But let me give Trueman's reasoning a chance. Reason one: bloggers attend previews to save money (but then undermine this by stating that the lack of discount entitles them to blog). Let me use my example of buying Hamlet tickets this week. I booked for a preview performance because it will save me £10. Ten pounds for me is half of my weekly travel budget. Any discount (however small) is a good thing when you see as much theatre as the

---

[3] Corinne links to: https://www.theguardian.com/stage/theatreblog/2011/feb/10/bloggers-review-previews-theatre.

average theatre blogger does. I still paid £17.50 for my ticket though. That's not an inconsiderable amount for me (even living in London there's still a lot of other things I could do with that money). Am I less entitled to write about that show than when I've paid £10 for a dayseat at the National? Or when I've paid £8 to go to Southwark Playhouse? Or £12 to the New Diorama? Or when I've been papered? What Trueman's statement doesn't take into account is that a discount is HUGELY important on a financial basis when you're paying your way but this discount doesn't mean you're not giving out a sizeable chunk of your weekly budget to this theatre.

[There's a bigger question about previews that I'd like to note. As long time blog reader will know, for 18 months I was a Duty Manager for the West Yorkshire Playhouse. The WYP have previews that usually last for 4–5 shows. Every time there was a preview we'd pull out a big PREVIEW SIGN that bruised my ankles on more than one occasion and generally got in the way of everyone. And I lost count of the number of times an audience member asked me "What does preview mean?". These were people who'd bought tickets and didn't understand what a preview meant. In truth previews only mean anything for people who regularly go to the theatre or for the people who make it. For anyone else, given they've paid for their ticket, this is the show "concrete" (to borrow a word). At the point that you charge people to view your work this is the inevitable reality.]

The second reason given for blogging previews being "cynical" is that they are "chas[ing] hits". And y'know what? It's nice when you get hits. And writing early in a run means you're more likely to get them. However, if I were really after hits I wouldn't be writing about theatre. I'd write about Justin Bieber EVERY DAY. Or I wouldn't, because I only know who he is because of twitter, I'd write about David Tennant a lot more than I already do. I can only marvel at those bloggers who keep up with their viewing in a less chaotic manner than me. I've pointed out before that theatre blogging takes effort and rushing out to see every show first and then rushing home to write about it rather than sleeping or going to work or spending time with your family or friends just so you can get some hits which only you will know about (because it is 2011 and no one has a stat counter visible any more) seems utterly ridiculous. Moreover in terms of effort and reward that's a pretty skewed equation. Writing that blog post and getting hits isn't the reason theatre bloggers go to the theatre (something that Trueman's post forgets). They go to theatre for the theatre.

My disbelief doesn't, however, stop there. I'm bewildered by the notion that theatre bloggers must have "ethical responsibilities" to productions. As a blogger I have ethical responsibilities to my family and my friends and the people I care about. I have ethical responsibilities to the theatre that pays my rent. I have ethical responsibilities to my reader (in terms of those productions that I may write about which involve people I know, or when, as sometimes happens, I get sent free stuff). Personally (and this is just me from my own experience as a writer) I have ethical responsibilities to companies/writers if I'm at "Scratch" event (either for free or for some nominal fee). If you invite me into your rehearsal room I have ethical responsibilities to you. If I come to your dress rehearsal I have ethical responsibilities to you. If you charge me £10, £17.99 or £35 or more for a ticket and I do not know anyone involved and have no connection to the building or company I have no ethical responsibilities to you other than arriving on time, paying attention and being polite to the

Theatre Blogging

FOH staff. I am a paying customer. I make no claim for my writing being the official view of anyone other than my own subjective, meandering self. My blog isn't a newspaper or a carefully curated academic journal to be preserved in someone's archives.

I also can't help but feel that Trueman conflates some of his own reasons for blogging with those of other theatre bloggers. I'd suggest that few bloggers want the same "respect" as critics (if we take respect to principally mean industry acknowledgement). I just want as much respect as anyone who has paid to see your show, has bought things in your bar, has supported you. Which I'd suggest deserves at least as much respect as any critic (if we take respect here to mean something much more important).

It's nice in some ways that Trueman considers theatre bloggers to be influential enough to merit such a post (bloggers are most useful to smaller theatres/companies/those who are not in the London centric gaze of the "dead white male", thus those who are least likely to have extensive previews). In other ways it's laughable that Trueman felt the need to expend the effort on the post – a futile attempt to hold back the sea by wagging a finger at it and pulling a stern face. Theatre criticism isn't the same as it was ten years ago. Bloggers and web forums and twitter and onwards. Who knows what it will look like in ten more? Bloggers are here to stay, bloggers reviewing previews (for all the reasons listed above) are here to stay. It might not be the brave new world that Trueman would like to envisage but it isn't for us to adapt to the existing system – it's for us all to invent something new.

Why Isherwood Should Just Blog Instead

Don Hall, *Angry White Guy in Chicago*
10 October 2011
Now available via: https://web.archive.org/web/20111010114315/http://donhall.blogspot.com/

NYT theater critic Charles Isherwood has issued an interesting idea.

Turns out he's just plain tired of Adam Rapp's work.

> "Adam Rapp won't have me to kick around anymore.
>
> Oops. I think I got that backwards. I mean I won't have Adam Rapp to kick around anymore.
>
> Fear not, admirers of this almost absurdly prolific playwright. I don't mean to suggest that Mr. Rapp is heading off to Hollywood for good, hanging up his hat as a theater man. (In addition to writing and directing for the theater, Mr. Rapp publishes young-adult novels, has written for the HBO series "In Treatment" and has written and directed two films, "Winter Passing" and "Blackbird".) Given his superhuman output, he'll probably have a new play in production by next month.
>
> What I mean is I think it's high time I stopped reviewing his plays. I suspect Mr. Rapp would heartily endorse this idea."

As far as I understand it (and a distinction that the lovely Kerry Reid has taken the time to point out to me), paid theater journalists do not get to decide whose work they will or will not cover. Bloggers, on the other hand, can pick and choose based on their subjective opinions. If Kerry is assigned to cover a play by a playwright she thinks sucks balls, she still goes – gotta pay the rent, of course, but there is also a journalistic contract at play. I, on the other, never have to witness another House Theater show again if I so choose. Because no one pays me to write a freakin' thing. And because I've been through the eighth grade.

Isherwood writes for New Yawk Tides. He is a JOURNALIST. I write for myself and maybe 800 regular readers. I am an ASSHOLE WITH A COMPUTER.

So, what happens if Isherwood is granted by the Old Grey Lady to begin to selectively deciding who gets the ink and who doesn't? Well, first, he automatically joins the club chaired by Hedy Weiss (who has gone on record in her views that "certain types of theater should not be covered by a major paper") and joins my raggity club called "Just Another Asshole Who Has a Blog".

Not that I mind. He might class up the joint.

Second, like me, eventually no one will care what he thinks of theater because the lack of even a hint of objectivity (yeah … I know … but you have to try, right?) makes him a shill rather than a critic. He will become essentially irrelevant and I'm not sure his ego could handle that.

So, I think Isherwood should just suck it up and continue to cover another "tediously outlandish dark comedy …" written by Adam Rapp and quit the whining. Or quit his gig at the NYT and get a tumblr account.

A Response, From a young and unpaid critic (or theatre blogger – up to you)

Eve Allin, *Walking With Headphones*
16 December 2016
https://walkingwithheadphones.wordpress.com/2016/12/16/a-response-from-a-young-and-unpaid-critic-or-theatre-blogger-up-to-you/

Right. I'm writing a response. And maybe no one will read it but what the hell, I'm putting off my first summative 3,500 word uni essay and this seems like worthwhile procrastination.

For those who are unaware, Matt Trueman posted an article[4] in The Stage today about the decline of theatre blogging.

So I have a done a bit of blogging and bit of criticism here and there, some NSDF stuff, some unpaid online newspapers, some reviews on here that only my parents read … But I wouldn't say I am an established theatre blogger. I haven't been doing it for a long time but I have seen as many shows as I can and I have really really loved it.

---

[4] Eve links to: https://www.thestage.co.uk/opinion/2016/matt-trueman-why-im-worried-about-the-decline-of-theatre-blogs/.

Theatre Blogging

I'm not paid for this and I have personally always felt like I've never wanted to be paid for it. When I was 16 I knew that I could and wanted to write about theatre but I didn't want to be a "critic". Being a "critic" meant that you went to shows you weren't always passionate about, you had to meet gruelling deadlines, and you were surrounded by musty middle-aged men. In no world did that sound appealing. What I wanted (and I hope many other bloggers want) was to get really angry about theatre – so angry that all I could think about on the train home was how to form that first sentence about the mindnumbingly patriarchal binaries of that show which got press because it had a celebrity in it. Or get so inspired by a show that I write a blog about it, and then I write a play inspired by it, and then I see more shows like it and all I can think about is how theatre is this incredibly visceral art form that requires you to respond. I wanted to experience again and again how liveness of theatre makes it unavoidable to have some kind of response.

But often, that response is filtered, or edited, or set back in some way once the writer decides it needs to be put out into the world. There's a kind of struggle over whether your review will be ironic and funny, or heartfelt, or scathing, or profound – and where does it fit into the blogosphere? Has someone already said what you want to say, and have they said it better and have they been paid for it? Is your passionate outburst somehow less legitimate now? Is your review an artform in itself, and does it, therefore, have to be carefully constructed? Might you have the opportunity to work with these artists later on and therefore you can't say what you really think? I constantly rattle these questions around in my little echo chamber of a brain but come to no real conclusion. And then, because of that, the review sometimes doesn't get written. I don't think that's the problem for everyone and I don't think that's my only problem, but I think it is a contributing factor.

So, Matt, I think there is more to this than simply that the blogs are fading away. From my perspective anyway, there's kind of a 'standard' you have to be at to be considered a theatre blogger – maybe your review was retweeted by Andrew Haydon (nice, you're in), maybe you were followed by @TheStage (good one), or maybe you were mentioned in an article about the decline of theatre blogs . . . Anyway for young critics this can often seem intimidating and impenetrable. Also, Matt talked about how the conversation doesn't seem as fraught anymore, and everyone is stepping away from criticism to their real life jobs in theatre (?) but maybe they just got kind of, complacent? Because the lack of debate in the sphere has as much to do with the readers as it does with the critics. Maybe it's not about getting critics more passionate its about getting people to read and legitimise that passion.

Then, as also mentioned by Matt, there is the Bloggers vs Critics argument which has kind of died out as well. I disagree – I think that generally people think that if you're paid you're a critic, if you're not you're a blogger. I actually think that if you're unpaid you're more likely to be a critic – less constrained by press releases and the deadlines and the strict guidelines of what to say and what not to say. Again, why I always said I never wanted to become a 'Theatre Critic'.

Also – it feels kind of disheartening to see an article like the one in The Stage today. I kind of am constantly feeling like I just missed the bandwagon – the amazing companies that came out of my university are just a little old for me to know and be involved with. And now I've missed the criticism bandwagon too? I'm not so sure. I think there's still time for the game to be changed. Maybe there is some truth in the article – there most likely is a lot of truth in it. But I hope this new, snapchatting generation of kids can fight back. And who knows, maybe this will get retweeted by someone important and then what, I'll become someone worth listening to? Or just someone who now happens to be on your radar, and is therefore worth reading?

Thoughts on The Writer and this DANG INDUSTRY

Ava Wong-Davies, *Ava Talks About Theatre*
25 April 2018
https://avawongdavies.wordpress.com/2018/04/25/thoughts-on-the-writer-and-this-dang-industry/

All-round Good and Smart Boi James Varney tweeted something earlier.

"it's things like this that make me think theatre is broken and serving the wrong people

tied closely to thoughts that "theatre" and "art" aren't actually useful/can't do the work that i expect from them and maybe i should care less about them"

(This was in reference to his earlier tweet re the London theatre scene and its inherent exclusivity.[5] That's a Whole Other Post)

I RTed it to indicate my enormous social awareness, obv.

We then had a fruitful (but also probably ultimately fruitless) DM convo about how the industry is fundamentally flawed. (Was it even helpful? Was it just us airing our grievances and bitching? Because that's fine too but we need to do more than that) Eventually, The Writer came up. It's odd, seeing that tweet from James and seeing all this gushing, excitable chat about what sounded like a properly radical, properly Dangerous show, all in the space of about an hour.

What is a dangerous piece of theatre? What does that actually fucking mean? Seriously?

I'll get to that.

There are times when theatre twitter gets wrapped up in all this really detailed and esoteric chat about How To Make This Industry Better and part of me relishes it because it feels great and encouraging cos I can see that like there are people Like Me! who actually want to make theatre/art/whatever that is accessible and diverse etc etc. But then at the same time there's this voice in my head which goes

what good is this actually doing?
I mean maybe
Maybe we shud just burn it all down

---

[5] Ava links to: https://twitter.com/mrjvarney/status/989078076716978177.

Theatre Blogging

why r we focusing so much on this bullshit?
Why don't we just destroy this whole thing?
Like seriously i dunno if we should even rebuild it after we destroy it
Let's just raze it dance in the ashes redistribute all the money that gets poured into subsidising the NT in Actual Practical Ways instead of us fannying around pretending to be other ppl honestly

I should probably not be this cynical at 22. But I don't think I'm Being cynical, honestly, I think I'm just Being a product of this trash society that has truly fucked my generation etc etc. So hear me out for a sec.

I want a much broader demographic of people to start going to the theatre than are going now. People of colour, the queer community, working class people, disabled people – I want them all to go to the theatre and sit there and feel comfortable and like they belong in that space and I would like them to feel Seen.

But when we talk about accessibility schemes – when we talk about creating a scheme of £5 tickets for first time theatre goers – yeah that's ace, that will get Some new people in but ultimately, when we think about it, what is the aim? Because surely what you're going for there is an introductory type of thing that will entice first time audience members in the hopes of making them regular audience members who will eventually start paying full prices at a semi-regular rate to watch people walk around onstage and pretend to be things that they're not. That's not accessibility, surely!! Accessibility would be having £5 tickets for fucking EV ER Y ONE. At risk of sounding like a mad bitch WE'RE ALL PART OF THIS FUCKING SYSTEM THAT IS GOING TO EAT US ALL ALIVE.

Audiences are fundamentally customers. That's fine. (Like it's not. But it is. Ya get me) So that means that attempts at diversity and accessibility end up feeling like they're playing into this big system that just wants more bums on seats, more tickets sold, more money made. This industry is part of the free market (I guess?? I am Not Sure eek) and maybe I don't want the stuff I make to be part of That Market. (Sorry James I took that from u)

I dunno what to do because it almost feels like everything is playing into this big upper hand (we're getting controlled by The Man, don't u know). I've been making arguments for better PoC representation onstage and heard myself saying things like "but don't you want bigger audiences??? You'd make so much more money!!". I co-organised a BME festival at UCL last term and it was the fastest selling drama society show of the year. That's fucking amazing. I'm so proud and also so Not Surprised At All. Of course it sold out within a day. Of course your dry-ass Ibsen revival didn't. But that's how I justify bringing that festival back next year – by saying "well you know it sold incredibly well!!". Why is that the arbiter???
It's depressing af.

This leads me onto The Writer.
(that was all just massive preamble, don't u know)

I think I thought it was great but I also think I thought it was bad and flawed. And that's fine, it can be all those things. Before I went in I was standing across the street looking at the white stone of the theatre and watching people filter in holding glasses of white wine in the evening sunshine and I thought to myself – I think the Almeida has my least favourite audience in London.

There's something about watching a play about sexism and feminism (ooh that word, that word feels too small and so stupid nowadays) and the Almeida audience chuckling knowingly and yet oh-so-shallowly at jokes about the patriarchy and capitalism and Waitrose. Jokes which are pointed at them. Hickson wrote for this space, didn't she? She knew which audience she was writing for. It's pointed at them and it's slipping off their backs like water on duck feathers. It's not fucking hard enough on them. You're not necessarily a progressive bunch of people just because Corbyn is your MP, I want to screech.

I've thought for a while now that I dislike and distrust audiences and now I realise that it's not audiences in general, it's audiences at the National and the Almeida that I don't trust – these people who pride themselves on their progressiveness, their open mindedness but betray themselves through their laughter. Why are we still writing for these people?

Enough about the audience.

(On another note – there's something about a show which acknowledges its poshness and its whiteness but then doesn't actually do much about it that does irritate me. I don't think that's totally fair though. Hickson wanted to write this specific story and she did and she acknowledges her limitations and that's Fine but I just don't know on a gut level if that actually is Fine. Ack)

There's this fundamental disconnect between the play and the world outside it, I think, which is strange considering how influenced it is by the mundanity of everyday sexism. The Writer is unique, I think, because it talks about feminism (god there's got to be a better word, everytime I say feminism nowadays i just see taylor swift and those notebooks with the word FEMINIST embossed in rose gold) and the way it, or rather patriarchy, intersects with capitalism. The beginning of the play has a young woman essentially saying that she wants to dismantle the patriarchy and bring down capitalism. She says it in the same breath because you can't separate the two. Gosh that got a big laugh. And it is funny because the scale of it is ridiculous and incomprehensible but it's also funny because she's just a 24 year old girl, how adorably naive of her.

I take this play and its message seriously and I appreciate the seriousness with which it approaches the systems that it critiques. But what does that mean when I'm sitting in a theatre where ticket prices can go up to £50? What the fuck does that mean? How can this be a radical, dangerous thing to say when you are speaking from this seat of wealth and power? That laugh was indicative of so much. At the end of the play, these two old white ladies got up in front of me and said "God that was terrible". Is something radical, did something succeed because it made two Islingtonites a little bit uncomfortable and annoyed?

What is the point of making something this intelligent, of pouring your energy into making something this detailed and nuanced and beautiful and putting it onstage for people to say in front of a backdrop, only for the audience to laugh and smile and then leave, clutching their wine glasses and swaying gently on their way back to the station? Surely there is something more practical we could be doing with our time?

Theatre Blogging

What do I want, fundamentally? I want a fairer, more equal, more generous society. How do we get that? Really simply, I guess, through a redistribution of wealth from the top down. So why aren't we doing that instead of theatre? Why am I even writing this instead of actually Doing something productive and helpful with my time? What is the fucking point of all this metatheatre and intertextuality and navel gazing if the fact of the matter is that the theatre cannot Really change anything?

I got cynical and I apologise. Maybe it's exam season. But seeing work as angry and vibrant and desperate as The Writer sometimes, weirdly, makes me feel more hopeless than anything else.

CHAPTER 8
REVIEWS AND REVIEWING

Forumitis
Alison Croggon, *Theatre Notes*
2 October 2005
http://theatrenotes.blogspot.co.uk/2005/10/forumitis.html

On the train home from today's forum[1], I opened Giorgio Agamben's book of essays, *Means Without End: Notes on Politics*, to this serendipitous passage:

'Primo Levi has shown . . . that there is today a "shame of being human", a shame that in some way or another has tainted every human being. This was – and still is – the shame of the camps, the shame of the fact that what should not have happened did happen. And it is shame of this type, as has been rightly pointed out, that we feel today when faced with too great a vulgarity of thought, when watching certain tv shows, when confronted with the faces of their hosts and with the self-assured smiles of those "experts" who jovially lend their qualifications to the political game of the media. Those who have felt this silent shame of being human have also severed within themselves any link with the political power in which they live. Such a shame feeds their thoughts and constitutes the beginning of a revolution and of an exodus of which it is barely possible to see the end.'

It was almost startling, since it articulated something of the complexity of what I was feeling at the time. There I was, being an "expert", in a context in which my position behind the microphone and the attendance of an audience made a constituency of authority. And within that constituency, with the authority, however spurious or legitimate, conferred on us as panellists, we spoke about the act of theatre criticism.

I have no wish to impugn my fellow panellists, who are neither dishonest nor unintelligent, however I might disagree with them on occasion. Nor do I wish to exculpate myself. My sense of disturbance was much more subtle than any easy *j'accuse*, and difficult to track because it was also familiar, like one's own body odour. For whatever reason, a miasma of depression rose gradually inside me as the discussion progressed. There was nothing overtly wrong with the talk; it was unexceptionable, at worst boring. It was well-intended. It was agreeable; at times even jovial. I am not sure what the eighty or so good people who attended might have learned: that theatre critics like going to the theatre, that they have varying opinions on the point and value of what they are doing, that they have varying relationships to those they criticise and their employers, that they consider themselves informed commentators.

---

[1] Alison links to: http://theatrenotes.blogspot.com/2005/09/empanelled.html.

So what was this inarticulate scream, this "silent shame", which gradually oppressed me? For there was nothing to put my finger on, nothing overtly objectionable: nothing, you might think, to remind me of anything so extreme as a concentration camp. The connection, I suppose, is in the expression "the vulgarity of thought". The vulgarity does not lie necessarily with the individual critics speaking, but in the tacit contexts which constrain discussion, so that it may never reach any pitch of disturbance. The vulgarity twists around, I suspect, the very DNA of our culture. Is it partly that very Australian fear of intellectual seriousness, which makes its very expression a matter of defensive anxiety, as if to be too serious were a breach of propriety? Is it that our very passions are muted, as if they were swaddled in cotton wool? Or is it that any designation as "expert", as part of a group of "experts", taints one inevitably with complacency?

I am not quite sure what I am attempting to say. All I know is that if I am honest with myself, I felt a kind of shame, sitting there behind the microphone. I have sat on more than a few panels in my time, and it is always an experience fraught with dubiety; but the panels on theatre criticism have always had this particular flavour, which today I was able to identify. It seemed to me that, for all its display of culture, what we did today had nothing to do with art. It is perhaps not going too far to say that I felt, in some way that is not, in fact, easily identifiable, that it seemed to negate the very possibility of art itself.

This begs the question of what I think art might be. I can't answer that question; I can think of no general definition which is remotely adequate. It is not enough to deny that art is a commodity; of course it is a commodity. To claim that art is a created thing with a quality of excess that escapes commodification feels closer to what I mean. And yet we seem incapable of speaking of art except in terms of its value as a commodity – as a consumable item which may be "rated" (three stars or five?), in all its forms from a basic "entertainment" to the kind of product which confers less tangible benefits, such as social or intellectual status. Not only does this seem to miss the point; it obscures it almost beyond rescue. For there is a point, ungraspable as it may seem, which may hold value in its very ungraspability.

I realise I am very close to saying that art is the same as the sublime. Given I can't abstract art from its material nature – theatre simply wouldn't exist without the sweaty temporality of the human bodies which enact it – I clearly can't quite mean that. This materiality seems to me in fact art's redemptive vulgarity, a certain crudity which is very different from that vulgarity of thought Agamben refers to. Perhaps, within this sublime vulgarity, I find a kind of hope. The problem is that it's not hope for anything: just hope itself, ridiculous and naked. And it is, like all ridiculous and naked things, an embarrassment, a fracture of ease, which may admit then another possibility – joy? grief? play? life? Maybe it was the lack of this very fracture which made me feel so infinitely and yet so indefinitely hopeless. For lack of unease, I was ashamed; I felt I had participated in the imprisoning of something I think of, not as an *expression* of freedom, but as freedom itself.

I certainly couldn't have said anything like this at the event today. I could not have even thought it, and nor would it have been "appropriate". After all, we were only talking about theatre reviewing.

Attempts on Her Life at the National

Andy Field, *The Arcades Project*
12 March 2007
http://thearcadesproject.blogspot.co.uk/2007/03/attempts-on-her-life-at-national.html

With the body of Jean Baudrillard still relatively warm, it is fitting that Katie Mitchell has managed, to such a large extent, to craft her stupendously, courageously ambitious version of Martin Crimp's Attempts on Her Life in the great man's image.

And image is the important word. From the moment that the safety curtain crunches open to reveal a set-less Lyttleton stage littered with recording equipment it is clear that the production will rely heavily on the moving image, a feeling that is confirmed by the dauntingly huge screen that drops into place after the first scene; what is not immediately apparent however, is quite what a fascinating deconstruction of the medium the show will become.

With staggering precision Mitchell presents Crimps disjointed scenes and their ambiguous heroine using cinematic jump cuts, 360 pans, cross fades and split screens, documentary interviews, live press conferences, dubbed foreign language advertisements, television panel shows and rock and pop music videos – all of which are realised beautifully *live* on stage and then projected onto the giant screen above the seamless ensemble who scuttle across the cluttered stage, hauling lights, cameras and instruments with a grace and naturalness that is breathtaking.

On an aesthetic level what they create is wonderful. The images that rear up on the screen are almost universally breathtaking. Delicate compositions, perfect digital altering and editing and some simply superb acting that manages to be at once theatrical and cinematic and never less than utterly convincing.

And yet without intelligence and intent all this magnicent(ly complicated) visual experimentation would be showy but meaningless. What Mitchell's dense storm of genres and mediums lay bare is the artificial, superficial and essentially constructed nature of the film and television as a means of representation. Crimp's elusive narratives allow Mitchell to deconstruct the apparatus through which truths are told to us.

Baudrillard is most remembered (in the US at least) for once bodly asserting that the Gulf War did not take place, in part because it consisted almost entirely of images that stand in for (and hence, necessarily replace) reality. He described the war as:

a masquerade of information: branded faces delivered over to the prostitution of the image, the image of an unintelligible distress.

Such a description is a fitting summation of the production and it could be similarly argued that in Mitchell's hands Crimp's play does not take place. It is always displaced, dislocated and rendered entirely artificial. And yet such a treatment feels entirely appropriate to Crimp's haunting, ambiguous text. For what is at the heart of Crimp's play – underneath all the representations and simulations? Precisely nothing. A woman who is 'an absence' and a large red bag that is only full of stones. Crimp, like Baudrillard, believes only in the surface, the object.

Theatre Blogging

Mitchell seems to grasp that Crimp's text is so seductive precisely because it is constantly evading meaning, reason and depth. The protagonist is an empty red dress that drops into view as if from the gallows. Occasionally it is worn by one of the ensemble but it is always apparent that it is the hollow dress that is the character with actor inside it. In one magnificent scene Mitchell harnesses Crimps voices into a televised *Newsnight Review* style panel (replete with stand-in Tom Paulins and Germaine Greers who bought guffaws of laughter from certain sections of the audience) who critique scenes from an experimental film that are created on the other side of the stage without pastiche or parody. Both the panel and the film are projected onto the giant screen without bias. The piece becomes at once the film and its opposite, the criticism of the film, and both are demonstrated to be equally constructed. In another scene of similar evasive beauty, what begins as an English press conference with a Spanish translation is slowly transformed to the point where the English press conference is a translation of the Spanish. Opposites colide and are demonstrated to be the same.

It all only *feels* real.

The play and the ensemble become trapped in this procession of images, in this apparatus of representation. They are at once the apparatus and the subject. Indeed it is significant that all the actors are recognizable from film and television; from the start their faces already feel incorporated into the all-consuming multi-media simulacrum that we are fed every day as news, documentary, information and entertainment. By the end their language (and the viewer) is so exhausted that we have ceased to imagine there is meaning in their superficial play; and as they sink into the stage still talking it is quite conceievable that they could continue to do so indefinitely.

As has already most likely become apparent, for those (and there are many) who find Baudrillard unbearable, this piece will likely be equally so, for all the same reasons. It is ironic, evasive, glib and contradictory, and it doesn't have an interval. People continued to walk out throughout the two hours it ran for and the old man sitting beside us tutted and wrung his hands until I thought he might chew one off and throw it at the actors.

I however loved almost every moment. It was a wonderful, challenging and effortlessly entertaining exploration of the loss of self in an era that is ever more dominated by the moving image. It is also the kind of bold, theatrical experiment that, technically and financially, could only happen at the National, so hats off to Mitchell and Hytner for putting together such a memorable show. With this and Faust Hytner's serious faith in some wonderful young artists has resulted in undoubtedly my two favourite shows of the last twelve months. Go see it. Now.

A major event in our theatre

David Eldridge, *One Writer and His Dog*
15 March 2007
No longer online

An edit has been made to this post at the request of the publisher.

Reviews and Reviewing

At times sitting in the Lyttleton Theatre at the NT last night for the opening night of the revival of Martin Crimp's 'Attempts on her Life' I had to pinch my self. Once again at the NT with Nick Hytner at the helm a glorious night at the theatre was further dazzlingly amplified by the sensation that never in my dreams did I think I would ever see a piece of theatre this modern on the National's stages.

I had such a good time. At times I felt like leaping out of my seat or starting *a Mexican Wave*. At one point I was on the verge of tears of both *delirious delight* (sorry Richard Bean) and again *pride that I was finally in and part of a National Theatre that I wanted to be in and part of.*

The play/show directed by Katie Mitchell and the company felt even better than it did when saw it at the Royal Court in 1997. As Paul Taylor wisely reflected elsewhere *in watching (and indeed in making) a piece of theatre, context is everything*. At the Court in 1997 the formal experiment seemed much less exciting than in the Lyttleton. But that is small beer compared to the resonance of the text which a decade later feels visionary and written for now. Post 9/11 terror and in a truly post-Soviet age of rampant consumerism, eastern European sex trafficking and of 'Big Brother' and Blair this play has found it's place in our culture.

It's a determinedly post-modern evening so don't expect even a narrative as such let alone a plot or a play or characters or scenes in any conventional sense at all. As Lance Woodman noted it took me too a few minutes to tune into the thrillingly disorientating and witty front line dispatches for our time. I won't elaborate further on it than to guide you towards Andrew Field's quite brilliant blog on this brilliant show here.[2]

And for all the Baudrillardian play with questions of reality the evening for me became finally a moving argument for society amongst humans and the theatre's place in that. We end where we began – without images projected on to screens – and return to the scale of the human form communicating with it's Lyttleton audience. The play is too full of the joie de vivre to be ground down by the existential crises of modernist expressionism. In a show full of technology it is finally the actor who is celebrated.

As Field implies in his blog and as cries emanate from the same old reactionaries on the theatre discussion boards – *they hate this show*. The sounds coming from the early reviews aren't great either this morning. Michael Billington as usual wants more politics. Paul Taylor's stand in at 'The Independent' sounds too scared to have an opinion in case she stands out from the crowd and once again Quentin Letts disgraces himself in 'The Daily Mail' calling it *two hours of debasing trash*.

I mean you wouldn't ask a navvy to perform root canal treatment on you would you? Perhaps theatres should just ban Letts from coming as Dominic Dromgoole once blocked Nicholas de Jongh from The Bush …

Actually I am interested to see what de Jongh makes of it as he sometimes really gets behind the shock of the new (*pace* Caryl Churchill and Debbie Tucker Green recently) but so far it is

---

[2] David links to: http://thearcadesproject.blogspot.co.uk/2007/03/attempts-on-her-life-at-national.html (the previous post).

Theatre Blogging

only Michael Coveney that has really grappled with and rightly cheered what the evening in the theatre has to offer.

The conservatives will mewl and puke as they once did at 'Waiting for Godot' and turn away from the NT in droves. But their places in £10 seats will be filled a hundred times over by the young professionals that laugh at the inanities of modern TV advertising, that fly to the cities of Eastern Europe for stag and hen weekends and pay to fire Ak-47's on former Warsaw Pact army bases, nodding to MP3 players to the strains of Franz Ferdinand's 'The Dark of the Matinee' on budget airlines as they pass the time with 'Hello' and 'GQ' and the rest.

And this generation will *revel* as their decadence is both celebrated and skewered in equal measure. They will *marvel* as they spill out on to the South Bank that they've seen at last a piece of theatre that neither *lectures nor patronises* but simply has the measure of them and is able to treat them with both *the wit* and *contempt they know they deserve*.

The word is out. This production of 'Attempts on her Life' is a major event in our theatre.

Review – Love Never Dies, Adelphi Theatre

Andrew and Phil, *West End Whingers*
2 March 2010
https://westendwhingers.wordpress.com/2010/03/02/review-love-never-dies-adelphi-theatre/

The Whingers could think of many reasons not to see *Love Never Dies*, the long-awaited (although by whom is unclear) sequel to *The Phantom of the Opera*.

Phil was impressed with the spectacle of the original when he saw its first preview a zillion years ago but when he then revisited it with Phantom virgin* Andrew years later he was shocked by how, well, tedious it actually is.

On the plus side if you really must do a follow-up then a storyline set in Coney Island sounds just up the Whingers' alleys. Just think of the visual possibilities! The Whingers' inner juries were definitely going to examine all the evidence before deciding whether or not another crime against musical theatre had been committed. Phil even admitted to being quite excited about going.

But word-of-mouth from die-hard Phantom fans wasn't encouraging: there are 53 pages (and still counting) of largely negative comment on the WhatsOnStage forum, largely from *Phantom* fans. If *they* didn't like it what chance would the Whingers have?

Still, there obviously IS a demand from the press at least because the nice people at Peter Thompson Associates who are handling PR for the show wrote a very nice email back to the Whingers to say that "due to the extremely high demand and a strictly limited ticket allocation we will not be able to provide you with press tickets for this show".

How cruelly dashed on the rocks of pecking orders were our dreams of endless first nights, unlimited free drink and casual hob-nobbing with celebrities at after-show parties. Bet Biggins got an invite.

So anyway, it was down to the Whingers to fork out their own money like the ordinary theatre-goers they once were, and are apparently again, for £37.50 EACH in the UPPER (oh, the shame of it) Circle of the Adelphi.

So let us examine the case for and against Lord Andrew Lloyd Webber's latest opus.

For: The title. Hacking the Bond movie producers off, one imagines, ALW has come up with a title that gets both love and death into it. We can just see Ms Broccoli taking a thick marker pen and crossing it off her list of potential titles, wishing she'd got in there first. On the other hand, what does it mean? Nothing. Of course love dies. Of course it does. What bollocks. But no, this is a "For". Good title. Good title.

Against: Merchadising. Andrew's first words on entering the Adelphi Theatre were "Let's go and look at the merchandising". The Whingers love having a look at a show's merchandise. Where was it? Nowhere. Not a mug nor a pinny in sight! We don't buy it ourselves of course, but it's comforting to know that it's there if we ever change our minds. Very disappointing.

For: The Prologue. Those very words bring back happy memories of Frankie Howerd squeezing them through pursed lips in *Up Pompeii*! Sadly there is no Frankie here but the opening scene looked rather spookily lovely with some marvellous forced perspective, some clever use of old bedsheets and held no little promise.

Against: It was a bit gloomy. So was the next scene and the one after that. In fact the whole thing was gloomy. Andrew's advice to people with contact lenses: take eye-drops and a high beam torch.

For: *Forbidden Broadway* summed it up brilliantly with their song about projected scenery. You don't really feel as though you're seeing your money up on stage, which here frequently looks a bit empty. No *Phantom of the Opera* here. But both Whingers confessed to finding the projections dynamic, depth-filled, impressive and indeed just about the best thing in an otherwise disappointing (and gloomy) design.

Against: The book. OK, Coney Island a great idea, but it took **four** people – Lord ALW, Glen Slater, Frederick Forsyth, and Ben Elton (who apparently "unlocked the story") to come up with it. That makes a contribution of one plot point each by our reckoning. Sometimes it didn't really make sense, or was that because we couldn't hear a lot of the lyrics? If Raoul is a drunken gambler doesn't that rather pull the rug out from under those who loved the original and went away thinking it had a happy ending? Ben Elton should have thrown away his key.

For: The scene in the Phantom's Aerie at the top of what looks like Blackpool Tower and which is dressed with freakish oddities such as a Medusa like singing chandelier and a half woman-half skeleton walking a hostess trolley (the Whingers *really* liked that), all played out to an appalling rock-ish music score. It's the most fabulous overwrought mess currently on view on the West End stage and *Wicked* is still running apparently! The Aerie's design over-wrings the worst excesses of Art Nouveau to produce the bastard child of sexual congress between a peacock and an owl in a Notting Hill antiques shop.

Against: The Phantoms's sidekicks, Fleck, Squelch and Gangle (or is it Guangle? – the programme** can't really decide) weren't established as characters at all. Fleck looked like she'd stumbled in from a ritzy production of *The Rocky Horror Show*. If only she'd done the time-warp again. With Biggins. We may be wrong but we imagined that they were supposed to be freaks. There was a lot of talk of Coney Island freaks but not one bearded lady, not one midget, not two Siamese twins. What kind of Freak Show was this? The Whingers would have been demanding their money back.

For: Raoul's line to Christine (Sierra Boggess) as she bangs out a few bars of the dreadful title song, "Must you make that racket?". At last, Lord Webber *has* got a sense of humour. But why were the Whingers the only ones who laughed?

Against: The Phantom's lyric "Time keeps moving on" had Phil looking at his watch. Was the Phantom sure? Surely it had stopped.

For: Poor Ramin Karimloo (as the Phantom) has a terrific set of lungs. Very impressive singing. Even if when he whips off his mask Phil was reminded of *Frasier*'s Niles Crane.

For: Poor Liz Robertson as Madame Giry, channelling Mrs Danvers.

Against: The climax to the end of act one involves Madame Giry throwing a jacket down a stair well. As climaxes go, it's not really up there with the bit in the film of *Chitty Chitty Bang Bang* when the car goes off the cliff before anyone knows it can fly. If it hadn't been such an eagerly anticipated event the Whingers would have thrown their towels in the stairwell after the jacket and departed to the nearest pub.

For: The bar scene at the beginning of Act 2. The combination of projection and scenery actually looks quite good and Raoul's drunken scene with the Phantom actually had bit of the tension which was sadly lacking elsewhere. But then lines like "one more drink sir" and "another drink" were playing to the Whingers in their Aerie seats.

Against: The big moments. The first appearance of the Phantom, his first meeting with Christine, the Phantom's unmasking. All thrown away. Christine's surprise suggested that the Phantom had bought a new pair of trousers since she last saw him rather than the fact that a disfigured kidnapper she thought was dead was in her bedroom.

For: Phil had another laugh at the interminably drawn out finale where little Gustave slips his fingers in the Phantom's disfigurement. Phil made a mental note that it's a while since he's handled a bowling ball and must book a ten-pin bowling lane soon.

Against: What a shameful waste of talent. Director Jack O'Brien did such a brilliant job on *Hairspray*, choreographer Jerry Mitchell similarly on the same show and with his direction and choreography of *Legally Blonde*. There's hardly any choreography in *LND*, but you can't blame them for accepting an offer to leap aboard an ALW cash cow, even if the udders appear to be somewhat dried up and the milk very much on the turn.

For: The very helpful expositionary snippets of dialogue – "I say that not just as your mother but as your producer" and "They say she's still pitch-perfect but it's like the flame went out or something". And the monologue – "That boy! His music! He plays like me!". We would have been lost without them.

Against: Sung-through shows in general and this one in particular. The Whingers want fun and *LND* is sooo po-faced. The Whingers only laughed at things which weren't meant to be funny. Note to selves: best stick to shows like *Legally Blonde*.

For: The bit where Christine performs her big number (can't remember what it was called or how it went) while the Phantom and Raoul watch from either Wing and the whole thing revolved. Andrew knew it reminded him of something but couldn't quite put his finger on it…

[Embedded video of a Shirley Bassey performance from 1971][3]

Against: The music. Obviously one doesn't go to an ALW in search of tunes but this one is particularly devoid of anything that might become hummable after repeated viewing. Even the heavy-handed repetitious leitmotif from *Phantom* began to seem desirable to the Whingers after half an hour. Andrew did enjoy one moment when he recognised the first four notes of the the very beginning of the *Star Trek* theme but by this time his mind – desperate for melody – may simply have been playing tricks on him.

For: Poor Joseph Millson (as Raoul) for mustering all his dignity and gamely going on and not pulling a sickie every night. We would have.

Against: Did we mention the po-facedness of it all? Just wait until you see the attempts at the "lighter" numbers involving squeaky chorines led by poor Summer Strallen. Shocking. There's an attempt to make life a bit interesting for the audience at one stage with a quick-change routine which hopefully will be competent by opening night. In the meantime, here's what a quick change routine looks like:

[Embedded video of an act from America's Got Talent][4]

Verdict: Dull. Like watching paint dry, and as we all know, paint never dries***.

Footnotes

* That's as in "new to Phantom" rather than "phantom virginity" a la "phantom pregnancy". Although actually …

** **Against:** The programme is a bit on the sloppy side. Gangle/Guangle isn't the only mistake: director Jack O'Brien's CV lists him as artistic director of the Old Globe Theatre in Sandiago

---
[3] See https://youtu.be/2Xvln035znM.
[4] See https://youtu.be/ p40L8amjjA.

rather than San Diego. You can get quite a lot of proof-reading done when you've nothing to distract you and Phil spotted oodles of mistakes during Love Never Dies.

*** Yes, alright paint DOES dry eventually but love does die too so we're quits with ALW.

Rating

2/5: slightly corked or vinegary

---

how you do this is up to you
Maddy Costa, *States of Deliquescence*
27 February 2012
http://statesofdeliquescence.blogspot.com/2012/02/how-you-do-this-is-up-to-you.html

---

[As you will probably work out when reading it, this post has taken me over a month to write. Add the fact that Open House – which was part of the first Transform season at the West Yorkshire Playhouse – happened in June 2011, and this is horrifyingly overdue. Apologies to Chris Goode: I really didn't expect it to take so long! And the deepest, truest thanks to Chris, Jonny, Theron, Emma and James for the welcome, the acceptance, the trust.]

Open House happened so many months ago that part of me questions the value in writing about it now, especially as Chris Goode did so, more eloquently and insightfully than I can, both in anticipation and retrospectively, over on Thompson's. But I've come to accept that it's a characteristic of this blog to be straggling along behind everybody else, even to enjoy the freedom I feel from the inexorable propulsion of theatre criticism, where the expectation is that you'll react to a show immediately then speed on to the next. My thoughts as I move from show to show are meandering and receptive to diversion, as themes and arguments are shared between them, or reflected in the films I'm watching or the books I'm reading or the art I'm seeing. It makes thinking about theatre a much less stuttery experience than it was when I was reviewing regularly. In any case, the second round of adventures with Chris Goode and Co is starting soon, and I wouldn't feel right embarking on that if I hadn't fully processed everything from round one.

So: my first impressions of arriving at Open House, West Yorkshire Playhouse, on Wednesday June 15, 2011, as I remember them in the cold glare of February, 2012. A weave of stairs and corridors to get to the rehearsal room. The resistant bulk of the door. Inside, a surprising brightness: the weather was stormy, the sky outside a burdensome grey, yet the rehearsal room felt spacious and light. Sheets of paper tacked haphazardly to the walls. Some quiet, absorbed activity close to a microphone: I can't remember how big the group was, but I think it was gathered around James Lewis, who was demonstrating how to fold, tuck, fold, turn, fold, open out, origami houses. Chairs, several. Small heaps of unmemorable clutter. Across the room, a low tent constructed from big sheets of white paper, two feet protruding from one side. (I later discovered they belonged to Theron Schmidt.) The tantalising sensation that the room, and everyone and everything in it, was waiting, for the minutes to tick, tick past, for a call to action. And, coursing through my veins, the excited but faintly neurotic feeling I've had when house-hunting, when you walk across a stranger's threshold and look at the rooms and the windows and the books on the walls and ask yourself: could I live here? Where might my stuff go? What do I need to do to insinuate myself into these rooms? Do I fit in?

I arrived at about 6pm, shortly before the first public showing of the company's work so far. The core team – Chris, Theron, James, Jonny Liron and Emma Frankland – had been there since Monday; the doors had been open to all throughout that time, but this was their first attempt at, not staging exactly, but re-creating something of their activity for seated spectators. Already the team had expanded to absorb visitor-performers; intriguingly, all of them were women. To my mild amusement, if no one else's, the core players appeared entirely wrong-footed by the audience beginning to pour into the room unannounced on the dot of 6.57pm, so they could be seated in time for a 7pm start. Such is the stuff of conventional theatre, concerned with rules and customs and established patterns of behaviour for performers and audiences: stuff that wasn't quite appropriate here.

I found the showing a little befuddling at first: enjoyable, but enigmatic. So much seemed to be happening with so few signposts. Possibly that says more about my residual love of narrative than it does about the showing itself, which was – and I'm not sure to what degree I appreciated this on the day, and to what degree I understand this in retrospect – clearly organised, neatly patterned with visibly demarcated threads of activity or thought. Storytelling coloured one set of threads: in particular, some of the joiners-in were given space to recount their impressions of the room. Theresa, who has been coming to see shows at WYP for years, is retired, and will take any excuse to get out of the house, said she felt out of her depth on arriving on Monday, and a bit scared to come back. But she had come back, promptly, every day since. She was critical, a little acerbic, but also admiring; I loved the way she said, faintly combatively: "I've come for the ideas." All I remember about Kylie is that she was younger; from her speech I scribbled down these notes: "when walked into room shocked by how silent it was / intimidated – but friendly – can come in, join in with own stuff".

More stories in the Blue Peter Badge strand: someone – James, or perhaps Emma – had genuinely earned a Blue Peter badge in their youth, and so the company whipped up several copies and distributed them, whether to random audience members or people who had been in the rehearsal room, I forget. Intermittently through the show, people stepped up to tell us about the special skill or remarkable deed for which they had/would have been awarded their badge. "For waving not drowning", said one, delightfully.

Harder to grasp immediately was the poetry, partly because its delivery was less concerned with making the words audible and more with communicating sensation: confrontational, romantic, melancholy. For one piece, Chris invited us to listen while lying down; I lay on my stomach, so when – as prompted by the text – I should have been gazing up at imaginary stars, instead I was counting the dust motes on the floor, which, I fear, reveals more about me than I would care to admit.

For all that it perplexed me, I found the poetry very moving – and the final section of the showing even more so. It began with a song: the audience clustered together, peering over shoulders to see the lyrics, Chris apologising that he hadn't thought to write out more copies, because he hadn't anticipated a crowd. As instructed, we flexed our happy-face muscles and sang, an exuberant chorus. When it ended, we drifted back to our seats and, just briefly, felt a little lost, forlorn at our separation. But then Pauline, who had arrived in the rehearsal room that morning, started dancing: a simple, repetitive dance, a few steps, flittering fingers, a turn, no more. Members of the core group started dancing. Someone I didn't recognise started dancing. Theresa took a stranger's hand and beckoned him to join in. Theron stopped doing this dance and started doing other moves. Pauline and Jonny broke out, then slotted back in to the rhythm. I couldn't tell who had been in the rehearsal room earlier in the day or week and who had only just arrived to watch, who was audience and who was performer – because if such a division had even existed, it had just been eradicated.

The showing ended in a blur: Theron hurtling around the room, displacing people's bags and coats, before pushing the piano violently across the floor; Emma ripping posters from the wall and hurling them up elsewhere. A transformation was happening, but of/from what, to what? I didn't understand, didn't know how all the pieces fit together, what the connections were between the strands. But what I did understand, adore, was the generosity of the invitation to others, however long they had been in the room, to perform, with all the instilling of confidence and rejection of obstacles inherent in that invitation; the variety of voices – not just oral but physical – giving those performances; the electrifying sense that anything was possible and the tangible energy this generated. I felt part of a community, not of spectators watching makers, but a united group of theatre-lovers working together to make something happen, even if we didn't necessarily know what that something might be.

I spent a long time fretting that I had approached Open House back-to-front: I should have started with the rehearsal and ended with the showing. But again, that's custom, conditioning; the pervasive but spurious notion that it's a final product – let's call it the show unveiled on press night – that counts, not the journey to get there (let alone the journey a show might continue to take long after it's been reviewed). Halfway through the rehearsal on Thursday, I scribbled this in my notebook: "seeing retrospectively how the showing is a representation of what happened in the room – not so much a created thing as an agglomeration of movements and multiple creations". To think of the showing as a final product is to approach Open House in the wrong spirit entirely.

A more useful thought is this: Open House was designed to be alive to chance. We want theatre to be alive – but anything living is constantly changing, so how do you allow for that mutability on stage? As in, night after night, so that the show is never a fixed entity but changes in accordance with the weather and the news and the people who walk through the door? (Coincidentally, I write this having just seen Uninvited Guests' extraordinary Love Letters Straight From Your Heart, which asks similar questions and finds astoundingly effective routes to an answer.) And how do you rehearse that liveness, that receptivity to chance and change? What are you doing in the room?

In a sense, Thursday was the perfect day to be in the rehearsal room, because the Wednesday showing had surpassed Chris and co's expectations – and now they had to repeat it. Or not. There was a tension in the room all day, between, as Theron explained to Pauline, "starting from scratch and showing something completely different, or being lazy and showing the same thing". Much of that tension came from a place of tiredness, a muscle-ache of frustration with what Theron, again, described to Louisa, as they lay together on the floor, as "quite a demand – burden – in rehearsal to create SOMETHING". It was assuaged with a lot of quiet, recuperative mooching and mulling. For minutes on end, nothing happened. Time passed and passed and passed. And then someone would move, and that would inspire someone else to move, and suddenly, breathtakingly, everything would happen.

For me, this was the most palpable tension in the room: the spine-tingling awareness that, any minute, the merest wisp of a thought might trigger an explosion of activity. It made me (and, I'm sure, other visitors) reluctant to walk out, even for a few minutes, for fear of missing anything. In my memory, music inspired a lot of that activity, be it Emma strumming aimlessly on a guitar or Theron putting on Sigur Ros and proceeding to read-rap lines from that day's paper as an accompaniment. (And – for someone who also writes about pop music – there was something particularly engrossing about Chris's later attempts to find the right piece of music to communicate with and draw out each action, witnessing for myself the changes in mood he achieved, for instance with Pauline's dance, by shifting the soundtrack from a jaunty but level pop song by the Coral to a more pulsing, quivering, soaring track by Orbital. There was a cherishable moment when he told the assembled group that he thought the Wedding Present were exactly what was needed for a proposed sequence of hurling across the floor on kneepads, and I was the only person nodding frantically in agreement, because I too have an indie-schmindie past – who am I kidding when I say past? – and I knew instantly he was right.)

The most mesmerising, exhilarating sequence of the day began with Jonny dancing, a jittery, tempestuous dance, to Bowie's Modern Love played at heart-pounding volume. As the music faded, James quietly narrated one of the pieces of text pinned to the wall (I think the one titled The Lover and the Revolutionary), while Theron, who had earlier divested himself of his jeans, transformed his trousers into a sculpture on the floor, folding and arranging them as though this, too, were origami. And then Theron held Jonny. They wrapped their limbs around each other so tightly, it was difficult to tell where each tangled body ended and began. Emma read from Thornton Wilder's Our Town (it was one of the inspiration pieces for Open House), finishing with the words: "You need to pass this on." And then a word poem began, Jonny and Theron taking turns to contribute a single word: "blue-heart-like-blossom-in-spring-soft-as-a-fire-sky-like-grinning-heather". It was strange, jagged, nonsensical, absorbing, beautiful. Emma transcribed their words, folded the piece of paper into an origami house, and James read out from it, the word-poem reconfigured into a new, random order. And on, and on, until they ran out of ideas, or their energy fizzled out, as though someone had pulled a plug.

Watching all this, it struck me that the core team shared a mindset, a thought process, that was, not private exactly, but particular to them, from which visitors – no matter how welcomed, how empowered to contribute – remained excluded. But the team rarely gave this difference open expression, and if they did it was when alone, checking in with each other after the showing, or before visitors arrived for the day's rehearsal. The rough notes I have about this weren't written at the time of speaking but of sudden remembering several hours later: "participation – but on our terms // something Emma talked about – still difficult, getting people to come into their world". Their world was naked, mercurial, impetuous, rigorous, uninhibited, abandoned. Visitors were clearly comfortable creating their own work, trying out their own ideas; as the core team, one by one, left for lunch and returned, they marvelled at how the room seemed to have an energy of its own, such that they could walk away and things would still be created. Visitors had confidence, then, but only so much; by comparison with the core team they were diffident, cautious, contained. It's worth emphasising that this was simply something I noticed, and not something voiced in the room. What the core team did articulate, sweetly, with a perceptible note of awe, was admiration and supportive interest – particularly for Pauline's dance exercises, impulses and routines. And if that "participation – but on our terms" thought was spoken aloud in any way, it was probably like this: in another of my favourite sequences of the day, Theron buzzed hither and thither, impish and preoccupied, taping pieces of paper to the floor, to the wall, pushing the piano below the central beam so he could climb up to stick the last pieces there. Written on them was a message, communicated piecemeal, to be understood by anyone curious enough to follow their higgledy path: "How you do this is up to you."

That curiously mobile piano became emblematic for me of another key feature of Open House: the fluidity of the space. Posters went up, fell down, were moved around; chairs were pushed against the wall, then tugged into a circle in the middle of the room. By the time Chris returned from lunch, the room had been reconfigured, redecorated. Individual personalities betrayed themselves in their interactions with the space, whether it was Theresa's incessant tidying, taking lunch plates back to the cafe and, more finically, moving posters back to what she felt to be their original positions, or Jonny throwing off his underpants, neglecting to put them back on when getting dressed again, and forgetting to pick them up for several hours. All small things, but all subtly affecting the perception of the people who entered there. And how vital, how heartening, that such extremes of personal approach could be simultaneously accommodated, that there was space for conservatism, even if it was, arguably, antithetical to the spirit of the room.

And me, what difference did I make being there, curled up like a small animal or squashed beneath chairs, failing always to melt into invisibility? It was piercingly odd, being still and silent in that room: I felt inimical. Not to the people: such was the atmosphere of gentle inclusivity, it was perfectly fine for visitors to sit and watch and not participate at all. It was the energy of the room I was denying, the tendrils of change and effect with a force of their own, which kept reaching out to me to take part, and which I kept pushing away. It wasn't until the end of my day, shortly before I had to leave for the train back home, that I got up and joined in, with a run-through of the dance that had whisked so many people to their feet the night before. The sense of relief and release in doing so was immense. Apart from that, my sole contribution was when Emma unexpectedly asked me to give her three words, words that had previously been spoken aloud in the room. What came immediately to my head were: "blue" (colour or mood?), "project" (noun or verb?) and "mystify". As he skipped off to make something of them, I felt as though I had unconsciously exposed myself.

There was another time Emma came and sat with me, just for a chat, when she asked me what I was thinking. I told her the truth: I was wondering, for the umpteenth time that day, how someone would feel walking in for the first time. She asked what had prompted this thought: I suspected she assumed it was watching Jonny take off his clothes and stand naked, crushed, trembling, clutching his jeans to his face. But it wasn't that. That was action, demonstration, externalised thought. As Kylie had intimated the day before, it was the lengthy periods of quiet, of calm and self-absorption, when everyone in the room seemed to be reflecting, or recharging, or simply resting, that were really intimidating. This is how I'd written the thought in my notebook much earlier in the day:

how would someone feel walking in here for the first time?

Emma playing guitar

Theron quavery singing

Pauline making tape outlines on the floor

Jonny at the piano

baffling

strange

inconsequential

Theron locking Jonny into chairs

You couldn't slip into that scene without feeling like an intruder, feeling faintly voyeuristic. No, that's not it: you couldn't slip into that scene without having to encounter yourself. You could hear your heartbeat in that quiet, feel each thought shiver across your brain. With nothing to watch, no complicated action to absorb, you inevitably turn inwards. As mentioned in an earlier CG&C post[5], I thought a lot about courage while I was in Leeds: the courage it takes to let someone build a cage of chairs around you; to strip yourself of all the carapaces you grow to shield you from the world; to try out ideas knowing they might fail; to reveal yourself – I mean mentally, more than physically – in the company of strangers; to accept an invitation; to decide that something is not for you, however much you long for it to be. The periods of silence demanded more of that courage, because they gave you nowhere to hide.

Although the rehearsal felt largely chaotic, as with the showing, that chaos wasn't wholly unstructured (although Theron, I think, would have been happier if it the showing especially were more free-form – the phrase he used, delightfully, was along the lines of "in a constant state of jam"). Intermittently through the day, Chris held check-in sessions, to find out how everyone was feeling, what they wanted to explore or achieve. Each time there was an emphasis on liveness: a desire to create in the moment, so that what audiences saw could only have happened at that minute on that day in that room. There was conflict: over how to position the chairs, what risks were being taken by stepping in front of the audience, how noisy and obstreperous they should be and how much they should be holding the audience's hands. But it was the conflict of competing theatrical ideologies that I can't pretend to have comprehended sufficiently to represent here. In any case, what impressed itself upon me more wasn't disunity but the harmony made possible by the selflessness of all participants.

---

[5] Maddy links to: http://statesofdeliquescence.blogspot.com/2011/06/come-on-chemicals.html.

Strikingly, in the later check-in sessions, when the group discussed ideas and actions that had emerged in the past few hours, no one spoke of their own work but passionately of everybody else's: Emma described how Theron had done this, Jonny related how James had done that. In the simplest, directest way it underscored how nothing in this piece was individual, everything was collective. The final check-in was devoted to sorting out a kind of set-list for that evening's showing. I had to leave for London an hour before it started, so didn't get to see how it played out, but Chris assured me later it was absolutely terrible.

Each day ended with the core group alone, without any of the new participants, decompressing, checking out. I was at the Wednesday check-out, and what I talked to the group about then is what I keep coming back to here. That incredible sense of community. That idea that anyone, at any point, could join in, could break away, could participate, could observe, and that every one of those decisions could be made autonomously, but with the profound understanding that it would affect the atmosphere and affect the group. How rare this is in the theatre. And the more I dwell on it, the more rare it seems outside of it, too.

I mean something quite particular by that. The final line in the song Chris wrote for us to sing went like this: "We all live every day in an open house." I can't say the words made much of an impression at the time: they were cheerful but, you know, pretty anodyne. But the more I read through my notebook from those 24 hours, preparing to write this, the more those words reached out to me. To live in an open house. To reject competition, selfishness, secrecy, all the back-stabbing and hidden corruption of our world. To think more widely than the nuclear family, or indeed the extended family. To think about the implications of our actions within the home on the planet (my husband works in climate change, and has coherent and terrifying arguments for why behaviour within the home needs to change if human life is to be sustainable). To think about our responsibility for each other. Not occasionally, but every single day. The final moments of Open House made me cry, and it's taken a lot of digging to figure out what made them so emotional for me. It wasn't just the feeling of community, but the implication of what you can achieve with community. Change.

On my desk I have a (fake) Blue Peter badge. I got it for being part of Open House.

Embedded

Andrew Haydon, *Postcards From The Gods*
16 April 2012
http://postcardsgods.blogspot.co.uk/2012/04/embedded.html

Strangely, this is a piece I've been quite interested in writing for a while now, but my fortnight at Forest Fringe @ The Gate seems to have made it feel a bit more focussed than hitherto.

The idea of "embedded critics" seems to have gained something a momentum recently. Perhaps the most interesting session (to me) at this year's Devoted and Disgruntled was the one called by Maddy Costa and Jake Orr on this very subject. Their basic question was: "What new dialogue can we set up between people who write about theatre and people who make it?" with the sub-question "Do we want to maintain a distance between the people who write about theatre and the people who make it?" (full report here[6]).

Only a couple of days after D&D, I went to Kurdistan with ATC and their touring production of Roland Schimmelpfennig's *Golden Dragon* (my first report on this is published in the paper version of *The Stage* this week – doesn't seem to be online yet). Being in Iraq and a journalist, jokes about my being "embedded" abounded.

And it is an interesting position for "a critic" to find themselves in. Indeed, the question of "embeddedness" is one that goes to the very heart of what we think a critic is *for*. Or what a critic's job is/should be.

I've written before about the slightly funny, symbiotic relationship between critics and theatre. Obviously there is a school of thought which holds that the critic is essentially a parasite, feeding off a host body and is incapable of surviving without it.

As a basic model, I think I prefer those birds that apparently hop into the mouths of crocodiles and pick bits of food from between their teeth. On occasion it's probably quite annoying for the crocodile and they might think, "Look, for God's sake, you can't kill these things that you're eating, so why the hell should I let you pick at my leftovers". And probably those birds *could* go off and eat something else, but mostly the crocodile benefits from have the bits picked from between their teeth. It improves their mouth just as much as it apparently sustains the bird.

Is that too much metaphor? (I do hope I haven't misremembered those birds – I think learnt about them when I was three and haven't really thought about them since.)

Anyway, my point is, critics aren't a cancer on theatre. Our survival and reproduction does not entail the death of theatre. We essentially have a vested interest in theatre's survival.

Beyond which, as I also said before[7], I think I've pretty much given up being a "proper" critic. There are a bunch of reasons for this, which I might or might go into at some length at some point, either in the future or indeed in this essay, but, for the time being, let's just say that I'm more interested in experimenting with new models of how to write about theatre (/performance).

I'm not going to say that the "old model" is broken, nor am I going to claim that I'm trying to *fix* it. I think (star-ratings aside) *normal* criticism, or "the old model" has its uses. And I think some mainstream critics are very good at doing it. I have to admit that, actually, I think a lot of my reasons for trying to find a different way of *doing criticism* are as much down to the bad-fit that I am for proper criticism as anything deeper or more philosophical.

Anyway, I seem to have got off the point slightly.

So, "embeddedness". Is it desirable? What are the problems? What are the benefits?

---

[6] Andrew links to: https://www.devotedanddisgruntled.com/blog/what-new-dialogue-can-we-set-up-between-people-who-write-about-theatre-and-people-who-make-it.
[7] Andrew links to: http://postcardsgods.blogspot.co.uk/2011/03/political.html.

Theatre Blogging

Obviously, there's an initial massive, potential problem with the "embedded" critic. And that is the problem of readers' trust. At root, before knowing anything about theatre, before being able to write, before even having anything like "good taste", the one thing a critic needs is the trust of his or her readers. Mostly, I get the impression that our critics do ok on that score. We might think, in various cases, that their taste is lousy and their writing is abysmal, but I don't think I've ever heard anyone ever really question whether a critic was telling the truth. The only one I'd question is sometimes Quentin Letts, who, I'd say, sometimes looks like he's second-guessing or rehearsing a political position more than actually saying what he really thought. I mean, it's possible that he really does think like that, in which case, God help him. But I think it's far more likely that he knows what he's expected to say and says that.

If a critic is "embedded" then there's the possibility that that relationship of trust is shaken slightly. The reader might conclude, in the words of Mandy Rice-Davies: "Well, he would say that, wouldn't he?"

I want to have a bit of a look at this assumption. And also at what it means for criticism.

Because, I think on one level, there's something in it. I don't think that the reader would be right to *mistrust* the "embedded" critic, and I don't think that the "embedded" critic is any the less truthful. But on the other hand, the relationship between them and the artist is plainly going to be different.

At various papers, there's an informal policy that if one critic writes an interview or feature about a company/director/actor to preview their forthcoming production, then it should be the/an- other critic who reviews it.

This stems from the somewhat puritanical conviction that a) the work should speak for itself, and b) it contaminates the critic's, I dunno, purity of mind, if they've had the director explain to them what they're driving at already.

I can see two answers to this. On one hand, yes, if someone's told you what they're going to do before you see them do it, or try to do it, then, well, you'll know what they're trying to do as you watch it happen. This is a different experience to working it out yourself from seeing them do it. Lyn Gardner has gone further and written about how she doesn't even read programme notes before watching a show.

As I've written before, this is certainly one approach, and I can see its value.

On the other hand, firstly, it is very culturally specific. I've now gotten over my surprise that German critics read the texts of plays they're going to see, before they see the productions. Of course, that approach is partly informed by the way that German directors treat texts, but I think it also bespeaks a certain thoroughness and rigour that Germany's theatre has that we don't.

That said, the not-knowing-what's-coming approach *does* fit the way a lot of mainstream British theatre operates. And there is an advantage to being made to jump in your seat, laugh, and squirm in the same way as the rest of the audience is.

At the same time, other members of the audience might read the director's programme notes before the show starts – theoretically giving them potentially more insight into the show than the critic who has denied themselves that opportunity.

There's also Tassos Stevens's maxim that states: "The experience of an event begins for its audience when they first hear about it and only finishes when they stop thinking and talking about it" (he's written a fuller account of that idea here[8]).

In one way, that very maxim, and the thought process behind it, ensures that the critic's experience of a piece of theatre is always going to be different to that of a regular audience member. As *The Reduced Michael Billington* blog[9] brilliantly skewered it some years ago: "critics are uniquely equipped to see through all of the PR and marketing that surrounds plays. They do this by going to theatres on special nights set aside for them, where they are met by the play's publicist, handed a handy press pack put together by the marketing department and given free drinks at the interval which come from the play's marketing budget. How could an ordinary member of the public possibly see through the marketing, which, from the theatre's point of view, I am a part of?"

As such, one sort of 'embeddedness' could just be framed as an extreme version of reading the programme notes before watching the script.

Actually, it strikes me I haven't really discussed what I even mean by "embeddedness".

Maddy and Jake's original D&D discussion seemed to focus on being present in the rehearsal room, doubtless informed in part by Maddy's involvement in Chris Goode's *Open House* at the West Yorkshire Playhouse last year, and Jake's subsequent attendance of (and upon) various companies' rehearsals.

I haven't done, or been doing that exactly. Granted, I did sit in on one run-though of *The Golden Dragon* in Sulaymaniyah, but since all but one of that company had already spent at least a month touring India with the production, that was far more of a run-through of a play (which I'd already seen in Edinburgh last year anyway) for the benefit of the one actor who'd just joined. As such, there was very little of the actual creative process on display – not so much of the emotional nakedness that one imagines might go on at the very start of a rehearsal process.

What I did do in Iraq/Kurdistan was spend six or seven days travelling about with the company, eating with them, sitting in the mini-bus with them, and, hell, experiencing a totally new country with them. Which obviously changes my perspective on those actors, and that director, stage-manager and producer. Apart from anything else, it humanises them. It strikes me that in the usual run of things, theatre criticism sometimes kind of requires you to forget the humanity of those about whom you're writing.

Or at least, it's helpful if you don't think about it too much.

Because, after all, you're writing about the art. About the achievement, or otherwise, not actually about the *people* who have made it.

But of course, it was made by people.

---

[8] Andrew links to: http://allplayall.blogspot.com/2011/12/experience-of-event.html.
[9] *The Reduced Michael Billington* was a short-lived blog active from 2006–7, which would rewrite/translate Billington's reviews and articles in order to critique his arguments. See http://billingtonslightreturn.blogspot.com/.

Theatre Blogging

It's a bit obvious to suggest that if critics were to consider their subjects as *people*, then they might be a bit nicer. Or more polite. Or might put things differently. But I think that's simplistic. I like to think that I'd be able to say everything I've ever written to the face of the people about whom I'd written it. Even if a couple of times actually doing so might have earned me a slap.

I think there are about four reviews I've written where I've probably gone too far (for the record, they are: *Sex Idiot*, *Behud*, *Off The Endz* and *Berlin*). Interestingly, they're also among the reviews that people have told me they've enjoyed reading most often. Because people do love a good pasting at someone else's expense.

In my defence, I do still stand by those reviews and maintain that they are still accurate records of just how cross some pieces of theatre have made me in my time. Also, for the record, Bryony Kimmings and I are now friends on Facebook and hung out a whole bunch in Edinburgh last year. And she's a really nice person. And I still don't think I'm ever going to like *Sex Idiot* (although, I do partly blame the way that it was framed at the Pulse Festival for the extent of the violence of expression in that review. That and the fact I might have subconsciously been feeling more removed than usual from considering UK artists as people, since I wrote the review after I'd returned to Berlin). But, if I saw it now, I'd have a lot more information at my disposal, as well as having met her in real life. It kind of goes without saying that I'd write the review differently. I'd still write it honestly, but there are a lot of different ways of saying the same thing, aren't there?

So, does that mean I've been compromised?

I'd say not.

There is an interesting maxim in theatre criticism that your first duty is to your reader. Having had a bit of a think about this, I've concluded that I disagree. I reckon one's first duty is to one's own humanity (which, I agree, is a sickeningly pompous way to put it). But, I don't think it's healthy to lose sight of how cruel one could be being simply because a lot of people enjoy reading critics being cruel.

That said, there's every chance I'll forget these noble sentiments next time I see something that I *really* hate, and realise that some bastard has just stolen three hours of my life to bore me to tears with their crappily performed, sexist/racist/homophobic/solipsistic rubbish, but, in the main, I don't think it's unhealthy to sometimes be reminded that you're writing about people. And people who are mostly acting out of good faith.

Another aspect of "embeddedness" that I think worth addressing is whether, if a critic gets "embedded" in some way or other, it will make them view the work more favourably.

Well, here's a thing. I reckon a critic's actual *opinion* of a piece is frequently the least important part of a review. Yes, some people treat reviews as some kind of consumer guide. I suspect many of them might be the same sort of people who grumble if they suspect a critic isn't "being objective". They're the people who prize the star-rating. And, having taken into account what I've said only a couple of paragraphs earlier about respecting the humanity of others, I still think those people are the wreckers of civilisation.

Ok, it is useful to know if something is good or not. But unless you're actually the person who's reviewed the show – or you have the magical good fortune to have a critic with whose taste yours corresponds exactly – the good/not-good question just boils down to that most mysterious of things; one's taste.

What *should* be useful in criticism is the expertise of the critic. Their insights and ability to cast light on a work; to describe what that work is doing; how it does it; etc.

Of course, all this involves value judgements too, but judgements that are a good deal less crass than the false binaries of good or bad. And it takes *words* to *explain* them. You can't just explain a plot, or a set of synaptic responses, or a philosophy, or a design with a number of stars out of five.

If you accept this as a view of criticism, then it makes the idea of whether a critic is embedded or not suddenly seem a lot less relevant. I guess, in part, that's why I'm interested in this as a possible new direction for writing about theatre.

Which brings us pretty much up to the present, which, as of this sentence, finds me sitting in the small ante-office of the Gate Theatre, sat next to Forest Fringe co-director Andy Field, writing a piece justifying why I believe this state of affairs is in any way acceptable. And why, moreover, I think it's *useful* and perhaps even *better*, than if I just turn up at half seven and scamper off as soon as the show finishes.

There are a couple of other elements which I haven't mentioned yet. These could usefully be filed under the headings: "Festivals" and "Friends".

I remember while I was taking part in the Festivals In Transition Mobile Lab, one of the elements that we spent a bit of time thinking about was that of the position of the critic at an (international) theatre festival. The vast majority of those festivals that we visited, as well as the Neue Stücke aus Europa festival in Wiesbaden, were distinguished by the closeness of the festival communities that quickly grew up within them – much more like the National Student Drama Festival here, than either the Edinburgh Fringe writ large or even the Edinburgh International Festival. And, as such, we did a bit of thinking about whether one writes any differently as part of a community rather than as an individual voice, more or less lost and anonymous in a metropolis as vast as London.

I don't think we concluded at the time that we thought we did, or would write any differently. And, hell, you only have to read my attempted evisceration of Superamas's *Big 3rd Episode: Happy/End*, to see what we meant (and that review, fwiw, was written at a festival in Rakvere, Estonia, a town where the festival existed in more-or-less total isolation from the rest of the town, with performers, audience and critics all eating and drinking together in a little arty bubble).

Actually, I think the impetus for the spirit in which I'm approaching my FF@TG has a lot more to do with the spirit of Forest Fringe itself. And the fact that some of the pieces are first scratches – which is a different sort of review again.

And then we come to the issue of writing about friends' work. Last week at Forest Fringe, I did know quite a few of the people performing, through various channels. I was at university with Chris Thorpe and Lucy Ellinson (and playwright John Donnelly, who came along on Tuesday night). Indeed, the first thing I ever directed as a student was a short play by John in which Lucy took the lead role. I've also known Andy Field for an aeon since he reviewed for

Culture Wars while I was still theatre editor there. I've known Ira Brand since I saw Tinned Fingers at NSDF '08, and subsequently recommended them to Andy for the first publicised season of Forest Fringe in Edinburgh, at which they were a huge hit, and their relationship with Forest has since blossomed. And, hell, I've known Chris Haydon for long enough for him to have stolen my made-up surname to be his made-up surname. Actually, and perhaps most relevantly to this argument, I shared a flat with him in Edinburgh the year that, while reviewing for the Scotsman, he effectively *discovered* the TEAM, five-starred them, got them awarded a Fringe First and, I guess, put in motion the chain of events that led to their storming hit *Mission Drift* last summer.

You'll notice that both Field and Haydon (Christopher) also used to work as critics, before they hopped over the fence.

Which perhaps explains another element of how and why I feel that this experiment in being almost a "critic-in-residence" for this fortnight makes sense. And I think, why I've been allowed by both theatre and resident/guest-company to do it. These are entities led by people who also understand first-hand the value of writing about theatre.

Embedded Criticism: some Arguments, an Offer and a Dare

Daniel Bye, *Pessimism of the Intellect, Optimism of the Will*
20 April 2012
http://www.danielbye.co.uk/blog/embedded-criticism-some-arguments-an-offer-and-a-dare

---

So, Andrew Haydon wrote an excellent post about what he calls "embedded critics". Jake Orr and Maddy Costa have both spent time in rehearsal rooms recently, reporting on process, and Maddy was the convenor of a D&D session on this topic, which she unpacks more fully in this post.[10] There must be something in the air, or it wouldn't have turned up in Matt Trueman's latest Noises Off column on the Guardian theatre blog. That sounds like a swipe at Matt, as though he's always the last to pick up on anything. It's not: his job in that column is to digest the things everyone's talking about. Everyone's talking about "embedded".

It's worth noting that what Andrew means by "embedded" and what Jake and Maddy mean differs slightly. Jake and Maddy have evinced a specific interest in witnessing rehearsal rooms in action, and have so much money in their mouths on the subject, we'll have to have a whip-round to buy them lunch. Meanwhile, Andrew is going to every single night of Forest Fringe at the Gate, which is a thrilling level of critical attention to bring to a small-scale operation, but in practice makes him little more embedded than, say, Joyce McMillan at the Traverse for the first three days of August. Andrew writes some of his reviews from a tiny office at the Gate, sure. But Joyce wrote the official history of the Traverse Theatre. And Danny Concannon has a desk in the White House. What's your point? There are loads of

---

[10] Dan links to: http://statesofdeliquescence.blogspot.co.uk/2012/03/devotional.html.

great things about what Andrew is doing, few of which I'm going to talk about in this post. It's the Jake-and-Maddy version I'm engaged with here.

—

An increased closeness between critic and artist is obviously problematic for the reviewer writing what Andrew calls "consumer guide" criticism, helping audiences to choose which play to see as one might select which wine to have with their roast lamb. Even if the critic is hand-on-heart sure they'd have loved the show whether or not it was written by their best mate, not everyone will share their confidence. Adam Werrity might be a great doer of whatever it is he does, but you'd be forgiven for thinking he wouldn't be doing it if he weren't friends with Liam Fox.

Closeness between critic and artist is just as obviously unproblematic if, like me, you're more interested in critical writing that in some way illuminates, rather than just swiftly evaluates the work. It's the difference between saying someone has "thighs of steel", and describing the science of muscle growth. The wine-guide approach, with its 300-word limits and star ratings, is obviously inimical to that, so let's just accept, like Maddy Costa at that D&D session, that we're talking about something else: a new space for critical writing, a form that is more than briskly evaluative.

From the point of view of the artist, it's easy to bemoan the state of theatre criticism.** Some artists spend more time doing so than making, you know, art. And they've plenty of good points. The wine guide approach, the tiny word-limits, the star ratings, the ridiculous glibness this and everything else about our culture cultivates. Yes, lots of theatre criticism is bloody awful. Artists have running jokes about most of it, and many critics laugh along.

So what could possibly be edifying about not only having your outfit criticised by this facile culture, but first inviting the critic into your bedroom to watch you get dressed? With the amount of idiotic criticism there already is, the last thing we need is more of it, in the room, while we're trying to work, eating all the bananas and typing during the nude scene. But the only way we can save criticism as an institution from the idiocy imposed on it by the marketplace and the broader culture is by giving it space, access and generosity. Criticism is in trouble as a serious form, and keeping it at a respectful distance from its subject isn't going to help, any more than Aggers broadcasting from a fort helped produce good commentary (as opposed to a whizz-bang story for the BBC). It won't get better if we shut it out.

And of course there are plenty of ways in which illuminating criticism can happen without a critic ever setting foot in the rehearsal room. Some of those are exactly what Andrew is doing over at Postcards – you know, the stuff I'm not talking about in this post. And I'd welcome more such long-form discursive writing on contemporary theatre that, say, considers a production as part of a continuing tradition, for example, or as part of a wider cultural discourse, or indeed as part of a social or political problem. Anything that does more, goes deeper than: it was well-written, tick, the acting was good, tick, I didn't like the set, cross, three stars – is A Good Thing. You don't need to know whether they did voice warm-ups or played knee tag in order to write those pieces, and write them well. Let's have more of this, please. This is what the blogosphere can do that the mainstream press can't, or won't, and it's heartening to see an increase of interest in this, and a burgeoning of spaces where it can take place. All I'm really interested in is what illuminates the form, and the work.

Thus, in one sense, the question about whether or not critics should spend time embedded in rehearsal rooms is a simple one: will it illuminate? The answer is obvious: sometimes. Sometimes a brilliant critic will enter a rehearsal room and see things no artist has ever seen about their work. Those insights will be revelatory for audiences, students, emerging artists and makers. Other critics will find their skills not as well-suited to this particular method of engagement, and make right tits of themselves. Some should stick to reviewing, some should write long discursive pieces about the formal kinship between Forced Entertainment and Beckett – but stay out of rehearsal rooms. And some will find that there's a whole territory here, uncharted by pretty much any critical writing.

But can critics really bring any insight? Surely artists write well enough about this for themselves, without the unnecessary degree of exposure? Well, I'm not so sure. Many artists, when asked about their process, will first say they haven't got one. Then when they've had a few hits, Nick Hern will ask them to write a book, and they attempt to formulate a process by describing a series of exercises. These exercises are in fact no more the process than a suit of armour is a soldier. What the artist really describes in these books tends to be the work's construction, it's architecture, while presenting the assumptions on which that construction rests as god-given universals.

So the obvious place to start this kind of critical enquiry is with the process's embedded assumptions about form. I think it gets even more interesting if considering its embedded assumptions about humanity. Eh? Well, the process is constructed of a complex web of assumptions about the ways people should and do interact with each other, how best they work under pressure, how they can be enabled to produce their best work. In this respect a rehearsal process is no different from any other human interaction geared towards a common end. And it's amazing to me how many processes work according to assumptions radically contrary to those the work is attempting to encode. How much work espousing collectivist left-wing politics is made under (benign or otherwise) dictatorships? Good critical writing about process could observe inconsistencies like this in a way artists might not – could observe assumptions and conventions so internalised we're not even quite aware of them. I hope they'd also observe the ways in which many artists in rehearsal rooms are open, generous, brilliant people, but you've got to take the rough with the smooth.

We've all learned that how our food is grown, or how our clothes are made, is of ethical concern to us. Why should this be any different for the theatre we watch? Sure, we're unlikely to find that the actors we're watching were treated in the same way as Chinese workers at the Apple factory – although you'd be surprised. But it'd be nice to know that work espousing or decrying particular social practices can live according to its own principles, just as it is nice to know that a politician practices what he preaches. If Mike Daisey taught us anything, it's that how the work is made can very quickly become part of the experience.

Of course, the rehearsal rooms that are most ethically problematic are exactly the ones that won't let critics in. Like Burma, or North Korea. But the very existence of a discourse around the practices and processes of a rehearsal room must be healthy for the form as a whole. It has to raise the bar, just a bit. Even then, artists won't necessarily talk about this stuff in public – that's my bedroom you're talking about – but at least they might start talking about it in private. At present, plenty don't even do that. Richard Eyre once said that "directing is like sex – everyone's curious about how everyone else does it, but they never get to watch"***. (He probably said that before the internet took off and enabled us all to watch the press night version of sex at any hour of the day or night.)

Many of you will be more interested in the embedded assumptions about form, about what theatre should be or do. I'd argue that's inseparable from what I've described above, but plenty of critics will separate it anyway and do pretty good work. An example. I've long been fascinated by the structure of Forced Entertainment's large-scale work. They obviously don't structure their work according to narrative conventions, and it seems to me they do so according to musical shapes: sometimes verse-chorus-bridge, sometimes something more akin to classical sonata form, but nonetheless the effect is of a rhythmic ebb and flow that provides shape to the experience. What I don't know is how, or even if that is articulated in the rehearsal room. I don't know whether it's intentional, or based on a set of assumptions I haven't been able to diagnose from the work alone. But observations from the rehearsal room would tell me more about this. I'd learn more about Barcelona's tactics by watching them train than I can discern from watching them play.

Now, I'd argue that the assumptions you make about the ways you choose to structure your work are inherently political assumptions. But I'm a bore, and anyway I don't propose to unpack that here. This is already quite a long post. Suffice it to say that valuable critical work can be done on process-work without getting too deep into its political assumptions, as I hope I've suggested above.

Finally, though, the key reason for discussing the rehearsal process as well as the product is to do with the status and nature of the artistic work itself. Thinking of a work of art as a "product" of its process, or even of its society, is a fundamental misconception. We've been sold the idea that we buy plays, or movies, or cups of coffee as perfected objects, smooth to the touch, no care unlavished: finished. Cobblers. However polished, works of art are no more or less than part of an ongoing cultural process. They're not *products* of the conversation society has with itself, separated from it by the label "finished". They are part of that conversation. And they aren't the last word on a subject, either, though if they're really brilliant they might be the first one. Thinking about the process that led to the creation of a piece of work (which process is itself not hermetically sealed from the outside world) can only help to correct this bizarre view of works of art as artefacts, relics clamouring for museum space as soon as they emerge into the world. I can't think of anything that exists purely as "product". Even shit's a fertiliser.

—

So, let's imagine critics start reporting from rehearsal rooms. Don't let's pretend there won't be problems along the way. The first and most prevalent of these will be writing about what's happening in this rehearsal room as though it's never happened before in any other. There was a little bit of this in Jake Orr's often excellent writing about Dirty Market's devising process at Ovalhouse. Things that emerge as difficulties in any devising process loomed larger than life, as though they were particular difficulties faced by *this* company. A flat afternoon after a vibrant morning. A frustrating slowness in the coalescence of constituent parts. To Jake's great credit, he acknowledged this slippage in his writing, but it will remain a danger for any newly-embedded critic who hasn't already been in several rehearsal rooms – by the same measure, a tried-and-tested rehearsal method could, to a green observer, make an ordinary director appear a genius. Plenty of us in any medium think we have invented the slicing of bread, only for an audience to tell us otherwise. To observe what's distinctive about one piece of theatre, it's necessary to have seen several others. The same is true of wines, poems and a good cover drive.

Mistakes will be made. Critics will confuse the particular with the general. Then sceptics will do the same, damning the whole critical enterprise as flawed on the basis of one flawed example, like those ludicrous people who hate telly because they once saw something on ITV. And many readers (and indeed writers) won't be at all interested in the sausage factory aspect of theatrical process, arguing that only the sausages themselves are of real interest. Fine. Such people shouldn't read this strand of critical writing. Just don't be like those people who seem to think football should be banned because they don't happen to enjoy it. And don't come running to me when you find out your sausages are made by grinding up testicles.

—

It will also, if we really want this to happen, take a lot of will on the part of practitioners. Some of us will be pilloried for three weeks before the usual pillorying,**** then get pilloried again on press night. Some of us rightly. In my rehearsal rooms, for example, there come times when it looks like nothing is happening at all. Some critics will laud this as valuable space for contemplation, others will damn it as dossing about. They will both be right. Some will praise my commitment to optimism in difficult times. Others will damn my persistent cheeriness as a glib mask insulating me from serious issues. They will both be right. And plenty, more, I hope, will say things I never even thought of. Artists will need to be open to this new sort of presence in the room.

So I'd better put my money where my mouth is. Here goes. Over the summer I'm making several new pieces of work. I will happily welcome any critic who'd like to come and spend a long period of time in the room with us. I don't like people being excluded from opportunities on the basis of inability to pay, and of course I don't have a budget for this. So I will support, to the extent of co-writing, an Arts Council application to fund the possibility. I think such an application would have legs: this is Quite a New Thing.

(I'm aware that very little is clear about what this work is, where and when it's being made, etc. This page[11] gives hints and links. We're working in the north east, for most of July and September. I suppose opening this offer and informing those interested as fully as possible demands a blog post about the, yes, process. But honestly, this one's taken me all day. I don't know when I'll get round to that.)

Dear Other Artists: go on. I double dare you.

---

[11] Dan links to the 'current shows' page of his website.

* Please do read that post by Maddy Costa, and not just because she's nice about me on an unrelated point in the last paragraph. She is responsible for galvanising all of this.
** Although it's not irrelevant that I spent a brief year or so, from 2002–03, as a critic myself, writing in Scotland for pretty much every publication in print while trying to put together my first professional fringe show and figure out what I should write about in my phd.
*** This is a paraphrase. It's in his diaries somewhere, but I've spent long enough on this post already.
**** Although I suspect a certain sensitivity will be required of people you're going to spend three weeks in a room with. It's only polite, right?

Translunar Paradise & Critical Distance

Catherine Love, *Love Theatre*

25 May 2012

Now available on: https://catherinelove.co.uk/2012/05/25/translunar-paradise-critical-distance/

If you'll forgive the cliché, sometimes less really can be more, as Theatre ad Infinitum prove with their delicate essay on love and loss. The plot is simple, the production accomplished through a blend of simplicity and ingenuity. The elderly male protagonist is coming to terms with the loss of his wife, still taking down two cups from the cupboard instead of one, rifling through suitcases brimming with memories; his wife's ghost looks on, gently but firmly wrenching herself from his grieving grasp. This is all told, over an hour, with no words. Instead we have the sigh and hum of an accordion, the narrative precision of movement. In a beautifully judged touch, masks are inventively used to convey age, whipped away to transport the couple back to their youth and lightly hinting at the deceptive proximity of these two states.

Through a series of smoothly executed flashbacks, we are given a glimpse into this couple's life together, from the moment they meet, through their small joys and disappointments, to the little tragedies that touch their existence and eventually wrench them apart. Into this moving story of the lives of one ordinary couple, Theatre ad Infinitum even manage to weave one of the most chillingly evocative visualisations of war and its traumatic psychological scars that I've seen on the stage. On real and dreamed battlefields, performer George Mann is pummelled by invisible blasts, painfully contorted, violently tossed about by nightmarish forces. Not all of Spielberg's mud and gore can quite match it for emotional force.

Speaking of emotional force, while watching I couldn't help thinking of *Lovesong*. While these may in many senses be two very different pieces of theatre, there are common elements that immediately leap out: the process of a man coming to terms with the idea of losing his wife, the centrality of physical movement, the melting of past into present. I found, however, that *Translunar Paradise* was more genuinely moving in its wordless simplicity than *Lovesong* was in all its none too subtle emotional manipulation. Sobbing is all very well (though not something I'm particularly susceptible to in the theatre, to my immense discomfort as everyone around me at the Lyric Hammersmith sniffed into their tissues) but an excess of tears can blur meaning beyond intelligibility.

While *Lovesong* sacrificed promising debates about the nature of time in favour of prodding at our tear ducts, here such underlying strands are given more nuanced exploration. Through what is, on the surface, an ordinary tale of two ordinary people, Theatre ad Infinitum delicately investigate the fluidity of time and, linked to this, memory. Form subtly reflects content; the flashbacks emerge as snapshots, flicked through with vivid energy. These elegantly choreographed scenes from the past rather appropriately have the stuttering quality of early film, jumping from action to action, meticulously wrought expression to expression. There is all the frenetic motion of memory and the seemingly speeded up time of youth.

After seeing this moving and beautifully assembled piece, however, I found myself thinking as much about how my impression of the performance had been refracted through my experience of speaking to creator Mann as I was thinking about the show itself. This is not to detract from *Translunar Paradise* in any way, but perhaps rather to detract from my own abilities and assumptions as a reviewer. As a result, this has morphed from a review into a not-quite-review with a bit of reflection on the distance between theatremakers and critics thrown into the mix.

This issue of distance was not something that had previously worried me. Yes, I sometimes review shows after writing features about those shows, but usually I still feel qualified to form an independent opinion; I don't know the creators of the theatre well enough from one short interview to be swayed by any personal connection to them, and often there is much about the piece that still remains to be discovered even after discussing it. While it might have put a slightly different slant on those reviews, I hadn't really thought about it in any great depth until recently.

Then the idea of 'embedded' critics started getting thrown around. A good place to get started if you're new to this discussion is Andrew Haydon's blog, where he has written twice about the idea of embedded criticism, with Daniel Bye's response making good follow up reading. Distilled down and somewhat simplified, embedded criticism denotes the deeper involvement of the critic in the piece of theatre they are writing about, be that a full immersion in the creative process or more of a surface paddle. There are lots of different ways in which this might function in practice, but the driving idea behind it is that being embedded in the process could provide illumination on both sides: critics bring their outside eye and in return gain insight into the process of making.

I'm not going to discuss embedded criticism and all its benefits and drawbacks here, partly because others have already done so fairly comprehensively and partly because I'm yet to fully make my mind up about it. I'm equally fascinated by, excited about and wary of the idea. Which brings me to the particular wariness I felt while watching *Translunar Paradise*. I think these concerns arose in relation to this particular production simply because Mann spoke in such eloquent detail about the process of meticulously piecing this show together. Through hearing about creative choices, I felt somehow involved in them, and the end product immediately prompted memories of the process that Mann described to get to this stage. As such, I was unsure whether I could trust my own critical perception of the piece and its effects.

There is always the danger, once you have been told what the intention is behind a certain creative decision, that as an audience member you will be unable to distinguish between whether this decision actually produces the desired effect or whether you are simply reading it in that way because you've already been instructed to. There are even occasions, such as I found with Headlong's confused and frankly bizarre touring production of *A Midsummer Night's Dream* last year, when explicit, laboured reasoning is required to explain a production's concept, which seems something of a failure of the concept itself.

Aware of this danger, doubts insidiously imposed themselves on my reading of *Translunar Paradise*. Was this really an exercise in precision, or did I simply see precision because I knew about the lengthy creative process? Here I feel fairly confident that yes, Theatre ad Infinitum's work was beautifully precise, but when it comes to other building blocks of the piece I am less certain. Would I have read quite so much into the choice of accordion accompaniment had Mann not spoken about the importance of an instrument that "breathes"? Would I have picked up on the influences of photography and graphic novels? How much would I have scrutinised the physical embodiment of age had Mann not admitted that it took him a lot of work to perfect the gait of an old man?

But for all my doubts, I also feel immensely grateful for the insight that I gained into the process that made this piece of work. Ultimately I found watching *Translunar Paradise* a hypnotically captivating experience, which I suspect was a mixture of the show itself and the tiny glimpse I had gained of its loving creation. I also hope that any insight provided by Mann's words might enhance the experience for other audience members. It's a lot like the magician and his illusions; magical as it might be to be tricked and dumbfounded, another part of the mind always wants to know how it works, to feel for the cracks. And sometimes being shown the process behind the illusion even makes the illusion itself all the more beguiling.

The Strange Undoing of Prudencia Hart
Dan Hutton
16 July 2013
https://danhutton.wordpress.com/2013/07/16/the-strange-undoing-of-prudencia-hart/

---

created by David Greig and Wils Wilson
at the London Welsh Centre, Monday 15th July 2013

"National Theatre of Scotland cannot be held responsible in the event of any member of the audience losing their head, their heart or their very self during the course of the performance"

Last night I was a motorbike.

Part the First

During the first act of *Prudencia Hart*
An actor pretended I was his kart.
Falling beside me he whispered "Give me your arms",

Theatre Blogging

Then rose up behind and clamped his palms
Around my wrists.
Then proceeded to drive me, bike-like, with all sorts of twists.
For a few short seconds I was not me
But had surrendered myself to become part of theatre's visual imagery.

Moments like this happen throughout the show
Which, reading this review you'll probably know,
Is written in rhyme.
Pretty much the whole time
David Greig's play is spoken in those things
We like to call couplets, which means the verse sings
And follows the structure of that ancient form:
The Border Ballad. This therefore is the norm.

Prudencia Hart follows the story of an eponymous Pru,
A somewhat traditional academic from Edinburgh who
Goes to a conference and looks a bit of a mallard
As she gets trounced in a debate subtitled "Neither border nor ballad".
At said meeting are scholars who feel
That the study of balladry is a far bigger deal
Than simply old songs. Here, the argument goes,
We can learn much more about folk and community from those
Aspects of pop culture like chants and X-Factor,
And in this discussion Pru's confidence lacked her.

The story is one which contains two clear sides
And around this debate the whole thing rides.
On one side the school of thought which believes
That old-fashioned ballads tell our national story best and leaves
The newfangled stuff out of academia.
Opposite them are those who fear
That ignoring the modern form of an ancient song
Is just plain wrong.

We see hear that academics are just
As petty and personal as the rest of us.
Though an intelligent, articulated reason may support
A far-fetched idea, it's really just short
For "I think this"
Based on personal preferences.

This dichotomy is played out
(In a style akin to a fencing bout)
On Georgia McGuinness' traverse-style staging in a hot sticky pub;
We become the regulars there and get to rub
Shoulders with this motley crew
And, like them, are invited to "have a few".

Part the Second

After the much-needed interval in the boiling, muggy bar of the London Welsh Centre, the tone of *The Strange Undoing of Prudencia Hart* changes. She has been led off a B&B with an enormous library on one cold, snowy midwinter's night by a suspicious looking man who doesn't leave footprints. And Prudencia's studies come true as she [SPOILER ALERT] gets locked away in hell for eternity. Here, the production really comes into its own as the mania of the first act gives way to the intensity seen here, rhythm and rhyme discarded in the vaults of hades. Melody Grove is allowed to plunge to new depths in the expansive role of Hart, whilst David McKay and Paul McCole take turns at playing a slimy but charming devil, proving true the folklore that our protagonist has spent her whole life studying.

In this section, Alasdair Macrae's thumping, joyous music is conspicuous by its absence as we come to note the importance of music and the collective action of singing, even when it is Katy Perry at a karaoke bar. All that Prudencia has in this vast cavernous library in hell is her books, and she lacks the vitality of those academics she once scorned. And then, slowly, she comes to understand the importance of finding poetry within yourself, in the present.

And then as the devil comes to resent
This new-found ability to rhyme
Prudencia decides that it's the time

To try to break free. But it isn't quite this simple, as the devil fights back. And here, orally and visually, a battle is enacted between living in the present and living in the past, as we are asked to chant, football-style, in order to save her.

One Colin Syme
There's only one Colin Syme
One Colin Sy-ime
There's only one Colin Sy-ime

And then, as we work together as one
It becomes clear that the right person won.
And Wils Wilson's direction allows us to see
That even though we may disagree
On the things we hold highly
Sometimes all you need is a bit of folk-y Kylie.

None of this really explains the show one bit
Not least 'cause my writing is a little bit shit.

[Embedded video of Kylie Minogue's Can't Get You Out Of My Head][12]

---

[12] See https://youtu.be/c18441Eh_WE.

Theatre Blogging

Criticism Redux Redux Redux

Jill Dolan, *The Feminist Spectator*
10 January 2014
http://feministspectator.princeton.edu/2014/01/10/criticism-redux-redux-redux/

There's a bit of a firestorm on Twitter and on line these past few days about criticism (again), prompted in part by P. Carl's HowlRound post, "A New Year's Diet for the Theater,"[13] in which he cites my essay on "critical generosity" from *Public*. The offending phrase from my piece seems to be where I take Ben Brantley and Charles Isherwood of the *New York Times* to task for not being responsible to the "deleterious effects" of their criticism, and where I suggest that criticism is "always political", whether or not it's "masked by the 'objectivity' that power bestows on their work".

The offending moment in Carl's piece seems to be where he argues that we should be "nicer": "Let's be nicer this year," he proposes. "There is a growing critical edge to social media conversation that is beginning to wear on me."

Some commentators on Twitter quickly conflated "critical generosity" with "nicer" and protested that being nice has nothing to do with criticism; that it gives feminism a bad name; and that daily critics don't have the leisure to have an extended generous (whether or not "nice") dialogue when they write about theatre.

George Hunka, in his blog post, "We are All Victims Now", admitted, "Nobody likes a good round of *Times*-bashing more than I do", but chastised me for not citing any of Brantley or Isherwood's reviews "that would lend substance to [my] accusation of political, aesthetic, and 'objective' motivations for negative critical verdicts". Then he digs up the old Arlene Croce debate in *The New Yorker* from 1994 about Bill T. Jones's piece *Still/Here*, which Croce refused to review because she dubbed it "victim art".

A peculiar gender bias haunts this conversation which, as Carl might note, blew up in edgy and quickly accusatory ways on Twitter (a format I find pithy but not really conducive to thoughtful and, I admit, generous commentary). That is, "nice" is quickly equated with a kind of sentimental, non-evaluative, dishonest, non-confrontational, frankly and stereotypically "feminine" kind of engagement. And daily critics – whether or not, I should say, they are men or women or any other mix of gender identifications – are positioned as the brawny, masculine laborers being stalwart and honest and clear as they do the difficult and sometimes painful but always necessary work of telling consumers where to spend their money on theatre.

That's too bad.

I agree with Carl. The arts are beleaguered. We're not "victims", as Hunka accuses me and Carl of suggesting (I think). But I would expect most of us to agree that when money dries up for artistic experimentation and innovation and the nourishing of new voices, we should

---

[13] Jill links to: http://howlround.com/a-new-year's-diet-for-the-theater.

all be worried. I believe that we need to take care with the work we see and engage, to honor the impulse that produced it; to see it in a broad context of social relevance and meaning; to consider it through a variety of aesthetic and taste traditions; and whether or not we "like" it, not to dismiss it out of hand, even when we see its flaws and failures. That's what I mean by critical generosity. Word count and daily deadlines shouldn't excuse derogatory dismissal.

Critics – good, professional critics – are experts. We know a lot about theatre and performance. We know its history, its debates, its forms, genres, and contents. Many of us are experts in particular kinds of theatre and performance. I know a lot about feminist theatre, queer theatre, women playwrights and directors, self-avowed political theatre, contemporary American theatre, solo performance, and a few other things. But that doesn't make me *superior* to the work about which I write. I don't want to stand above the work. I want to see myself in conversation with what it means, how it feels, what other people thought about it, what it *does in the world*. And yes, I do want to engage with kindness and rigor. I don't think they're mutually exclusive. A performance can make me angry and I still want to write about it carefully and I hope kindly. That's also what I mean by critical generosity. (See this story[14] about a new blog that documents random acts of kindness by academics. It's relevant.)

Any critic also has a *perspective*, a way of looking that guides their engagement. I would propose that ways of looking are *always* ideological, never objective (see John Berger's foundational series and book, *Ways of Seeing*). But then, I'm a feminist. I don't think power is equally distributed. The *Times* and its first- and second-string critics have a certain influence, power also determined by their relative status at the paper. Anyone writing for a daily paper has visibility that gives their words weight and meaning. And obviously, they negotiate with the editors and advertising managers who supervise them, and are beholden to deadlines and word counts that constrain their writing.

Arts critics' positions are also being reduced or de-funded at daily papers all over the country, a trend that will certainly affect the discourse about arts in this country. How can we proactively reimagine, then, how we stage our conversations about theatre and performance?

I started this blog (nearly 10 years ago now) because I wanted a place for a counter-discourse, one in which I could participate in a different kind of conversation about the theatre and performance to which I'm committed. My writing *isn't* beholden to editors, word counts, or advertisers; I have that beautiful freedom and leisure. My writing is political and ideological; but then, because I'm a feminist, I believe all writing is marked by position and power, that all writing is rhetorical and wants to persuade. Why else would we write?

I look at theatre and performance – and film and television – with an interest in what and how it tells me about gender and sexuality, about race and class, about how we're hailed as citizens of the world. I'm interested in how form and content and context complement each other around those themes. I'm interested in reception and production, in how artists frame their arguments and how audiences see and hear them. I'm interested in talking about the arts as though they have a real effect on our lives and what we're capable of imagining for ourselves and others – because I believe they do.

---

[14] Jill links to: http://www.insidehighered.com/news/2014/01/09/blog-aims-normalize-kindness-academe.

Theatre Blogging

Other critics look at and for other things. I'd love to have a real conversation – not an accusatory conversation – about the *work* of criticism and what it makes possible for artists and audiences. I don't think I'm always right.

On that note, I'll apologize to Brantley and Isherwood (whom I don't know) for suggesting in my *Public* essay that they "revel in their power to destroy productions they don't like". I don't know if they really *revel* in that power; perhaps it keeps them up at night. Sometimes, when I read their work, I don't sense much concern for what their criticism might do to the artists whose work they're evaluating. But as I've admitted, I'm sensitive to biases and to power inequities. My own words about Brantley and Isherwood in that essay come from too many years of frustration with the lack of audible alternative critical voices in public forums with the power to shape the public arts conversation.

But what I said wasn't very generous. So I'll follow my own injunction. I didn't mean to be mean; I respect daily and weekly and monthly critics, as well as those who blog frequently or irregularly. I feel connected to other people who write about the arts and appreciate their labor; I want to be in dialogue with them, as well as with artists and audiences.

When I teach my students how to write criticism, they assume they have to be negative. I'd rather teach them how to be rigorous and generous about what they see, how to refrain from ad hominem attacks and respect the artists about whom they write, and use their words to create a dialogue about what works and what doesn't and why, and *what it all might mean.*

Am I sentimental? I don't think so. Are those of us in the arts victims? Not at all. Are we people with a common purpose, which at least in some small part is to champion the arts and the diversity of stories that deserve to be heard and explored and contested and provoked under its auspices? I hope so.

Got life, got music, got theatre
Maddy Costa, *Deliq.*
5 November 2014
http://statesofdeliquescence.blogspot.com/2014/11/got-life-got-music-got-theatre.html

---

I am old now and so drunk on just two glasses of wine and in the past six days I've had the kids on half-term and moved back into my family home that doesn't suit me and left London three times and right now I'm sitting on a single bed in a twin room in a B&B in Malvern with my head swimming and my heart racing because tonight in a stupidly big room with an audience of not enough people tonight at Malvern Theatres I saw Uninvited Guests' new show This Last Tempest and my body isn't big enough to contain it, I can't hold all at once everything it made me think and feel. I am trembling, every inch of me vibrating, with how much I love this show. Two weeks ago I was in Bristol with the company because they've asked me to be a board member and anyone who thinks that in some way this invalidates my response to it can right this minute just fuck right off, another time I'll have a more temperate and articulate argument but just now the idea that what a FAN thinks is somehow less trustworthy than what a "distanced" "dispassionate" observer thinks can take a flying fucking jump. Have you seen the Nick Cave film 20,000 Days on Earth? There's a bit in that where Cave and Warren heart Ellis talk about Nina Simone, about the transformational power of live performance, that reminded me (partly because I'd been talking to Peter McMaster not long before seeing the film about whether or how art can transform those who encounter it) of a very specific night in an upstairs room of a pub in Camden watching Tortoise play, I guess in 1994, and knowing that I would never need to take drugs, because I would always have live music to recalibrate my body and take over my brain; tonight watching This Last Tempest I had a bit of that again, heart so swollen I could hardly breathe and blood flowing with the cadence of the stage. This Last Tempest begins where Shakespeare's Tempest ends – there's a part of me that doesn't want to go into too much detail because I know I'm seeing it again in Colchester on November 27 and by then already it will have changed/honed/found its rhythm, and because I want everyone to go in with the same not-knowing, to experience the same wonder/surprise, but also there's a part of me that wants to sit up until 3am dissecting every moment of it one by one – it begins with Prospero leaving the island and Arial and Caliban needing to learn how to live for themselves; it begins with that same speech by Gonzalo that was also the fulcrum of Chris Goode's The Forest and the Field, the speech in which he envisages a non-hierarchical society that has no commerce or trade, no magistrates, no riches or poverty, no power to overthrow, a speech no teacher of mine ever adequately addressed; it begins with an awareness of climate change, our responsibility to change our intemperate behaviour, the (im)possibility of returning the earth to itself; it begins with the faltering attempts to love, to feel, of two creatures who have been shown scant love or compassion, the appropriation of others' language to express those burgeoning emotions, the blossoming of empathy that comes with love; it begins with a longing for change, a desire to destroy and through that to create; it begins with the 2011 riots, with Crack Capitalism, with the fear of living in the end of times; it begins with sound, with frequencies just slightly beyond human hearing (how delicious to see this within a few days of Dickie Beau's equally testing/enrapturing Camera Lucida), with an immense love of Nick Cave and My Bloody Valentine; it begins in my exploding fucking heart, and weeks of not really needing to write about theatre, and knowing this show is special because I couldn't brush my teeth or sink into bed before vomiting words into a computer screen (honestly, if they'd set out to make a show that would be everything I love to distraction, they couldn't have ticked more boxes). And there's something so correct and pleasing and stupidly meta in the fact that this is me writing like Megan Vaughan writing like me, in response to Uninvited Guests reshaping Shakespeare to think about the weight of history – oh! I haven't even mentioned the weight of history yet, the fear that however willingly we attempt to shape what could be, we will always be too scarred by what was – and the power of language to rule and ruin, divide and oppress. And all the things it reminded me of: something else by Chris Goode, on want and desire[15] in theatre, that I just read last week, and all the thinking I've been doing about class with/ alongside Harry Giles (Shakespeare's Miranda will weep for princes, but not the ordinary slaves), and the fact that from now until the end of the year women are effectively working for free because unequal fucking pay, and oh my god the whole sequence where gravity is destabilised, and somewhere at the heart of it, this song:

---

[15] Maddy links to: http://beescope.blogspot.com/2010/05/house-of-future.html.

Theatre Blogging

[Embedded video of Ain't Got No, I Got Life by Nina Simone][16]

But now it's 12.12am and my train leaves in exactly seven hours and there are still teeth to brush and pyjamas to pull on and a bed to climb into and I can't write it all, all I can do now is marvel and shiver and wait for next time, impatiently and full of joy.

[Embedded video of To Here Knows When by My Bloody Valentine][17]

[Embedded video of Gamera by Tortoise][18]

Behaviour: Lippy and Western Society

Gareth K Vile, *The Vile Blog*
7 April 2015
http://vilearts.blogspot.co.uk/2015/04/behaviour-lippy-and-western-society.html

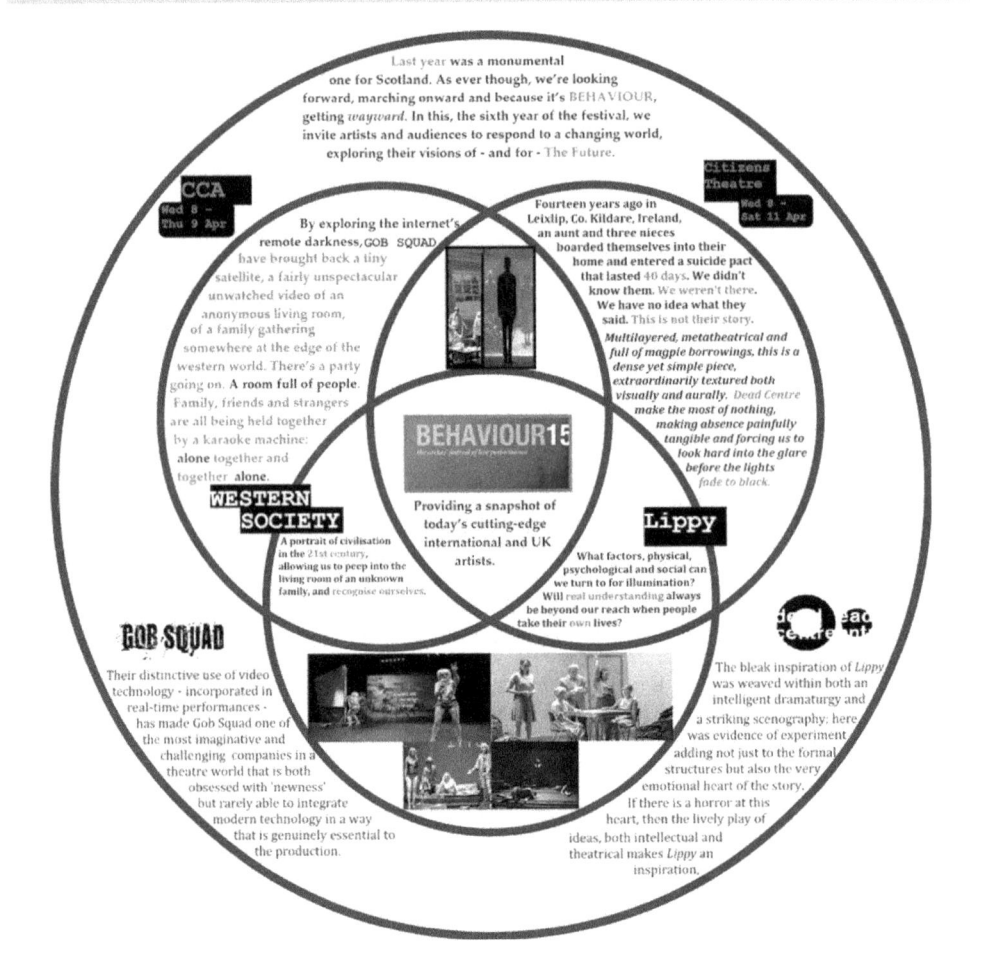

---

[16] See https://youtu.be/L5jI9I03q8E.
[17] See https://youtu.be/chaYm2TqfHM.
[18] See https://youtu.be/OLCgcp83Tfg.

> ## Application for review
> Megan Vaughan, *Synonyms for Churlish*
> 15 July 2015
> http://synonymsforchurlish.tumblr.com/post/124105363393/application-for-review-reviews-a-b-and-c-of

Reviews A, B, and C of The Trial (Young Vic) are now available online for successful applicants only.

To submit your application to the committee, please complete Form Q31A.

—

The post linked to the following online form. Responses were automatically emailed to me, where I could determine if the applicant had been successful or not.

The Trial – Application for Review Q31A

This is Application Form Q31A, regarding The Trial (Young Vic). For Application Forms Q27A to Q30BK, please contact the Helpdesk.

Complete the application form truthfully and in block capitals. Applicants will be notified within 48 hours if their request has been successful. Applications not completed in the spirit of the law will be rejected. By submitting Application Form Q31A you agree to the Terms and Conditions. To request a copy of the Terms and Conditions, please submit Data Request Form K77ii. To request a copy of Data Request Form K77ii, please contact the Helpdesk. (Helpdesk contact information can be found in the Terms and Conditions.)

* Required

1. Name:
2. Date of birth:
3. What do you do for a living?
   ☐ Think
   ☐ Count
   ☐ Worry
   ☐ Pretend
   ☐ Other:
4. Please enter the diameter (to nearest cm) of Rory Kinnear's perfectly-shaped head:
5. Think about the last 5 years of your life. Please order the following activities according to their frequency:

Theatre Blogging

Responses are limited to one per column.

	Most often	Quite often	Sometimes I guess	Not very often	Least often
Envy	☐	☐	☐	☐	☐
Loneliness	☐	☐	☐	☐	☐
Austerity	☐	☐	☐	☐	☐
Impotence	☐	☐	☐	☐	☐
Middle-management	☐	☐	☐	☐	☐

6. Please skip to question 7.*

7a. What is the worst thing you have ever done? Please provide appropriate context.

7b. Do you repent?
   ☐ Yes (go to question 8)
   ☐ No (go to question 9)

8. And what good has that done exactly?

9. Is this because you are:
   ☐ Selfish
   ☐ Too tired
   ☐ Unfeeling
   ☐ Rational
   ☐ Other:

10. What do you think about during sex? Please include URLs of any relevant reference material.

11. Which review of The Trial (Young Vic) are you applying to read?*
    ☐ A
    ☐ B
    ☐ C

12. Please enter your email address.*
This is where you will be notified regarding the success of your application, so please ensure you spell it correctly.

—

According to the applicants' preference, links to the following reviews were sent via email:

Review A

You can imagine the first meeting can't you.

"So the central design feature is going to be a conveyor belt. It's the perfect metaphor for the relentlessness of modern life and Josef K's complete lack of control. It'll get people talking, seamless scene changes, a motif that really focuses the whole production. Kinnear's gonna be on stage basically the whole time, so the travelator whatsit will propel the action quite literally. Or perhaps it's better to say it'll *prolong the struggle* . . ."

A conveyor belt running right through the middle of The Trial is a brilliant idea. Honestly, it really is. It's the perfect concept.

But this is a shit conveyor belt. It's too noisy; whirrs into life like an extractor fan. The SM team still need markers for the set but, instead of little glow-in-the-dark blobs or white tape or whatever, they've got massive numbered stickers with (!!!) *pink running men on them*. Times I'd be so distracted by them I'd be like "Ooh, running man number 34. He last stopped in front of me with the Charles Manson photo back when Josef was fucking that kid..."

And, of course, they want to reveal the conveyor belt to us when the show begins, not before, so it's necessary to employ some form of lid for the preshow. Remember A View From The Bridge, in this very space? Those black walls that rose slowly to reveal Mark Strong having a shower? (I'm still gutted that they thought his dick would've been "too distracting" for British audiences. DISTRACT ME MARK, I PROMISE I CAN HANDLE IT.) Anyway, conveyor belt lid. Not for Miriam Buether, the tasteful black walls of Mark Strong's STEAMY POST-GRAFT SHOWER CUBICLE. The Trial has this ridiculous orange box with a massive keyhole cut into it. The colours of the whole thing are a nightmare. It can't decide if it's going for the claustrophobic retro office vibes, or dayglo surrealism. Wheelie bins and wobbly doors and neon yellow jiffy bags. Mad Men down the rabbithole. Every so often a clock decends (I guess to justify cutting that keyhole shape) and at one point the words THEY KNOW scroll past like big wooden subtitles. They're like those pieces of shit people buy from garden centres or Argos or wherever; letters spelling out LOVE or HOME SWEET HOME or whatever vomity bollocks the total fucking *basics* are into these days. What are they doing *here*? This design should be just a conveyor belt (a silent, un-juddery, un-*numbered* conveyor belt), and a series of searing, sharp, angular, unpredictable shafts of light. Gimme the clock as a ticking sound design, or that digital Oresteia business or something. Fuck all this fucking *stuff*.

That said, if you can mentally tunnel your vision onto Kinnear or Kate O'Flynn, or even close your eyes completely and focus on the modernist rhythms of the inner monologue Nick Gill has written for Josef, this show is pretty fucking boss.

Kafka: a brilliant timeless bastard. This design: outdated 40 years ago.

Review B

Let's spake um of Michael Billington's review[19], all Kafka built un asken glance. On firsten view ee airpunchen much: "Oh joy ay celebrate um Tynan storylol!"

Ay share ay love ay chat biggen smiles for MB's cut loose funface. The Trial withstanden reshape playtime, is great text enough for riffen regular, especho from Godfather Billo mit weekend hairdown glee.

But Nick Gill, mine knickers soakem right through at your frenetic Josef headspeak! Ee musten revisit Ulysses on headphone-pages after this staccatum modernist bambambam. Ee

---

[19] I link to: https://www.theguardian.com/stage/2015/jun/28/the-trial-review-a-punishing-kafkaesque-experience

Theatre Blogging

lookback to MB cheekface now and lazybum smugdick no no no. How did Billodad ever choose repliKafka over light un quickenpace of pure Gillumtext brain muscle...?!

NG ist trophy arm heroman thinkscribe. MB error-looken to wrongem source matter.

Review C

It's just a shame she had to play so many sexual victims in this show.

Revolt. She Said. Revolt Again.

Kate Wyver
19 August 2016
https://katewyver.wordpress.com/2016/08/19/revolt-she-said-revolt-again/

When we were in school they used to show us a video of a group of school kids on a tube train. One of the kids would be on a different carriage and encourage the others to join them there. So one by one they would jump over from their carriage to the next, leaping over the gap between them and being pulled through by their friends. Then one of the kids, I think it was a girl, goes to jump but she's nervous. Her friends yell at her and she is pressured to jump, and then there's a sort of crackling and crashing and the video changes to one of a watermelon being squashed into thousands of squelchy little pieces as it gets trapped between the tube carriages and smashes to the ground, the tube racing on ahead. That watermelon was meant to be that girl's head.

Watching that video is what the script of *Revolt. She Said. Revolt Again.* feels like.

[Embedded video of Salt-N-Pepa's Let's Talk About Sex][20]

Revolt. is a piece of fiercely strong feminist theatre that would have much of Twitter exploding with calls of feminazis. *Revolt.* is about how we talk about sex, gender, and consent. It's about

---

[20] See https://youtu.be/ydrtF45-y-g.

how we deal with women, and how we deal with being women. It started its life at the RSC in 2014 with a series of other plays that had the provocation: 'well behaved women rarely make history'.

So I'm going to talk a bit about women, and consent, and being well-behaved.

A few weeks ago I had sex (woah IKR – I swear this gets more interesting). Then – for various reasons that are explained probably too openly in the link below – decided I didn't want to have sex and asked him to stop. More than once. He did not. I saw, and still see, this as a form of assault because it was non-consensual. I wrote something about it,[21] and it was clear that not everyone agreed with me. I was sent a few messages.

> **[username removed]**   12m
> @KateWyver that's a helluva moan for deciding right before climax that u didn't want to have sex after all 😒 😒 😒

> **[username removed]**   2h
> @KateWyver This attention-seeking self-proclaimed victimhood is an insult to feminism and women who have suffered sexual violence.

Which was fun.

But that's not the point, I'm not the point of this. The point is – yes, it's a tricky subject, and yes, what happened to me "could have been worse". But that doesn't mean that it's okay. If that's okay, where do you decide draw the line? Is it only not okay if the girl is crying? If she's bleeding? If she's shouting for help?

What *Revolt.* does is say this isn't okay.

Revolt. reveals the language of control between genders that might make us think these things are okay. Because if we have an unbalanced language we use for sex, how can we expect people to know that those words translated into physical actions aren't okay too? When I said stop, I was no longer a person having sex, I was an object being had sex with. By inverting the language and switching up how we talk about sex on stage, *Revolt*, stands up and says, look, do you see these things aren't acceptable?

Which I really needed to hear.

So perhaps this production will mean more to me than others, but there are plentiful reasons why I think it is still an inspiring play for a wide audience.

'*I want to make Love to you*

Or

With?'

(This article on the patriarchy of sex[22] is great too.)

---

[21] Kate links to: https://katewyver.wordpress.com/2016/08/08/zero-something-important/.
[22] Kate links to: http://www.huffingtonpost.com/amber-genuske/the-patriarchy-of-sex_b_1924743.html.

Theatre Blogging

I hadn't read *Revolt.* before seeing it, but interviewed director Erica Whyman for AYT about it when it premiered. (I particularly remember because Lyn Gardner retweeted it and that was very exciting.) In that interview, Whyman said this:

"On the one hand [this provocation is] an interesting thought about women now, and whether we're still expected to behave differently to men, and whether we have to behave badly in order to get noticed. But the other provocation is that their plays don't have to be well behaved and can experiment with form."

Birch's script does both of these things. It swears and spins and screams and says this which is stunning:

'Lie down and become available. Constantly. Want to be entered. Constantly. It cannot be an Invasion, if you want it. They Cannot Invade if you Want It. Open your legs and throw your dress over your head, pull your knickers down and want it and they can invade you no longer.'

The script also has a form similar in style – when looking at it on a page – to the work of Sarah Kane. The power of *Revolt.* undoubtedly lies in it's script and its revolutionary call to celebrate vaginas in a way that manages to make the audience rock with laughter. It twists the norm and makes you reconsider the way you speak, and what you expect from others.

So then, the production. It has ups and downs. It's like it chokes you and holds you up against a wall and you can't breathe and then suddenly drops you, runs away to get a Sainsbury's meal deal or something, then comes back a while later and picks you back up.

Everyone in Edinburgh is talking about Lucy McCormick's *Triple Threat*, the play about sex and gender with lots of on-stage fingering. (I haven't seen it but everyone who has is *very* keen to discuss.) Next to *Triple Threat*, it feels like little else at the Fringe could be called radical, but the staging of *Revolt.* – which by it's very nature, and the provocation it's responding to, should be radical – doesn't even get close to claiming the word.

(But it's on at the Traverse so perhaps that's not unexpected? Or is that unfair on the Traverse? But that's a whole different conversation.)

The staging for the first few sections of the script revolve around beams of light, which I think look pretty cool, but apparently this has been done a lot before, better.[23] It puts the focus on the words, the subtleties of action, the swing of a chair or the writhe of a hip. Anyway, I like it.

But the light beams aren't used very much and afterwards, any sense of coherent style evaporates. The script suggests no props should be used but Whyman's staging disobeys this, bringing on all the objects the script vaguely refers to – watermelons and bluebells and potatoes rolling around the stage – and it feels a bit GCSE.

In Birch's script she has headings, great headings like:

REVOLUTIONIZE THE LANGUAGE (INVERT IT).

---

[23] Kate links to: http://postcardsgods.blogspot.co.uk/2016/08/revolt-she-said-revolt-again-rsc-at.html.

which they project onto a massive screen in this production. It feels a little too easy. Shouldn't we have to guess these, aren't they sort of stage directions rather than words we should see or hear?

Then there's the ending. It was building well, the cast were saying things that made so much sense. Then they laid the table and suddenly became a grandma, mum and child and what they were saying didn't seem to mix with what they were doing. The passion had suddenly disappeared and it wasn't weird enough to be swept up in nor naturalistic enough to believe. I'm still not sure what we were meant to think of that scene. Finally all of the individual sections are thrown together in a conglomeration of cries and rants and a spinny chair. It feels thoughtless, it's simultaneously not messy enough and too messy, it's organised fun. Watermelons are smashed all over the place and I don't understand why, and all I can think about is that video of the girl's head as the watermelon as it's smashed between the tube carriages.

I want to leave the theatre feeling invigorated, wild, like I do after the first two scenes (particularly the first), but instead I'm a little confused, a little deflated, a little unsatisfied. I hope I get to see this play again in the future in different hands, and perhaps those final scenes will make sense to me. But I'm very grateful to have seen this play, because I needed something bigger than another person to look at me and say it isn't your fault, that's not okay.

Revolt. She said. Revolt again. And again please.

(Seen on 17/08/16 at the Traverse at the Edinburgh Fringe)

---

revew: Walter Meierjohann – Uncle Vanya

James Varney
22 November 2017
http://www.jamesvarney.uk/revew-walter-meierjohann-uncle-vanya/

Uncle Vanya/
by Anton Chekov/
vers by Andrew Upton/
dir Walter Meierjohann/
HOME/
3-25/11/2017//

i swear the most precious and beautiful and Must Be Repeated part of *Uncle Vanya* at HOME is Leaf Boy. he plays the accordion at random intervals for no reason, at the start of the second half he comes onstage and JUST STARTS TIPPING LEAVES EVERYWHERE I LOVED IT BEST PART OF THE SHOW STRAIGHT UP – I don't know who anyone is or why the play is even named after this Vanya bloke but LEAF BOY?! UGH HE'S PERFECT. He has like three words in the whole sodding play its like he's just a particularly obnoxious member of the stage crew he's just hanging around on the stage not saying or doing anything, occasionally he's sent to fetch someone and All The Time he lookes pissed off and bored he is the best Every Play Needs A Leaf Boy

who is he?!

mate whats actually sposed to be happening in Uncle Vanya? i swear

Uncle Vanya's funny. I swear I don't know what the plot was sposed to be. I go in being all 'oh this is Chekov he's supposed to be good I saw *The Cherry Orchard* ages ago and that was alright, kind of miserable. So what, Chekov's miserable and Russian and dead but he's pretty held up right? He's like a Russian Ibsen, people like him, Michael Billington's probably seen at least a hundred of em let's go.

So what I understand is that Uncle Vanya lives in a big old house with his Niece and two older women and an older man and I don't really know what the last three are there to do but Vanya and Niece look after the estate and the books and things. But the house is all crumbling and also Niece's Dad is here with his Wife, who Vanya is in love with (because she walks across the stage in a particularly attractive way (was that bit supposed to be funny?))

so what does Vanya harbour in his heart a secret desire to move to Africa?

I've No Idea which bits in Vanya are supposed to be funny. I found loads of bits funny because they were naff and made no sense. There was a rumbling sensible chuckle when the script made a joke about Gogol's *The Government Inspector*. This was, of course, An Approved Joke, but when I laughed at Vanya wistfully talking about a better life then turning to a map of Africa, a woman sat behind me whispered 'disrespectful'. Fukin hell. And of course, if I'd turned around to stare at her and her mates so as I could effectively take my cue as to when was an Appropriate Moment Of Sophisticated Comedy, I'D have been the rude one. Bloody theatre.

Maybe it's an illusion but I've noticed a Marked difference between the audiences at the Royal Exchange and at HOME. (they're both pretty white n old n posh, but) When I saw *King Lear* at the Exchange last year, the audience were laughing all over the place, it was great. Lear wanders on talking nonsense because he's gone mad because everyone and everything he loved and owned has been taken away from him and there's just giggles everywhere. It was beautiful. Everyone laughing at the poor mad man and Don Warrington possibly getting a bit pissed off that the house isn't full of weeping.

But HOME audiences are stuffy, is my point.

Obviously that's this specific audience n this specific play n that night and all that but but

but I just want to be allowed to laugh if I fucking feel like laughing when I'm watching a play and its funny.

how old even is this girl/woman whos hiys niece anyway? Like 17? 38? 11?

So Niece is referred to as something like 'being almost a woman' or 'on the cusp of womanhood' or one of those other creepy phrases. But she's also running some kind of stately home? And she makes reference to years and years ago helping translate papers for her Dad's work. So was she like 7 doing that? And I swear Doctor says something like

'5 years ago I might have considered her'. So is she actually young or is everyone just mad infantilising her?

The gender politics in *Uncle Vanya* are shit. Not that I'm surprised the women in a play that's idunno maybe 100 years old(?) are a bit flat but GOD the men are fukin creeps. Like almost to a man the men are creeps. The only one that avoids being a creep is the man whose function I don't know that I think they called Waffles(?) But he's not a character as much as just a random bit of light humour. Every action he performs is a bumble. He bumbles here, he bumbles there. He's the only non-white actor in the cast. I don't know what his function was.

The Doctor's function seems to be to be a big virile lech. Uncle Vanya's function seems to be to be a big impotent lech. They both really really want to have sex with Wife. Who makes it clear she doesn't want to have sex with them, she has a husband, thank you very much. But surely she can't really love her husband? They say. He's old and a bit thick. You want to have sex with me. They both say. Vanya fetches her flowers, Doctor grabs her and traps her against walls.

And then in a quivering OH-I-was-just-playing-coy-and-sexy-and-hard-to-get way, she gives in to her inner passions, which were never a part of her character before but I guess cos she's wearing a playsuit we can assume she's just a temptress and a sexpot idunno so that doesn't need to be a part of her character cos she's a woman onstage duh (dont laugh at this bit this is the way the world works silly boy). So she snogs him a bit and gives him a hug.

I guess I can't blame her for wanting to have a bit of the Absolutely Awful Doctor Who Everyone Onstage Is Attracted To (definitely including Vanya) Despite The Fact He's A Right Knobhead. Because in an earlier scene her husband (Dad) is upset and she tries to nosh him off to cheer him up, and THAT doesn't even go right. So she gets upset because if she can't nosh off her husband to cheer him up what can she do? (i swear she said some words to this effect).

and i KNOW i could just look on Wikipedia but surely if I've seen the show i ought to have learnt these things??

WHO is this dude who keeps bumbling on for no reason? WHO IS HE?

Something else I understand from Vanya is that the men (Vanya & Doctor) are SO PURE AND VIRTUOUS but they've been corrupted by Dad and HIS AWFUL WIFE and their miserable surroundings. Doctor has an indulgent speech about how he and Vanya are Very Good Men who have been ruined and made coarse by other people. I think I laughed at this bit cos I thought throughout they were both knobs. Also I was very confused cos I didn't even think they were mates? Like they're these weird love-rivals, Doctor is a cocky wolfish dude and Vanya is a very wet blanket who thinks he's better than everyone and then suddenly they've got some sort of intimate history?

So there's obviously this big sort of metaphor at work that probably relates to the Russia Chekov was writing in and if you wanted you could make a boring 'crumbling house of Britain' Brexit comparison (y'know if you're the sort of 'critic' who wants their 'reviews' to be read and make sense lol). There's a kind of power-tension between Dad who *sort of* runs the house and Niece who *technically* owns the house and Vanya who *just really cares about it all*

Theatre Blogging

ok? And I guess I can infer that there were some big scary shifts in economic power at the time. But yknow that's always a fear of people who have big houses and money (omg is that what people mean when they talk about 'universal themes'? Houses and Money. Oh it all makes sense now(?)).

I don't know if the original Russian is this clunky but there are so many lines that are like 'I'm SAD now BECAUSE THIS HAPPENED' or 'YOU are making ME ANGRY'. And oh. Ok, maybe I should just listen to what the characters literally say instead of trying to decipher what their interactions mean. Actually maybe that would be a good technique because the script has a tendency to have the occasional exposition dump in case you're not sure what's going on. There's a big scene around a table where Dad just explains the economic situation and what he wants to do with the house and then Vanya explains that Niece actually owns the house and I wasn't sure if I was supposed to already know any of this.

I'm going to go and read a synopsis after posting this but if anyone wants to tell me what was actually going on then I'd be v grateful.

so ive only seen two Chekovs now but is his thing 'people leave a house at the end of a play'? like The Cherry Orchard ended with people leaving a house and so does this Is That A Thing?

VERDICT: sexist and confusing but very very funny if you dont mind people getting annoyed at u laughing

PS: Leaf Boy 5ever 2k17 idft

CHAPTER 9
REPRESENTATION AND VISIBILITY

> **On Women Directors**
> Jill Dolan, *The Feminist Spectator*
> 7 February 2013
> http://feministspectator.princeton.edu/2013/02/07/on-women-directors/

The status of women directors has received relatively less airtime and press space compared to the perennial woe expressed over the paucity of women playwrights represented on Broadway (or Off, for that matter) and in regional theatre seasons.

Patrick Healy's recent New York Times article, "Staging a Sisterhood"[1] (2/3/11 issue, print edition), draws important notice to a crop of women now working more frequently on higher profile productions. Wonderful artists like Leigh Silverman (*Chinglish* and the upcoming *The Madrid*, with Edie Falco), Anne Kauffman (*Detroit*), Pam MacKinnon (*Clybourne Park* and *Who's Afraid of Virginia Woolf*), Anna D. Shapiro (*August: Osage County*), Rebecca Taichman (*Luck of the Irish*), and many more seem to be finding their way into broader public consciousness, often by collaborating with the host of talented women playwrights now populating the American theatre scene. Annie Baker, Amy Herzog, Kirsten Greenidge, Bathsheba Doran, Madeline George, Katori Hall, Lisa D'Amour, Lisa Kron, Lydia Diamond, Tanya Barfield, and many more women writers are galvanizing audiences with their stories and widening our sense of how theatrical narrative works and the people on whom it can focus.

But when Roundabout Theatre's Artistic Director Todd Haimes tells Healy, "I don't feel an old boy's club exists any more," I fear he's being disingenuous, even though he admits, "but statistics might disagree." While the women interviewed for Healy's article paint a generally hopeful picture of their career prospects (only Tina Landau, who most recently directed Paula Vogel's *Civil War Christmas* at New York Theatre Workshop, calls directing a "male-dominated tradition"), let's admit it: the glass ceiling persists.

"'Can we call it growth when we say the 2011–12 season saw three women directing plays on Broadway as opposed to one woman in 2001–2?' asked Laura Penn, executive director of the union representing stage directors and choreographers." (Healy, NYT, 2/3/13)

No, we frankly can't call it growth. Is the current "trend" a happy bubble that will burst at the next sign of recession, when producers worry about declining profits and fear they can't entrust women with their budgets? And if women directors' fortunes are tied to those of the

---

[1] Jill links to: https://www.nytimes.com/2013/02/03/theater/female-directors-more-prominent-in-new-york.html.

talented women playwrights with whom they collaborate, can we ignore the statistics that continue to track these playwrights' compromised, constrained successes, which rarely happen on Broadway? Theresa Rebeck remains the only woman playwright able to open a play on Broadway without years of development workshops and productions that move from Off-Off to Off- to maybe London to, on the rare occasion for playwrights who aren't Rebeck (or Wendy Wasserstein before her), Broadway.

The *New York Times* also reports that stars like Al Pacino and Scarlett Johansson increasingly wield the real power to bring shows to Broadway, but are mostly interested in revivals that allow them to attempt the roles they've long wanted to play. Pacino felt he was ready to take on Shelly Levene in David Mamet's *Glengarry Glen Ross* and Johansson, too, said "now felt like the right time for me" to play Maggie in *Cat on a Hot Tin Roof*; both are now starring in Broadway revivals. Because Pacino got a hankering to do Mamet, producer Jeffrey Richards bumped his planned Broadway production of Lisa D'Amour's *Detroit*, which was produced (beautifully) last fall at Playwrights Horizons instead.

What does this "star casting" trend mean for plays by women and their collaborating women directors? Richards admitted it was much easier to raise the requisite money to do Mamet, with Pacino in the lead, than it was to finance *Detroit*. And the *Times* article underlines how much power these stars accrue given how hungry producers are for hits in an economic environment in which only 25% of Broadway productions turn a profit. Which producers will risk new plays without star casts – especially those written and directed by women?

Women directors who run theatres perhaps have a bit more sway. Healy cites for example Lynn Meadow at Manhattan Theatre Club and Sarah Benson at Soho Rep. Scanning the regional theatres, we could also mention Diane Paulus, who is interviewed in Healy's article and directs on Broadway mostly by transferring productions from ART, the theatre she runs in Cambridge. Emily Mann, the longtime artistic director at Princeton's McCarter Theatre, transferred *Having Our Say* in 1995 (receiving three Tony nominations in the process) and recently directed *Streetcar Named Desire* with an African American cast on Broadway. Garry Hynes and Mary Zimmerman, two of the handful of women who've ever won the Tony for Best Director, both transferred to Broadway productions they developed with their own companies (the Druid and the Lookingglass, respectively, for *Beauty Queen of Leenane* and *Metamorphosis*).

Women directing new plays somehow seems a natural fit, but how often do we see women directing the canon, especially on Broadway? Karin Coonrod has directed in the Public Theatre's Shakespeare cycle and mounted classics at ART, but for Broadway, Daniel Sullivan gets the nod (*Merchant of Venice*). Susan Stroman and Kathleen Marshall can successfully direct Broadway musicals, probably because they're primarily known as choreographers, which is a more gender-neutral or even female-friendly field. But they've never, to my knowledge, crossed over to direct straight plays (certainly not on Broadway).

The high profile Julie Taymor/*Spiderman: Turn Off the Dark* debacle haunts this scene, too. I don't think Taymor's plight *caused* problems for women theatre directors, but it underlined the issues that already exist. Taymor is enormously talented, a truly visionary theatre and film artist. But the *Spiderman* producers got away with calling her "difficult" and "emotional" in ways that would never pertain to a male director, even if he was being stubborn and highhanded and running millions of dollars over budget. Gender stereotypes continue to haunt women theatre artists of all stripes in ways that keep that glass ceiling hovering low.

For those of us interested in innovative theatre; in plays that tell new stories in new ways; in directors with a visual sense that makes something vivid and new out of the old proscenium stage, Broadway might not be the best place to expect the women artists we admire to succeed. But the resources available on Broadway, not to mention the salaries, working conditions, benefits, and essential visibility, make it difficult for women directors, playwrights, and designers not to aspire to those mid-town stages.

As Healy's article demonstrates, women directors and playwrights are flourishing elsewhere, as they have for so long. I loved writer/director Tina Satters' *Seagull (Thinking of you)* at the New Ohio Theatre during January's Coil Festival in New York. Satter created stunningly original stage pictures, and her colloquial, queer adaptation of Chekhov's play sounded poignant and new, performed by a female and gender-ambiguous cast that she directed with warmth and empathy. I'd be delighted to see Satter write and direct in a large, resource-rich forum like Broadway.

I also love the work created by Page 73, and the now-disbanded 13P, and the thriving, determined Clubbed Thumb, and the increasingly well-received, significant, venerable Women's Project. Their production of Laura Marks's *Bethany*, directed by Gaye Taylor Upchurch at City Center, is a smart, beautifully executed production of a play with a razor sharp, feminist critique of the American economy. The Women's Project even makes its own bid for star casting in *Bethany*, with America Ferrera (of TV's *Ugly Betty* fame) proving her stage chops in the leading role. Why doesn't this production transfer to Broadway?

Like it or not, even in 2013, our stereotypes of "the theatre director" continue to be male. *Smash*, the NBC TV series created by Theresa Rebeck, began its second season last night. The preview press touted its new show runner, Josh Safran, fresh from *Gossip Girl*, and promised a new and improved run of episodes. But all the old tired theatre stereotypes persist so far. Derek (Jack Davenport), the mercurial director of *Bombshell*, the musical suffering development hell, gets called out for sexually harassing his cast members, after bedding one would-be leading lady and then almost seducing the other. He's "the director" writ large, the auteur whose vision won't be tamed; the cruel taskmaster whose exacting standards "get" the requisite performances from his women, even after he makes them cry; and of course he's white, male, and heterosexual.

This stereotype *isn't* true – we *know* that all Broadway directors aren't Derek. But the point is that the stereotype persists. When people think of a Broadway director, the image of someone like Derek is already there, intractable, resisting efforts to erase it or to remake it into something more diverse. Those stereotypes can be very persuasive in the imaginations of people bankrolling risky, expensive projects.

It's not that women directors don't have the pedigree. Of the directors profiled in Eric Grode's sidebar, "Meet the Directors",[2] which accompanies Healy's *Times* article, many refer

---

[2] Jill links to: https://www.nytimes.com/2013/02/03/theater/female-directors-present-past-and-future.html.

to graduate degrees from Yale School of Drama or NYU's Tisch School of the Arts. These women have impeccable credentials and they're impressively talented. What else could explain their relative lack of power and Broadway exposure *but* the glass ceiling?

Don't you wish we could retire that old metaphor? Don't you wish the glass ceiling would shatter like a trick stage prop, never to be reassembled? Without that barrier, what kinds of stratospheric success might women directors and playwrights accomplish? Wouldn't it be great to know?

Imagine if women were employed regularly and visibly at all levels of American theatre. Imagine if they were routinely trusted to share their talent, their vision, their methods, their dramaturgical skill, and their emotional, political, and intellectual acuity. How might American theatre change?

Of course, many of us have been practicing that "what if" exercise for decades. Are we still stuck here, excited about articles that feature women we've followed for years? Wouldn't it be something if we *didn't* have to applaud simple attention to women, if their theatre work was expected, typical, *unremarkable*? If we could just talk about the work, instead of about the fact that it's been produced at all? Years ago, I wrote a piece that took an ungenerous swipe at Julia Miles, the founder and then artistic director of the Women's Project, because she imagined a time when her theatre's advocacy for women would no longer be necessary. Decades later, I have to say I know what she meant – and I agree.

Would that companies like the Women's Project could persist not because they *have* to, but because they *want* to continue creating fertile space for women theatre artists to learn and grow. Would that the glass ceiling could be smashed and replaced by a ladder on which successful women would help one another into positions of increased power and visibility and that they could all *stay there* and thrive. Would that the persistently unequal demographics that describe the gender (let alone race and ethnicity) of those working in the theatre would finally balance out, so that we wouldn't be so thankful for just a few women's successes. 50/50 in 2020 indeed.

Call me liberal; call me utopian; call me, maybe. Or call me a feminist critic on a life-long mission that's not over, yet.

"a fiercely provocative, insightful mediation on race"
Mike Lew
16 May 2013
http://www.mikelew.com/thoughts-on-the-theater-blog/a-fiercely-provocative-insightful-mediation-on-race

---

I keep seeing these plays that get heralded as "a fiercely provocative, insightful mediation on race". But invariably I come away from those plays feeling disappointed and somewhat appalled. The thing is, I'd *love* to see a fiercely provocative, insightful mediation on race. It's just that I haven't seen many.

Everyone's aesthetics are different, and what seems hollow to me just might be revelatory to others. So I think it's worthwhile to go ahead and define what – in my book – would constitute insightfulness, in the hopes of pushing the dialogue forward a little. I don't mean to sh*t on any one play in particular. Rather, just like how one critic felt compelled to draw attention to the trope of the "manic pixie dream girl" in film, I feel compelled to point out certain tropes and patterns that are being repeated in race plays. Because I think we're settling for too little complexity, and we keep telling the same old story.

Here are my thoughts on that, in four parts.

1) The plays we herald as "a fiercely provocative, insightful mediation on race" tend to keep coming from one race. Let me be clear on what exactly I'm saying: I'm not saying that white people shouldn't talk about race. They should absolutely talk about race and have important insights to offer. Also, I'm not saying that other races *don't* talk about race. It's just that those plays don't as often end up in the zeitgeist. Inevitably, the most prominent, talked-about, celebrated race plays are most often plays by white dudes. But if we hope to glean further insights on race, we ought to be hearing and championing more than just one perspective. Artists are going to create the art they're most passionate about. But we as audience members (and producers and critics) need to be far more omnivorous in what we want to consume.

2) A play in which male protagonists devolve into racial epithets is not provocative or insightful. It's *sensationalist*, but not insightful. Too often with race plays the critics and audience conflate a *strong emotional response* with *insight*. These racial epithet scenes are essentially a melodramatic, hollow depiction of race in extremis designed to elicit a gut response from the audience. But in my heart of hearts I just don't believe that at base we're all a bunch of incorrigible bigots who would happily scream racial epithets at each other were it not for the polite veneer of society. The trope of "everyone is a deep-down racist" is hundreds of years old. Seeing it onstage again and again only reinforces our sense of "the other", deepening our animosities and suspicions. Sure, it's titillating and dramatic, but what's going to move the dialogue FORWARD?

3) Most onstage depictions of race politics in America are far too simplistic. Invariably these plays consider black-white relations only. Which is fine – that's a powerful subject with deep historical resonance. But if our entire canon of "fiercely provocative, insightful mediations on race" consists entirely of black-white relations, where do Asians and Latinos fit into that picture? What about immigrants, and the effects of immigrant populations? What about the after-effects of colonialism? Most importantly, where does biracial/multiracial identity fit into that picture? Biracials are the fastest-growing ethnic group in America, but you rarely ever see it depicted onstage, because we like to categorize people as one-race-only. In other words, when it comes to depicting race, we're thinking too binary, too black-and-white.

4) This is true for all plays, but for race plays in particular, I think we need to consider VERY CAREFULLY: what is the *meta-narrative* that is being presented in this play? Ultimately at root, thematically, does this play further our understanding of race, or does it play into our already-held assumptions? These heralded plays have a whole lot of craft: good characters, strong emotions, plot twists, etc. But that craft distracts us from a dangerous meta-narrative

that's providing very little in the way of real insights. From an analytical perspective, by and large you'll find that a whole lot of race plays are essentially telling the exact same story, which is this:

"I don't mean to be racist. But sometimes I say stuff that you think is racist. But hey: you're a little racist too. So let's just call it square. Are we square??"

Our race relations are far too complex and the pains too deep to just wash over everything, call it post-racial, and essentially say, again and again, "Hey this political correctness stuff is a burden: can't we all just move past that?" It's the same dangerous argument that we place onto women in regards to our gender politics. "We did all that women's lib stuff! These culture wars are exhausting! So let's just call it square. Are we square??"

No, we're not square. And it's not going to be square, ever. And the worst thing we can do given the still-persistent racial (and gender and sexual) inequities in this country is keep presenting narratives that essentially gloss over the problem. The worst thing we can do is champion a set of plays that provide only the narrowest of perspectives.

We settle for too little when it comes to a race play. We see a big fight with a lot of dirty words and we gasp and we call it insightful. But what would actually provide insight, what would actually be provocative would be hearing perspectives and stories we haven't heard before, so that we can adapt our ideas about race, so that we actually learn something. We move on from racial tensions not by pretending we're past them, or by pretending that race doesn't exist, or by relying on stale old tropes. We move on by addressing race in a thoughtful, considered, proactive, nuanced way. Pluralistically.

Wondering about The Fiddler On The Roof at Arena Stage

Jill Dolan, *The Feminist Spectator*
17 December 2014
http://feministspectator.princeton.edu/2014/12/17/wondering-about-fiddler-on-the-roof-at-arena-stage/

The 50th anniversary of *Fiddler on the Roof* has been celebrated amply this past year, including with a Princeton symposium Stacy Wolf (FS2) and I organized last fall. Alisa Solomon's marvelous book, *Wonder of Wonders: A Cultural History of Fiddler on the Roof*, beautifully chronicles the musical's origins and its evolution into a cultural touchstone for American Jews, one that often replaces or stands in for religious knowledge and practice.

I anticipated Molly Smith's production of *Fiddler* at Arena Stage in Washington, DC, where she is the long-standing artistic director, because she's done very well directing other classic Golden Age musicals. Her production of *Oklahoma!* during Arena's 2011–12 season was gorgeously re-imagined, with a multiracial cast that added thrilling new dimensions to the story about farmers and cowmen on the American prairie. Using the challenging theatre-in-the-round architecture that gives Arena its name, Smith managed to bring vital new life and resonance to the show.

Likewise, her production of *My Fair Lady* at the Shaw Festival at Niagara-on-the-Lake in 2011 made that show much more than an old chestnut. She instilled in the musical a vivid sense of ironic humor, brisk pacing, and characters with a lot of feminist verve, making it, like her *Oklahoma!*, come alive with new meanings and colors, as well as a whole lot of pleasure. That production, too, was cast with people of color in major and subsidiary roles, making the show look relevant and contemporary.

Smith says in her program note for *Fiddler*, "Many of you know I often cast in a cross-cultural way because I believe this is the world we live in." What a shock, then, to see her production of this musical performed by only white actors. She says that for *Fiddler*, "I was very interested in casting in a culturally specific way – through the Jewish and Russian point of view. In this way we go from the individual to the universal."

What a fascinating idea! But, with respect, I'll say I was hard pressed to find the "culturally specific casting" in the production, since very few of the actors seemed to be Jewish. Okay, I know: how can we tell? And isn't it essentialist to assume from a name or an actor's photo in a program, or even from their appearance on stage, who's Jewish? Especially if "Jewishness" is more about culture and religion than it is about race? (Although this is an on-going debate and point of discussion in Jewish studies.) Or by "culturally specific", did Smith mean Eastern European in origin?

I ask these questions as a Jewish woman whose name is "Dolan", after all. My grandfather's family name was Dolinsky. He was born in Poland, but when his family immigrated to the States and he was later drafted to serve in the First World War, the Army changed his name to Dolan. My father tells me that my Zedie Jake was fond of his new name. He enjoyed having an Irish name because he thought it made him sound more American (since, of course, the Irish became white before the Jews).

For me, the misrecognition of my name as Irish has meant a lifetime of trying to convey my Jewishness through identity performance. I use my hands a lot, I raise my eyebrows, and I inflect my sentences in such a way that I hope will *read* as Jewish to my interlocutors. Being recognized as Jewish always seemed to me better than passing as gentile. I was afraid of what people might say in front of me, if they assumed I wasn't Jewish. I was afraid that what I might hear would make me feel a traitor to my race or might scar my own sense of self. Nonetheless, all that hand-waving wasn't enough to keep me from overhearing anti-Semitic jokes when I was in high school theatre classes at the Pittsburgh Playhouse because my fellow actors thought there were no Jews present. And despite the hand-waving, I still have to come out as Jewish whenever it seems important and necessary, or when I feel people dancing around that part of my identity, wondering.

So what does it mean for Smith to cast her *Fiddler* as "culturally specific", with actors named Jonathan Hadary (Tevye), Ann Arvia (Golde), Dorea Schmidt (Tzeitel – could be Jewish?), Hannah Corneau (Hodel), Maria Rizzo (Chava), Shayna Blass (Shprintze – most likely Jewish!), and Maya Brettell (Bielke – maybe Jewish?)? Any of them could be Jewish, for all I know. But when Yente is played by Valerie Leonard, the cast member who most seemed to miss the musicality of the (contrived) Eastern European lilt Joseph Stein (book) and Sheldon Harnick (lyrics) wrote for their characters, what does this signal about cultural specificity?

Leonard could be Jewish and simply tone-deaf to the character's Yiddishisms. If the actor can't *play* Jewish and/or is not "really" Jewish, why not have her played by an African American actor adept enough at *acting* to perform the authenticity required to make this musical succeed and make sense? Because black skin isn't culturally specific to the Russian shtetl? But swarthy Italian complexions and curly black Italian hair can better "pass" as Jewish?

I really do mean to wonder (no pun intended) and not entirely to criticize. I note that Jenna Weissman Joselit, a Jewish Studies scholar who runs the program at George Washington University and spoke (beautifully) at our *Fiddler* symposium at Princeton, receives special thanks in the program. And Dr. Yohanan Petrovsky-Shtern (who is, I find via Google, a professor of Jewish Studies at Northwestern University and recently published a book called *The Golden Age Shtetl*) is also thanked. Ariel Warmflash, an Arena Theatre teaching artist whose blog post[3] on the Reconstructionist Rabbinical College web site leads me to believe she's Jewish, is listed in the credits as a "cultural consultant". Perhaps she helped dialect and vocal coach Lynn Watson with the rolling r's and intonations of the Russian accents the cast affects with greater or lesser success. But does *accent* signal cultural specificity, especially when the songs that compose *Fiddler*'s soul aren't written that way?

Does being Jewish even give you a special cultural purchase on the musical, when Solomon's book and Harnick's quote in Arena's program insist that the point of the musical was to show that "Jews are just like everybody else"? (See also Robert Brustein's New Republic discussion of the show[4] and Solomon's book.) Given Smith's directing history and Arena's location in a predominantly African American city, foregoing multiracial casting to be "true" to what seems to me a misbegotten sense of cultural authenticity represents a theatrical and political misstep.

But what does the production bring us in any case? All the pleasure of *Fiddler* remains intact, from the pedagogical and rousing beauty of the opening song, "Tradition", to the mournful resignation of "Anatevka", when the shtetl-dwellers round up their belongings and leave their humble homes before the pogrom burns them down. Hadary, a man slight of build and fairly short for a role typically cast with a rounder, more physically imposing type, underplays Tevye. He's casual with the glorious "If I were a Rich Man", refusing to embody Zero Mostel's iconic hands-above-his-head hip-shaking da-da-dee's and deedle-dums, which makes the number feel tossed off instead of heart-felt. He speaks in a Brooklyn accent, underlining perhaps, as Solomon argues in her book, that the musical was meant for those who had already assimilated to America and for whom it provided a nostalgic rereading of the shtetl from which many of the musical's Jewish audiences' ancestors might have come.

But Hadary's New York-isms and his rather fey interpretation of Tevye aren't fleshed out enough to be refreshing or original. Because he's determined not to imitate Mostel (or Topol, the Israeli actor who played the role in Norman Jewison's popular film adaptation), he throws away many of the character's best lines and performs the patriarch as though he's already

---

[3] Jill links to: https://www.ritualwell.org/blog/odds-are-dont-look-far.
[4] Jill links to: http://www.nybooks.com/articles/2014/12/18/fiddle-shtick/.

cowed by his daughters' impossible marriage requests. If Tevye has no fire or fight, his debates with his daughters and with his god seem beside the point, pleading little performances whose endings are already known.

And of course, they are. Most of the audience at Arena during the matinee I saw knew how *Fiddler* ends, except for perhaps a few of the children. After all, it's a classic. The suspense isn't in what happens; it's in how the actors and director and designers get there. Hadary missed opportunities to surprise us with his interpretation, and because of his size, Tevye often seemed the least, instead of the most, important person on stage.

Sometimes, that worked to the production's benefit. "Do You Love Me?", the love song between Tevye and the dubious Golde, was sweetly understated. Arvia's Golde was the larger of the couple in Smith's production. Her ample heft softened Golde's edges and she played the archetypal Jewish wife without the fatigued sarcasm many interpreters bring to the role. Their duet allowed Tevye to truly wonder if his wife loves him, and let Golde acquiesce to what felt like the warm surprise of admitting it, after 25 years.

"Sabbath Prayer", too, felt more familial than magisterial, as Tevye and Golde stood on opposite sides of their simple wooden table to offer their benediction, with their daughters and Perchik, the Kiev revolutionary, gathered around. The set design and Smith's use of the stage lent themselves to this more intimate, domestically focused interpretation, as scenes were decorated with few props and several benches that were moved easily around. Red apples in a basket or clutched in a character's hand supplied some color and texture against the muted tones of Paul Tazewell's ragged shtetl costumes. In "Sabbath Prayer" and in the wedding scene, actors carried candles that also warmed the space and provided flickering adornments to lighting designer Colin K. Bills's sharply crafted spaces. Smith amplified the sense of community by placing actors with lit candles above the audience around the back of the theatre, too.

"Anatevka" benefited from a similar warm under-playing, as Tevye and his neighbors slouched on the wooden floor boards and benches that comprised set designer Todd Rosenthal's stage, underlining the resigned but somehow stalwart determination that the song implies. Lacking the revolve that typically moves Tevye and his family and their cart away from their home, Smith directed the cast to walk in an ever-expanding circle around the low ramps that encircled the stage, finally leaving the shtetl by stepping off the platform into the aisles of the audience and disappearing through the auditorium. It's a nice touch, representing the Jews of Anatevka dispersing around the globe.

But aside from the perhaps purposefully diminished Tevye and Smith's attempt to render cultural specificity, this production doesn't add anything very new to the canon of 50 years of *Fiddler*. It all works; the daughters are especially good in "Matchmaker" and in their individual numbers, begging their father to let them marry whom they wish (and singing beautifully). The women and girls who play them convey their affection for one another, and for their ambivalent father and warm mother, very well. But they don't add new notes to their characters, nor do they offer much in the way of the performance of Jewishness.

That said, I was struck in this production by how pedagogical the musical is, and by how much of it performs Jewish rituals. Perhaps this is what Smith meant by cultural specificity, though I still don't find those ethnic particularities in the performances so much as in how the scenes are constructed by Stein, Block, and Harnick and directed by Smith. "Tradition" is such a good way to instruct the audience about ritual garments like *tallit* (prayer shawls), and in what it basically means to study Torah, and in the strict gender division of Orthodox Jewish life (although Anatevka's residents always look more Orthodox than they really are, since the creative team was writing for assimilated, secular Jews).

The wedding scene, too, is pedagogical, as Tzeitel and Motel are lifted on chairs, the stage bisected by stanchions that keep the men from the women until Perchik insists on challenging tradition and dancing with Hodel. The Bottle Dance, which Solomon explicates brilliantly in her book, is a tradition the original choreographer Jerome Robbins invented, through his ethnographic observation of Jewish weddings in preparation for the show. Though fabricated, the muscular, masculine dance – which insists on the heteronormativity of *Fiddler*'s wedding scene even as it performs a lovely, queer homosociality – has been adopted as a Jewish ritual tradition that persists even now at weddings and bar and bat mitzvahs.

I had fun at *Fiddler*. How can you not? Talk about essentialism: I cried through the whole thing, moved by the music, the dialogue, the predictable, inexorable situations, and by the man with the fiddle who haunts Tevye's every decision and goes with him to America, carrying a bit of home and a continually diminishing sense of the shtetl along. Is it my Jewishness that causes me to cry through *Fiddler*? Is it my own nostalgia for singing the score around the piano with my family through the years? Or my nostalgia for singing "Sabbath Prayer" with Stacy at the occasion of one of our nieces' baby-naming ceremonies? Or my memories of performing in our family living room as each of the characters when I was growing up, regardless of gender, and acting them all out the way I thought best? Or my second-hand recall of Stacy's stories about staging the Fruma Sarah dream-sequence with her sister, Allie, when they were kids?

(By the way, Smith stages that scene beautifully here. The characters in Tevye's dream wear surreal animal masks. When the dead Fruma Sarah appears, she rises from the middle of the bed in a column of tulle as a monstrous, huge figure that towers over Tevye and Golde to proclaim her curse on Tzeitel's marriage to Lazar Wolf. Then she disappears back into the bedding the way she came. This was the most brilliant interpretation of this number Stacy and I have ever seen. It was terrifying and exhilarating all at once, even when you know exactly how the iconic number ends.)

In the theatre's on line dramaturgical notes, Hadary claims,

> "I grew up hearing the Tevye stories of Sholem Aleichem. In fact, my family members could well be characters in the play. So there was a lot of connection to the material. This whole production, of Fiddler on the Roof, here, for me, brings together an awful lot of threads in my life – my ancestry, my whole life as an actor, my family, my Washington roots, plus it's simply as good a role as has ever been written for a man in the theater."

Okay, so he's Jewish after all. Does that secure something authentic about his performance? I don't really think so.

I can't quite explain my "Jewish" nostalgia for *Fiddler*, or why exactly I care whether its characters are played by Jews. There's something about ethnic spectacle that Smith's production both panders to and explicates, a bid for authenticity in which multiracial bodies might have gotten in her way and taken focus from the "real" Jewishness she thinks she's invoking here. But if Smith is going to attempt cultural specificity, then I suppose I can revert to ethnic form and say that most of these actors didn't "feel" Jewish, that the production didn't evoke anything particularly authentic in its rendering of shtetl life, cultural consultants and scholars aside. But then, Solomon would say it was never meant to be authentic, but was crafted as an American memory of an unknowable past, one safely left behind with the Russians as Eastern European Jews immigrated to the new world and looked forward, never back.

Why I Wrote True Brits
Vinay Patel, *shut up and deal*
3 February 2015
https://vinayskpatel.wordpress.com/2015/02/03/why-i-wrote-true-brits/

I'm fucking terrified.

True Brits opens tomorrow and as the writer it's a funny sort of helplessness to that terror. At this point, pretty much nothing you can do will change anything, save for you pulling some "oh captain, my captain" speech out of your arse if necessary. I've hauled boxes with texts, sat it in final rehearsals and, to busy the writing side, I've responded to a fair few interviews. A question that comes up more often than I thought has been: "Why did you write this play?". Each time I answered, I talked about wanting to capture certain feelings but it is a bit more complex than that and I wanted to elaborate on a few of them here. Not all of them are good-minded artistic or social reasons but I will try to be honest.

Contains Minor Spoilers

REASON 1) BROWN DUDES BEING NORMAL

Not just in the life of the character, but in the action of a piece of drama. I can't tell you how sick I was of seeing entirely regressive families, drug dealers, terrorism, arranged marriages, honour killings etc. It was as if these were the only spheres you could have a main Asian character (no, that doctor character with a few lines every episode doesn't count). Not that these don't have a place or aren't interesting to delve into but none of it chimed with the reality of my life or young people like me that I knew ... at the very least, where was the funnies? Where was the getting on with it? Of course there's a sort of confusing cultural violence to being an integrated kid of immigrant families. You get pulled every which way from a young age and after events such as 7/7 you are made to choose in lots of tiny little ways – but honestly, most of the time you just want to hang out with your mates and you don't think about it. And I hadn't really seen that reality portrayed (Ishy Din's *Snookered* a notable exception) in a play.

It wasn't until I watched a rehearsal yesterday that I remembered how much that frustration has fed itself into the form of the show. What you get for the first half is a slight mis-sell to the blurb. Yes, it talks about the Olympics for a bit, but it's mainly just a kid doing what kids do. His background inflects Rahul's life, there's a little in every scene, but it never dominates until the second half. Even then, it's much harder to be treated as a normal kid by those around you than it is for him or to, say, resist an urge to hop off to Syria or escape an arranged marriage.

Not, perhaps, the most radical thing in the world for most people – to have a character be normal – but I can't stress how important this was to me to have snapshots of a complex emotional life in a different sort of Asian character that's fun to be with in a theatrical space (mostly anyway . . .)

Following on from this . . .

REASON 2) BROWN DUDE BEING KINDA MIDDLE CLASS

It's a small one this but I'm always amused when people tell me they're glad that theatre's trying to get past its "middle-class moment": ask anyone of a minority background if it ever existed for them.

In timely fashion, Kayvan Novak has written about similar in the Guardian yesterday. This in particular struck a chord for me:

> I think I decided . . . that I was not prepared to have my identity dictated to me. That simply "being myself" was never going to satisfy me or get the job done. That the odds were stacked against me somehow, that the world was not about to adapt to me, but that I needed to adapt to the world. I had to fool the world into accepting me. I didn't seem to fit the mould of my idols. My idols were all white or black, for a start, and working class, and northern, or American, drug addicts, rock stars, the same as anyone's. But definitely not brown. I wanted to belong. But I never did. I was lost.

I felt all of this as a young man, and it was the loneliest place to be in since I had no way of expressing it to people who didn't quite get it. Writing *True Brits* and seeing the responses to it have made me feel a little less lost and a lot less alone.

REASON 3) I WANTED BOTH THE FEAR AND THE HOPE TO EXIST IN THE CULTURAL MEMORY BECAUSE I THINK IT WILL, IN A TINY WAY, MAKE THIS COUNTRY A BETTER PLACE TO LIVE

So this is the wankiest of the three but I can't say it wasn't part of my process. I think a lot about how our cultural memories are affected by the arts. I'd wager the way a lot of people think about Vietnam is affected by the movies about it. It's why there's so much discussion around *American Sniper*. I hadn't seen anything that captured what it was like to be a brown teen in this country but in London specifically after 7/7. Stuff like see-through backpacks, relentless stop and searches and people seeing a beard and moving seat will fall away from people's minds as it probably **should** but you want to be able to look back and have some repository where it can be recalled. If you don't, you're not moving on from something, you're just sort of erasing it. I wanted to be able to point to a piece of cultural work and go "I feel like a well-integrated fella but fuck me, sometimes it was bloody hard work to be the (relatively) nice guy that I am today, and likely harder than you might otherwise comprehend."

BUT, and this is perhaps the most important thing behind this play for me. I am hopeful about my place in this country. In fact, in a slightly unfashionable way, I think I love it here. Not ironically, and not in a "God Bless America/All Hail The Motherland" way. Rather, like an album that catches your heart when you're young and remains the soundtrack to your life, I feel it's always going to be a part of me. I'll always step off a plane after a holiday and whilst I'll complain about the weather I'll secretly want to wrap myself in the inevitable cold blast. It's home.

Being repeatedly called a 'paki' as a kid, having my nose smashed in by various goons as a teenager, being told by sniffy posh bastards that I deserve airport searches as a young adult … this has all tested that feeling, but I've come out of it with a strong affection. I know this is not unproblematic. Britain's ridden with problems, with corrosive ideologies, and its worse instincts are almost sort of an integral part of it. But I also know I want to be responsible for doing something about that. I want to do what I can to make it better. I think attempting to create a mostly harmonious ethnically and culturally diverse country is one of the nobler projects that can exist, we do do it relatively well here and y'know, it's basically the future of the planet.

There's a knobby, aggressive way to do this kind of thing (Bobby Jindal, I'm looking at you). But erasing difference will never sit properly. The post mass-immigration world is necessarily messy and confused and it's hard to deal with that for some, but embracing and becoming comfortable with that confusion (confusion is a big part of *True Brits*) is the only way to go. Zadie Smith, a person far cleverer than me, frames this idea well in her lecture about Obama.[5] Speaking in different tongues isn't deceptive – it's how we really operate, so seeking to polarise identity into "this is genuine, this is not" is how you end up with extremists in every sense. They claim to provide solidity and easy comprehension but really give nothing but a purist fantasy that isn't honestly human. Confusion is scary, but it's not a mush or a nothing, nor only endorsed by the tabloid-favourite "cosmopolitan, multicultural elite". Being comfortable with confusion shouldn't be something that's out of the hands of, say, a white dude from Birmingham who's had a trauma free upbringing. It goes all ways. To my mind, if something exists where you live, it's all fair game to embrace and love and claim as a part of you. I feel like the reverse of that glorious Goodness Gracious Me sketch – Kebab shop? British. Italian Deli? British. Not wrap-it-in-a-flag British, just "you're both here, you're both each others to enjoy, and you're both re-shaped by each other in a combination unique to where we are" kind of way where the British imagery and terminology becomes the platform on which to host all of that.

In the play the Olympics stands in for that desire because my experience of it was seeing people wanting to be able to love the smorgasbord country they lived in, and refreshingly without a lot of the jingoistic shit or old markers of 'True' Britishness. Welsh and don't fancy singing the national anthem – fine. A black Muslim immigrant – super. Mixed-race from Sheffield – love it. Both sides of your family been here for yonks – fab. All of these are us and ours.

---

[5] Vinay links to: https://soundcloud.com/nybooks/zadie-smith-speaking-in-tongues.

Theatre Blogging

That's what I hope the future of this place looks like and it's what a lot of British Asians want and strongly believe too, if you look at the research. I don't prescribe whether that hope is naive or worthwhile or necessarily interrogated enough – but it seems like a good place to start and I just needed to show it exists, even if it's just to myself.

> **In the Depths of British Theatrical Racism @the_printroom**
>
> Erin Quill, *fairyprincessdiaries*
> 16 December 2016
> https://fairyprincessdiaries.com/2016/12/16/in-the-depths-of-british-racism-the_printroom/
>
> *An edit has been made to this post at the request of the publisher.*

The Fairy Princess would like to wish everyone a happy and healthy Holiday Season and is cheerfully slamming the door on 2016.

There have been some good things happening in terms of Asian Americans on Broadway – for example, the opening of **IN TRANSIT** on Broadway, featuring the wonderful **Telly Leung** in a lead role.

There was the announcement that the Broadway cast of **GROUNDHOG DAY** is complete and is featuring **Raymond J. Lee** and **Vishal Vaidya** (making his Broadway debut) in the cast.

The first shots of **Philippa Soo** as the lead in **AMELIE**, which will make it's Broadway bow in 2017 are out, and they are *charming*.

And *FINALLY*, TFP's *favorite*, **Miss Isabella Russo** was featured in **THE TOYCRACKER** extended theatrical commercial for a major retailer, where she co-starred along with Chrissie Teigen and John Legend! (**TFP** knew this already but could not let the cat out of the bag, but she did say that this was a kid to keep an eye on!)

So of course with all that goodness abounding, there has to be some *abject f*ckery* coming our way, and of course, it's coming at us from a few different angles.

First off, **The Hollywood Reporter** did one of their year end wrap up discussions at a table, and they asked a bunch of white guys how to not make an animated film not chock o block full of stereotypes.[6]

The only bright light in this conversation which boils down to **"All the White Guy had to do to appease the other people in the world and what a drag that was . . ."**

is that apparently John Lassester, the Disney Animation Chief, chose to demand that his team on **MOANA** (which, truly is beautiful), do actual research on the culture that they were going to be exploring in this film.

---

[6] Erin links to: https://www.hollywoodreporter.com/features/animation-roundtable-seth-rogen-6-more-avoiding-ethnic-stereotypes-creating-ugly-cute-princ.

Seemingly the recipient of that 'enforcement', kind of resented it, but it wound up enhancing the film!

Imagine! Knowledge is actually good for you! This is soooo *anti-alt-2016* this concept, but there you go.

Asking and employing actual Pacific Islanders to inform on a film that is about Pacific Islanders can help make the film deeper.

It is still a 'Pan-Pacific Islander' take on this story, however it is not a documentary, and it is closer than they have gotten since **MULAN**.

They had sensitivity with the casting of the voice actors and there is no forced romance in **MOANA**, which is *great* for little girls to have as an image in their heads.

Although it seems like he much preferred the non-research his team invested in when they did **ALADDIN** – had they done that research, they may have learned that that particular story was *not* part of the original Arabian Nights, but was added later by a Frenchman.

Also that the story of Aladdin was supposed to take place in a border town along The Silk Road in . . . wait for it, China.

Also, **TFP** does **NOT GET** how asking Seth Rogan about sensitivity in animation really is justified since, in his animated film coming out, he has a character named *FIREWATER*.

Think about it.

So there you go, Hollywood enjoying the perks of having people of color in their stories, but not having people of color direct those films, or even inviting them to the conversation.

Where was the Director of **KUNG FU PANDA 3 – Jennifer Yuh Nelson?**

Where was the Director of **SANJAY'S SUPER TEAM – Sanjay Patel?**

Tired. So tired.

Also hot on the heels of the aftermath of **BREXIT**, comes this offering from the U.K. – **In The Depths of Dead Love, presented by The Print Room at The Coronet coming in January.**

It is a play. Ah, a play. **TFP** loves plays.

Enjoys plays. Does plays.

Where, she wonders, is this play set, perchance?

Specifically? Let us go to their website:

> **Set in ancient China,** *In the Depths of Dead Love* **tells of a poet exiled from the Imperial Court & the favour of the Emperor, who scrapes a living by renting his peculiar property – a bottomless well – to aspiring suicides. Among these is a married couple who exert an appalling influence over him. Told through Barker's celebrated exquisite language and affecting humour,** *In the Depths of Dead Love* **is the witty and poignant tale of a man facing an impossible dilemma.**

Ah, a play set in **CHINA!**

OF COURSE! WHY NOT?

CHINA of course, had a ton of intrigue and politics, and is one of the oldest countries around from which to draw cultural inference, and stories about China should of course, be told.

One problem.

There is no one, **NO ONE** in this play on the stage, who happens to be of East Asian heritage.

Again, this is a play **SET IN CHINA**, telling a story of **CHINESE PEOPLE**, and *there are zero British East Asian Actors in the play*.

How many?

Zero.

Do we really have to go through this *again?*

Do we really have to try and figure out that China is a real and actual place?

Do we need to again, look at map?

All right, esteemed playwright Howard Barker, here is a map of CHINA. **TFP** will even pick a Dynasty.

Here is one from the HAN Dynasty. BOOM!

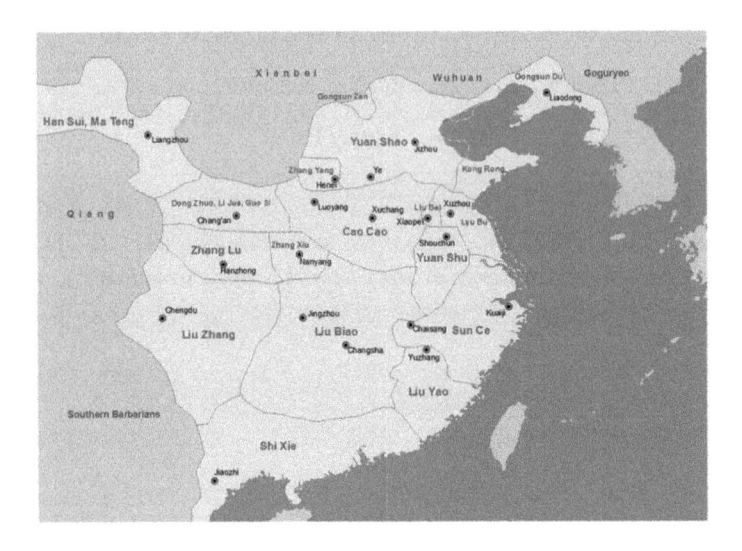

WHY do we need, *again*, to look at images of Ancient China?

Also, *which specific part of Ancient China*, my dear Mr. Barker?

Because ... not listed. Not listed in the information **TFP** was able to glean – so it's just some *ephemeral* part of Ancient China – *no Dynasty*, no actual researched period – which, btw, are all available to find out.

List of Chinese Dynasties to 600 C.E.
- Prehistoric Times–1.7 million years – the 21st century BCE
- Xia Dynasty – 21st–16th century BCE
- Shang Dynasty – 16th–11th century BCE
- Zhou Dynasty – Western Zhou (11th century–771 BCE)
- Eastern Zhou – Spring and Autumn Period (770–476 BCE)
- Warring States Period (476–221 BCE)
- Qin Dynasty – (221–206 BCE)
- Han Dynasty – Western Han (206 BCE–24 CE)
- Eastern Han – (25–220 CE)
  - Three Kingdoms Period – (220–280)
  - Jin Dynasty – Western Jin (265–316)
    Eastern Jin (317–420)
  - Northern and Southern Dynasties – Northern Dynasty (386–581)
    Southern Dynasty (420–589)
- Sui Dynasty – (581–618 CE)

On the magic of the Interweb.

So we know a few things – aside from no British East Asians on the stage – we know that the costumes are going to be wrong. Why?

Because it's *Amorphous Ancient China*.

In *Amorphous Ancient China* anything can happen. It's like an Animated film. Wardrobes can talk. Dragons appear from nowhere and cause documented events to occur.

Matt Damon can save China in *Amorphous Ancient China*.

Tilda Swinton becomes an Ancient Asian One in *Amorphous Ancient China*. *(Which is potentially when Tibet's status which all the fighting is currently about was more or less defined, but let's recognize that really doesn't matter to them)*

In *Amorphous Ancient China*, Scarlett Johansson can become Japanese – it is just THAT Amorphous and magical!

Because where countries lie on maps simply does not matter when words like Ancient and China are in the same sentence.

Let's put it this way – *in Amorphous Ancient China, Elvis is probably still alive and ruling over it from a tricked out rumpus room in a basement room in The Forbidden City!!!!!*

It. Is. Magical.

People fly in *Amorphous Ancient China*.[7]

Why not? It's Amorphous.

---

[7] Erin includes an image from *Crouching Tiger, Hidden Dragon* (2000), in which two characters fight while hovering in treetops.

Theatre Blogging

The air is different in an 'exotic' and 'ancient' way which causes Caucasians to become inebriated with the possibility of co-opting every bit of the Chinese experience and then white-washing the Chinese faces from the stories they want to tell!

After all, why have Chinese faces tell stories about things that happened in China?

That just makes it all far too Chinese, right?

Too many Chinese people in China and what DO you get?

Like, over a billion Chinese people.

Who can devalue the US dollar any time they choose.

Just sayin'.

How DARE 'we' think that British East Asian faces should represent heritage that actual British East Asians have?

Why, we are upstarts! We are non-Public School, non-gentrified Gentlemen's Club out of order!

The bravado of us! The notion!

Why, the sentiment that British East Asians should portray East Asians is enough to send the women to the powder room in a fit of the Vapors!

Corset strings must be loosened!

The whale bone industry will be in jeopardy!

What WILL the mere presence of these faces lend to the proceedings, anyway?

Just veracity.

Just dignity.

Just authenticity.

In the theater, we fight, don't we? We fight for veracity. We fight to find the dignity in characters. We fight to be 'authentic' in our portrayals.

Here, the Creative Staff and the Theater Company have done something completely different. They have invested in lies. Investing in lies is *not* theater. Investing in falseness is a betrayal of all that theater has become. The characters are betrayed. The text is not worth hearing.

Why?

Because you are starting with the absurdity that abject racism can be forgiven within the context of the play, simply because white people wanted to do this play.

Read that again – you cannot ignore the foundation and setting of the play, which is specific, just because your personal hubris believes that being a Caucasian gives you the right to decide when and where ethnic faces will be allowed.

Representation and Visibility

What was it the great Mick Jagger often sang? Sing it with **TPF** now, *SING, DAMMIT:*

> *You can't always get what you want, but if you try sometimes, you might find, you get what you need.*

No, you cannot, oh denizens of **THE PRINT ROOM, always get what you want.**

You cannot decide upon a portrayal of China in which there are no British East Asians to tell the tale. It is categorically racist. It is unquestionably absurd in premise, and it is the epitome of elitism in British theater.

Sorry, *theatre*.

Would you do this if the play was set in Ancient Africa?

Would you?

If there was intrigue in Amorphous Ancient Africa would you be comfortable with portraying an Ancient King of Africa? Would you invite friends?

Would you consider it 'your right' to get onstage and proclaim that you were, indeed, an Ancient King of Africa?

Likely not.

Which is the point.

TFP could continue to go on and on, but the simply truth about racism is – people like it.

Artists like it. They must. Especially Artistic Directors, Producers, and Writers of a certain stature. They perpetuate it with glee. They *delight* in telling Actors and Writers of minority status where their 'place' is, they love the premise that we all exist when and where they say we do. That they 'allow' our stories to happen. They also 'allow' us to appear in them when they say so.

They hide their preferences about it – chalk it up to *'well, this is who came in'*, or *'an actor should be able to portray any role'*, or *'we had no qualified people of color'* – but that is all a lie.

You can find any actor.

Repeat – **YOU CAN FIND ANY ACTOR YOU NEED.** There are things called 'recommendations', there are people called "Casting Directors", there are places to advertise, there are Drama Schools to call – *any actor of color needed can be found*.

In this case, they simply did not want to. ███████████████████████
██
██
███████████

It is societal, and it is both unconscious and conscious – the simple truth about why there are more working Caucasians in theater, and why their stories get told more, is because there is bias – they 'default' to themselves.

Theatre Blogging

"Loving a heritage other than your own is no excuse to culturally skin us and wear us like a coat" - Erin Quill

What we have learned in America this past election, is that white people – and **TFP**, again, is ½ white – do not like to admit their biases.

They KNOW it is wrong, they know it is small minded, and ignorant. They know their perceived moral and genetic superiority is a fallacy – but they like it. It makes them comfortable. They want the world to remain horribly pre-disposed in their favor.

Theater artists are no different from anyone else. In fact, sometimes they are worse, because they are mostly politically liberal, they are mostly believers in equality – or that is what they tell you.

However this is not what we, the Artists of Color in the world are being shown. We are not being given an opportunity lightly – it is always conditional. We are not given the benefit of the doubt with our knowledge or experience – it must always be proven.

Look at the plays of the West End – how many tell the stories of people other than Caucasian? Look at Broadway – same thing.

We are all talking more, yes. But are we changing things?

> *When someone shows you who they are, believe them the first time* – Maya Angelou

TFP is giving The Print Room the benefit of belief – they are showing her their bias and prejudice, and she is simply going to believe that is who they are.

Congratulations Old Chaps, you are Bigots!

200 Smacks of the Wand to all at The Print Room – you are whitewashing the Chinese from China!

The audacity of that speaks volumes as to your worldview.

Also – you are hereby banned from entering any Asian food eatery!

Why should we feed you when you erase us?

Oh yeah, this includes curry – how DARE you think it does not?!?!

TFP OUT.

Feature: Scenes From A Yellowface Execution

Daniel York Loh, guest post on *The Play's The Thing UK*
18 December 2016
https://theplaysthethinguk.com/2016/12/18/feature-scenes-from-a-yellowface-execution/

Before we go any further, let me lay a couple of things out there:

Howard Barker is a first-rate dramatist.

The Print Room in Notting Hill is a great small-scale theatre.

But they have epically and catastrophically screwed up their casting choices in Barker's latest offering, *In The Depths Of Dead Love*. According to the theatre's website, the play is set in 'Ancient China', concerns an "Emperor" and "Imperial Court" and features characters called "Chin" and "Mrs. Hu", with an entirely white cast who (without wishing to sound too ironically stereotypical) one would normally expect to see on TV taking tea with Lady Mary Crawley in Downton Abbey.

It's also doubly ironic that in post-referendum, post-truth Brexit Britain, we've spent the last few months being told that you simply cannot call people stupid or racist.

Well, here's the deal. We don't actually have to be stupid to do stupid things and we're all perfectly capable of perpetuating systemic racism without actually being consciously racist. Yes, it's a subtle one, folks, and interestingly, I can honestly say, hand on heart, I have never once heard the immortal words "I don't have a racist bone in my body" said by any person of colour. Not one. Because people of colour are ten times as aware of racism as white people. It's just a fact.

Now, what that hotbed of London fringe theatre that is the Print Room have done, in a play by one of Britain's most eminent playwrights, is perpetuate the practice of "yellowface", i.e. when a person who is not of East Asian descent plays a *character* of East Asian descent. Yellowface, like blackface and brownface, is a remnant of a time when actors of colour were simply not allowed on our stages.

There's often confusion about a couple of things here. People like to kid themselves that blackface only ever happened in some bygone Edwardian hinterland and only then because there were no black actors around to play Othello. However, this isn't actually true. The last blacked up Moor of Venice on our stages was as recently as 1990. The practice was only ended by protest from black actors.

Yellowface has lingered on a lot longer, unfortunately. We did however think we'd finally laid the culturally appropriated beast to rest (on British stages at least) in 2012 when, after the Royal Shakespeare Company elected to cast only 3 (out of a cast of 17) East Asian actors in minor roles (including a dog and a maid) in the Chinese classic, *The Orphan Of Zhao*, a mass social media protest that went viral globally caused considerable embarrassment to both the RSC and the British theatre industry as a whole.

Since then we have seen a whole slew of productions in major theatres: *Chimerica*, *#AiWeiWei*, *The World Of Extreme Happiness*, *Yellowface*, *You For Me For You*, *P'yongyang, Shangrila*, *The Sugar-Coated Bullets Of The Bourgeoisie* – in major venues, achieving enormous success with casts of real-life East Asian actors, not Caucasians doing an "ethnic turn". We will also shortly see *Snow In Midsummer*, at the RSC no less, and *Chinglish* at the Park Theatre. These are cast with actors who can actually trace their roots to Eastern Asia.

The other confusion that lingers about yellow (and black and brown) face is that if you don't have the make-up on, the taped eyelids and the dodgy Mickey Rooney in *Breakfast At Tiffany's* accent, this somehow ceases to be dodgy theatre practice and magically becomes instead a perfectly valid form of "colour-blind casting".

But this is the deal. If you take an East Asian character and cast it with a white actor, you're effectively saying there is no East Asian actor who was good enough/clever enough/talented enough/capable enough to play it.

Or they simply did not exist.

In other words: erasure.

The "Playwright's Intent" and the Dangers of the "Purist"

Melissa Hillman, *Bitter Gertrude*
13 July 2017
https://bittergertrude.com/2017/07/13/the-playwrights-intent-and-the-dangers-of-the-purist/

It's always exasperating to see people scolding directors for "desecrating" a canonical play or a canonical playwright's "intent" because they cast actors of color, cast a disabled actor, or removed something racist (or sexist, antisemitic, ableist, etc) from the work. It's exasperating because it's the smallest and least artistically viable point of view to have about modern stagings of canonical work.*

Our "canon" has deliberately shut out women and people of color for a great many generations. Until fairly recently in western history, it was very difficult for women and people of color to become playwrights (lack of access to education being a significant bar), and for those who were playwrights, it was very difficult to get produced outside of certain theatres. Even if produced, the work of women and people of color was rarely considered "important" or "universal" enough to be included in the kinds of awards, articles, books, and university courses that created what we consider to be the "canon". Plays that were considered "universal" reflected specifically white and male points of view; plays that differed from that were considered specific to a cultural subgroup rather than "universal" in the vast majority of cases. Even today, most works in a traditional survey course are written by white men while "Black theatre" is its own category, often represented by a single play. In my undergrad education, that play was the short piece "Dutchman" by Amiri Baraka – we didn't even read a full-length play. "Asian Theatre", "Chicano Theatre", and "Feminist Theatre" are still often brief mentions as classes move directly to more important, "mainstream" writers such as Sam

Shepard and David Mamet, with Caryl Churchill the lone female voice in an otherwise very male reading list.

Scholars and theatremakers have begun the process of interrogating the formation of the canon, as well as reframing the works we consider "canonical" within their specific sociohistorical context rather than continuing to pretend these works are 'universal'. This is vital work.

You only get answers to the questions you ask. Scholars and theatremakers are asking new questions about "canonical" works and the formation of the "canon".

When we stage canonical work, we have two choices. The first is what is mistakenly referred to as the "purist" approach. This approach holds that works should be preserved untouched, performed precisely as they were first performed. There's some educational value in performing work in historically accurate ways – at least as far as we can reconstruct that level of accuracy. Those who advocate for this approach believe they are defending the "playwright's intent", which means they somehow believe that their interpretation of the "playwright's intent" is the only accurate one. These people are, in my experience, overwhelmingly white and male, and, as such, have been taught from birth that their experience of the world is universal, and their interpretation of the world and its processes and symbols is "correct", so it's not entirely surprising that they believe they are the only ones who understand the "playwright's intent" and can therefore separate what is a reasonable interpretation of a work from page to stage from what is a "desecration".

There are many problems with the purist approach. First of all, no one knows the playwright's intent if the playwright, as is the case with most canonical plays, is dead. Even if the playwright wrote a 47-paragraph screed entitled "Here Is My Intent: Waver Not Lest Ye Be Tormented By My Restless Spirit", no one knows what the playwright's intent would be if he had knowledge of the cultural changes that occurred after he died. The audience for whom he wrote the play – the culture that understood the references, the jokes, the unspoken inferences; the culture that understood the underlying messages and themes; the culture to whom the playwright wished to speak – is gone, and modern audiences will interpret the play according to their own cultural context. Slang terms change meaning in months; using a 400-year old punchline that uses a slang term 90 per cent of the audience has never heard seems closer to vandalizing the playwright's intent than preserving it. Would Tennessee Williams or William Shakespeare, masters of dialogue, insist that a line using a racial slur now considered horrific still works the way he intended? Still builds the character the way he intended? It seems dubious at best, yet this is the purist's logic. The playwright's intent on the day the play was written, the logic goes, could not ever possibly change.

It's important to continue to *study* these works unchanged. We must not forget or attempt to rehabilitate our past. But to claim that lines written decades or even centuries in the past can still work the way the playwright originally intended is absurd.

We have begun to understand that the "canon" and its almost exclusively white male point of view is not "universal", but is a depiction of the cultural dominance of a certain type of person and a certain way of thought. We have begun to re-evaluate those works and the "canon" as a whole as part of a larger historical narrative. **This is why it is of great artistic interest to stage "canonical" work in conversation with the current cultural context.**

Theatre Blogging

When staging, for example, *The Glass Menagerie* in 2017, one must consider the current moment, the current audience. We can choose to present the work precisely as it was presented in 1944 as a way to experience a bygone era, or we can present the work in conversation with its canonical status, in conversation with our own time, in conversation with the distance between its era and our own, in conversation with the distance between the playwright's intent and the impossibility of achieving that intent with a modern audience, simply due to the fact that too much time has passed for the original symbols, context, and themes to work the same way they once did.

What does *The Glass Menagerie* – or any canonical work – mean to an audience in 2017? What can it mean? What secrets can be unlocked in the work by allowing it to be interpreted and viewed from diverse perspectives? What can we learn about the work? About the canon? About the writer? About ourselves?

The meaning of any piece of art is not static. Whether the piece of art is a sculpture created in 423 BCE or a play written yesterday, the meaning of any piece of art is created in the mind of the person beholding it in the moment of beholding. The meaning of each piece changes with each viewing, just as the meaning of what we say is created in large part by the person to whom we're saying it, which is why we can say "Meet me by the thing where we went that time" to your best friend but need to say "Meet me at the statue across from the red building on the 800 block of Dunstan" to an acquaintance. To insist that there is one "correct" meaning – always as determined by a white male – is to deny the entire purpose and function of art. **You cannot create a "purist" interpretation without the play's original audience in attendance.** The closest you can come is a historical staging a modern audience views as if through a window, wondering how historical audiences might have reacted, or marveling at the words and situations historical audiences found shocking – or did not. How many audiences in 2017 understand *Taming of the Shrew* as a parodic response to the popularity of shrew-taming pieces? Shakespeare's audience is gone and the cultural moment to which he was responding is gone, so the possibility of a "purist" staging is also gone.

This is 2017. Our audiences live in 2017. It's insulting to them to present a play written generations in the past as if nothing about our culture has changed since then, as if a work of genius gave up every secret it had to give with the original staging, **as if art has nothing whatsoever to do with the audience viewing it.**

We know better. Art lives in our hearts and minds, whether those hearts and minds are white and male or not.

*Of course I am only referring to interpretations that have received permission from the writer or estate, or stagings of work in the public domain. This is not – at all – an argument in favor of running roughshod over someone else's IP.

Road @ Royal Court: Somehow a Somehow
Harry R McDonald
04 August 2017
https://harryrmcdonald.wordpress.com/2017/08/04/road-royal-court/

Representation and Visibility

Why did the Northerner cross the road?

TO GET A DECENT FECKING PART IN A PLAY.

*

Jim Cartwright's Road holds an almost mythic place in the pantheon of modern classics. It is so often cited as an example of the Royal Court firing on all cylinders, messing with form and content, transforming the theatre physically and metaphorically. Some of my favourite northern actors have been influenced by it – Maxine Peake recalls it being the first play she read at school and was able to recognise herself.

I only knew it by reputation. I'd never read it, never seen it. It was one of the things I was most looking forward to this year. Ultimately, it wasn't what I expected.

It's a series of vignettes, and soliloquies. Snatches of conversation and speeches are heard, as we hurtle down this unnamed road in sort-of Bolton (Brothel on wheels. Peake knows what's up,[8]) and all this is emceed by the aimless Scullery (Lemn Sissay,) a man with a deep affection for the people living on this road. Characters are barely characters, they are voices. They are individuals, but also a "whole kind of person", as Kushner might say. It's like 'Not I' but with social context. They call out into the dark, not for help, but just to be heard. You can certainly see how this was so arresting in promenade.

Inevitably, some bits work better than others, and most of the best bits are in the second act. I did find myself wishing that someone had taken a pair of scissors to some of the scenes, although I'm sure even simply speeding it up, and running it straight through without an interval might have added a momentum that's hard to generate when you simply move from speech to speech. But under it all, there's a quiet rhythm and a quiet poetry to it. Most surprisingly, it's political with a determinedly lowercase 'p.' You don't hear any speeches denouncing Thatcher or her policies; no sense that the circumstances of these people can be attributed to anyone – except maybe everyone.

And there are some gorgeous moments. There's a wonderful scene where Michelle Fairley's Helen is trying to seduce a drunk, younger soldier. It's pathetic, and hopeless. He's barely conscious and she's desperate. She kneels in her plate of chips to dodge his vomit – the most convincing stage vomit I've seen since Adler and Gibb, incidentally – and you can't help but wonder how the hell it got to this point. These characters can't afford to have a past or a present, they can only afford to live quid to quid, in the moment.

It's in the moment that the joy of the piece takes flight. These characters aren't seeking anything but an ear. They want to be heard; they want everything to change and nothing to change. When Scullery dances to Swan Lake with an old trolley, the collision of absurdity and realism meant I couldn't help but grin. It's ridiculous, and somehow completely recognisable. Which is true for the whole piece, whenever I was worried it was falling into caricature, I'd remember someone I know who is exactly like that character in manner or attitude. I know everyone in this play, somehow.

---

[8] Harry links to: https://youtu.be/cq6Wq-qdmss.

Theatre Blogging

I can forgive the dodgy scenes in Road because of the last one. Two lads and two girls, as the morning approaches. Everyone's nervous, worried to make the first move. When the girls threaten to leave, the lads promise them something different. They drink a considerable amount of red wine, then stand, facing out, and we listen to Try A Little Tenderness in its entirety, as it swells from ballad to a thumping R&B blare. There's the urge to move, to release the tension, but they just listen. The release comes after the music is over, and they begin to talk. They shout into the theatre, demanding to be heard, their dreams and their hopes.

And they start to chant, to incant even, "somehow a somehow might escape. Somehow a somehow might escape." It's a plea, and a prayer. It's genuinely quite painful to listen to, at least to me. I thought about Tony's line in Billy Elliot "we can't all be fuckin' dancers", the idea that there are so many people doomed to spend their lives on this road, and knowing there's no shame in that. But then somehow I have to reconcile my own desire to get as far away from my own road as possible, with my love for the people that live there still. The sheer fucking guilt you feel when you escape, but that you have to ignore in want of something else. And it's all carried in that line.

*

John Tiffany's production seems at first to expose the theatre for the skeleton that it is, but when you look closer, you see the back wall is a recreation, the poles at the side are fake lampposts . . . It's simultaneously interior and exterior, nowhere and everywhere . . . It also seems very traditional.

When you put a piece like this, so overtly confrontational, in a proscenium arch space there's inevitably dead air between the performer and the audience. There's more effort in pushing the voice out into the space, and it somehow rings slightly hollow. It sounds like acting.

It's not helped by the glass box designer Chloe Lamford uses to facilitate the quick scene changes. This sterile cube that is spat forth from the stage floor, revealing lonely figure after lonely figure to be watched. It does isolate the character, but to a fault. You hear the voice from the speakers, you know there's a barrier between you and them. When those characters are asking to be heard, it lets the audience off the hook, because you can sense the separation.

There's also the movement, actors sweeping across the stage removing and setting up props as they go. Sometimes they linger at the side of the stage, watching. At the end, this escalates into dance, and I'm not convinced it has the effect intended; it's almost as if Tiffany doesn't trust the words, and feels he has to create a visual magic on top of the linguistic. I use the word magic deliberately, because I did find it reminding me of his work on Harry Potter and the Cursed Child quite a lot. In mood, in atmosphere . . . even in aesthetic, although this was brick where Potter was wooden panels.

But Tiffany has assembled a great company of actors. They act entirely without ego – this is a play that would disintegrate if anyone tried – but with quiet dignity, and more importantly, you can tell they're having a blast. Liz White and Faye Marsay (in her STAGE DEBUT ffs) are especially good, there's a warmth and a wit to their portrayals that in other hands might feel contrived. White in particular can carve years into her expressions as she despairs over her husband and then ditch them as she scoffs chips on the edge of the stage at the end of a night out.

Also, excellent wigs throughout.

*

Periodically, I ask myself when was the last time I saw a northerner on stage. It's often months in between occasions. If I ask myself when was the last time I saw a Scouser that wasn't nicking something, I have to go back 3 and a half years to Educating Rita. You might argue that this isn't the responsibility of the London theatres, as there are regional theatres that do this, and do it excellently. I beg to differ. The theatres in London have a status that privileges them. They get more money, and their reputations are more widely known. When that money is derived from taxes collected from all over the country, they have an obligation to represent the voices of those people.

Not only is Road a piece of the Royal Court's history, it does exactly this. It puts the voices of working class northerners in direct conversation with the audience. I think to argue against this because of the affluence of the audience, and the location of the theatre (there's a sodding Hugo Boss next door) is a cop out. Does it feel like the audience is laughing at the people Road portrays? Occasionally. For what it's worth it didn't bother me nearly as much as the audience at Ink did.

But it does raise the question, why do they need to revive it? Why isn't the Royal Court putting on new plays that are dealing with the lives of working class northerners today? They're doing it next season too, going back to a 35 year old play in Rita, Sue and Bob Too instead of commissioning new work. The only northern voices you hear are echoes from decades ago.

Because even at the Royal Court, with its reputation for being at the forefront of every theatrical shift, RP remains the standard. Take Anatomy of a Suicide, for instance (which I loved, before you start,) why did those women have to talk like that? Why couldn't they talk with a Geordie accent? Or a Lancashire accent? Or Scouse? What about Bodies, upstairs at the moment. Middle-class people live in Yorkshire, too. And yes, there was a Scotsman in it, but Justine Mitchell couldn't use her Irish voice? Escaped Alone, Unreachable, The Children ... I'm sure there's others. I'm probably being a bit harsh, or even unfair. But it seems to keep happening.

Put voices on stage that you will actually hear on the street. It's not like by putting northerners on a stage you're denying opportunities to cockneys, because you never hear them either. It doesn't have to be about people from those areas. Just do it. It won't destroy any world you're meticulously trying to create, it just makes it sound more real.

Maybe I'm being old fashioned. Maybe what I'm suggesting is a version of realism that went out of style years ago. But it still lingers. And that pisses me off.

CHAPTER 10
ON *MY NAME IS RACHEL CORRIE*

A quick word about this section before you start. *My Name Is Rachel Corrie* is a play which explores a complex political situation. Just as you can read or hear Rachel Corrie's words and understand which side of the Israel–Palestine conflict her sympathies lay, you can read the blog posts reproduced here and get a sense of where their writers stood on the subject back in 2006. I want you to know that in selecting posts for this section, however, it was never my intention to make an argument about the Middle East, only to represent the energized and fast-moving debates about New York Theater Workshop's cancellation of this play and how the theatre blogging community responded.

Censorship Comes To Downtown

Garrett Eisler, *The Playgoer*
28 February 2006
http://www.playgoer.org/2006/02/censorship-comes-to-downtown.html

What are we to make of New York Theatre Workshop's cancelling of a seemingly anti-Israel one-woman show? (Which even the celebrity involvement of Alan Rickman couldn't save!)

That the play, *My Name Is Rachel Corrie*, was originally produced by London's Royal Court says something – and *not* that the British theatre hates Jews. It says they believe in the very idea and possibility of a *political theatre*. Such commitment entails staging something, giving voice to a play that just might piss people off – including yourself! – if you still believe in it as provocative and powerfult theatre. When NYTW head James Nicola whines, "It seemed as though if we proceeded, we would be taking a stand we didn't want to take", he pretty much misses the point, doesn't he? I mean this is New York Theatre Workshop for chrissakes. How sad.

If Culture Project is smart they'll swipe it up and make a huge hit out of it while the once-alternative NYTW continues to twiddle its thumbs for a year, waiting for their alarmist subscribers to calm down.

NYTW

Garrett Eisler, *The Playgoer*
28 February 2006
http://www.playgoer.org/2006/02/nytw.html

On *My Name is Rachel Corrie*

While we await more official statements, backtracking, and gossip from the fallout of NYTW's announcement to cancel a play for perceived anti-Israel views, let us also consider the following...

Whatever the provocations of the play, it relays the testimony of an American activist protesting one of the most brutal military face-offs in the Gaza conflict. Without knowing more about the script, to me it seems there should be enough room here for some criticism of the Sharon government without crossing "sensitivity" lines. But as Nicola himself puts it (highlighted by Cashmere in the "comments" below): "we were more worried that those who had never encountered her writing, never encountered the piece, would be using this as an opportunity to position their arguments". So I guess the specific content of the play is irrelevant. (And, hey, not knowing the script makes me even more qualified to comment!)

Second, keep in mind a mass rebellion of subscribers is not necessary to make a nonprofit company shiver. It takes just one big donor, one prominent board member to object. One wonders if the very idea of a woman denouncing Israeli militarism and supporting Palestinian statehood from the stage of NYTW would be enough to rub some v.i.p. the wrong way. Or, being that board is made up of nothing if not good businessmen, someone advised a little caution and "risk management".

Also, think about this... London-based conservative critic/blogger Clive Davis asserts: "*My Name Is Rachel Corrie* is a painfully mediocre piece of agit-prop" – presumably based on seeing the Royal Court premiere in London. Now he may have his own political biases in the matter. But this does throw into focus the question of *why* NYTW decided to program this piece to begin with. *Either* they belived wholeheartedly in its value (message included) or ... At this point I have to wonder about the Alan Rickman factor. The lugubrious-voiced and wildly successful thespian isn't the first type one would imagine mentoring and co-directing this activist barebones piece. But there you are. And it is hard not to imagine NYTW being ... impressed by such an association.

So as a Blog with no journalistic ethic to stop me from recklessly speculating.... is it *possible* Mr. Nicola signed onto the piece sight unseen, dazzled by just the catchphrase "*Harry Potter's* Alan Rickman presents new Political Play!" (And with just one actor, it's cheap at that!)

Rickman's side of the story?

> "I can only guess at the pressures of funding an independent theatre company in New York, but calling this production "postponed" does not disguise the fact that it has been cancelled," Mr Rickman said in a statement. "This is censorship born out of fear, and the New York Theatre Workshop, the Royal Court, New York audiences – all of us are the losers."

See more on the Brit background and perspective here.[1]

And finally – "Jew York City" or not, if such a play cannot happen here, where else will there be the freedom of discourse for this? And please don't say Syria.

---

[1] Garrett links to: https://www.theguardian.com/world/2006/feb/28/usa.israel.

Theatre Blogging

(As a mildly self-disliking half-Jew, Playgoer reserves the right to employ any phrases and/or rhetoric that could possibly be construed as anti-semitic. So there.)

It Just Gets Worse and Worse
Isaac Butler, *Parabasis*
7 March 2006
http://parabasis.typepad.com/blog/2006/03/it_just_gets_wo.html

Anyone who wants to keep following the ongoing **My Name is Rachel Corrie** controversy should keep reading The Playgoer who is doing a really great job of holding NYTW's feet to the fire.

I have to say that it just looks worse and worse for NYTW's version of events. They claimed that there wasn't really a definite production in place and they had just postponed it, but tickets were on sale at Telecharge weeks prior to the yanking of the show, and according to the Royal Court, press releases had been written, flights booked etc.

Furthermore, there are some details about this whole thing that I hope the hive-mind out there can help me with:

1) Which organizations did James Nicola poll, and which leaders did he meet with? I don't believe the original article in the NYTimes says, although it's now on pay-per-view which means that I can't re-read it. I remember it having quotes from Jewish Community leaders, but none of them actually said they met with Nicola. And furthermore, I don't see anyone in the press really sticking up for NYTW and defending their decision now that the controversy has grown a bit. Certainly those who urged Jim Nicola to "postpone" the show would now be cheering the decision in the pages of newspapers like the New York Times, right?

2) Nicola claims he wasn't worried about subscribers cancelling subscriptions but rather was worried about activity from people who weren't going to see the play. With *Corpus Christi* there were specific bomb threats. With *Sensation* Rudy Giuliani threatened to cut funding. With the NEA 4 and Robert Mapplethorpe, it was congress. Who exactly was he worried about, and what did they say they would do?

3) What do Ariel Sharon's stroke and the recent election of Hamas have to do with anything? These excuses seem to be red herrings as far as I can tell. It's always going to be some variation of crazy-go-nuts out there. As this blogger[2] put it, what is he waiting for, the Messiah to come and peace to be declared? Under what geopolitical conditions would NYTW do **My Name Is Rachel Corrie**?

4) Jim Nicola makes specific references frequently to "preparing the community" for the play, and creating an environment in which the play can be seen as apolitical. I really doubt the

---

[2] Isaac links to: https://www.richardsilverstein.com/2006/03/04/new-york-theatre-workshop-drops-my-name-is-rachel-corrie-as-too-political/.

second one is possible, or would have ever been possible, and as to the first ... I have a suspicion that Nicola is using the buzzwords of audience outreach and responsible art making to justify what he's doing here. What steps were they planning to take to prepare the community?

5) Did any board members raise a stink about the show? Nicola has specifically ruled out subscribers in the media, but no one has mentioned the board.

6) Where are the other artists on this one? I am a very small fish in the very large pond of NY Theater Artists (although I am a shockingly large fish in the rather small pond of NY Theater bloggers!), and therefore I guess I have a kind of foolhardiness on this one. I don't expect to be directing at NYTW any time soon, and I'm not elligible for their directing fellowships. Christopher Shinn is the one established artist I know of to have spoken out about this, I know many established artists who I've talked to who are outraged, but haven't said anything publicly. Where are the artists? Where is Tony Kushner, who has been at the forefront of many of these issues? Where is Doug Wright, who is on their board and has written a play about censorship that was shortlisted for the Pulitzer? What about the other artistic directors? While people might want to avoid publicly lambasting a colleague, this is a public issue with ramifications on the public sphere of ideas, and it needs to be handled publicly.

7) Where are pro-Israel, pro-freedom of expression bloggers on this one? Why isn't Andrew Sullivan raising a stink about it? Where are the Conservatives who rail against the PC Left all the time? Isn't this a great example of said left-wing PC bullcrap that you're always whining about as destorying our culture? Or is it because they aren't capitulating to Muslims, the conservative blogosphere's favorite whipping boys, and thus it's less interesting?

8) Is this censorship or not? Scott argues that for something to be censorship, it must be done by the government, George argues that this is the new censorship, powerful private institutions being pressured into using that power to control what is and is not acceptable in the private sphere. I'm starting to agree with George.

If anyone has any ideas, or any facts as to any of this, please feel free to comment or e-mail me at parabasisnyc@yahoo.com, especially if you happen to work for NYTW. All information will be kept private, of course.

UPDATE: Andrew Sullivan apologist Mac Rogers (just kidding, Mac) points out that Sullivan in fact did write about the Corrie thing in a post about creeping self-censorship. DAMNIT! Just when I thought I had his goose cooked with the same cheap move he uses on everybody else!

The saga of Rachel Corrie

Matthew Freeman, *On Theatre and Politics*
8 March 2006
http://matthewfreeman.blogspot.com/2006/03/saga-of-rachel-corrie.html

Theatre Blogging

The main places to find the continuing and ever widening blog-orgy about Rachel Corrie are Playgoer (leading the charge); Superfluities and Parabasis. I bowed out rather early.

It's my view, though, on a very basic level, that the issue here has been overstated by very interested parties. Producers are calling each other liars. Israels military actions are being discussed. People are throwing around that deadly word censorship. Over beer with a few bloggers (lovely gents, both) I heard one of them say that the New York Theater Workshop has "given up the moral high ground". And even today, I'm wondering if the story hasn't become the story. And if anyone really knows what they feel the desired result is. Is it an end unto itself to take the "moral high ground"? Or do we want the New York Theater Workshop to scream mea culpa in the streets?

What are we angry about? Is it that NYTW bowed to political pressures? If so, then they claim to have gone out and *looked* for those pressures. Are we upset that they didn't hold up their end of the deal with Alan Rickman (who we all like to watch in movies)? Is it because the Royal Court seems to be calling the NYTW dishonest? If we're shocked that a theater producer pulled out of an obligation and doesn't entirely explain itself for it, we're living in a fantasyland.

I'm curious how many people have read the play. I certainly haven't. I also don't have personal connections that the New York Theater Workshop like Jason Grote does, so I have no inside information about this, nothing to add but my own anger, which just isn't there. This play will certainly be seen in NYC eventually, it will make more money than it would have otherwise (due to the contraversy) and someone will write a letter to the editor about it. If NYTW was smart, they'd change their minds right now and let the contraversy sell tickets.

The fact is, not producing a play that has a particular political subject matter is weak. But it is incredibly common. That is because our "not-for-profit" theaters are beholden to Board Members, audience interest, ticket and subscription sales ... *money*. They are not funded like theaters in London, and therefore can get cold feet due to market and world forces.

The problem is not that the NYTW wants to shut down discussion about Israel and Palestine. The problem is, why is it worried about this? More than likely, the decision was financial.

That's the boring part. We can cry censorship all we like, but I think that Rachel Corrie's literary martyrdom is doing her message more good than if they play had just gone up next year, or or if it was being performed, right now, to your standard battery of reviews. Perhaps (here's a thought) the decision makers at the NYTW want the play to undergo some changes, or they don't feel strongly about it for quality reasons/content reasons but they didn't want to burn a bridge by saying so publicly. It could be as simple as that. Yet again, we don't know.

Maybe I'm lukewarm about this issue because I find the politics of the play a bit unsettling and I'm not sobbing that a play that puts a upper class white teenage girl from Washington State in front of an Israeli bulldozer isn't being used as propoganda in NY.

Or maybe I'm lukewarm because I feel like this is simply a function of an art that needs funding in order to make more independent artistic decisions.

Or maybe I feel a bit like an internal struggle at the New York Theater Workshop about a play I've never read has been latched onto and exploited on the blogosphere, to attack and cajole and shame producers I've never met, who made a decision I don't know the details about.

I don't feel this is censorship, it's much more complex than that. As I said on *Superfluities*, I feel like using the word censorship here is like using a sword to perform major surgery.

The rambling conclusion to this rambling essay is: Let's *think* for a minute. It's easy to become the mob. I think it's better to look for a solution. What do we want from this outcry, beyond just a chance to cry foul?

Response to Walter Kabak
Isaac Butler, *Parabasis*
13 March 2006
http://parabasis.typepad.com/blog/2006/03/response_to_wal.html

---

This week, the President of NYTW's board had *this* to say in the New York Times:

> To the Editor: Since its inception, New York Theater Workshop has taken risks that few other theaters take and has provided support to artists who might very well not have found it elsewhere. It has pursued its mission with artistic integrity and intellectual honesty.
>
> I am dispirited by the shrill chorus of voices publicly condemning New York Theater Workshop for its decision to request a postponement of the production of "My Name Is Rachel Corrie" for a relatively brief period. It is destructive of an institution that warrants the support of those truly committed to the theater – even though they may take exception to this particular decision.
>
> Wayne S. Kabak
>
> New York, March 8, 2006
>
> The writer is president of New York Theater Workshop.

I've got one words for this letter: classy.

Okay, I've got some more words . . .

This letter seems . . . well . . . desperate. The first indicator is its use of right wing Iraq war defense rhetoric, namely that the critics of NYTW are "shrill" (a derogatory term used for left wing, anti-Bush bloggers) and that it is a betrayal of our values to even criticize the Workshop. So . . . we shouldn't criticize regardless of what we believe, and we're shrill. Does this sound familiar?

It also contains the obviously false "brief postponement" meme. Once again, if this was a brief postponement, why did everyone involved in the show think that it was cancelled? Why didn't they decide on another date with the UK people and announce it? When were they thinking of doing it? Not a single public statement from NYTW can answer any of these questions satisfactorily.

This letter is completely devoid of any actual argument in support of the Workshop's actions. First, it sticks up for NYTW's long history of artistic bravery and excellence. NYTW indeed has the kind of institutional history I would die for if I was a theater. That doesn't mean that they can't be criticized for actions taken today. As Oskar Eustis said, Jim Nicola has done an amazing job leading the Workshop, he just happens to have screwed up this time. So presenting NYTW's history in no way is an argument in its favor on this one.

Next he moves on to ad hominem attacks of those of us who would dare criticize a powerful off-Broadway theater. We must not care about the theater – *must not* be "truly committed". This is offensive in the extreme. I would argue to Mr. Kabak that those of use who are truly committed to the Theater must not be truly committed to any of its instutitions if we want it to become an important and vital art. I would also argue that those of us who are truly committed to the theater and the ones who are brave enough to open our mouths and criticize the Workshop, even though it could have deleterious effects on our burgeoning careers. It moves me that Jason Grote[3] would post what he does on his blog. I know few people more committed to the theater than Jason, and I know few bloggers who could realistically hope to actually work with them sometime in the near future. To post what he posts about it, and to be as involved as he is is an act of bravery.

I would also argue that those of us criticizing NYTW are *more committed* to its mission that Mr. Kabak is. To whit, NYTW's mission is:

> New York Theatre Workshop **produces challenging and unpredictable new theatre** and fosters the creative work of artists with whom we share a vision. With a community of artists and audience members, we explore perspectives on our collective history and responses to the events and institutions that shape our lives.
>
> New York Theatre Workshop is dedicated to nurturing artists at all stages of their careers and to **developing provocative and thrilling new works**. In addition to staging full productions, we maintain a series of programs specifically designed to provide artists with the support they need and a venue within which to hear their works.

The emphasis is mine. I emphasized those two passages because it is exactly those qualities about *My Name Is Rachel Corrie* that got it pulled – the worry that it would be too challenging, that audience reaction would be too upredictable, that it would be too provocative and possible cause a reaction that was too thrilling.

Mr. Kabak, I am saddened and angered by NYTW's actions. My main theater professor in college was a director whose talents had been nutured by the Workshop, so I was imbued with a love for your particular theater at an early age. Furthermore, you introduced many important theatrical voices to New York Theater, from playwrights like Tony Kushner to

---

[3] Jason's blog is no longer online, but a selection of posts from March 2006, including his promotion of the *Rachel's Words* staged reading, can be found on the Internet Archive's *Wayback Machine*: https://web.archive.org/web/20060322002804/http://jasongrote.blogspot.com:80/.

directors such as Ivo Van Hove and have changed theater history by doing so. It is specifically because of the high standards of your actions that the "postponement" of *My Name is Rachel Corrie* is so upsetting.

Matt Freeman asked on his blog what my ideal outcome of all of this would be ... To me, The Workshop needs to agree to participating in the town meetings that are going to be held at the Culture Project and New Dramatists (if they haven't already). In those meetings, they need to explain specifically and clearly as to why the show was "postponed", who did they meet with? who put pressure on Jim Nicola to cancel the show? what were they afraid of? What was the process by which such a decision was made? And then, if they will not or can not choose a date in the future to produce the play, they need to help get it produced somewhere else in New York. That to me is what I would like to see happen. I have no desire to punish New York Theater Workshop. They made a mistake, mistakes can be made up for and forgiven. A moment of tarnish on their reputation doesn't have be the be-all-and-the-end-all. We shouldn't forget that this is a moment of friends criticizing friends, not enemies warring over territory and principles.

(UPDATE: thanks to Josh for the spelling correction. Eventually they'll make a spell checker for mac ... really they will ...)

Infamous Words

George Hunka, *Superfluities*
27 March 2006
Now available via: https://web.archive.org/web/20060402221604/http://ghunka.com:80/

News from Garrett Eisler this morning that the first American theater to announce formally a production of *My Name Is Rachel Corrie* is David Esbjornson's Seattle Repertory Company. Until 1999, Esbjornson was the artistic director of the Classic Stage Company here in New York; currently the Seattle Rep is running Esbjornson's production of *Tuesdays with Morrie* as part of their mission to produce "plays that excite the imagination and nourish a lifelong passion for the theatre".

And with that, and with a production of *Rachel Corrie* no doubt in the near future here in New York, *Superfluities* will close this particular chapter of its long-running book. The groundswell of support for the play from the progressive left has guaranteed that the play will finally receive a delayed hearing, so she will speak (as she has at several events all over the city); the New York Theatre Workshop is now concentrating on arrangements for its 10th anniversary celebration of *Rent*; Jim Nicola and the NYTW have been castigated, defended and will emerge to stage plays again.

As Walter Davis writes in his new essay here,[4] this may have been expected, though Mr. Davis's coy suggestion that this was all a *Producers*-like plan cooked up by the Royal

---

[4] This essay is no longer online, but Davis uses the discussion around *My Name Is Rachel Corrie* and censorship as the starting point for a later book: *Art and Politics: Psychoanalysis, Ideology, Theatre*.

Court to puff up the play is one of the most intentionally funny things said by any of the commentators on this matter over the past few weeks. More importantly, Mr. Davis demonstrates that, as a post-capitalist democracy that requires an outlet for its own conflicting ideologies, the psyche of a community absorbs its oppositions to repeat, in a circular manner, its conflicts, thereby defusing them.

The NYTW is a theater whose mission is to develop "challenging and unpredictable... provocative and thrilling new works", therefore the work it develops is by definition challenging and unpredictable, provocative and thrilling. (And, like many a post-capitalist institutional theater dedicated to the free speech of its artists, they retain the services of a public relations firm to make sure they're perceived that way.) The progressive confrontational left has embraced *My Name is Rachel Corrie*; the play has become the darling of the progressive confrontational left, therefore the play is progressive and confrontational. The challenges of the play have been absorbed and reified, acted out in the public arena. Where do we go from here?

Inward, one hopes: it's the only place we can go if we're truly dedicated to a meaningful theater and its redemptive possibilities. But neither the NYTW nor the progressive left, both engaged in what Catholic theology calls "immanentizing the eschaton", to wit, the creation of heaven or hell in this world instead of waiting for it in the next, has pointed to the truly provocative possibility of this play, which is located in a short paragraph that Corrie wrote about a month before her death:

> It's just a shrug – the difference between Hitler and my mother, the difference between Whitney Houston and a Russian mother watching her son fall through the sidewalk and boil to death.... There are no rules. There is no fairness. There are no guarantees. No warranties on anything. It's all just a shrug, the difference between ecstasy and misery is just a shrug.

Forgiving the somewhat adolescent self-pity and worldweary sigh this constitutes, it is not a sentiment inclined to give either the New York Theatre Workshop or the progressive left much hope for success in their world-changing missions. As Davis notes, "Here is an experience that neither the humanist nor the political activist can contain.... Experience often erupts in an existential contingency that eradicates all guarantees. Authentic subjectivity is defined accordingly by anxiety and dread and through a deepening of the knowledge of the world that flows from those moods. Their development thus issues in a Voice that shatters all extant dramatic forms by exposing the ontological fallacies on which they depend. But for this to happen anguish must be sustained. The beauty of the political choice is that it delivers us from that task. The world seen in the indifference of the 'shrug' is sacrificed to the calcifying clarity of political commitment."

This requires a theater that contemporary aesthetic ideology, with its insistence on a form of emotional and narrative closure (true even in "verbatim drama" which seeks to present and finally frame the questions it raises about the behavior of governments and the fragility of human individuals, finding a presumed authenticity in the mere parroting of seemingly unfiltered first-person documents), can't contain. Progressive political ideology is just as much a closed system, though obviously not nearly as closed, as the decision-making process at the New York Theatre Workshop, and to say a good word for that progressive left, its bounds are wide enough to contain a play that the NYTW found too challenging and provocative for containment even by its own mission statement.

So good for everyone, I suppose. But is the cause of a truly radical, not merely progressive, theater and drama served? I would suggest: not really. The wider political community of New York has absorbed and temporarily resolved its conflicts and can feel good about itself: the censor has not succeeded, the controversial voice has been heard. The NYTW has been scapegoated (properly so, by the way). And, on the morning after, nothing has changed, about our theater, our world or ourselves. The truly transgressive and soul-redeeming work has yet to be done. In the meantime, the stages of our institutional theaters are busily rebuilding themselves as the recent firestorm as passed; perhaps some other dramatist is preparing a new play, a life-affirming drama that "excite[s] the imagination and nourish[es] a lifelong passion for the theatre". I even have a title: *Tuesdays with Rachel Corrie*. I await a call from the New York Theatre Workshop.

Ideas and text, the body and Rachel Corrie

Ben Ellis, *Parachute of a Playwright*
11 April 2006
No longer online
Content warnings: religious violence, sexual violence, racism, Islamophobia

---

Be prepared: this is a long post.

Been in mad professor mode, hiding in my studio for the most part this last week, writing about 100 pages of preparatory outline/scenario for **My Father Fell From a Helicopter Above Bougainville**. In the meantime, the only posts I've made have related to my obsessive disdain for the political direction of Australia. Now it's time for me to try to combine a bit of theory and practice.

Others have been busy working on manifestoes (manifesti?). Walter A Davis[5] via George Hunka along with George's responses[6] in particular, but one should also check out Lucas Krech's perspective on transfomation and its relationship to the mundane and magical thing we commonly call light.[7]

Adding my two bits' worth to all of this, having attended the Pierre Bonnard exposition myself, George Hunka's musings on it[8] from afar crystallised many of my vague thoughts about the exhibition and how Bonnard's tableaux could relate to a playwriting process which places emphasis on the lyrical: that in the theatre the body provides the weight, the anchor to

---

[5] Now available via the *Wayback Machine*: https://web.archive.org/web/20080517182616/http://mwcnews.net/content/view/5848/26/.
[6] Now available via the *Wayback Machine*: https://web.archive.org/web/20060413152918/http://www.ghunka.com:80/.
[7] This post is no longer online.
[8] Now available via the *Wayback Machine*: https://web.archive.org/web/20060402221604/http://ghunka.com:80/.

our reflections made through language. My first thoughts about Bonnard, especially upon seeing "Le Peignoir" (forgive me for not tracking down a decent enough re-pro on the web), were that Bonnard is important to us in that he paints somewhere between figuration and abstraction, that is, between the body and abstracted forms and patterns. The body fascinates Bonnard, and haunts the canvas (or the wood), as a pattern in itself. If the self is represented by the body, but the body can be turned into a kind of pattern like the pattern of a cloak, dissolving into its surrounds, what effect does this produce on the self? That's a major point of fascination for me, at least, in observing Bonnard's work.

Bonnard's less successful work is in landscape or in the large scale theatre-curtain work. Where the body is lost or becomes simply a figure (or one of several) in a larger scheme, intensity dissipates and the work, I feel, lacks balance. (This makes for a strange contrast with, say, the work of Cezanne and Pissarro. At the d'Orsay, a recent exhibition has pitted Cezanne's work against that of Pissarro. Strangely enough, Pissarro's landscapes always included a human figure – and during a certain period, Cezanne often painted beside Pissarro and painted the same landscape, but he depopulates the paysage. Yet the energy of Cezanne's work, its total balance of colour achieves a better effect than Pissarro's, which seems to divide the scene up into objects, so that the effect is of several recognitions rather than a transfer to the viewer of a total effect.)

But what could this suggest for our playwriting work?

Interestingly, the Pompidou Centre's exhibition of modernist art, "Big Bang", (see my post below[9] for more details) begins with a room devoted to the "disillusioned body". Each room in the exhibition is devoted to concept central to the artists' progression from earlier ideals of art, and ripe for mutation. There are 8 major categories. Destruction, Construction/Deconstruction, Archaism, Sex, War, Subversion, Melancholy, Re-chantment (basically Bill Viola's Five Angels for the Millenium series).

Under Destruction, you're led through the following sub-category ordered themed works of art: Disillusioned Body; Disfigurement; Chaos; Abstract City; Transition to the Horizontal; Geometric Scale; Grid; Monochrome.

Destruction here can be understood as an explosive possibility within modernist art. One doesn't experience the destruction as destructiveness. Rather, destruction of ideals and a liberation towards the materiality of forms and their material. In the terminology used by Davis in his essay, it is the destruction of the ego towards the release of the agon, the destruction of secondary emotion, perhaps, which leads us to a confrontation with those he identifies as primary.

Of course, this 20thC art has, within its overwhelming plurality, its limits. For example, in the Sex area, we find a masculinity on display, or attempting to confirm itself, which serves to limit, including the following themes: Sacrilege; The Bride; Transgression; Obscene; The Prostitute; Voyeurism.

---

[9] No longer online.

On *My Name is Rachel Corrie*

The works here display what I would term as implosive possibilities. The obsession with the existential basis of 'woman' being only bride or prostitute is mistaken for creative transgression. For me, not so: it collapses the existential possibilities of existence for half of the audience. The figure of the prostitute looms large still for many playwrights wishing to explore social transgression, but the hooker with the heart of gold is about all we continue to get, allied to the inference that the heart of gold is what we (or women) universally share and therefore, in a bizarre syllogism, all women are prostitutes. I realise that I haven't included the works to back this assertion up, but I'll attempt to do so in an update.

For now, I'm interested in the possibilities of the "disillusioned body". And I'll do something which I don't normally do (but which Adam Szymkowicz and Zay often display the courage to do): that is, put up some work of mine. To keep things nice and circular, it's related to Rachel Corrie.

First, my reservations about it ... it's a touch of verbatim work.

For the most part, I believe verbatim theatre a reductive enterprise which posits a false authenticity to directly quoted speech or utterance, which thereby denies the transformative agency of a playwright's imagination. The theatre of the verbatim thus is a ritual which is underscored by the following collective act: the audience denies the authenticity of their imagination also, and of their power to imagine other futures and histories, and to engage in a dialetic with these in a social forum. The unspoken idea that the world as is, as spoken through 'unmediated' language, is all we need for theatrical investigation is an imaginatively and thus politically implosive one.

Now that's out of the way, mea culpa: I have applied the idea of the "disillusioned body" to text I've sourced on the web about Rachel Corrie. There's not only the Nomadics poetry posting board (thanks to Alison Croggon) that saw some very ugly stuff indeed posted about Rachel Corrie, but I stopped counting at around 60 the number of anti-Corrie web pages (discussion boards, notice boards, groupmails, etc.) which contain this sort of material.

For my experiment's sake, I've transposed, with minor adjustments, the posts which focus upon Corrie's body in their language. I've taken words which don't use evidence – they're imagined "facts" these posts are speaking – plus the source, from the web, which is supposedly bodiless leads us to the physical. This is an invented Corrie which the posts discuss, an invented Israel, an invented Palestine – which is my own way of justifying the usage of the verbatim material: it's fantasy.

I've tried shaping it as a fugue for 5 voices, (and it's free for other people to experiment with in performance as long as they seek to inform me first.) I simply wanted to find a way to investigate language which focused upon the body ... it reads at about 10 minutes (in my sotto voce) so here we go, with apologies for the length of this post in toto:

* *

NOTES: Where the text indicates "text," the actor should indicate a quotation mark with his or her fingers, sarcasm, eyebrows ... or a combination of the three.

While there are only five voices, there are many more characters – which is in part how we experience internet space – so contradictions within voices' arguments are there to be welcomed.

The only restriction on casting is that **E** be male and that **C** be female.

START

Silence.

A– She was protecting terrorists
B– She was standing on top of a tunnel used to smuggle weapons
C– Maybe, just maybe, Rachel Corrie knowingly aided and abetted cold-blooded murderers
D– A blindingly obvious fact about Rachel Corrie and all the other objectively pro-terror swine of the International Solidarity Movement: they know perfectly well what they are doing
A– She and others converged on Israeli territories and knowingly supported terrorists
B– Corrie and her friends would have had to be blind not to notice
C– ISM members accused the driver of the murder even before the military had time to investigate the incident.
D– When you lie down in front of bulldozers to help terrorists smuggle weapons, you might die.
A– Rachel Corrie lived the life of a terrorist
B– and died the life of a terrorist.
C– The driver of the bulldozer may not have seen Corrie
D– ISM'ers who stayed with Gaza families might have seen the tunnels themselves.
A– During deliveries, people would have been hauling the goods out of the homes.
B– Maybe Corrie herself did some heavy lifting.
E– Young Rachel. .plain. .rebellious. .naif. .
C– But it also seems possible that Rachel Corrie was clueless
purposely left that way so that she would feel more motivated to let herself be bulldozed
E– Rachel meets an older man . . . with a handsome Edward Said mask. .
he seduces her. . . . hallals her hard as can be in her behind . . .
C– I'm not defending her, but I think she was doomed by her education
and by a family who were obviously schooled in the same trash
E– Said abandons her . . sends her to her inevitable doom. . . .
D– But . . . but . . . they weren't helping "terrorists". They were assisting "freedom fighters" in their battle against white capitalist and imperialist oppressors who were tools of the American colonialist war machine . . . Sarcasm off now. I read she was a member of Hamas.
E– Rap sound track . . pink panther motif. . . . .
in the last scene . . . the Said character takes off his western mask
puts on his fanged Pan-Arabic one
while sodomizing her dead body and ululating to the cheers
A– The most hateful, poisonous, anti-Semitic individuals I have encountered.
E– the cheers of the London glitterati
D– No. She despised America and Israel and romanticized "palestinian" terrorists.

E– You're right i'll have to change the ending . . .
Rachel wakes from a bad dream.
the Edward Said masked figure put his 10 inch weapon in her mouth. chomp chomp. . . . .
D– She was no innocent flower.
E– chomp chomp chomp. chomp . the masked figure becomes Othello . . who strangles her to death. . . .
D– She knew the score.
A– People only care because she was blond and American
D– Impeach Rachel Corrie.
B– They act as lookouts for Israeli helicopters coming to arrest Palestinians involved in the mass murder industry
A– They attempt to stall soldiers at checkpoints thereby allowing terrorists to pass
B– They call in the positions of Israeli troops to Palestinian terrorists
C– who then use the info
D– to attack Israel
C– I would get mad too if I thought Israel had no reason to be bulldozing houses.
D– The ringleader was happy to let her stand in front of a bulldozer, but I guess he didn't feel much like doing it himself.
B– I see what you mean. She was either – one, complicit; two, far too stupid to live.
A– Still gotta go with choice number one.
D– Every islamic pal or useful idiot has their "expires by" "this date". Corrie matched the criteria for that day. Next! Step right up: death awaits.
B– Put up that pic of her peacefully destroying a poorly made US flag.
E– Which do you folks think is more awesome? A dead old man's face on webforums just to get people, or cheering on the gruesome bulldozing to death of a young American woman?
B– You mean the old man who actively supported and planned the death of Jews
A– and the young woman who actively supported terrorists?
D– Do I think Saint Pancake got what she deserved?
B– No screaming Rachel pictures?
C– More pancake jokes, please.
E– For my 2 cents Edward Said is responsible for killing Rachel Corrie
Cold blooded foot-noted academic murder . .
C– She wasn't run over by the bulldozer. .
E– the only kind there is . . .
C– but critically injured by debris being knocked over by it.
B– Rachel was only a tool.
D– So she was killed with a Catepillar D-9
A– The ISM doesn't bother to update their website regularly on her: this just confirms she was a tool.
D– I met someone yesterday who works for Catepillar.
E– I would erase anyone with the D-9, and I have demolished plenty.
D– He was somewhat familiar with Corrie – his term was 'stupid' – but not as informed as we are here.
E– I wanted to destroy everything. I begged the officers, over the radio, to let me knock it all down; from top to bottom.

Theatre Blogging

D– By the way, CAT revenues and profits are up!
B– Some day if I'm in the area
E– For three days, I just destroyed and destroyed.
B– I'm gonna piss on her grave.
E– I didn't see, with my own eyes, people dying under the blade of the D-9. But if there were any, I wouldn't care at all. If you knocked down a house, you buried 40 or 50 people. I had lots of satisfaction in Jenin, lots of satisfaction. No one expressed any reservations against doing it. Who would dare speak?
C– Poor Rachel
E– If anyone would as much as open his mouth,
C– she ran and ran
E– I would have buried him under the D-9.
C– but just couldn't get away from the evil bulldozer.
B– I remember a bus bombing in Israel and the ISM rep showing up at the scene almost immediately Coincky dinky, don't you think?
A– It was before the Rachel Corrie pancaking. I think.
C– That reminds me, I'm out of maple syrup.
D– Since you're asking, I'll favour "gruesome bulldozing to death of the young American woman".
A– Rachel Corrie was giving aid and comfort to terrorists who soak shrapnel in rat poison then wrap it in explosives and detonate it in school buses and pizza parlours because they hate Jews.
E– Wait a minute guys. While I expect that RC was knowingly aiding and abetting Hamas, and not just a loon or a useful fool, we haven't provided any hard information to confirm that.
D– Probably not all that important, given that she was just small potatoes.
B– I have on another computer . . . I can't access it now
Emergency room photographs that prove that she was not run over by a bulldozer. I mean, she was in an emergency room. She was pretty mangled but the defence force didn't do it, seeing as she was not run over by a bulldozer. It appears that she ran scared from the bulldozer and found refuge in a moving pile of dirt that was being displaced by the bulldozer
She was crushed by moving dirt, which caused her injuries that, together with Palestinian medical care, eventually led to her untimely death.
A– If Rachel Corrie was intentionally crushed, they would not have squeegied her off the dirt and brought her to the emergency room,
C– because she would be dead.
E– Her internals would be squirted all over the surrounding ground.
B– The opposing side's theory is that Rachel Corrie basically stood in front of a bulldozer and protested as it rolled over
A– her feet
B– her legs
E– her thighs
D– her midsections
C– her abdomen

On *My Name is Rachel Corrie*

A– her ribcage
B– and her head
D– Only a Muslim government would do that to a person.
E– Put up the photos! You know which ones!
A– The photos showing Corrie talking before the bulldozer with a megaphone are not time sequential.
B– She died for nothing other than to be a pain in the ass
C– and to help the PLO terrorists
D– Whatever she suffered in dying doesn't compare with Jews maimed and killed by the weapons smuggled through the tunnels by the most vile, disgusting, blood-thirsty and fascistic people to come along since the Nazis: the Palestinians.
E– Ugly, dead flat bitch Rachel Corrie is one less Nazi in the world.
D– I sincerely hope that lots of ISM scum lie down in front of the dozers and join the Palestinian worm farm in hell.
A– Don't play with matches
B– Don't play over the railroad tracks.
A– Don't play in front of moving bulldozers.
E– Corrie's parents, who raised a daughter to aid in the killing of Israeli babies by helping terrorists to smuggle weapons from Egypt will be appearing at this Church in Barkly.
D– We should mount a demonstration outside.
C– It wouldn't hurt to flood their phone lines asking for information
E– This is their number.
D– This is their website.
B– I have long suspected that Corrie was killed in the arab "hospital" but I have started to wonder if she was also raped and sodomized there as well,
A– and if that helped lead to her death:
E– are the autopsy photos on the net anywhere?
C– I vote for she died on the operating table, as she was worth more as a martyr than a cripple to ship home, and provided invaluable propaganda merchandise
E– Keep the pancake jokes coming!
D– You know which picture I mean?
E– Can you put it up?
A– My heart goes out to the driver of the bulldozer.
B– Rachel Corrie who wanted to help blow up Jewish babies
A– He was the real victim.
C– A blindingly obvious fact
E– The comments section is now closed.

Silence

END

* *

Of course, I'm interested in responses not only to this text, but to the ideas. I'm not particularly interested in whether you like it or not. I'm more interested, for example, in what principles could we use, if we are placing an emphasis upon body-language over plot-structure, to give order to the events? I think that's my main concern following the difficulty I experienced in editing the above. What is to happen, and when, and to which precepts? A heartbeat? An orgasm? A breath – in two acts, inhale and exhale? "The seven ages"? It's all very well to place on emphasis on language, but how are we then to deal with the consequences this deals to our employment of time? (These are not rhetorical questions. And if you've made it this far, you get a chocolate frog.)

CHAPTER 11
ON *THREE KINGDOMS*

> **Three Kingdoms – Lyric Hammersmith**
> Andrew Haydon, *Postcards From The Gods*
> 10 May 2012
> http://postcardsgods.blogspot.co.uk/2012/05/three-kingdoms-lyric-hammersmith.html

[this piece is more of very long failure to do justice to something I loved than a review]

If you're going to see one production of a new play by a British writer this year, it should probably be this one. If you've never seen any German theatre before, here is a pretty good place to start. If you have any interest in how a director can work with a script, this is essential viewing.

Put another way: the first half of this play is 1hr50. When the interval turned up, it felt like little more than an hour had passed. Overall, this three hour play felt like an hour and a half. Tops. Given that theatre is a medium that is often able to prolong one hour indefinitely, this is no small achievement.

At root *Three Kingdoms* is a detective thriller. The action opens in Hammersmith, London, with the unlikely-ly named detectives Ignatius and Charlie interrogating a young man who has been picked up on London's ubiquitous CCTV system throwing a sports bag into the river. The bag contains a head. The head, it eventually transpires, belongs to a trafficked sex-worker. The two detectives, apparently on a whim and independent of any formal hierarchy, decide to follow a lead which takes them first to Germany and then to Estonia.

The set is an oblong boxy room on the stage with the fourth wall cut off. It's painted in a very stained, neutral duck-egg blue or sky grey. There's an open door and a massive serving hatch (really huge – more like a landscape window that has been taken out) at the back. These give onto the kind of communal corridor common to tenement buildings across Europe. This space variously becomes police interrogation cells, departure lounges, hotel rooms, hotel lobbies, brothels, porn studios and yet more hotels, departure lounges and police cells again. It feels at once spacious yet somehow claustrophobic. The lighting tends to be artificial, variously suggesting strip-lights, or neon, or the gauche pink lighting of strip clubs and brothels.

Onto this script, and into this set, director Sebastian Nübling pours his talent for invention.

[You know all the stuff about the production, yes? Co-prod. between Munich Kammerspiele, Tallinn's Teater NO99 and Lyric Hammersmith – British writer Simon Stephens, German director Sebastian Nübling and Estonian designer Ene-Liis Semper. Actors from all three countries. Multi-lingual production. Lots of sur-titles.]

Theatre Blogging

In the first scene, set in England, the English actors do English acting. The opening scene of police interviewing a young suspect is at once totally familiar and utterly different. There is no table; the room is the wrong size; there is no tape-recorder on the no-table. When they show the suspect photographs – a scene familiar from a hundred police procedural TV shows – one of the officers stick them round the walls not on the table. It's still perfectly played, and yet the differences somehow make you see it differently; makes you watch it harder from the off. It is suddenly like seeing theatre again, rather than like watching TV done live.

I *think*/It looks like the English actors in the section have also been encouraged into some more gestural (what I'll call with a massive generalisation) *German* acting. But already this scene has been preceded by an eerie version of an Estonian song, sung to a minimal, slightly trip-hop-sounding backing track by a tall, skinny, gaunt man in a slim-fitting white suit.

There's a lot to talk about and think about in *Three Kingdoms*; both in this production and in the text itself. In a lot of ways, even making that distinction feels a bit like failing the production. On the other hand, German critics tend to read the text of a play before they see the director's *version* of it. And this is the cultural context from which Nübling comes, so while feeling like the most organic synthesis of directorial vision and text imaginable, it is also possible to regard the two entities as entirely separate. For the record, I didn't read the play before I saw the production and haven't read it since. I would like to, but much more, I would already like to see the production again.

Without reading the text, however, my distinctions of who is responsible for what might be slightly off – I'll either correct in the text, or add footnotes later when I have – because we know that Nübling hasn't just staged every word in Stephens's script and heeded nothing but his stage directions. It feels embarrassing having to point this out, but having had a glance through the MSM reviews yesterday, it appears that it's still a point worth highlighting.

Indeed, the *seeming* near-binary opposition between this première of *Three Kingdoms* and Katie Mitchell's première of *Wastwater* last year feels usefully instructive. Where with *Wastwater* you came out feeling like you'd had every word of the play precisely underlined, here it seems surprising that there even are words sometimes, and it feels like you're absorbing something much more organic. This isn't to disparage Mitchell's approach one bit, by the way. But simply to note what a different experience *Three Kingdoms* is.

Part of the reason for this, of course, is that more than half the play (a guess) is performed in German and Estonian, so one is receiving language-based information not only as speech but also as written text.

Another part of the reason, however, is the way in which Nübling has directed the production. As I already suggested,[1] it's pretty much impossible to describe the way that Nübling works better than Stephens himself does in the Lyric's trailer for the show:

> "Unlike a lot of British directors, he doesn't work from the inside out, but he has a kind of visualised realisation of the play that he imagines. And he stages that as a means of

---

[1] Andrew links to: http://postcardsgods.blogspot.co.uk/2012/04/trailer-park.html.

travelling into the play. He's never asked me what I'm trying to say with a play. It's not been anything he's interested in . . . He just wants to make a kind of musical energy, a kind of visceral muscle on stage, but he does it with tremendous intelligence and sensitivity."

The best way I can think to articulate the way I understood the production is by comparing it to a sculpture. On one hand, yes, you can see the wood. The whole damn thing is wood. But at the same time, you're not just looking at a piece of wood, you're looking at the thing that the wood has been made into by a controlling intelligence. You can see the chisel marks, but at the same time you can marvel at how one thing has been made into another thing.

Except "a sculpture" might wrongly imply a kind of inertia. That would be wrong. There's a tangible energy here, not just that which is demonstrated by the electric physicality of the performers, but also in the spark of ideas – watching *Three Kingdoms* is like giving your synapses an electric shock.

It's worth talking about the "plot", or the "narrative" or simply "the things that happen one-after-the-other".

The script breaks down into an easily discernible three act structure – in fact, amusingly, on this level it's actually quite formally conservative as a play. Each of the acts is set in a different city and follows detectives Ignatius and Charlie as they try to track down the killer of Vera Petrova, a trafficked Estonian sex-worker, through a series of interviews, interrogations and meetings.

The tone here, though, is less the suspenseful police procedural, and much more like an increasingly hallucinatory involuntary journey. They interview one of Petrova's colleagues, a silent sex-worker, dressed in high heels, underwear, fur coat and a deer's head, with the aid of a Home Office Russian translator, and you start to feel the naturalism of their world slide away as their grasp on the situation gradually turns into the situation's grasp on them – an inexorable drag deeper and deeper into an increasingly sludgy world.

I should mention at this point that as well as being intelligent, surreal and all that other stuff, it's also very funny indeed. Much is made of lost-in-translation jokes and the detectives themselves have a fine line in pop cultural banter.

By the time the interval turns up, the two detectives have found themselves in a porn factory in Germany – still no nearer to their goal and surrounded by actors wearing strap-ons, a naked camera-man roaming around the pink-lit corridor, with a dull repetitive soundtrack of mechanical moaning. Squirty cream stands in for faked ejaculate, while another naked man wipes tissues of excrement on the wall. It's at once bleak, funny and also far sexier than more or less anything the British put on stage. Ever.

After the interval we arrive in Estonia and there is another change of pace. In a subtle way, the production offers portraits of each country through a kind of distilled essence (perhaps even gentle pastiches) of their theatrical cultures. Where Britain opens with an almost Pinter-y dialogue, and where Germany inevitably collapses into mess and nudity, Estonia is represented by a violent athleticism and physicality. The four main Estonian actors conjure their country by pummelling the walls of the set with boxing gloves.

It is also here that the narrative's debt to the later films of David Lynch really kicks in, seeming to offer the sort of plot twist that makes a kind of non-iron-able Mobius Strip of the plot. Suddenly, from linear, it becomes circular but with a twist in it that means it can't be logically made back into a straight line.

[NEXT PARA POSSIBLY A BIT SPOILERY]

This is perhaps the hardest thing in the piece to process. Assuming I haven't just got this totally wrong, it seems by the end, that Ignatius, the detective who speaks no other language but English, has become his own quarry. He might have woken up in an Eastern European hotel room with a dead girl. He is interrogated, tortured – a domestic iron is pushed onto his hand, echoing the bandaged hands of ___ who he is interrogating in the first scene.

[END OF POTENTIALLY SPOLIERY BIT]

When a play takes this sort of jump outside the realms of the possible, it suddenly seems to become much more difficult to talk about. "What does that mean?" suggests itself as a question. Or even simply "What just happened there?" Are we meant to reconstruct our ideas of what happened through this new development? Is this sudden transformation intended as A Big Metaphor that we're meant to Get? It is disorienting in all these ways. Being willing to allow that disorientation to be a part of the whole experience of the play feels crucial.

I suspect, in part, this might be what other critics have objected to: the fact that, on one level, the play does stop "making sense" altogether – although I would argue that this precise moment actually generates a lot new *senses*. But it's not immediately pin-downable. And if someone believed their job was to pin down and explain, then this sort of thing is inevitably going to get on their wick.

There are plenty of screamingly obvious ways for an audience member to read this slippery final twist, and I have no intention of imposing any of my many, quite vague, and far from definitive impressions as to what it "meant". In a way, this point, more than any other in the play, doesn't even demand "understanding" so much as "experiencing". You can feel it rather than overthink it.

Of course the play does have "themes". Many of them common to those in *Wastwater*, and, in a strange way, *The Trial of Ubu*. These themes seem to be on a continuum with Stephens's growing concerns – at least in his plays – about the size of the world and the way that the world operates as a global concern. Ideas about travel, cultural difference and globalisation recur. And behind all that, the internet, making the world at once feel like a much smaller, more accessible place but also emphasising its vastness; and within the internet, the pornography that seems to be almost the life-blood of the internet.

[As a side note, I'd say these particular preoccupations, and the way in which *Three Kingdoms* articulates them, puts Stephens into an artistic line-up alongside Chris Goode, Chris Thorpe, Chris Haydon and Andy Field much more interestingly, perhaps, than categorising him as a writer of New Writing like, say, Richard Bean, Mike Bartlett or David Eldridge.]

Beyond discussing the work in terms of the playwright – as is, of course, traditional with a new play by a British writer in Britain – it's also worth thinking about the production in terms of where it sits both in relation to Nübling's work (of which I haven't really seen enough: the première of Stephens's *Pornographie* and Feridun Zaimoglu's *Alpsegen* (video trailer here[2])) and theatre more generally. Actually, in relation to these other two pieces directed by Nübling the comment I can really make is that it's very different to both those other pieces, which were also both very different to each other.

If Nübling has *a shtick*, then it's undetectable between these three productions. Which might not seem a point especially worth making, but I'd hate for anyone to go away thinking that he just does this to every play he directs – it's not just a case of stick everyone in animal masks, chuck in a bit of nudity, add some *movement* and off we go. Those precise elements were specifically chosen for *this* production of *this* play. In fact, the only thing I noticed being re-used from anything else that I'd seen was that some of the incidental music also features in the video trailer for Nübling's production of *Pornographie* (and presumably the stage version, although I don't remember it).

Visually, *Three Kingdoms* reminds me much more of moments from Gisele Vienne's *I Apologize* – which also featured animal masks, stage mess and similar qualities of frenetic movement or deliberation.

Admittedly, these elements are not especially unusual on the German stage – the Deutsches Theater production of Dennis Kelly's *Taking Care of Baby* had one character wearing a duck mask, for example, while their *Othello* made great use of a gorilla costume. Similarly, it seems almost futile to try to point to a specific example of the use of cumulative big mess on the German stage (I think this one was the first example I saw[3]). That said, just listing a couple of examples I happen to have seen feels shallow and perhaps as pointless as a fledgling German critic coming to London and totting up the number of actual kitchen sinks they see in any given month. It would be a novelty for them in much the same way as these elements are to the British.

If, in actuality, animal heads and mess are quite normal strategies, it feels like they should be either considered as part of the whole or not at all, in much the same way as we tend not to obsess over the sinks in domestic drama. The idea being propagated elsewhere that doing something this way is "self-indulgent" while having a set that features working taps is "normal" displays such a catastrophic level of self-satisfaction that their dismal failures of engagement can be dismissed out of hand (for the record, I'm not dissing working taps. Those are perfectly nice).

What's fascinating about *Three Kingdoms* is the way that it anticipates its critics and possible criticisms. There is actually enough said on stage for Michael Billington to have sketched out his usual précis of "what the playwright is saying" had he so wished. But at the same time, that's not how you actually do experience the play. Instead of drily noting the way that the Estonian gangsters typify a new globalised understanding of commerce – and in this case, the trade in women – these moments occur within a production that exists more as a series of feelings than thoughts.

---

[2] Andrew links to: http://www.youtube.com/watch?v=g0vtaZZLLkg.
[3] Andrew links to: http://postcardsgods.blogspot.co.uk/2008/06/hamlet-ist-tot-keine-scherkraft.html.

Theatre Blogging

While the play deconstructs or even attacks its own potential process of Orientalising (as it were, I nearly went for "Othering") of Eastern Europe, the production and the performers almost deconstruct the text's deconstruction. Perhaps more problematically, I'm not fully convinced it quite clears the hurdle of how to portray subjugated women. There are not enough women in the cast, and the re-gendering only runs one way – i.e. a naked man with a head can double as the mortuary slab body of a beheaded woman and later turn up in drag/as a woman, but no women ever conspicuously play men (not least because there aren't enough in the cast to do so). At the same time, making this point feels like a peculiarly British sort of PC over-worrying, and oddly, something I'd have worried about a lot less in Berlin (it plays at Deutsches Theater on 7th June, where it'll share a building with a woman playing Othello and more full-frontal male nudity than you can shake a strap-on at).

Perhaps the most interestingly contradictory thing about *Three Kingdoms*, however, is how joyous and freeing this parable about misery, suffering, sex-slavery, brutality, cruelty and murder feels. And perhaps this is its finest achievement. Rather than simply showing us that forced sex and violence against women is a Very Bad Thing and that Europe, still living through the traumas of its history, is riven with darkness and violence, and that beneath the veneer of civilisation there is a rot so deep you'd be better off burning it – sending us into the night saddened and a bit depressed – it instead shakes us, makes us feel something and fires up our brains in entirely unpredictable ways (although that might be down to *us*, in this instance, being an audience of excitable Brits rather than coolly analytical Germans).

Still, it's bloody brilliant. Go and see it.

Three Kingdoms: New Ways of Seeing, Experiencing, Expressing

Catherine Love, *Love Theatre*
12 May 2012
Now available from: https://catherinelove.co.uk/2012/05/12/three-kingdoms-new-ways-of-seeing-experiencing-expressing/

If it is possible for one piece of theatre to be an argument against the traditional model of theatre criticism, then *Three Kingdoms* makes that point rather comprehensively over its messy, anarchic, thrilling three hours. Despite wrenching the obligatory, paltry 400 words[4] out of my still slightly dazed brain, a part of me wants to go back and smash them apart again. Simon Stephens' latest play actively resists being weighed up and judged with a neat star rating within a tidy word limit; it sticks two fingers up, as it were, to the well made review.

To be completely honest, I left the Lyric Hammersmith on Tuesday evening in a state of confusion, disorientation and uncertainty. It was as though I had been submerged for three hours in a strange and baffling yet oddly captivating dream, one that frustrated at some turns and delighted at others. If someone had asked me, in the immediate moments after I

---

[4] Catherine links to: http://www.fourthwallmagazine.co.uk/2012/05/review-three-kingdoms-lyric-hammersmith/.

vacated my seat in the auditorium, whether I liked *Three Kingdoms*, I would have struggled to answer them. "Like" strikes me as a word from a completely different vocabulary to the one in which this piece of theatre operates. In fact this whole production, directed by Sebastian Nübling in an extraordinary British, German and Estonian collaboration as part of World Stages London, seems to speak a different language to the one we are accustomed to in British theatre.

The strange irony of describing *Three Kingdoms* as dreamlike – which is the closest I can get to evoking its loopily surreal quality – is that I did in fact dream about the production in anticipation of seeing it. Yes, I was that excited. But my subconscious was incapable of creating anything as bizarre, visually imaginative and downright bonkers as what appeared on the stage of the Lyric Hammersmith. Women don deer heads and are pursued by wolf-masked men; a gang of boxers violently pummel the soiled set; a strangely haunting, white-clad figure sings chilling pop song accompaniments; there is more lurid sexual content than you can shake a strap-on at.

I should perhaps point out that within the hallucinatory kaleidoscope of images there is a plot of sorts, and a detective plot no less, but this is far from your average whodunnit thriller. We begin in the middle of a police interrogation, as detective duo Ignatius and Charlie question a young man who has inadvertently thrown a severed human head into the River Thames. The forensic evidence points back to Europe, where the decapitated sex-worker has been trafficked from. With odd suddenness, the two detectives follow the trail back to the pimps and pornographers of Berlin and later – with Charlie inexplicably disappearing from the scene – to an Estonian sex-trafficking gang.

Without knowing much about European theatre – a lack of knowledge that I'm keen to remedy off the back of this – I would ignorantly speculate that the style and tone of the production shifts appropriately with the geographical location. Never is the writing more central than in the early London-based interrogations, reflecting the new writing culture of British theatre, with more than an echo of Pinter in the detectives' swift back and forth of dialogue. As the action moves to Germany and later to Estonia, we are offered increasingly audacious visual imagery and an escalating physicality, as performers tumble through windows and spring startlingly from suitcases. It certainly feels many miles from British theatre, and bracingly so.

In this way, Nübling manages to create a disorientating visualisation of the dislocation of foreign travel, immersing us in cultures that are strikingly different to our own through the conduit of Ignatius, a man severely lost in translation and persuasively, energetically portrayed by Nicolas Tennant. In this sense, the perplexing surreality of the production is a resonant metaphor for the clash of cultures in an increasingly globalised world, where Europe is both sister and other.

Through the piece, Stephens and Nübling make us aware of our own strangely separate and insular status as an island nation, a culture that is supposedly part of Europe and yet distinctly divided from it. Our perceptions of this continent, and particularly of the still largely alien society of Eastern Europe, are both channelled and challenged. While the practice of sex-trafficking may be this play's overt subject, the relationship between East and West demands an equally prominent place on the stage.

Theatre Blogging

Related to this, language is another key concern, perhaps surprisingly in a production so anchored by the sensory. The very experience of having to read surtitles for much of the evening already puts a different slant on how this play is received, with the audience having to do the mental leg-work of reading and connecting both spoken and physical language. Translation also throws up its own issues, particularly as Ignatius is forced to rely solely on what German-speaking Charlie chooses to tell him, a potent illustration of the power of words and the fluidity of their meaning. Even when we are dealing only with English, words are important. Ignatius and Charlie verbally play with synonyms before finding the right fit, while a sentence such as "they sawed it not sliced it" (in relation to the woman's decapitation) is an excruciating demonstration of how a slightly different word can have a vastly different effect.

While Nübling has clearly transformed Stephens' script into a theatrical creation that is as much his own as it is the playwright's (the word collaboration here feels fully justified), the words still dazzle on their own. There is a sharp precision to Stephens' writing, conjuring an incisively perceptive vision of the world that emerges most powerfully through the short monologues that various characters speak. One character's description of the market economics of sex trafficking is brutally wounding in its calculated logic; the analogy of a toilet to convey the message that "shit doesn't go away" is a painfully apt one.

Dealing with Stephens' script also brings me onto the relationship between writer and director, which is here figured strikingly differently to how we are used to it in this country. The respective places of the writer and the director in British theatre demand a whole other blog post, but it is worth briefly pointing out the extraordinary free rein that Stephens has given to Nübling, placing huge levels of trust in the director's hands. Anyone interested in this area should read Alex Chisholm's excellent essay for Exeunt,[5] in which she questions the imposed division between "new writing" and "new work". It is certainly worth considering whether the model posed by Stephens and Nübling could provide a way to bridge this gap in British theatre.

Moving on, in the multi-lingual environment that Stephens has created, pop music emerges as a common language. This clearly reflects Stephens' own interests, but it also seems an appropriate demonstration of the wide-reaching penetration of some elements of culture and not others. There is a sinister irony to the way in which music is used, with romantic lyrics often clashing with the global commodification of sex and sexual violence that is being portrayed. One particularly haunting rendition of the Beatles' *Golden Slumbers* still has yet to release its grip on me.

As heart-pumpingly exhilarating as this production may be, however, I cannot quite offer *Three Kingdoms* my wholly unfettered praise. My main problem with the piece is the way in which it treats its female victims (a word I use with caution). Is silence the way to give these women a voice? Before criticising, I can wholly appreciate and understand the perspective of this production, which is itself a primarily male product. (To briefly digress, the word "product" here feels significant. As in the sentence I have just written, products

---

[5] Catherine links to: http://exeuntmagazine.com/features/the-end-of-new-writing/.

are actively created by men – the product is the object, the men the collective subject – while women in this play are referred to by the Estonian sex traffickers as the passive "product" that they trade.)

On one level, it makes perfect sense. *Three Kingdoms* is shocking in its treatment of women, thereby shocking us as a result. The women in the piece are largely silent because the women they represent are living in enforced silence; it seems appropriate, authentic (another word that is tainted through its particular, unsavoury use by Stephens – see my earlier point about the importance of language?).

But doesn't this just compound the problem? Here I'd like to refer you to an exchange on Twitter between Chris Goode (@beescope) and Stella Duffy (@stellduffy) that caught my attention before I had even seen the show myself and that sums up pretty comprehensively what I'm trying to get at:

> @beescope: Three Kingdoms is hugely impressive, a near-perfect match (collision?) of writer, director and intrepid actors. Still frustrating though that nobody wanting to work in those modes wholly within the British system would ever get past the gatekeepers. Also wish it didn't revel quite so much in the misogyny it's describing.
>
> @stellduffy: @beescope the difficulty of representing that which we're trying to counteract/deal with.
>
> @beescope: @stellduffy Yeah, for sure. But it's extra troubling when the work so completely reproduces the malaise that there's no critical leverage. If you make the victims essentially voiceless you can come awfully close to appearing not to have noticed there's a problem.
>
> @stellduffy: @beescope women are abused in life. re-creating a problem is not the same as creating an alternative. sigh.

(Apologies for the awful formatting of the above, I couldn't get a decent screenshot)

There is something to be said for exposing an issue in all its brutal ugliness, but it is disturbing and worrying that it is so rarely exposed from the perspective of those upon whom it most impacts. Women are rendered speechless throughout, either by language barriers or by fear. In one of Nübling's many powerful images, a half-clothed female figure silently irons in the background while men watch porn on a phone screen; another woman is unable to even communicate with the men who viciously insult her.

The production also seems to revel somewhat in the sexual violence it portrays, which is upsetting and troubling on the one hand but intriguing on the other. Such is the level of dazzling visual spectacle that we are invited to become complicit spectators; Stephens and Nübling recruit the audience as a living example of the dark forces within human nature that drive the acts they are depicting. Thought of in such a way, Michael Coveney's protestation that anyone to enjoy this experience must be "debauched beyond redemption" takes on a slightly defensive air.

Also complicit are the two detectives, whose common gender – while it may exclude greater involvement from female characters – becomes darkly significant. At the same time as doggedly pursuing their case, they are implicit participants in the industries responsible for this murder. In a chilling scene in which they watch a recording of the young woman's beheading, they become tainted spectators, and their attitude towards the women they encounter on their investigation hints at deeper problems. The concluding twist, which I am still wrapping my head around, seems to enhance Ignatius' guilty complicity in what he is attempting to destroy; there are no heroes here.

Another potential criticism is the plot's gradual descent into incomprehensibility, as we are assaulted with unfathomable image upon unfathomable image in a hedonistic Estonian finale that becomes increasingly hard to follow and digest. This frustrates the very British aim of getting to the bottom of what a play is "saying", but perhaps it is the critical approach that is at fault rather than the production. We can be determinedly blinkered as a theatrical culture and have nurtured a sort of suspicion towards theatre that asks its audiences to feel and experience as much as it asks them to think.

The very lack of meaning here seems to create a new kind of meaning. Stephens has said that Nübling never asked him what he was trying to say in his script, and perhaps we should not ask either (I am aware of the hypocritical irony of making this statement several hundred words into a piece of writing that it is, on some level, doing just that). This is theatre that demands a new way of watching and I found myself feeling hampered by the nagging knowledge that I would have to write a formal review, pestered by the panic-inducing question of how I was going to critique it. I almost wish that I could have experienced this production without the critical handcuffs binding me.

Value judgements are usually, at least by the standards of the conventional review and the purpose it serves, what make a piece of critical writing. Readers want to know whether the reviewer thinks it is "good" or "bad" theatre (note the inverted commas); they want to know whether or not they should buy a ticket, which is a valid expectation to have from a review. In this case, although I obviously did give one in the form of a star rating, I felt to an extent incapable of offering my value judgement, my thumbs up or down. But as for whether others should go to see the show, I can only offer a resounding YES. This is theatre that needs to be consumed on an individual basis, and I suspect that it may be divisive, but it should be experienced. It is made to be experienced.

As if to prove my opening point about *Three Kingdoms*' inherent challenge to mainstream theatre criticism, the majority of the mainstream press have struggled with it and, in some cases, condemned it. This style of theatre is clearly not to everyone's taste, but it saddens and frustrates me that many of the reviews do not even attempt to engage with it on the most basic level. Instead, there has been a startling dichotomy between the verdicts of what we might call the traditional critics and the response that the production is receiving through Twitter and online critical outlets. Perhaps this heralds the realisation that we need new ways of seeing, of experiencing, of expressing. And perhaps that isn't such a bad thing.

For some other interesting approaches to Three Kingdoms, try taking a look at reviews by Andrew Haydon and Daniel B. Yates. And for anyone wanting a more visual impression of the production (as only seems appropriate), see the Lyric's trailer below:

[Embedded video of the trailer][6]

> **Three Kingdoms**
> Dan Rebellato, *Spilled Ink*
> 12 May 2012
> http://www.danrebellato.co.uk/spilledink/2013/3/12/three-kingdoms

Three Kingdoms is a new collaboration between German director Sebastian Nübling, Estonian designer Ene-Liis Semper, and British writer Simon Stephens. Respecting the equality of that collaboration, the show is performed in three languages, and the words, production, design are all balanced, none given priority over the others. The production opened in Tallinn in September last year, moved to the Munich Kammerspiele a month later and now has begun a run at the Lyric Hammersmith, prior to its move to Berlin.

Let me start with the headline. This is intense, nasty, dark, funny, haunting theatre. I doubt I'll ever forget it. I loved it.

What's *Three Kingdoms*? This is a delicate one. I could describe the plot – in which two British detectives, exploring the beheading of an Eastern-European prostitute, journey to Germany and Estonia, to find her murderer and uncover a world of pornography, prostitution and people trafficking. But that's not really the show. The show is a journey into the underside of our cultural imaginary; it's a performance that explores the newly permeable boundaries between nations, between people, between desire and the possible, between right and wrong, between self and other, between who I am and who I am. The first 'scene' of the play is an extended interrogation scene between the detectives and a young guy, caught on CCTV throwing a holdall containing the prostitute, but as the investigation proceeds the tone and style become increasingly dreamlike and then nightmarish. By the end, the very idea that there is a simple distinction between perpetrator and investigator seems absurd. As the story unfolds and uncovers the global patterns of pornography, criminality, and violence, this network comes to characterise the performance itself.

It's so boring to do battle with the critics all the time, but the minor furore that has been kicked off tells us something about our peculiar new writing culture. To read some of the critics, you would think that what has happened here is that a play has been seized unwillingly by a director who has obscured its plot by piling all sorts of irrelevant and shocking imagery on top of it, including a meaningless series of animal heads. Thus, the result is a mess, the triumph of director's theatre, and a laughable departure from settled and sensible British theatre convention.

None of that description is true. None of it.

---

[6] See https://youtu.be/VpGsgU1XOp4.

First, the play was written *for* Sebastian Nübling. Simon Stephens has been developing a writing style that leaves space for the director. The published text is large, generous, sprawling; it asks to be intervened in, to be selected from, to be cut. It reminds me of Howard Barker's *The Ecstatic Bible*, a play that would probably take 12 hours to perform and has never been performed in its entirety. But even in more conventional theatre, J B Priestley always deliberately overwrote his plays, on the understanding that a particular production would find its own path through the material, its own emphasis, its own interests and could therefore cut it accordingly. *Hamlet* is enormously long in its fullest textual variant and is almost always cut, without demur.

Second, and following from the previous thought, if Simon's intention is to offer a text to be cut about, interpreted, selected from and collaborated with, Nübling has been doing the good old-fashioned British thing of respecting the playwright's intentions.

Third, the production's imagery is entirely drawn from the text. In that sense, it's a very conventional piece of work. Simon Stephens has written a play – I reckon – in a very uncensored way; it feels to me like he's pushed on through the writing, not wanting to decide to protect arcs and realist anchors, but just to follow the imagery and his imagination, no matter where it takes him. And the production respects that, producing its imagery the way that our dreams are studded with randomized fragments of the previous day. An early reference in the interrogation scene to The Beatles provokes a strange series of aggressive puns from the detectives. This already serves to dislodge language from literal meaning which is amplified later on when the German detective who is their liaison in Hamburg goes into raptures about the White Album, culminating in his painfully slow phonetic performance of one of that record's least essential moments, 'Rocky Raccoon'. Later the curious otherworldly riddler played by Risto Kübar sings a slow, ethereal version of 'Golden Slumbers', summoning up a sudden wealth of feeling, sentiment, and affection, that the show's dirty bare walls never otherwise see. None of this is 'realistic', of course.

Fourth, nor are the animals. The image that is reproduced everywhere is of a woman in underwear and fur coat, with a deer head. Some critics seem to have been embarrassed by this image, because they dismiss it with those ghastly half-jokes that critics like Quentin Letts seem to specialise in. And yes it's embarrassing; it's unsettling. It's a strange image because it's frightening and it's also sexy. The heels, the fur coat are classic fetish items. The woman walks on like a deer, her vertiginous heels making her look like the animal just before the lion attack of so many nature documentaries. Vulnerable, beautiful, timid, haunting. In the third act, the Estonian gang taunt a woman as 'Pitsu', the Estonian equivalent of 'Fido' – she's a dog, an animal, a lower form of life, and thus available to be used. While I found my own feelings about the image engaged in all their confusion, I don't find it a difficult image to understand. The play begins with a distinction between the methodical investigation of the police and the animal brutality of the murderer. But these categories blur as the show goes on and the boundaries between brutal instinct and rational enquiry, between desire and restraint break down. It works by acknowledging the theatre's visual dimension, its transactions between stage and auditorium; why are we watching this show? Do we want to see the killer brought to justice? Or are we, just a little, or quite a lot, interested to see more of this violence, this degradation, this abuse? Are we high-minded theatregoers or voyeurs?

None of the production's imagery is particularly obscure, by the way. As I was watching it, I wondered what the critics who puzzled over the deer's head would make of Donnie Darko ('a perfectly simple story about adolescence in the American suburbs, obscured by some confusing flashbacks and a silly actor in a rabbit suit') or even Monsters Inc. ('a potentially powerful thesis about the evils of corporate America, weakened by a reliance on some rather implausible technology and a mystical belief in the existence of monsters').

Fifth, has Nübling obscured the plot? No. The plot is an opportunity to enter into a world that undermines the architecture of plot – causality, distinction, morality, justice – and instead gives us a vision of our cultural imaginary in which our own world is sustained by cruelty and horror. One review, describing the complex plot, compares it to Raymond Chandler or Dashiell Hammett, but worries that this production obscured the details of it. These are very pertinent reference points: does anyone, seriously, read or watch *The Maltese Falcon* and follow exactly what's going on? And does anyone, seriously, think that's the point? The hard-boiled detective story, film noir, and the David Lynch thriller use the metaphysics of crime to launch us beyond a world of blame and responsibility to something much more troubling, the dependence of innocence on guilt. And that is a picture of our world, the way that transnational movements of goods, labour and services have conspired to allow the New Global Slavery, the world-spanning networks that deliver to your hotel room an Estonian woman who is guaranteed to do A-Levels and CIM, or, to your computer images of the same. To complain that the plot is too convoluted is really to complain that the world is convoluted. It's like blaming war artists for war.

Sixth, is it a mess? It's messy, certainly. There's a disgusting series of faecal handprints on the rear wall. The stage floor is variously smeared with apple juice, lubricant, cream, coffee, alcohol. The walls bear the marks of its previous performances; in the upstage left corner we see faint spatterings of blood that is only actually spattered in the last half hour; downstage left two jagged patches of grey made up of pencil lines are explained when the detective measures his and the English detective's height against the wall. There is excess, yes of course, grotesque excess. Most notably, the scene where the detectives interrupt a pornographic film shoot and we are shown an impressionistic riot of symbolic perversity, enormous strap-ons, anal penetration, facials, fetish gear. But it's a depiction of excess, rather than excess in itself. Or rather – because that suggests something rather distanced – it's an experience of excess that is intended to immerse us in the disorientation of stepping into that room. It's also very funny, in a Bakhtinian sense, a kind of grotesque lower-body riot of organs, objects and their interpenetration. But it's very precisely chosen and placed; it marks a sharp gear change in the performance, around 75 minutes in. It also creates the dreamworld by showing a kind of terroristic attack on Global Gender Security, after which the sexual and gender identity and propriety of none of the characters seem stable. Are the English detectives seducible? By men or women? Are they seduced? It becomes impossible to say. There is one moment where I did think it was messy and excessive, a lengthy physical sequence set to a stripped down version of P J Harvey's 'The Last Living Rose'. But even here it's properly placed: it's the complete breakdown of narrative movement, of spatial organisation, of character. We can no longer know who is responsible, whether distinctions of place are meaningful, if we're dreaming or awake, and the imagery places us at the heart of this collapse.

Seventh, is this the triumph of director's theatre? No, if you think director's theatre is always the crude violation of a play. I'm sure that has happened, but it happens, too, in British theatre within the new writing tradition, where a bit of bad casting or a misjudged set, a tin-eared or tone-deaf director, fail to convey the virtues of the writing. But here, Sebastian Nübling is responding generously to the writing: not just to the story, but the feel of the writing, the way it was written, what the writing does not what the writing means. It's a really sophisticated and impressive piece of work.

Eighth, is this a departure from good old British theatre practice. No it isn't. Yes, it's a departure from what we say we do, but it's not a departure from what we do. The caricatured British practice is to perform the play 'properly' as the author intends. But we know don't we – we know this – that any play worth putting on is worth putting on again, in a different way. We go to see new productions of plays because we want to see something different. Good plays contain multitudes. They can't be performed properly; they are always interpreted. Now, there are good things about putting on plays the way the author intends, in the sense that playwrights learn from seeing some of their half-formed ideas realized in performance. It's a system that allows playwrights to get better, to write more richly, to be more daring, because they can learn from performance. But a playwright, qua playwright, does not have an intention about every detail of the performance. If they do, they are a director. In this instance, as I've said, Sebastian Nübling is following Simon's intentions in getting inside the play, turning it inside out, shaping and unshaping it in rich, complex ways.

Finally, I'm a playwright and I'm really, really into playwriting. Boy, do I ever love playwriting. I like Simon Stephens as a playwright and I always love seeing and reading his plays. But I feel that the debates about this kind of performance suggest a deep misunderstanding, indeed mystification, of what playwrights, directors, designers, and actors do. We always collaborate. A play is both a complete literary object and a fragment that needs to be completed in performance (that's why plays are such fascinating and strange objects). A production must – and always does – add things that aren't in a play. It's always an interpretation. This is as true of Sebastian Nübling as it is of Max Stafford-Clark.

In this instance, a particularly bold and successful collaboration has created a stark, frighteningly persuasive picture of the sexual atavism of the globalising world and the way our own desires are part of that, however we might tell ourselves otherwise. If the critics could only see it, Simon Stephens, Sebastain Nübling, and Ene-Liis Semper have revived the state of the (inter)nation play.

POSTSCRIPT:

The broadsheets have, mostly, fumbled the ball on this one. Much better commentary here:

- Daniel B Yates on Exeunt
- Matt Trueman on his blog, Carousel of Fantasies
- Miriam Gillinson on her blog, Sketches on Theatre
- Catherine Love on her blog, Love Theatre.
- Andrew Haydon on his blog, Postcards from the Gods.

Andrew tweeted earlier this week 'Is Three Kingdoms the next online generation's Katie Mitchell *Attempts on Her Life*?' and, as someone who blogged combatively about Attempts in

On *Three Kingdoms*

2007, I think he might be right. In fairness the papers usually have little space to discuss a very big experience, but thereby hangs the tale. Is online the only space that can deal adequately with these experiences?

Catherine addresses very well the problem that the production may reproduce the misogyny that it's trying to critique. I haven't addressed that directly, except that I think the performance is trying to engage our own voyeurism – if voyeurism there is – as a way of engaging our responsibility. But that could be a very conservative move. It's certainly the case that the women on stage feel like victims of the production almost as much as of the characters. But take a look at Catherine Love's blog for a much more developed discussion.

Review: Three Kingdoms, Lyric Hammersmith

Matt Trueman, *Carousel of Fantasies*
13 May 2012
Now available from: http://matttrueman.co.uk/2012/05/review-three-kingdoms-lyric-hammersmith.html

---

About halfway through the first half of *Three Kingdoms* on Tuesday night, probably an hour and fifteen minutes in or so, I scrawled the following in my notebook:

> "Stop everything. Storm the National Theatre. Tear down the Donmar Warehouse. Torch the Royal Court. Redact the entire history of the RSC and fetch me Trevor Nunn's head on a plate."

In retrospect, this was probably an over-reaction born in the heat of the moment. Not because it over-praises, but because it does the great work at those theatres a disservice. Let's blame the adrenaline flooding my bloodstream. Let's blame the breathlessness and the dizziness; the disbelief and the sheer fucking thrill. I was putty. I was windswept. I was in love.

Three Kingdoms is a joyride.

And like any joyride, it's possible to jump into the back seat or stand on the pavement and disapprove. So let's not get carried away too quickly. It's not helpful. Far better to take a step back and assess, than scream in your faces until you're spittle-flecked and angry.

It's true that, next to most British theatre – and it's very consciously aimed at a British audience; more of which later – *Three Kingdoms* looks like an enfant terrible. It's behaving badly and it knows it. However, there's nothing so radical that you'll sit there baffled and cursing its pretentions. Quite the opposite, in fact. It's actually pretty conventional, even if it looks unfamiliar. It's certainly not inaccessible. Whatever the mainstream critics say, you know exactly how to watch this. You just need to jump in the back seat.

Co-produced by the Lyric Hammersmith, the Munich Kammerspiele and Estonian company NO99, *Three Kingdoms* brings together a British playwright, a German director and an Estonia designer in a head-on collision. Simon Stephens has written a play. Its narrative is, more or less, linear. Sebastian Nübling has directed it, using a blend of techniques adopted from Peter Brook, Pina Bausch and – without wanting to scare you off – live art. Ene-Liis

Theatre Blogging

Semper has designed it. Boldly, but certainly not uncomfortably so. No more so than a Richard Jones directed opera or a West End musical. No more than one might Alice in Wonderland. It's just that the Wonderland in Stephens's play is not an imaginative space, but mainland Europe. But I'm getting ahead of myself again.

Since I'm trying to ease you in, the relationship between these elements is not dissimilar to that of Mike Bartlett, Rupert Goold and Miriam Buether for *Earthquakes in London*. It just goes further: the text doesn't demand such a theatrical approach, though it leaves room for it. Stephens's text is characteristically muscular. Nübling and Semper run a massive charge through it and, rather than disintegrating, it comes thrillingly to life.

Admittedly, the production's spirit is one of excess, but only insofar as Nübling and Semper have turned *Three Kingdoms* up to 11. Call that self-indulgence if you will – and almost every mainstream critic has – but really it's a matter of making every moment count to its fullest. It's about maximising its theatricality. I've been watching a lot of *Great British Menu* recently and *Three Kingdoms* reminds me of some of the cooking techniques. This week, one of the chefs made a spherification of some pea puree. That involves making semi-solid spheres of a liquid and the end result looked rather like peas, but with an intense pea flavour. Another chef infused lobster meat with lobster stock, doubling the taste. Sebastian Nübling – generally dubbed a maverick, but I'm not so sure – and Ene-Liis Semper have done the equivalent to Simon Stephens' play.

That play looks like a detective thriller, but it's not. It's a journey narrative and a loss of innocence play. It just so happens that the journey in question is that of DI Ignatius Stone (Nicolas Tennant, brilliant), a detective in the Metropolitan police, and it runs in parallel with an investigation he's conducting. The difference is that the former is all about the investigation itself (the detective is basically a flavoursome cipher), while the latter is all about character.

However, *Three Kingdoms* is still a detective thriller by proxy. It starts with a police interrogation; a standard good-cop, bad-cop affair. We've seen a thousand before. Stone is bellowing into the ear of a young local lad in an empty warehouse. His partner DS Charlie Lee (a professorial Ferdy Roberts) looks on coolly. We know what happens in these scenes and we know the narrative patterns they fit into. The first scene conforms and Stephens tricks us into watching *Three Kingdoms* as a detective thriller. But it's not. That detective thriller stops conforming; it breaks apart and fragments. Yet the core character-driven play retains the pulse of a whodunit.

A head has washed up on the Chiswick Eyot in a rucksack. It belonged to a prostitute, who, it turns out, had been trafficked into this country. It was removed with a hacksaw. There's a video on the internet. We're told her head was held in a vice while a man masturbated into her hair before decapitating her with some difficulty. We hear the screams screeching from a digital camera. (The gore is always kept from us; proper In-Yer-Head theatre, but, boy, does it retain its impact.)

Setting out to solve a murder, Stone and Lee find themselves chasing down a sex trafficking ring run by a man known as 'The White Bird'. They track him first to Germany, meeting Detective Steffen Dresner (Steven Scharf) and visiting the industrial porn factory that produced the incriminating video. From there, Stone and Dresner go to Estonia, seeking the root of the trafficking gang.

Structurally, the play does much the same as *Wastwater*, only using a single narrative rather than three distinct scenes. It grows increasingly violent, dragging us into the depths. The first act hums with menace; the second pulsates, and, by the third, the play has reached Richter Scale forces. The joyride screeches out of control and careers off the road.

It's also worth nothing that *Three Kingdoms* is the inverse of most sex trafficking narratives. It runs backwards: retracing the victim's journey, rather than travelling it. As a result, it also looks wider than most such narratives and is not confined to the tragic experience of one individual (like, say, Roadkill) that only starts halfway down the causal chain. It heads towards the root cause, rather than the end effect. It doesn't exemplify the whole. It goes after it directly.

In fact, it looks wider still, at the entire cultural system into which trafficking fits. *Three Kingdoms* is largely not a play about sex trafficking at all. It is about globalisation. Its just that the products being shipped around are people and, as such, the play hits home in a way that one about coffee beans or bananas simple couldn't manage.

Stephens is basically accusing us, to borrow a phrase, of wilful ignorance. We are entirely complicit in propping up the system. He shows us it's unseen side-effects; both those that exist underneath our noses – the hyper-local narrative starts across the road, in the William Morris pub opposite the Lyric Hammersmith – and its far off effects.

Nübling plays with the first of these themes particularly elegantly. Early on, a white-suited man (Risto Kübar), whom we presume to be the White Bird, squeezes through a crack in the wall, darts across the stage and disappears in similar fashion. It's as if London's underworld exists in two-dimensions, only visible from a certain angle. That world is also chameleonic. Still in the first act, Stone and Lee are cramped into a train compartment with the killer they're seeking.

As for the second strand, as the Estonian detective puts it to Stone: "When you go to the toilet, you think your shit just disappears . . . Shit doesn't disappear." It winds up, apparently, in Estonia; London's sewage system. Of course, this is not a revelatory point, particularly not in theatre, but it's rarely said with so much force and élan.

First, Stephens takes us to Germany, where the porn our 12 year olds watch, according to the Daily Mail, is made. Nübling makes Germany into a conveyor belt of porn. Men and women in strap-ons stride around, lubeing one another up and joylessly sucking each other off. They masturbate coffee containers and straddle baseball bats. The occasional casual cry of 'cam-er-a' goes up to catch the imminent money shot. Shit and squirty cream and KY jelly goes everywhere. It's repulsive. (It's also – guiltily – the opposite.)

Stone starts to fray, and feel – as Lee puts it, in one of Stephens's characteristic linguistic pointers – "a little dislocated". The girl he meets at his hotel looks disarmingly like his wife in England and they have a frisson of sexual chemistry. Nübling plays one of their conversations in an exploded scene, such that Stone seems to swirl in and out of the actual conversation and his headspace. He also captures the sensation of feeling utterly alone and adrift in a foreign city. It's somewhere between *Lost In Translation* and that *Simpsons* sequence in which Bart and Milhouse overdo the All-Sryup Squishies. Stone seems to reel drunkenly, unable to speak the language and tempted by the repercussion-free sleaze on offer. (Interestingly, David Lan told me beforehand that deep beneath *Three Kingdoms* is Christ in the Wilderness.)

By the time we reach Estonia with Stone, this has – in keeping with the *Wastwater* model – the ante has been well and truly upped. Semper makes Estonia a grey world of sheeny suits and rampant, savage misogyny. So noxious are its fumes (smell is key to the script and Nübling draws it out further, hence the deer and wolf masks for prostitutes and pimps) that DI Stone – who seems more bumptiously naïve than ever – unravels. The play does likewise, and it's often hard to keep track. Are we the White Bird? Is Dresner? The Estonian gang wear boxing gloves and pound the walls with a barrage of punches. Speaking about the shift of global economic power Eastwards, imagining a world where Western Europe girls are trafficked into Asia, the trafficking gang turn slowly, terrifyingly, our way.

In all this, our experience mirrors Stone's journey. As he travels Eastwards, Stone becomes increasingly disorientated. As we travel alongside him, what we see gets wilder, more fantastical and more extreme, particularly in its violence. Stone unravels and so do we. There are scales tumbling from eyes all over the place. (This is why I feel that Stephens is writing for a British audience, and Nübling is following suit, by gradually moving from naturalism to uncaged metaphor. It is about the Little Englander complex; and that applies to our theatre as much as it does to our wider worldview. Here, the play becomess an accusation of its audience, in a way that elsewhere, it is aimed, to a certain extent, at an absent party.)

However, Stephens makes clear that Estonia is not the Soviet hangover we might presume it to be with our English island mentality blinkers on. Like any of us, it survives by whatever means are its disposal. Stephens carefully structures each act as an echo of the others, moving through the same pattern with actors doubling in the same role (romantic interest, key lead, hunted) each time. It's quite amazing; the same choice can both disorientate and suggest parity.

However, in the two messages, Stephens comes awfully close to having his cake and eating it. He suggests we're completely to blame for their situation and also that we're all ultimately the same. Yet, the production – whether from Stephens's text or Nübling's direction – is fully aware of this. Its coda – in which Kübar challenges Tennant to make a swan out of origami, scrunches his own paper and shakes his head when Tennant does likewise – admits the two-sided coin and the (near) impossibility of our own situation. Head it wins, tails we lose. It's also quite possible to argue that the production, at some point, becomes the very thing it sets out to critique, and it exploits its subject matter for its voyeuristic charge. This, however, seems an unavoidable byproduct of its scoring its hits so powerfully and, for me, the ends wholly justify the means.

As for Nübling's direction, it's just unbelievably good. Nübling is not a maverick. He's a master. As I suggested above, he has a tonal control that I've never seen rivalled. In the main, he employs Peter Brook's theory of 'empty space' – that theatre's representational system is analogical, not literal – but with a fiercely contemporary approach. So, individual signifiers work not simply as signifiers, but as real objects and actions with their own charge

On *Three Kingdoms*

independent of the fiction they create. It's a question of focus and he draws out the essential information, about character or location or action, with an intense minimalism.

He can bring out the brutality behind clincal post-mortem results in the slicing, dicing and juicing of an apple. He'll stretch the luridity of pornography with synthetic strap-ons and squirty cream. After moments of heart-thumping tension and speed, he slams on the breaks with a soft, soothing, breathy lullaby. He makes a concertina of Stephens's text expanding some moments and contracting others, trusting us to get the plot and adjusting the colour filter to bring out embedded themes.

In fact, it's worth looking at *Three Kingdoms* as an supped up equivalent of Brook's 1970 (!) RSC production of *A Midsummer Night's Dream*. For Sally Jacob's white box, we've got Semper's grey one, which has a more complex layout that enables a more layered staging. Where Brook used spinning plates and diabolos, Nübling uses knives and dildos. Where Brook kept the playing fairly straight, Nübling brings in textual layers of dance and song, which carry both information and tone. (In fact, the mainstream rejection of *Three Kingdoms* starts to look all the more inexcusable in this light.)

Nübling might be auteurial, but not one of his decisions detracts from Stephens's text at all. Rather they bring it thrillingly, vividly to life, while drawing out its essential, underlying contents with a stunning clarity.

I could go on and on, but essentially, I'm saying this: *Three Kingdoms* will change the course of British theatre. It comes at a time when certain young directors – Bijan Sheibani, Polly Findlay, Joe Hill-Gibbins among them, but plenty more further down, are starting to look to Europe for a clinical viscerality – and it goes much further. If you have any interest in theatre, in its potential and in its future, you must see *Three Kingdoms*. It is an extraordinary, powerful, rapturous combination of theatrical spectacle and dramatic intensity. You have one week.

An incitement to smash some fucking shit up

Megan Vaughan, *Synonyms for Churlish*
14 May 2012
http://synonymsforchurlish.tumblr.com/post/23221501522/an-incitement-to-smash-some-fucking-shit-up

---

This blog post has been partly written in German and Estonian.

Dieser Blogeintrag wurde teilweise in deutscher und estnischer Sprache geschrieben.

See blogi on osaliselt kirjutatud saksa ja eesti keeles.

I was supposed to go to see Babel last night. I'd bought the ticket about a million years ago because everyone in theatre still had a massive boner for Michael Sheen's Passion thing in Port Talbot and I thought I'd see what these Wildworks guys were all about. I watched the documentary about the Port Talbot Passion recently and it looked like an actual real-life

Theatre Blogging

outreach triumph, even if I did hear of the involvement of (*shudder*) "community groups" and "local people". (Excuse me – think I was just a bit sick in my mouth.) I would've gone along to Babel quite happily; enjoyed the knitted cityscapes and tree-dwellers and shit, but then Three Kingdoms happened.

I don't really pay attention to what proper theatres do with proper scripts and actors these days. I've got too little money to waste it on sitting in a dark room without either a) guaranteed glitter cannons and mass tap-dancing, or b) someone basically asking me to be *in the show* with them, but then all these people on twitter started going HAAAAAAAAA THREE KINGDOMS WTF WAS THAT AMAZING AMAZING AMAZING and pictures of women wearing nighties and DEER HEADS started appearing and I was all like "I *really* can't be fucked with Simon Stephens but, well, look at all the women in the fucking DEER HEADS" so I sacked Babel off and went to that instead.

I have never been so stimulated in all my life (ex-boyfriends, I'm looking at *you*).

So there were these two detectives, Iggy and Beardy, and they were investigating the murder of a woman whose head was covered in jizz then sawn off and dumped in the Thames. They followed this porn/sex slavery ring to Germany and then Estonia but none of that really matters. What matters is ALL THE STUFF THAT WAS GOING ON. They say that you shouldn't really notice a show's direction but Three Kingdoms was *directed to fuck*. Guys would just leap over walls and run into things and throw chairs. Throw suitcases through windows. There was the dude who re-enacted Rocky Racoon by The Beatles and the other guy with a bale of hay on his head and teine mees, kes tembeldatakse kurgi viilud and the other guy who masturbated a foot-long strap on dildo and the guy who wrapped the whole set in hazard tape and the guy who said "fuck you you piece of fuck" and die Frau, die sich ergab einen Schwamm Bad and the bit where everyone clinged to one wall as if the whole place was tipping over nagu hukku laeva and every so often everything would come together in the most beautiful fucked-up musical bit with a guy singing or half-singing or mumbling maybe and Glitter an den richtigen Stellen and shadows in the right places and it was just really really really BEAUTIFUL to watch.

It was like hyperreality. Like, why do we all insist on just fucking *meandering* through life when we can leap-frog through it and walk up walls and wear a fuck-off great-big dildo under our clothes? I'm writing this in a coffee shop near Victoria Station right now and when I pay my bill I'm going to flash the waitress then hurl the empty tea pot right through the fucking window.

LASST UNS GEHEN UND TATSÄCHLICH LEBEN MEIE FUCKING ELU

---

on walking out of Three Kingdoms
Sarah Punshon, *Taking Things Too Seriously*
17 May 2012
http://takingthingstooseriously.blogspot.co.uk/2012/05/on-walking-out-of-three-kingdoms.html

On *Three Kingdoms*

So. A Russian prostitute has been murdered in a spectacularly brutal way for attempting to inform on her "owner". The British police track down the killer in Germany because his sperm was in her hair: he'd wanked on her head whilst it was held in a vice, then sawed her head off with a blunt hacksaw. Whilst she was alive. But he isn't the big baddie. No, that's his Estonian boss, who made him do it.

Now we meet the boss, and his gang of sex-traffickers. They discuss the realities of market capitalism: the fact that very soon the traffic will be going in the opposite direction. They'll be getting girls from Amsterdam, Berlin and London, and selling them to Beijing, Moscow and Rio de Janiero. In between, they mock the silent prostitute who sits in the room with them: calling her stupid, giving her a name like a dog, discussing the smell of her. Then they're violent towards her.

Does this sound like fun entertainment yet?

I mean, we've seen something a bit like this before, right? We've had ordinary, sordid, naturalistic versions of this story before. On stage. On TV. I myself got into a terrible state by stupidly watching the whole of Abi Morgan's Sex Traffic in one go whilst on my own, with no-one to reassure me that no, all men do not despise all women. All women are not helpless, silent, at the mercy of whoever's the strongest and most violent.

Ah, but this is different. This is a brilliant, genre-changing, horribly funny, nightmarish version of the story. It's been made as an international collaboration between three amazing companies.

So the predatory men sometimes wear wolf masks. The mostly silent women sometimes wear deer head-dresses. People sing, and dance. The blonde, muscular Estonian gang come on like some kind of Aryan fantasy in white vests and boxing gloves, and beat hell out of the set whilst having their chat about market capitalism. The silent prostitute in the corner is wearing a very expensive and restrained green silk dress and carrying a silver platter. When the men talk about getting girls from London, they clock the audience, checking out some of the women and smirking at us. A chunk of the audience giggles at their theatrical naughtiness.

Or perhaps at the idea of being trafficked by these men. Because that would be great fun, hey? When they're violent towards you, they just spit cucumber at you, or stamp on it in a theatrical demonstration of violence. It's not actual violence. No women were harmed in the making of this play. It's all just a play, Sarah. Stop taking it so fucking seriously.

So I left. I walked out from the front row and went home. And I wish I'd gone earlier, because then I would have fewer of these images in my mind. And I would feel less disturbed about what all those middle-aged middle-class white men who made that piece of work really feel about women. When they put eleven strong male actors on stage, of all ages, shapes and sizes, and only two young, slim, beautiful and mostly silent women. When they let the men on stage look at me the way the scary men on street corners in Brixton sometimes look at me when I walk home late at night. When they fill my head with horror. And give me no hope.

Theatre Blogging

fanning the bonfire

Maddy Costa, *States of Deliquescence*
18 May 2012
http://statesofdeliquescence.blogspot.co.uk/2012/05/fanning-bonfire.html

None of this was supposed to happen.

I had an idea for what could happen. On Thursday May 10, the day after seeing Three Kingdoms, I sent an email to Andrew Haydon and Simon Stephens with a proposition:

Hi Andrew, hi Simon – i won't bother asking how you are bec frankly we're all in a 3 kingdoms place and such piffling questions seem irrelevant. Holy fucking christ i've had some intoxicating nights in the theatre but that was really something else. I want to propose something to the two of you: I really loved it, as I hope you can tell, but there is a bunch of stuff that I think is worth wrangling with and I would like to do that in company rather than on my own. Obviously there is a motive: the end point of this would be publication on Dialogue. The whole point of the site is to allow those dialogues to take place that aren't happening and this play, and particularly the critical reception of it, is perfectly situated to show what we can achieve with that. I've only read three reviews so far, partly bec I'm trying to preserve a little bit of my own headspace, but it strikes me that critical reception is falling into two camps: the mainstreams – and obviously things wld be quite different in that camp if Lyn had been allowed to review this – who just don't see the point, and the young bucks who absolutely see the point but, I would argue, are a little too ready to gloss over the stuff that's worth wrestling with in the desire to be supportive. In other words, I think we've got two entrenched camps standing off and to be perfectly honest I don't see what use that is to you, Simon, as the theatre-maker in the middle. That sounds like I've got all sorts of high-and-mighty ideas about critics and particularly myself as someone who wants to stand back a bit from this squaring up, but I don't – although if I do, i'll confess that I have been reading a book lately called Making Plays that was initially very annoying to me but has slowly pulled me in and given me lots to think about. It's a dialogue between these two seemingly patrician makers, the playwright Richard Nelson and the director David Jones – forgive me if I'm telling you a bunch of stuff you already know – that dissects every relationship in the making of new work. And there are about four really fascinating pages in it that deal with the role of critics: as people who can support new work, explain it, set up questions that fuel the writer in their continuing work, and so on and so on. So that's where I'm coming from too. . . . Simon: I totally appreciate that during the run this is the LAST conversation you might want to be having. Equally, I totally appreciate it's not a conversation you want to have at all. So please be honest about whether or not you'd like to take part. Haydon, you turn this down and the metaphorical wrestling [mooted on twitter] is going to become real.

*

They both agreed, so on Friday May 11, I sent them a second email. I'm going to edit it a bit, but only because it was 2000 words long, chunks of it were reused in the Guardian blog, and it was full of spelling mistakes:

On *Three Kingdoms*

*

Having agreed it's brilliant, let's start by having some fun with that. One of the things I've been thinking since I saw it is about the use of music in the show [the iPod shuffle of music and then film references I talk about in the Guardian].... To me it makes it feel like a production that couldn't have been made at any other time than now, you know? Like in pop reviewing, the holy grail is the album that sounds totally of the moment, that couldn't have been made in the 50s or the 80s or whatever.... Maybe it's just that I haven't seen enough German/continental theatre, maybe they've been doing this there since year dot, but over here multi-textuality of that sort feels new, which says so much about how stuck in the past our theatre is. It also made me feel very exasperated with everyone who described the plot as "labyrinthine". Haven't these people been to the cinema in the past 20 years? On the one hand, it did mean that there were occasions when I wasn't sure why I was seeing this on stage and not in a cinema. But my answer came every time something happened – the incredible leaps out of the window, that ASTOUNDING moment near the end when Ignatius realises whatsisname is the white bird and the three men fall oh so gracefully to the floor – that made it clear this story could ONLY happen on stage.

One of the things I'm confused about in the negative critical response is Michael Billington's enthusiastic review of Gross und Klein and the exhausted, disappointed dismay he projected about this. Both shows share a kind of hallucinogenic quality, both operate within a continental rather than British tradition, yet he loved the one and hated the other. I've been thinking about this particularly bec I spoke to someone at 3 kingdoms who really enjoyed it, but hated Gross und Klein. And I didn't understand that either. Except to think that it must be about connection: whether or not you feel connected to the characters. The central character in Gross und Klein feels really disconnected from society, she's stumbling around unable to get a footing anywhere. The irony is, we as an audience feel really connected to her, but we aren't in her world, we are outside peering in, just as she is outside all these other worlds peering in – at several points literally, through windows and doors and down telephone wires, startling people to such a degree that they can't bring themselves to form a relationship with her. I adored her but can see people finding her annoying. There's something similar happening with Ignatius in 3 Kingdoms: there's this almost estrangement from his wife who finds the idea that they might actually go to bed at the same time insane, there's his inability to communicate with any of the people he meets abroad, there's his feeling of isolation even from Charlie, who can communicate and only feeds him the edited lowlights of every conversation, there's the disconnect from nature and his true love of botany, all these things. Just as in the Strauss, this stuff is obfuscated, you kind of absorb it rather than comprehend it at face value, because it's put in there so subtly.

There's a question in all this for me about anticipating critical responses and the value of criticism. I think some of this thinking comes from a couple of tweets Simon sent out that really amused me: one was when you read Michael B's list of no-nos in theatre and said gleefully that 3 Kingdoms ticked a lot of the boxes, one was when you described the triumvirate of you, Sean H and Sebastian N as "three middle-aged men who want to be the Clash"... It makes me wonder how much you in the writing and Sebastian in the staging are deliberately goading a certain critical response ... But the thing is, when you get the reaction you expect, what use is that to you? This is kind of what I'm saying when I suggest that the reviews I've read so far seem to represent two entrenched positions, and what's been happening is that critics are squaring up against each other rather than actually squaring up to the play/production. Because the other side of it is that you get Andrew and Daniel B Yates glossing over the women thing. So before I get to the women thing, a question: what is the value of criticism to a production like 3 Kingdoms? I mean, assuming that criticism has a value beyond getting a few more bums on seats. Simon, is there anything you feel you would like to discover about that play from what critics write about it above and beyond what you've discovered about it through Sebastian's staging? Is it impossible to discover anything from the critics because the writing and the staging are so symbiotic that we all echo Andrew in saying: we don't know what Simon's responsible for here and what Sebastian is?

And so, to the women question. The only way I can broach this is by describing my journey through it, by which I mean the Tassos Stevens journey of before/during/after. Before: I read Chris Goode's tweets [about British directors not being allowed to do this, and women], and then later got an email from him in which he talked a bit about the show being problematic as regards women, even misogynistic. So I felt very forewarned/forearmed going into the theatre. And perhaps if I wasn't wearing so much armour, I'd have reacted differently – certainly the female friend I went with was very distressed by what she instantly described as the misogynistic treatment of women when we talked about it in the interval – but during the whole of the first half ie up to interval point I didn't balk at all. I was so intoxicated by the whole thing that yes, of course I found the description of the woman's death sickening, and of course I thought the woman wearing a doe's head and all the connotations of that – fawn, easy prey, beautiful but dumb animal, at the mercy of men/hunters/wolves – disturbing, and of course I found Alexander's cunt this cunt that language reprehensible, but at the same time it was OK. It was – and I feel like I'm stabbing the sisterhood as I say this – what the story needed to get across how wrong and foul and fucking shit the treatment of women is. I even, God help me, almost found it sexy at times, just as Andrew says. In fact, the only moment when I got really genuinely upset about the staging in the moment of watching was when the Estonian guy chews the cucumber and then spits it over the woman in the green dress. That, to me, was the moment that was unnecessary, because by then we had established the place of women in this world, and this wasn't required to communicate that.

What happened after was a slow burn that grew from mulling over the one other bit of the show that made me cross. The other cross bit was the speech from the policeman to Ignatius, criticising his attitude to the Europeans, condemning him for finding them (I can't remember exactly so forgive my crappy paraphrase) sleazy and shady and etc etc. For me it was the moment when the play took a swerve into good old-fashioned British naturalism and I just got really angry about that, without quite being able to pinpoint why. Thinking it through on the way home, the conclusion I came to was this: that diatribe about Ignatius being anti-European didn't attack something I felt to be within that character, but something I felt to be imposed upon him. There was something Ignatius very clearly said he was disgusted by, early in proceedings, and that was the trafficking of women. Yet by the end, the trafficking of women wasn't the "issue" in the play. The "issues" were globalisation and the closed-mindedness of British men.

What troubles me about this is that if you subsume the trafficking of women in that way, it becomes a mere plot contrivance, a trigger for the action and nothing more. Basically, the play uses women to tell a story about men who use women to get rich. No, the one thing isn't as bad as the other – but it's coming from a dangerously similar masculine-dominant headspace.... [And] it is not OK that women, in not being presented as sex objects, are instead seen as silent does, cleaners and bodies functionally washing themselves from a bucket. That just denigrates the women still further. Basically, the question I ask myself is: how would this play read if the commodity being trafficked were drugs or weapons and not women? Because if you're only going to mention once, and in passing, that the trade of women is revolting, I'm not sure that's enough to justify everything else.

*

There was a bit more after that, but conversational mostly. I felt nervous sending it: it was direct, and it was chewy, and I thought it likely that both would back out. In the event, Simon decided that a lot of this stuff was too raw to talk about now, but that he would like to come back to it later, and we agreed this was a good thing. And I was going to leave it there. I actually wrote in another email to them that I'm not so egotistical that I felt the need to publish my ha'penny-worth on the show. But then a lot of things happened in very quick succession. There were lots of tweets about empty seats at the Lyric. There were lots of tweets about irrelevant/anachronistic writing about theatre on the Guardian blog site. Simon tweeted that he was considering moving to Berlin. Are you seeing a pattern yet?

I haven't been on Twitter very long and I find it dangerously seductive. Instead of paying attention to my kids as they whinge about who's the winner and having to eat rice instead of pasta for dinner, I can scan through Twitter and find grown-ups I love and admire talking about Einstein on the Beach, or form vs content, or the appointment of Vicky Featherstone to the Royal Court. Of course my phone is now glued to my palm. But it also frustrates me so much. I want the dialogue to be longer: bonfires, not the brief flare of matches.

And the dialogue around Three Kingdoms is longer, spanning blogs and days' worth of tweets, reaching across the country. It's thrilling. I'd love to collate all the material into something like Diana Damian's Post: Critical site, but this week, with five Guardian deadlines looming, I just don't have time, let alone the ability to do such a thing on the web (although I know a man who probably can: reason 258 to love Jake Orr). (BTW, anyone who has some time on their hands who fancies doing the collating, please please let me know on twitter: you will earn my undying respect and a large box of maltesers.) So I just end up doing the same thing as everyone else: blogging.

I'm not sure I respect my motives in blogging for the Guardian site: at root was a knowledge that far more people would read me there than here. But there were also more altruistic impulses: I wanted there to be something positive about Three Kingdoms published in the Guardian, I wanted the site to feel more alive to what's happening in theatre right now, and I wanted Simon Stephens to stop wanting to move to Berlin.

That makes me sound like a right fan-girl, and I am, but I'm also not. I haven't seen all of Simon's work, but I've seen a fair bit, and often found myself wrestling with it. Motortown was my first and in my memory the irritation grew from a feeling of not being told anything I didn't already know, and as it happens wrapped up in that was a frustration with the portrayal of violence towards women, the way it was so clinical and inevitable. Punk Rock was thrilling to watch, Sarah Frankcom's direction and the performances were electrifying, but at the end I felt the investigation that had taken place into why children take guns and shoot other children was glib. Pornography completely, without question, blew my mind: I watched the entire thing in a sharp intake of breath. Ubu was tricky and subtle and about halfway through I decided it was brilliant. And Wastwater I've struggled unsuccessfully with here before:[7] like Chris Goode, I'd love to see Wastwater directed by Nubling and Three Kingdoms by Katie Mitchell, to see how it affects my experience of both plays.

Simon is a writer who fascinates me, who challenges me, who increasingly makes me see new possibilities for how theatre can be. And now I follow him on twitter I've discovered we like a lot of the same music to boot. But what I come up against time and again in his work is the issue of connection that so troubled me when writing about Wastwater, and indeed troubled the friend who came with me to Three Kingdoms. She and I talked hard in the interval about how she didn't feel connected to the characters, and I knew what she was saying but in this case I just didn't mind. What's so difficult about Simon's best writing, I'm starting to think, is that it mostly operates below sea level: characters and themes raise their heads above the surface but the full body of them is shimmering underneath, always moving, difficult to spot. And maybe I've started thinking this because of the Making Plays book I mentioned in the email to Simon and Andrew: in it, Richard Nelson talks about writing so that only the tip of the iceberg is visible, and how easy it is for people to misread the tip as the whole thing, and thus criticise the play for a lack when the problem isn't the play or the production, it's the audience (by which he specifically means critics) mistaking a fraction for a whole. There's an incredibly moving passage when he talks about his 1986 play Principia, and thinking it might be the last play he wrote, because "I didn't think my work was making sense to a lot of people". And then he read Michael Billington's review, which was very positive, and being overwhelmed with relief. "It wasn't satisfaction," he says. "It wasn't like, 'Oh boy! I got a hit show.' It was, 'I'm not mad. And what I'm trying to do was understood and someone articulated this back to me, and I read it.'"

This feels especially pertinent because I think I do this with Simon's work – especially after reading Andrew Haydon's review of Wastwater,[8] which not only excavated the entire fucking iceberg but examined every solidified water molecule compacted to make it. I did it again with Three Kingdoms: it wasn't revealed just at the end that it was about globalisation and the British male mindset, dummy, those things were present through the whole thing.

But then, this is my other problem with Simon's work. Like Andrew, my brain really snagged on Chris Goode's distinction between theatre that (thinks it) shows things and theatre that (knows it) makes things: I haven't yet fully figured this one out, but I want to apply it here, because the issue I had with Motortown and Punk Rock, and that others have with Three Kingdoms, is that these plays show the world as it is, not how it could be. The thing is, I already know how the world is. I know horrific things happen in the name of war that warp

---

[7] Maddy links to: http://statesofdeliquescence.blogspot.co.uk/2011/05/you-should-see-how-many-bodies-are.html.
[8] Maddy links to: http://postcardsgods.blogspot.co.uk/2011/04/wastwater-royal-court.html.

people's brains, and that kids shoot each other, and that men commit horrific violence towards women, and that people are abused within the capitalist system. But what is changed by you showing me this? Another project upcoming for Dialogue – and if it weren't for thinking constantly about 3Ks I might have gotten on to it by now – is talking to Tim Crouch at length about The Author. Because this is exactly what The Author is about: OK, you're putting this stuff on the stage – what next?

The past 10 days have been so intense I feel like my brain is frying. I've now reached the point with Three Kingdoms where I no longer feel I can write about it with any confidence, because I've read so much of what others have written I'm no longer sure what thoughts are mine and what has been planted in my brain by other people. But then, it's been a bit like that from the start for me. Sitting in the auditorium, I had Chris's email about misogyny in my head, and a conversation I'd had with Lyn Gardner the day before in which she'd told me it's a play to watch in a different way, using your subconscious, and I was sitting next to a friend whose very body language screamed her discomfort and dislike of the show. Even the email reprinted above contains some thoughts soaked up from other people, yet it's now the closest I get to a personal response. Everything since then has been response to other people's responses.

And now there's Andrew's new post about misogyny to respond to. And quite honestly, I'm just not up to it: partly because my brain is exhausted and needs some rest, partly because in the next few days I'm writing about The Ragged-Trousered Philanthropist, Romeo and Juliet, Sigur Ros and Ragtime, and editing two interviews about Torch Song Trilogy, and I'm not going to be able to do that with 3Ks clogging up all headspace. What I can say immediately is that when I rewrote the original email to Andrew and Simon as a blog – and that was matter of expediency: I came home buzzing from Tenet (and how I wish I had found time this week to write about Tenet), spent two hours reading every review I could find of Three Kingdoms, and ended up writing it in the early hours of Tuesday morning, finally stumbling to bed at 4am – I didn't think about how differently my scrabbly thoughts would read in a mainstream context. Reading Andrew pick the blog apart sentence by sentence was bracing. I suspect he'd have done exactly the same thing if our discussion had all remained on email. But when I wrote the email, I thought I was just mouthing off a bunch of opinions to see what happened. As Andrew points out, on the Guardian it all looks like statements of fact. But this brings me full circle to the underlying question I have about newspaper criticism and indeed all criticism: the extent to which reviews are expressions of taste and opinion, masquerading as statements of fact.

I disagree with Andrew about one thing: that the word misogyny closes off discussion. Mostly I disagree because that hasn't happened. What has happened is a whole lot of passionate debate about a really important aspect of the play. What that word does do is make anyone who didn't find 3Ks misogynistic – and much as I would love to fudge this one, the fact remains that the friend I saw it with emphatically and repeatedly said she did, whereas I haven't used that word in reference to my own thoughts once – feel very uncomfortable. No, I'll rephrase that: it's made me personally feel not only uncomfortable but immoral for enjoying the play. Reading Sarah Punshon's incredibly moving blog, I found myself thinking: why didn't I react like this too? What is wrong with me? This isn't a moral judgment Sarah is making of me, just as my friend spent the interval marvelling that I didn't find the first half misogynistic but never once judged me or accused me of anything. It's the feminist in me demanding an account from myself.

The questions that all this discussion about Three Kingdoms has opened up are massive: they deal with form versus content, how we watch and how we write. I'm so excited that these debates are happening, but at the same time I feel sad. Because this isn't how I wanted to engage with Three Kingdoms myself. I wanted to discuss it with critics – and I chose Andrew because he is much better at understanding Simon's work than me – and most of all I wanted to discuss it with Simon himself. Dialogue is a massively important project for me: it's where I get to reinvent the hamster wheel on which I've been running for the past 15 years. At this moment in time, have no idea whether that dialogue with Simon will ever happen. I feel as though I've spent 10 days in a very noisy place, full of voices, but the one voice I really want to hear is silent.

Simon, if you're still listening, I'm still waiting patiently, with my ears open wide.

Revisiting Three Kingdoms
Catherine Love, *Love Theatre*
21 May 2012
Now available from: https://catherinelove.co.uk/2012/05/21/revisiting-three-kingdoms/

Here we go again . . .

On Saturday, the final night of the run, I went back for a second viewing of *Three Kingdoms*. Drowning in superb but brain-frazzling criticism and starting to feel, much like Maddy Costa expresses in her wonderfully honest blog, uncertain which thoughts were my own and which I had accidentally borrowed from others, I needed to see it for myself again. I needed another hit of that visceral punch that can only be gained from the production itself (though Megan Vaughan evokes it pretty forcefully for anyone who wasn't there).

And it was an ecstatic rollercoaster of an experience, even second time round – perhaps even more so second time round. I surrendered myself to the dream and awoke three hours later, dizzied and wondering where all that time had gone. I also realised how utterly stupid my first impressions of the production were and how much I had missed. There is simply so much going on, and a second viewing only compounded the feeling that it would be futile to attempt to write about the production as a whole. This conceded, I'm not going to make such an attempt, but there are a few points that I feel the need to return to.

Critical response – By now it's fairly clear that, whether or not you believe *Three Kingdoms* will change the face of British theatre, it has had an extraordinary response. For me the past couple of weeks have been a brain-melting whirlwind, and I'm still not sure I've read everything out there on the internet about this show. I personally have never seen such an overwhelmingly vocal response or such a volume of responses to one show – and this is all despite a fairly dismissive attitude from (the majority of) the mainstream press. I can only echo Maddy in hoping that someone will find the time to collate everything that has been written in one space.

As a result, I feel that much of my own response to the show has been bounced off of what other people have said about it. Which isn't necessarily a bad thing, as I find it valuable to test my own thoughts against those of others and continue to weigh up my reaction to a show for some time after, but it did make me begin to lose sight of what moved me to engage so much with this production in the first place. For that reason I feel as though a repeat viewing is vital, although even now the intervening hours since that second experience of the show have widened the gap once again between the thoughts that are purely my own and the thoughts that are responding to the opinions of others.

But I'm beginning to think that maybe this is what theatre is all about. I firmly believe that objectivity is a fallacy, because the way in which any of us view a piece of theatre is inevitably coloured by our own identity, experiences and opinions no matter how hard we try to discard these, and perhaps the truly individual response is much the same. Unless we are to view and critique a production in complete isolation, without access to any form of marketing material or even so much as the body language of the audience member sitting next to us, we are going to be influenced, however minutely, by those around us. I'm hardly the first to quote Tassos Stevens on this, but it seems appropriate and helpful to recruit his point here:

> "The experience of an event begins for its audience when they first hear about it and only finishes when they stop thinking and talking about it."

Within this extended experience, as Stevens sees it (and I happen to think he's hit the nail on the head), there are lots of other voices involved. The marketing material that alerts you to the production, the feature or interview you might read in the paper before going to see it, the programme notes, the background buzz of the theatre bar, the conversation with your friend in the interval. No critic can be completely impervious to this trickle of outside influence.

As long as we do not find our own opinions indistinguishably mingled with those around us, which I have felt is a real danger for me with *Three Kingdoms*, I'm not sure there's anything particularly wrong with taking on board the opinions of others. Engaging in dialogue afterwards is fast becoming one of my favourite parts of the theatrical experience and I frequently find myself refreshingly challenged by hearing or reading the responses of others. While I sadly don't have the time or, quite frankly, the mental capacity to respond to everything else that has been written about *Three Kingdoms*, I can only jump for joy that so much has been written and that so many people are having these conversations. This is, of course, where online criticism comes into its own.

Text and production – Coming back to the production itself after veering off on that slight tangent, I'm still intrigued by this question of how *Three Kingdoms* has been pieced together. If you can get your hands on a copy of the playtext (which might be difficult as I nabbed the Lyric's last one on Saturday night – sorry!) then I would strongly recommend taking a look at it. I've yet to read it cover to cover, but a cursory skim is enough to establish that this is a world away from the final production. As well as making it clearer which elements have emerged from the collaborative process with Nübling and the rest of the creative team, it has also made me think a lot about the relationship between text and production and playwright and director.

There are many, many differences between the original text and the final production it has morphed into, but two jump out. Firstly, reading the playtext reveals that Ignatius was originally conceived as a bilingual character, a fact that was only changed to adapt to a casting alteration during rehearsals. I was surprised by this, because Ignatius' deep sense of linguistic disconnection and cultural disorientation felt absolutely vital to the final production; as an audience, we too are enveloped in the surreal sense of dislocation that he experiences. It would not be the same play without it. Which raises questions about the value we put on deliberate design versus happy accident or fruitful experimentation. Is a play ever really finished until it reaches the stage? (Going further, we might ask if it is ever finished even then.)

Secondly, another integral element of the production does not appear in the written script at all. Here I'm talking about the character listed as 'The Trickster', the strange, ethereal, white-clothed figure who lopes on and off stage with his microphone and leaps athletically through windows. Stephens writes in the introduction to the playtext that this character, created by Nübling, was inspired by a figure from European myth who "takes many guises and is able to release the subconscious of those he meets and the underbelly of his world", a description that fits perfectly with his elusive role in the production. While he may seem incidental to the plot itself, he is central to the way in which we understand it and provides a striking demonstration of how script and production are melted together.

But perhaps it is a false division to keep talking about script and production as though they were two divorced entities. Yes, there exists a playtext version of *Three Kingdoms* that Stephens sat down and wrote and that we can now read, but it was never intended to be performed in this incarnation. It is misleading to talk about Nübling's treatment in the same way in which we might describe a radical reinterpretation of a classic text by a maverick director, because Stephens wrote this play for Nübling. As Dan Rebellato so effectively hammers home, this was not the director poaching the text of the writer and running amok; Stephens deliberately left room for the direction and actively collaborated in the rehearsal room process. So really, there is nothing but the production.

Structure – One thing that leapt out and slapped me on the face second time round – apart from the production's extraordinary visuals – was the overarching structure of the piece. It made me wonder how I could have missed so much of it initially (I'm inclined to blame all the deer heads, strap-ons and full-frontal nudity, which have the tendency to be a little distracting). It also made me doubly frustrated at all the mainstream reviews that point to the piece's meandering self-indulgence, as beneath all the deer heads, strap-ons and naked actors there is a carefully planned play full of eerie symmetries and striking symbolism, from which all of those supposedly self-indulgent elements essentially spring.

I could go into all of this in detail, but Matt Trueman has beaten me to it, comprehensively and analytically picking apart the structure and the symbolic use of deer, wolves and grass. It is (duh!) the food chain, the cycle of life. The idea that "shit doesn't go away", graphically illustrated by the faeces smeared on the set, also slots into this natural, cyclical structure and resonates powerfully with the issues that Three Kingdoms is grappling with. We go through every stage of the cycle and cannot escape it, thus being, as I spoke about before, somehow complicit in the sex-trafficking trade being shown on stage. We are all a part of the system in which this trade operates. It is about demand and supply, with sex becoming a commodity that has a demand as stable and constant as that for food and water. As one of the Estonian gang puts it, "the real advantage in our market is that demand is always, has always been and will always be stable".

One severely neglected area in my previous write-up was the play's massive inherent criticism of capitalism and market economics, which I touched upon only in relation to the discussion of the market that takes place during the first scene in Estonia. This was mainly because my mind was taken up by other thoughts at that point, but I feel it should at least be mentioned if not fully unpacked. Because this is what is really at the rotting heart of this tale. The industries of pornography and sex-trafficking that are depicted here are symptomatic of a larger problem, facilitated by a world that is dictated by market forces; again, demand and supply.

By watching one of the pornographic films in which the murdered Vera appeared, the two detectives become not only complicit in the abuse of women (more on this below) but also in the commercial circuit that has allowed this industry to thrive in the first place, a cycle reflected by the cyclical nature of the food chain. And then of course the play is also cyclical, with the interrogation of Ignatius by the Estonian police at the end mirroring the opening interrogation of Tommy – this was clear first time around, but the symmetries are even more resonant than I had initially realised. Three Kingdoms is nothing as tidy as a circle, but it does loop back around in a shape that, going back to mirrors, seems to perfectly reflect the content.

Women – This is the biggie. First of all, I'm using the word women and not misogyny because, despite this being raised by a number of separate individuals in relation to Three Kingdoms, misogyny is not a word I ever used myself and I tend to lean towards Andrew Haydon in thinking that this word has a nasty way of closing down discussion, or at least making it difficult to respond. Also, despite the concerns I raised in my initial write-up, I would certainly not want to make the accusation that anyone involved in this production comes from a misogynistic standpoint, because in fact I believe that the opposite is the case.

Even so, this has been one of the most emotive and pressing issues to crop up around the production. Perhaps the most upsetting blog I've read on the matter was Sarah Punshon's, which articulates a very personal reaction to the violence against women that is depicted throughout Three Kingdoms and subsequently made me question my own experience of the play. Yes, I was troubled and felt the need to raise such concerns when writing about the production, but this was more retrospective than anything. Only on reflection did the majority of my worries rise to the surface, and this was in any case influenced by the conversation that I had already read on Twitter between Chris Goode and Stella Duffy. While watching the play itself, a few grating moments aside, I was mostly swept along in the thrill of the production. Where this places me as a woman and a feminist I'm not sure.

So where to begin when addressing the question of how women are portrayed in Three Kingdoms? Firstly, I think we have to accept that some level of violence against women is inevitable when tackling subject matter such as that presented here. To attempt to deal with sex-trafficking without exposing the abuse at its core would be just as much of a betrayal, if not more than, portraying the victims on stage. Diagnosis, after all, is the first step towards cure. Whether or not it has to be portrayed quite in the way it is here is another question, although the violence is nowhere near as gratuitous as it might have been. This production wisely chooses to leave the majority of the brutality to our imaginations, and it is easy to forget amongst all the concern being expressed that we see far worse on our television screens nightly.

I was initially disappointed that we see so little from the perspective of the women upon whom the sex-trafficking trade being depicted most impacts, but now I am less sure how this would fit into the production that Stephens, Nübling et al have crafted. Although it precludes the possibility of a more even gender balance in the cast (that is if we accept that casting must be done along gender lines, which is a whole other question in itself and one that is particularly interesting in relation to a play in which a male actor at one point takes on the role of a female prostitute), it feels vital to the production that this is a male dominated environment. If one or both of the detectives investigating the case had been female it would be a very different play and perhaps a less powerful one; grubby complicity takes on a big role here.

In dealing with this question, on whatever very basic level on which I am able to do that, I'm aware that I owe a response to Chris Goode, who commented on my original write-up as well as on Andrew Haydon's blog. If I'm honest, I'm still grappling with his distinction between showing and making in theatre. Do we see theatre as simply depicting a situation or do we take that a step further and accept that theatre is also making that situation? This also goes another step further to what we think theatre is essentially for; is it there to hold up the mirror to life, as Hamlet would have it – to show us the state of things as they are – or to offer an alternative? Theatre can be powerful as a tool for exposing disgusting and unjust situations and making us feel that injustice, but if we're already aware of those situations then what is the function of a further depiction? I'm asking a lot of questions, because I really don't know.

Separately but related, Chris also suggested the need for a moratorium on the use of the word "exploring", in response to marketing material that described *Three Kingdoms* as "exploring human-trafficking". It all comes back to the idea I touched on previously about the precision of language, something that I sense Stephens is particularly attuned to in his writing. Exploring can mean a lot and suggests something fairly extensive, while it is questionable to what extent any work can fully "explore" the subject matter presented here. Words such as this are dangerous and I wonder if this is tangled up with the problem (if, that is, we perceive it as a problem) of the representation of women. Seen as an all-encompassing "exploration" of sex-trafficking, *Three Kingdoms* clearly falls short by denying the women involved a voice. If we view it more precisely as pulling apart the driving market forces and male complicity behind this disgusting trade, it seems a lot more successful.

In this argument I'm neglecting the many aspects of Nübling's direction that confuse gender and representation further. Men frequently play women (although, as others have asked, why not vice versa?); a male corpse provides the backdrop for the scene in which Vera's decapitation is graphically described; red herrings are dropped left, right and centre. I've also failed to mention that, though they might be outnumbered by men, there were of course women involved in the creation of this production. To simplify it all to the extent to which I am in part guilty of seems to be missing the point somewhat. Nothing in *Three Kingdoms* is simple, as my aching, slowly unravelling brain can attest to.

Despite the time I've given to the above, which is something I feel I should address as it's become such a big issue and my earlier write-up was pointed to by others in relation to this issue, I worry that it is a reductive argument. This is undeniably an important element of the production and one that deserves our consideration, but not above and beyond everything else that's going on in *Three Kingdoms*. It seems deeply unfair to everyone involved that this is what has grabbed arguably the most attention when, as I've said before, there is so much going on here. I only wish I had time to address it all in the detail it deserves, although I suspect that would require a book (or several).

[note: since writing the above, Exeunt have produced a much more thorough and intelligent discussion about the gender politics at play in Three Kingdoms, which I'd recommend anyone interested in this issue to have a read of][9]

~

I realise that this has mostly been a lengthy, meandering failure to articulate and work through thoughts that have been troubling me for the past few days, and that I have no solid answers. All I can say is that certainty is overrated. But I hope it's clear that *Three Kingdoms* has got me thinking, thinking harder than I have in a long time, and it's got plenty of others thinking too. If there is one thing to be certain about, it's that this is not the end. If this production leaves no other legacy, which is hopefully not the case, it will at least have set a lot of minds into motion. And that alone seems worth celebrating.

---

[9] Catherine links to: http://exeuntmagazine.com/features/critical-girl-on-girl-action/.

BIOGRAPHIES OF WHATSAPP DIALOGUE PARTICIPANTS

Anne-Marie Peard worked in arts festivals for many years before eventually starting to write. Now she's an arts journalist, blogger and teacher in her chosen home of Melbourne. She's been blogging since 2006 and is an occasional contributor to *The Age*, *The Music*, *Time Out* and *ArtsHub*. sometimesmelbourne.blogspot.com

Ava Wong Davies is a student, theatre writer and playwright. She has maintained her blog since 2017 and is a regular contributor to *The Stage* and *Exeunt Magazine*. avawongdavies.wordpress.com

Bob Bullen blogs at *Chicago Theatre Addict*, which he founded in 2009 to cover Chicago theatre of all shapes and sizes: storefront, big budget, black box, splashy musicals, gritty dramas, Broadway in Chicago, broken folding chairs in a basement. Bob has also contributed to the *Huffington Post*, *Chicago Like A Local*, and other local tourism sites. chitheatreaddict.com

Daniella Harrison is a recent Queen Mary University of London graduate, and has written her blog *The Mortal Fool* since 2016. She has also written for *Fest* and *Noises Off* magazines and won the Theatre Record Critics Award at National Student Drama Festival 2018. themortalfool.wordpress.com

Ian Foster is a blogger, or a critic, or a reviewer, whatever you want to call him really. Based in London though willing to travel, he has been reviewing any manner of plays, musicals, comedy and more (nothing with puppets though) since 2009. oughttobeclowns.com

James Varney is a writer and theatremaker based in Manchester. He has been maintaining his website since late 2014. In that time, he has also written for *The Stage*, *Exeunt*, *Le Monde* and *The Real Story*. jamesvarney.uk

Janice C. Simpson (Jan) writes the theatre blog *Broadway & Me*, which she created in 2007, hosts the BroadwayRadio podcast *Stagecraft* and was one of the revolving guest hosts for the TV show *Theater Talk*. She also directs the Arts & Culture Reporting program at the Craig Newmark School of Journalism in New York City. broadwayandme.com

Katharine Kavanagh (Kate) is a circus writer and researcher who transitioned from a career in theatremaking in 2012. Since setting up her blog *The Circus Diaries* (a.k.a. 'the UK's only publication dedicated to circus critique'), she has moved from the West Midlands to South Wales, where she's been ESRC funded to undertake a PhD in circus discourse at Cardiff University. thecircusdiaries.com

Kevin Jackson is an actor, director, teacher and blogger based in Sydney. After a long career working in Australia and the US, Kevin now teaches at the International Screen Academy and

Biographies of Whatsapp Dialogue Participants

The Hub in Sydney, recently directing *Mum, Me & the IED* alongside devised projects with community disability organizations. He has maintained his *Theatre Diary* since 2008. kjtheatrereviews.blogspot.com

Mary Nguyen founded the opera and theatre blog *Trendfem* in 2013. She previously wrote for online publications *LondonTheatre1*, *CultureVulture*, *FringeOpera*, and *LDNCard* as well as *Theatre and Performance* magazine. As a blogger with no academic experience in opera, classical music or theatre, she hopes her blog encourages new audiences to see shows for the first time and proves that so-called 'elitist' genres are accessible to everyone. Mary works full-time in a media agency. trendfem.com

Molly Norman is founder of *The Theatrical Board*, which specializes in opinion pieces about theatre written specifically by people who aren't old, straight, white men. With correspondents all over the United States, local productions to the big ticket shows in New York City are all covered and considered. thetheatricalboard.com

Shanine Salmon is blogger and founder of *View from the Cheap Seat*. In an age of £100+ West End seats, she tries to prove that it is still possible to see the best shows at bargain prices. Shanine is based in Croydon and is looking to expand the site's presence beyond London. viewfromthecheapseat.com

Stacey Meadwell set up *Rev Stan's Theatre Blog* in 2010 as a place to record her thoughts on the theatre she sees. Since then she's branched out to include opinion pieces, and interviews with writers, directors and actors. She'll watch anything, from something performed on a stage the size of a tea tray to big West End productions, but not musicals – she's tried them but doesn't like them. theatre.revstan.com

ACKNOWLEDGEMENTS

To everyone whose work is reproduced in this book, thank you so much for your trust and generosity. I hope I've done your work justice: Adam Szymkowicz, Alex Swift, Alison Croggon, Andrew and Phil Whinger, Andrew Haydon, Andy Field, Ava Wong Davies, Ben Ellis, Catherine Love, Chris Goode, Corinne Furness, Daniel Bye, Dan Hutton, Dan Rebellato, Daniel York Loh, David Eldridge, Deborah Pearson, Don Hall, Erin Quill, Eve Allin, Frances d'Ath, Gareth K Vile, Garrett Eisler, George Hunka, Harry McDonald, Isaac Butler, James Varney, Jill Dolan, Kate Wyver, Laura Axelrod, Mac Rogers, Maddy Costa, Matt Trueman, Matthew Freeman, Melissa Hillman, Mike Lew, Sarah Punshon and Vinay Patel.

To everyone who participated in the WhatsApp dialogue in July 2018, it was a joy and an honour to have you all living in my phone for a week: Ava Wong Davies, Bob Bullen, Daniella Harrison, Ian Foster, James Varney, Jan Simpson, Kate Kavanagh, Kevin Jackson, Mary Nguyen, Molly Norman, Shanine Salmon and Stacey Meadwell.

To everyone who gave up their time to be interviewed, thank you for putting flesh on these bones so honestly and candidly: Alison Croggon, Andrew Haydon, Catherine Love, Chris Goode, Chris Haydon, Dan Rebellato, David Eldridge, Garett Eisler, George Hunka, Isaac Butler, Jessica Foley, Jill Dolan, Laura Axelrod, Maddy Costa, Natasha Tripney, Nicole Serratore and Phil Whinger.

To everyone from the Something Other writers' group, whose peer support network (and free counselling service) I absolutely fucking *cherish*: Diana Damian Martin, Eirini Kartsaki, Ellen Wiles, Flora Wellesley Wesley, Griffyn Gilligan, Karen Christopher, Mary Paterson, Paul Hughes, Rowan Lear, and especially the unrivalled good cop/bad cop team of Maddy Costa and Simon Bowes.

Thank you everyone who attended the reading group on Duška Radosavljević's *Theatre Criticism: Changing Landscapes* convened by me and Alice Saville in summer 2017. Our conversations made a huge difference to my thinking about some of these issues. I will forget some names, but loads of love especially to: Frank Peschier, Hannah Greenstreet, Laura Kressly, Maddy Costa again, and Mary Halton. And, of course, *enormo*-thanks to Alice, and to Duška.

Thank you to all the bloggers I spoke to in 2016 and 2017 for my separate PhD research into online theatre criticism. The listening I did in our conversations has absolutely informed this book.

Thank you to Ben Ellis, David Eldridge and Laura Axelrod for sharing archived versions of their blogs.

Thank you to the team at the National Theatre Archives for all their help accessing *Attempts On Her Life* reviews and documentation.

Thank you to the Internet Archive's *Wayback Machine*, without which researching this book would have been demoralizing as fuck.

Thank you to Alex Lauck, Amy Taylor, Andrew Haydon, Andy Field, Ben Kidd, Bill Russell, Bridget Minamore, Bush Moukarzel, David Baltzer, David Greig, Diana Damian Martin,

Acknowledgements

Duncan Macmillan, Emma Frankland, Eve Nicol, Hannah Fallowfield, Jeremy Abrahams, José Miguel Jiménez, Keith Pattison, Laura Kressly, Maddy Costa *again*, Margherita Laera, Miranda Debenham, Nicole Serratore, P. Carl, Ruth Oliver, Stephen Sharkey and William Drew for answering my questions, making useful suggestions, saying yes to things, and otherwise helping me out along the way. And thanks to Metafilter users 'brainmouse', 'holgate' and 'oclipa' for their knowledge on tech corporations and legislation.

Thank you to Andrew Haydon and Matt Trueman, for being inquisitive, challenging, and generous sparring partners, and helping me work out where I stood on all this stuff long before I ever thought about doing a book. It's been an honour to argue with you both.

Thank you to Dan Rebellato, for endless patience, encouragement, diplomacy and cheerleading, but especially for reading my drafts – both of the book and of the proposal which got it off the ground back in 2017.

Thank you to Anna, Camilla, Meredith, Lucy, Ian, Laura and Vivien at Methuen Drama, for (a) letting me get away with this in the first place, and (b) replying to all my slightly panicked emails with care, goodwill and professionalism. Thanks to Dan, Merv and team for copyediting and typesetting, and thank you to Charlotte for taking on board all my cover worries and designing something that works so perfectly.

Finally, all the love in the world to the biggest influences in my life: Mum, Dad, Carl, and Twitter. 🤍 🤍 🤍

REFERENCES

American Theater Critics Association (ATCA) (2017), 'Apply for Membership'. Available online: http://americantheatrecritics.org/apply-for-membership/ (accessed 15 September 2018).
Bano, T. (2014), '9 Moments When Teh Internet Is Serious Business Really Was Serious Business', *Totaltat*, 14 October. Available online: https://totaltat.wordpress.com/2014/10/11/9-moments-when-teh-internet-is-serious-business-really-was-serious-business/ (accessed 26 February 2019).
Bano, T. (2015), 'The Encounter – A Review', *Pursued By A Bear*, podcast audio, 29 September 2015. http://exeuntmagazine.com/podcasts/the-encounter-a-review/.
Barrett, C. (1999), 'Anatomy of a Weblog', Camworld, 26 January. Available online: http://camworld.org/1999/01/26/anatomy-of-a-weblog-2/ (accessed 10 August 2018).
Billington, M. (2007a), 'I might be a white male, but I'm not dead yet, Mr Hytner', *The Guardian*, 14 May. Available online: https://www.theguardian.com/stage/theatreblog/2007/may/14/imightbeawhitemalebutim (accessed 15 September 2018).
Billington, M. (2007b), 'Who needs reviews?', *The Guardian*, 17 September. Available online: https://www.theguardian.com/stage/theatreblog/2007/sep/17/whoneedsreviews (accessed 10 August 2018).
Blood, R. (2000), 'weblogs: a history and perspective', *Rebecca's Pocket*, 7 September. Available online: http://www.rebeccablood.net/essays/weblog_history.html (accessed 10 August 2018).
Body of European Regulators for Electronic Communications (BEREC), 'All you need to know about Net Neutrality rules in the EU'. Available online: https://berec.europa.eu/eng/netneutrality/ (accessed 27 November 2018).
Borger, J. (2006), 'Rickman slams "censorship" of play about US Gaza activist', *The Guardian*, 28 February. Available online: https://www.theguardian.com/world/2006/feb/28/usa.israel (accessed 15 September 2018).
Boyd, C. (2006), 'The Sour Grapes of Wrath: A Short&Sweet Festival Reader', *The Morning After*, 8 December. Available online: http://chrisboyd.blogspot.com/2006/12/sour-grapes-of-wrath-shortsweet.html (accessed 15 September 2018).
boyd, d. (2006), 'A Blogger's Blog: Exploring the Definition of a Medium', *Reconstruction*, 6 (4). Now available from: https://www.danah.org/papers/ABloggersBlog.pdf (accessed 10 August 2018).
Brantley, B. (2011), 'Good vs. Evil, Hanging by a Thread', *New York Times*, 7 February. Available online: https://www.nytimes.com/2011/02/08/theater/reviews/spiderman-review.html (accessed 15 September 2018).
Brown, G. (2007), 'The worst play I've ever seen', *Mail on Sunday*, 18 March: 77.
Butler, I. (2006), 'It Just Gets Worse And Worse', *Parabasis*, 7 March. Available online: http://parabasis.typepad.com/blog/2006/03/it_just_gets_wo.html (accessed 15 September 2018).
Caines, M. (2007), 'Why does Edward Albee hate directors?', *The Guardian*, 2 March. Available online: https://www.theguardian.com/stage/theatreblog/2007/mar/02/whydoesedwardalbeehatedir (accessed 15 September 2018).
Chok, V. (2016), 'Whitewashing at The Print Room?', *Chok Notes To Self*, 20 December. Available online: https://beautifulbitchmonsteridiot.com/2016/12/20/whitewashing-at-the-print-room/ (accessed 15 September 2018).
Chok, V. (2017), 'More Thoughts On The Print Room', *Chok Notes To Self*, 14 January. Available online: https://beautifulbitchmonsteridiot.com/2017/01/14/more-thoughts-on-the-print-room/ (accessed 15 September 2018).
Coleman, B. (2017), 'The Ever-Evolving World of Twenty-First Century Musical Theatre Criticism', in J. Hillman-McCord (ed.), *iBroadway: Musical Theatre in the Digital Age*, 331–50, US: Palgrave Macmillan.

References

Collins, E. (2010), 'Theatre reviewing in post-consensus society: Performance, print and the blogosphere', *Shakespeare*, 6 (3): 330–6.

Costa, M. (2011), 'on peut toujours ecrire', *States of Deliquescence*, 11 April. Available online: http://statesofdeliquescence.blogspot.com/2011/04/and-so-to-business-and-primary-purpose.html (accessed 15 September 2018).

Costa, M. (2012a), 'What new dialogue can we set up between people who write about theatre and people who make it?', *Devoted and Disgruntled*. Available online: https://www.devotedanddisgruntled.com/blog/what-new-dialogue-can-we-set-up-between-people-who-write-about-theatre-and-people-who-make-it (accessed 26 November 2018).

Costa, M. (2012b), 'fanning the bonfire', *States of Deliquescence*, 18 May. Available online: http://statesofdeliquescence.blogspot.com/2012/05/fanning-bonfire.html (accessed 15 September 2018).

Costa, M. (2016), 'The Critic as Insider: Shifting UK Critical Practice Towards "Embedded" Relationships and the Routes This Opens Up Towards Dialogue and Dramaturgy', in D. Radosavljević (ed.), *Theatre Criticism: Changing Landscapes*, 201–16, London: Bloomsbury Methuen Drama.

Coveney, M. (2012), 'Three Kingdoms', *Whats OnStage*, 9 May. Available online: https://www.whatsonstage.com/west-end-theatre/reviews/three-kingdoms-4383.html (accessed 7 August 2019).

Crittenden, S. (2012), 'Now, Everyone Really Is A Critic ...', *Global Mail*, 6 February. Available online: https://web.archive.org/web/20120210182137/http://www.theglobalmail.org:80/feature/now-everyone-really-is-a-critic/23/ (accessed 15 September 2018).

Croggon, A. (2004), 'Apologia', *Theatre Notes*, 4 June. Available online: http://theatrenotes.blogspot.com/2004/06/apologia.html (accessed 15 September 2018).

Croggon, A. (2006), 'On being nice', *Theatre Notes*, 6 December. Available online: http://theatrenotes.blogspot.com/2006/12/on-being-nice.html (accessed 15 September 2018).

Croggon, A. (2012), '"Sh*t self-righteous theatre bloggers say"', *Theatre Notes*, 6 February. Available online: http://theatrenotes.blogspot.com/2012/02/sht-self-righteous-theatre-bloggers-say.html (accessed 15 September 2018).

de Jongh, N. (2007), 'Theatre wars – the dead white male hits back', *Evening Standard*, 15 May. Available online: https://www.standard.co.uk/go/london/theatre/theatre-wars-the-dead-white-male-hits-back-6582790.html (accessed 15 September 2018).

Dolan, J. (1988), *The Feminist Spectator as Critic*, Ann Arbor: University of Michigan Press.

Eisler, G. (2006), 'the bigger picture?', *The Playgoer*, 3 March. Available online: http://www.playgoer.org/2006/03/bigger-picture.html (accessed 15 September 2018).

Eisler, G. (2006a), 'Censorship comes to Downtown', *The Playgoer*, 28 February. Available online: http://www.playgoer.org/2006/02/censorship-comes-to-downtown.html (accessed 15 September 2018).

Eisler, G. (2006b), 'NYTW', *The Playgoer*, 28 February. Available online: http://www.playgoer.org/2006/02/nytw.html (accessed 15 September 2018).

Eisler, G. (2006c), 'Let's go back ...', *The Playgoer*, 13 March. Available online: http://www.playgoer.org/2006/03/lets-go-back.html (accessed 26 February 2019).

Encore Theatre Magazine (2006), 'Surprise Surfuckingprise', 29 November. Available online: https://web.archive.org/web/20070310140029/http://www.encoretheatremagazine.co.uk:80/?p=9 (accessed 15 September 2018).

Essential Drama (2018), 'Maddy Costa', November. Available online: http://essentialdrama.com/critics/maddycosta/ (accessed 20 December 2018).

Field, A. (2007a), 'Attempts on Her Life (part the third (and last ...))', *The Arcades Project*, 19 March. Available online: http://thearcadesproject.blogspot.com/2007/03/attempts-on-her-life-part-third-and.html (accessed 15 September 2018).

Field, A. (2007b), 'A script is a memorial, not a blueprint', *The Guardian*, 18 December. Available online: https://www.theguardian.com/stage/theatreblog/2007/dec/18/ascriptisamemorialnotab (accessed 15 September 2018).

Foley, J. (2017a), 'I am Not a Proper Critic: Rejection Letter from the American Theater Critics Association', *Foley Got Comped*, 25 October. Available online: http://foleygotcomped.blogspot.com/2017/10/i-am-not-proper-critic-rejection-letter.html (accessed 15 September 2018).

References

Foley, J. (2017b), 'Blogging About Theater For No Money: You Get What You Pay For', *Foley Got Comped*, 27 October. Available online: http://foleygotcomped.blogspot.com/2017/10/blogging-about-theater-for-no-money.html (accessed 15 September 2018).

Foster, I. (2011), 'A response to Matt Trueman', *There Ought To Be Clowns*, 11 February. Available online: https://www.oughttobeclowns.com/2011/02/a-response-to-matt-trueman.html/ (accessed 15 September 2018).

Freeman, M. (2006), 'The saga of Rachel Corrie', *On Theatre and Politics*, 8 March. Available online: http://matthewfreeman.blogspot.com/2006/03/saga-of-rachel-corrie.html (accessed 15 September 2018).

Fricker, K. (2015), 'The Futures of Theatre Criticism', *Canadian Theatre Review*, 163: 49–53.

Furness, C. (2011), 'I could have screamed but instead I wrote this', *Distant Aggravation*, 10 February. Available online: http://distantaggravation.blogspot.com/2011/02/i-could-have-screamed-but-instead-i.html (accessed 15 September 2018).

Garrett, J.J. (n.d.), 'About me', *JJG.net*. Available online: http://www.jjg.net/about/ (accessed 10 August 2018).

Goode, C. (2007a), 'Implausible jukebox #1', *Thompson's Bank of Communicable Desire*, 28 January. Available online: http://beescope.blogspot.com/2007/01/implausible-jukebox-1.html (accessed 15 September 2018).

Goode, C. (2007b), 'What's It All About Albee?', *Thompson's Bank of Communicable Desire*, 4 March. Available online: http://beescope.blogspot.co.uk/2007/03/whats-it-all-about-albee.html (accessed 27 February 2019).

Goode, C. (2018), conversation with D. Eldridge, *Thompson's Live*, S05 E03, podcast audio, 30 May 2018. https://chrisgoodeandco.podbean.com/e/thompson%E2%80%99s-live-s5-ep3-30th-may-2018-david-eldridge/

Habermas, J. (1989), *The Structural Transformation of the Public Sphere*, trans. T. Burger, Cambridge: Polity.

Halavais, A. (2013), 'Blogging as a Free Frame of Reference', in A. Delwiche and J. Jacobs Henderson (eds), *The Participatory Cultures Handbook*, 109–19, New York and London: Routledge.

Harvey, N., Grehan, H. and Tompkins, J. (2010), '"Be Thou Familiar, But by no means Vulgar": Australian Theatre Blogging Practice', *Contemporary Theatre Review*, 20 (1): 109–19.

Haydon, A. (2011), '2p', *Postcards From The Gods*, 14 February. Available online: http://postcardsgods.blogspot.com/2011/02/2p.html (accessed 15 September 2018).

Haydon, A. (2012a), 'Embedded', *Postcards From The Gods*, 16 April. Available online: http://postcardsgods.blogspot.com/2012/04/embedded.html (accessed 15 September 2018).

Haydon, A. (2012b), 'Three Kingdoms – Lyric Hammersmith', *Postcards From The Gods*, 10 May. Available online: http://postcardsgods.blogspot.com/2012/05/three-kingdoms-lyric-hammersmith.html (accessed 15 September 2018).

Haydon, A. (2012c), 'Three Kingdoms and Misogyny', *Postcards From The Gods*, 18 May. Available online: http://postcardsgods.blogspot.com/2012/05/three-kingdoms-and-misogyny.html (accessed 15 September 2018).

Haydon, A. (2013), 'Postcards From The Cods', *Postcards From The Gods*, 6 August. Available online: http://postcardsgods.blogspot.com/2013/08/postcards-from-cods.html (accessed 15 September 2018).

Haydon, A. (2016), 'A Brief History of Online Theatre Criticism in England', in D. Radosavljević (ed.), *Theatre Criticism: Changing Landscapes*, 135–51, London: Bloomsbury Methuen Drama.

Holmes, S. (2013), 'Maybe the existing structures of theatre in this country, whilst not corrupt, are corrupting', *What's On Stage*, 18 June. Available online: https://www.whatsonstage.com/london-theatre/news/sean-holmes-maybe-the-existing-structures-of-theat_31033.html (accessed 15 September 2018).

Horwitz, A. (2012), 'Re-Framing The Critic for the 21st Century: Dramaturgy, Advocacy and Engagement', *Culturebot*, 5 September. Available online: https://www.culturebot.org/2012/09/13258/re-framing-the-critic-for-the-21st-century-dramaturgy-advocacy-and-engagement/ (accessed 15 September 2018).

References

Hoyle, B. (2007), 'Dead white men in the critic's chair scorning work of women directors', *The Times*, 14 May: 3.

Hoyle, B. (2010), 'No love lost for the Lloyd Webber sequel', *The Times*, 5 March: 9.

Hutton, D. (2013), 'The Strange Undoing of Prudencia Hart', *Dan Hutton*, 16 July. Available online: https://danhutton.wordpress.com/2013/07/16/the-strange-undoing-of-prudencia-hart/ (accessed 15 September 2018).

Jancovich, M. (2002), 'Cult Fictions: Cult Movies, Subcultural Capital and the Production of Cultural Distinctions', *Cultural Studies* 16 (2): 306–22.

Letts, Q. (2012), 'No dialect can save the terrible Three Kingdoms that remains awful in all its languages', *Daily Mail*, 10 May. Available online: https://www.dailymail.co.uk/tvshowbiz/reviews/article-2142665/Three-Kingdoms-review-No-dialect-save-terrible-play-remains-awful-3-languages.html (accessed 15 September 2018).

Love, C. (2012a), 'Three Kingdoms: New Ways of Seeing, Experiencing, Expressing', *Catherine Love*, 12 May. Available online: https://catherinelove.co.uk/2012/05/12/three-kingdoms-new-ways-of-seeing-experiencing-expressing/ (accessed 15 September 2018).

Love, C. (2012b), 'Revisiting Three Kingdoms', *Catherine Love*, 21 May. Available online: https://catherinelove.co.uk/2012/05/21/revisiting-three-kingdoms/ (accessed 15 September 2018).

MacArthur, M. (2013), 'The Feminist Spectator As Blogger: Creating Critical Dialogue About Feminist Theatre On The Web', *Theatre Research in Canada*, 34 (2). Available online: https://journals.lib.unb.ca/index.php/TRIC/article/view/21425/24841 (accessed 10 August 2018).

Mackenzie, I. (2008), '10 questions: Don Hall', *Theatre is Territory*, 18 January. Available online: http://theatreisterritory.com/2008/01/10-questions-don-hall/ (accessed 26 November 2018).

Manthorpe, R. (2018), 'Childish Gambino and how the internet killed the cultural critic', *Wired*, 11 May. Available online: https://www.wired.co.uk/article/childish-gambino-lyn-gardner-internet-criticism (accessed 10 August 2018).

McKinley, J. (2006a), 'Play About Demonstrator's Death Is Delayed', *New York Times*. Available online: https://www.nytimes.com/2006/02/28/theater/newsandfeatures/play-about-demonstrators-death-is-delayed.html (accessed 15 September 2018).

McKinley, J. (2006b), 'Tensions Increase Over Delay of a Play', *New York Times*, 7 March. Available online: https://www.nytimes.com/2006/03/07/theater/newsandfeatures/tensions-increase-over-delay-of-a-play.html (accessed 15 September 2018).

Merholz, P. (2002), 'Play With Your Words', *Peterme.com*, 17 May. Available online: https://www.peterme.com/archives/00000205.html (accessed 10 August 2018).

Minamore, B., Mahfouz, S. and Dodds, G. (2018), 'Critics of Colour in 2019 (and hopefully beyond)', *Critics of Colour Collective*, 19 December. Available online: https://criticsofcolour.tumblr.com/post/181249377573/critics-of-colour-in-2019-and-hopefully-beyond (accessed 29 December 2018).

Morris, S. L. (2007), 'Is Edward Albee Softening with Success?', *LA Weekly*, 21 February. Available online: https://www.laweekly.com/arts/is-edward-albee-softening-with-success-2147453 (accessed 15 September 2018).

Nicol, E. (2013), 'Vinegar Tom – Warwick University Drama Society', *Edinburgh Furinge Reviews*, 12 August. Available online: http://edinburghfuringe.tumblr.com/post/58069062225/vinegar-tom-warwick-university-drama-society (accessed 15 September 2018).

Notional Theatre (2007), 'both pretentious and boring', 28 March. Available online: https://notionaltheatre.wordpress.com/2007/03/28/both-pretentious-and-boring/ (accessed 15 September 2018).

O'Reilly, T. (2005), 'What is Web 2.0', *O'Reilly*, 30 September. Available online: https://www.oreilly.com/pub/a/web2/archive/what-is-web-20.html (accessed 10 August 2018).

Pai, A. (2017), 'Remarks of the FCC Chairman Ajit Pai at the Newseum', *Federal Communications Commission (FCC)*, 26 April. Available online: http://transition.fcc.gov/Daily_Releases/Daily_Business/2017/db0427/DOC-344590A1.pdf (accessed 27 November 2018).

Perkovic, J. (2012), 'ah, but anyone can shit on a play', *Guerrilla Semiotics*, 8 February. Available online: https://guerrillasemiotics.com/2012/02/ah-but-anyone-can/ (accessed 15 September 2018).

Poll, M. (2016), 'When Little is Said and Feminism is Done? Simon Stephens, the Critical Blogosphere and Modern Misogyny', *Contemporary Theatre Review*. Available online: https://www.

References

contemporarytheatrereview.org/2016/when-little-is-said-and-feminism-is-done/ (accessed 15 September 2018).

Prescott, P. (2013), *Reviewing Shakespeare*, Cambridge: Cambridge University Press.

Punshon, S. (2012), 'on walking out of Three Kingdoms', *Taking Things Too Seriously*, 17 May. Available online: http://takingthingstooseriously.blogspot.com/2012/05/on-walking-out-of-three-kingdoms.html (accessed 15 September 2018).

Quill, E. (2016), 'In the Depths of British Theatrical Racism @the_printroom', *Fairyprincessdiaries*, 16 December. Available online: *https://fairyprincessdiaries.com/2016/12/16/in-the-depths-of-british-racism-the_printroom/* (accessed 15 September 2018).

Radosavljević, D. (ed.) (2016), *Theatre Criticism: Changing Landscapes*, London: Bloomsbury Methuen Drama.

Rheingold, H. (1994), *The Virtual Community: Surfing The Internet*, London: Minerva.

Sadler, V. (2016), '2016 Theatre in Review: Female Playwrights', *Victoria Sadler*, 21 December. Available online: http://www.victoriasadler.com/2016-theatre-in-review-female-playwrights/ (accessed 15 September 2018).

Sadler, V. (2017), '2017 in Review: The Lot for Female Playwrights Worsens', *Victoria Sadler*, 4 September. Available online: http://www.victoriasadler.com/2017-in-review-the-lot-for-female-playwrights-worsens/ (accessed 15 September 2018).

Sadler, V. (2018), '2018 Theatre in Review: Challenges for Female Playwrights Continues', *Victoria Sadler*, 4 September. Available online: http://www.victoriasadler.com/2018-theatre-in-review-challenges-for-female-playwrights-continues/ (accessed 15 September 2018).

Sans Taste (2010), 'Blogger etiquette: reviewing a preview', 27 October. Available online: http://www.sanstaste.com/2010/10/27/blogger-etiquette-reviewing-a-preview/ (accessed 15 September 2018).

Sans Taste (2011), 'Thoughts from the metro', 13 February. Available online: http://www.sanstaste.com/2011/02/13/thoughts-from-the-metro/ (accessed 15 September 2018).

Shenton, M. (2007), 'The power of dreams', *Sunday Express*, 18 March: 62.

Shenton, M. (2015), 'The past, present and future of theatre criticism', *Shenton Stage*, 5 April. Available online: http://shentonstage.com/the-past-present-and-future-of-theatre-criticism/ (accessed 10 August 2018).

Silva, H. (2012), 'Three Kingdoms: Simon Stephens and Sebastian Nübling', *Hannah Silva*, 16 May. Available online: http://hannahsilva.co.uk/three-kingdoms-simon-stephens-sebastian-nubling/ (accessed 15 September 2018).

Simmons, J. (2011a), 'Welcome to the site that tells you about theatre as it really is', *Shit On Your Play*, 10 June. Available online: http://shitonyourplay.blogspot.com/2011/06/welcome-to-site-that-tells-you-about.html (accessed 15 September 2018).

Simmons, J. (2011b), 'Belvoir's "The Seagull", written by Chekhov, butchered by Benedict Andrews & dissected by me', *Shit On Your Play*, 13 June. Available online: http://shitonyourplay.blogspot.com/2011/06/belvoirs-seagull-written-by-chekhov.html

Simmons, J. (2011c), 'STC's Baal, June 2011. Directed by Simon Stone and dissected by me', *Shit On Your Play*, 10 June. Available online: http://shitonyourplay.blogspot.com/2011/06/stcs-baal-june-2011-directed-by-simon.html (accessed 15 September 2018).

Spencer, C. (2007), 'Ageism is rife amongst theatre directors', *The Telegraph*, 15 May. Available online: https://www.telegraph.co.uk/comment/personal-view/3639900/Ageism-is-rife-among-theatre-directors.html (accessed 15 September 2018).

Supple, A. (2012), 'Shit on your Blog? No, I'd rather not', *Augusta Supple*, 6 February. Available online: http://augustasupple.com/2012/02/shit-on-your-blog-no-id-rather-not/#more-3218 (accessed 15 September 2018).

Tech Crunch (2009), 'JournalSpace Drama: All Data Lost Without Backup, Company Deadpooled', 3 January. Available online: https://techcrunch.com/2009/01/03/journalspace-drama-all-data-lost-without-backup-company-deadpooled/ (accessed 15 September 2018).

Thornton, S. (1995), *Club Cultures: Music, Media and Subcultural Capital*, Cambridge: Polity Press.

Thorpe, V. (2010), 'If even Andrew Lloyd Webber fears bloggers, is it curtains for the critics?', *The Observer*, 14 March. Available online: https://www.theguardian.com/stage/2010/mar/14/andrew-lloyd-webber-bloggers (accessed 15 September 2018).

References

Tripney, N. (2012) with E. Parry-Davies, D. B. Yates and D. Damian, 'Hardcore Critical Girl-on-Girl Action', *Exeunt Magazine*, 21 May. Available online: http://exeuntmagazine.com/features/critical-girl-on-girl-action/ (accessed 26 November 2018).

Trueman, M. (2011), 'Theatre bloggers must leave previews alone', *The Guardian*, 10 February. Available online: https://www.theguardian.com/stage/theatreblog/2011/feb/10/bloggers-review-previews-theatre (accessed 15 September 2018).

Trueman, M. (2012a), 'Review: Three Kingdoms, Lyric Hammersmith', *Matt Trueman*, 13 May 2012. Available online: http://matttrueman.co.uk/2012/05/review-three-kingdoms-lyric-hammersmith.html (accessed 15 September 2018).

Trueman, M. (2012b), 'Further reflections on Three Kingdoms', *Matt Trueman*, 16 May. Available online: http://matttrueman.co.uk/2012/05/further-reflections-on-three-kingdoms.html (accessed 26 November 2018).

Varney, J. (2015), 'Reading as Faith?', *James Varney*, 28 September. Available online: http://jamesvarney.squadsite.uk/reading-as-faith/ (accessed 26 November 2018).

Vaughan, M. (2012), 'An incitement to smash some fucking shit up', *Synonyms For Churlish*, 17 May. Available online: http://synonymsforchurlish.tumblr.com/post/23221501522/an-incitement-to-smash-some-fucking-shit-up (accessed 15 September 2018).

Vaughan, M. (2014), 'Teh internet is serious business', *Synonyms For Churlish*, 23 September. Available online: http://synonymsforchurlish.tumblr.com/post/98220912603 (accessed 15 September 2018).

Vaughan, M. (2015a), 'Application for Review', *Synonyms For Churlish*, 15 July. Available online: http://synonymsforchurlish.tumblr.com/post/124105363393/application-for-review-reviews-a-b-and-c-of (accessed 15 September 2018).

Vaughan, M. (2015b), 'Whether you whine or twine', *Synonyms For Churlish*, 18 March. Available online: http://synonymsforchurlish.tumblr.com/post/113978877618/whether-you-whine-or-twine-he-shake-it-up-right (accessed 15 September 2018).

Walker, T. (2007), 'An Angel's Kiss of Life', *Sunday Telegraph Magazine*, 25 March.

Walker Rettberg, J. (2003), 'final version of weblog definition', *jill/txt*, 28 June, updated 28 August. Available online: http://jilltxt.net/?p=227 (accessed 10 August 2018).

Weiss, P. (2006) 'Too Hot for New York', *The Nation*, 16 March. Available online: https://www.thenation.com/article/too-hot-new-york/ (accessed 15 September 2018).

West End Whingers (2006), 'Resurrection Blues: well it made us cross', 8 March. Available online: https://westendwhingers.wordpress.com/2006/03/08/resurrection-blues-well-it-made-us-cross/ (accessed 15 September 2018).

West End Whingers (2007), 'Two dead white males respond to Mr Hytner', 20 May. Available online: https://westendwhingers.wordpress.com/2007/05/20/two-dead-white-males-respond-to-mr-hytner/ (accessed 15 September 2018).

West End Whingers (2010a), 'Review – Love Never Dies, Adelphi Theatre', 2 March. Available online: https://westendwhingers.wordpress.com/2010/03/02/review-love-never-dies-adelphi-theatre/ (accessed 15 September 2018).

West End Whingers (2010b), 'Really Old, Like Moira Stuart', 11 March. Available online: https://westendwhingers.wordpress.com/2010/03/11/really-old-like-moira-stuart/ (accessed 15 September 2018).

Wong Davies, A. (2018), 'on criticism; or, what the fuck am i doing w myself???', *Ava Wong Davies*, 30 November. Available online: https://avawongdavies.wordpress.com/2018/11/30/on-criticism-or-what-the-fuck-am-i-doing-w-myself/ (accessed 20 December 2018).

Yates, D. B. (2012), 'Three Kingdoms', *Exeunt Magazine*, 10 May. Available online: http://exeuntmagazine.com/reviews/three-kingdoms/ (accessed 26 November 2018).

York Loh, D. (2016), 'Feature: Scenes From A Yellowface Execution', *The Play's The Thing UK*, 18 December. Available online: https://theplaysthethinguk.com/2016/12/18/feature-scenes-from-a-yellowface-execution/ (accessed 15 September 2018).

INDEX

bold = a republished blog post by the indexed author
italics = a republished blog post focused on this subject

About Last Night (Terry Teachout) 15
accessibility 3, 10, 28, 58, 72, 74, *125–8*
acting
    and cultural authenticity 182, 184
    developing a character 89, *92–3*
    differences between English and German styles 220
    industry pressures on actors 55
    and participatory art 118–19
    priorities for acting companies 85
    in *Road* (Royal Court Theatre) 200–1
actor training (*see* theatre training)
Adler and Gibb (Royal Court Theatre) 38, 199
The Age 116
ageism 28
Albee, Edward 23, 95–100, 101–4
Allin, Eve 71 n.1, 84, **123–5**
American Theater Critics Association (ATCA) 41–3
American Theatre 15
Amsbury, Zay 213
'Andrew and Phil' (*see* West End Whingers)
Angry White Guy from Chicago (Don Hall) 15
anonymity 17, 21, 25, 32, 33, 44
antagonism 9–11, 21, 25–7, 33
anti-Semitism (*see* Jews and Judaism)
The Arcades Project (Andy Field) 18
Armstrong, Mark 15, 20
Arts Council England (ACE) (*see* funding)
Attempts On Her Life (National Theatre) 24–5, 24 n.9, 27, 35, 82, *131–4*, 232
audiences 126–7, 172, 198
audio description (*see also* disability) 67, 74 n.5
The Australian 40
auteurism 24, 26, 89, 177, 237
autonomy 8, 9, 72
Axelrod, Laura
    on animosity towards bloggers 32 n.18
    on conditions for women theatremakers **90–2**
    foundations of the US blogosphere 15
    reflections on *My Name Is Rachel Corrie* 20
    on the relationship between playwrights and directors 82, **85–6**, 86, 87, 87 n.1, 89–90
A Younger Theatre (AYT) 34, 170

Bano, Tim 40
Barger, Jorn 4
Barrett, Cam 4, 5
Behaviour (festival) *164*

Berners-Lee, Tim 6
Billington, Michael
    on *Attempts On Her Life* (National Theatre) 133
    on *Big and Small (Gross und Klein)* (Sydney Theatre Company) 241
    critical approach 223
    on Hytner's 'dead white men' comment 28, *116–17*
    level of theatregoing experience 172
    on *Principia* (Richard Nelson) 244
    on theatre blogging 10, 22, 32 n.18
    The State of the Nation 25
    on *The Trial* (Young Vic) 167–8
    on *Three Kingdoms* (Lyric Hammersmith) 241
Blogger 5, 17
bloggers' nights 20
blogging
    definitions of (general) 5, 7–8
    definitions of (theatre) 8–9, 17
    disparagement of 10, 31–2, 32 n.18, 42–3
    history of 4–7
    hyperlinks within 4, 5, 7, 15, 28, 73–4, 84
    by theatremakers 9, 17, 18, 19, 50, 53–4, 77
blogrolls 4, 15
Blood, Rebecca 5, 5 n.3
Boyd, Chris 16, 21
boyd, danah 7 n.5
Brantley, Ben 31 n.17, 160, 162
British Council (*see* funding)
Brown, Georgina 24 n.9
Bullen, Bob 45–70
The Bulletin 16
bullying (*see* antagonism)
burn-out 51–2, 74, *105*
Butler, Isaac
    on the decline of theatre blogging 71
    establishing bloggers' nights 20
    foundations of the US blogosphere 15
    impacts of blogging on directing career 17
    on *My Name Is Rachel Corrie* 19, 83, **204–5**, *207–9*
    on online 'assholes' 21
    on the relationship between playwrights and directors 82, **88–90**, 90
Buzzfeed 40
Bye, Daniel 83, **150–5**, 156

captioning (*see also* disability) 58
Carl, P. 160–2

Index

casting
   celebrity 124, 176
   of *Seagull (Thinking of you)* (Coil Festival) 177
   of *The Fiddler on The Roof* (Arena Stage) *180–5*
   of *Three Kingdoms* (Lyric Hammersmith) 239, 250
   in Trevor Nunn musicals 113
   yellowface 43, 83, *188–95*, *195–6*
cat pics 38–40, 77
censorship 18–20, 202–11
Chicago Sun-Times 10 n.8
Chicago Tribune 10 n.8
Chok, Vera 43
Christian, Jude 38
circus 49, 54, 66
The Circus Diaries (Katharine Kavanagh) 41, 74 n.5
City Paper, Philadelphia 41
class 4, 74, 126, 186, 200–1 (*see also* diversity)
climate change 163
The Clyde Fitch Report (Leonard Jacobs) 40
Coleman, Bud 11
Collins, Eleanor 12
colonialism 14, 179
Comédie-Française, Paris 20
Comtois, James 15
conflicts of interest 17, 54, 66, 123
copyright infringement 76, 84
Corrie, Rachel (*see My Name Is Rachel Corrie*)
Costa, Maddy
   on critical expertise 77
   Criticism & Love newsletter 73
   embedded criticism 34–5, 75, 82, 107, 144, 147, 150, 155
   journalistic background 33
   on *Open House* (Chris Goode & Company) **138–44**
   on *This Last Tempest* (Uninvited Guests) *162–4*
   on *Three Kingdoms* (Lyric Hammersmith) 38, **240–6**, 246, 247
Cote, David 15
Coveney, Michael 37, 134, 227
Crampton, Hillary 116
The Craptacular (Laura Motta and Aileen McKenna) 29
Crimp, Martin 24–5, *131–4*
critical distance (*see* 'objectivity')
'critical generosity' 83, *160–2*
criticism
   affect and emotion 33, 36, 40, 48, 51, 60, 77
   of *Attempts On Her Life* (National Theatre) 24–5, 24 n.9, *131–4*
   critical expertise 77, *129–30*, 161
   democratization/diversification of 4, 10, 11, 12, 28, 34–5, 44, 46, 48, 56, 72, 77, *123–5*
   embedded 33–5, 38, 75, *138–57*
   experimentation with form/style 38–40, 48, 59–61
   feminist 12, 15–16, *160–2*
   of *Love Never Dies* (Adelphi Theatre) 29–31, *134–8*
   mainstream approaches to 117, 224, 228
   mainstream critic redundancies 10, 11, 12, 42, 48–9, 161
   'outsider' 9–10
   reviewing previews 30–2, 63–5, *120–2*
   of *Three Kingdoms* (Lyric Hammersmith) 36–8, *219–51*
Criticism & Love (Maddy Costa and Andy Field) 73, 73 n.4
Critics' Circle 43
Critics of Colour Collective 44, 44 n.25, 57, 77
Croggon, Alison
   on critical expertise **129–30**
   on Ming-Zhu Hii and Short + Sweet festival 21 n.7
   on *My Name Is Rachel Corrie* and the *Nomadics* poetry board 213
   Playbox Theatre controversy 16
   poetry connection with Chris Goode 28
   return to professional reviewing 40
   on *Shit On Your Play* blog 33
   Witness 72
   on writing for theatre 95, **101–4**
Croce, Arlene 160
crowdfunding (*see* funding)
Culturebot 34 n.20
CultureWars 150

Daily Mail 37, 133, 235
Damian Martin, Diana 73 n.3, 243
d'Ath, Frances 84, **115–16**
Davis, Walter 209–10, 209 n.4, 211, 212
Dead Centre 164
'dead white men' 27, 122
Dear Evan Hansen (Broadway) 56–7
Death and the King's Horseman (National Theatre) 38 n.22
defamation 81–2 (*see also* libel)
de Jongh, Nicholas 27, 117, 133
de la Puente, Gabrielle 60 n.2
Deliq. (*see States of Deliquescence*)
design-led theatre 27, 35, 38
devised theatre (*see* experimental performance)
Devoted and Disgruntled 34 n.20, 144, 147, 150, 151
Dialogue (Maddy Costa and Jake Orr) 34–5, 240, 245, 246
Distant Aggravation (Corinne Furness) 31
directing
   directing the 'canon' *196–8*
   directors' relationship with playwrights 23, *85–92*, 226, 228, 229–30, 232, 247–8
   European influence on 38
   by Katie Mitchell 24–5, 27, 220, 244
   Richard Eyre on 153
   by Sebastian Nübling 37, 223, 226, 228, 232, 236, 238
   by Trevor Nunn 112
disability 57–8, 67, 74, 83, 126 (*see also* diversity)
diversity 14–15, 44, 56, 57, 74, 77, 83, 90–2, *125–8*, 161–2, *175–201* (*see also* class; disability; race; women)

264

Index

Dodds, Georgia 44, 44 n.25, 77
Dolan, Jill 15, 29, 83, **160–2**, **175–8**, **180–5**
'dotcom bubble/crash' 6, 15

Edinburgh Fringe 41, 44, 62, 149, 170
Edinburgh Furinge Reviews (Eve Nicol) 38–40
Edinburgh International Festival 149
editing 72–3, 81–2, 84
Eisler, Garrett 15, 19, 20, 42, 83, **202–4**, 209
Eldridge, David
   on *Attempts On Her Life* **132–4**
   as emblematic of traditional approaches to playwriting 95, 96, 222
   foundations of the UK blogosphere 18
   on playwriting 14, 23–4, 25–7
Electronic Frontier Foundation (EFF) 76
Ellis, Ben 18, 20, 83, **211–18**
embedded criticism (*see* criticism)
emoji 40, 77
Encore Theatre Magazine
   online (2003–2006) 17–18, 23, 82, 95, 96, 98, 99, **112–15**
   print (1954–1965) 17
The Encounter (Complicité) 40
exclusivity (*see* accessibility)
Exeunt Magazine 37, 38, 40, 72, 84, 251
experimental performance 22–4, 25–7, 29, 98, 100

Facebook 9, 29, 148
FaceTime 3
Federal Communications Commission (FCC) 76
Felgate, Rebecca 29 n.15
feminism (*see* women)
The Feminist Spectator (Jill Dolan) 15–16
Fiddler On The Roof (Arena Stage) *180–5*
Field, Andy
   on *Attempts On Her Life* (National Theatre) **131–2**, 133
   as co-director of Forest Fringe 149
   Criticism & Love newsletter 73
   foundations of UK blogosphere 18
   as a maker of experimental performance 222
   on Michael Billington **116–17**
   on playtexts as memorials 25–6
file-sharing (*see* copyright infringement)
Foley Got Comped (Jess Foley) 41
Foley, Jess 41–3
Foss, Roger *117–20*
Foster, Ian 31, 45–70, 77
Freeman, Matthew 15, 19, 83, **105–6**, **205–7**, 209
free tickets 47, 50, 63–4, 73
Fricker, Karen 11
Fuel Theatre 22
funding
   Arts Council England (ACE) 22, 22 n.8, 26, 67, 74, 119, 154
   British Council 75
   crowdfunding 9, 11, 41, 42–3, 66–7, 74

   cuts to arts funding 22, 27
   donors, members, and subscribers 11, 19, 42, 43, 202, 203, 204, 206
   perceived inequalities of arts funding 27, 126
   venue finances 44, 112–15
Furness, Corinne 31, 84, **120–2**

Gardner, Lyn 146, 170, 240, 245
Garrett, Jesse James 4
Gasp! (Laura Axelrod) 15
George Jean Nathan Award for Dramatic Criticism 29
Get The Chance 58, 58 n.1
GIFs 38, 77, 83, 84
Global Mail 33
Gob Squad *164*
GoCardless 42
Goode, Chris
   on the decline of theatre blogging 71
   foundations of UK blogosphere 18
   as a maker of experimental performance 222
   Open House 34, **107–10**, *138–44*, 147
   on the social and economic context of blogging 15
   as a subject of embedded criticism 34, 75
   The Forest and The Field 163
   on *Three Kingdoms* (Lyric Hammersmith) 227, 242, 244, 245, 249, 250
   on writing for theatre 23–34, 25–7, 28, **93–101**, *101–4*
Google Ads 67
Google Analytics 68
Google Reader 73
Grehan, Helena 8, 11, 12, 21 n.7
Greig, David 17, 38 n.22, 157
Grote, Jason 15, 19, 206, 208
The Guardian
   article by Kayvan Novak 186
   articles by Michael Billington 10, 116–17
   coverage of *My Name Is Rachel Corrie* cancellation 18
   coverage of Edward Albee's *LA Weekly* interview 23
   as an example of mainstream media 3
   Maddy Costa's career at 33
   Matt Trueman reviewing previews article 31
   'Noises Off' column 28–9, 150
   'Theatre blog' section 25–6, 25 n.12, 240–1, 243, 245
Guerrilla Semiotics (Jana Perkovic) 16, 29

Habermas, Jürgen 26, 26 n.13
Halavais, Alexander 7
Hall, Don 15, 84, **122–3**
Hall, Justin 4 n.1
Hamilton (Broadway) 83
Hammerstein, Dena 20
Handke, Peter 20
Handspring Puppet Company 22
Harewood, Jamal 40
Harold Hobson Drama Critic Award 33
Harrison, Daniella 45–70

265

Index

Harvey, Neal 8, 11, 12, 21 n.7
hashtagging 29 n.15
Hawks In The Wings 44
Haydon, Andrew
    on embedded criticism 34, **144–50**, 150, 151, 156
    on the history of online theatre criticism 11, 26
    interest in European theatre 35
    response to Eve Nicol's *Edinburgh Furinge Reviews* 40
    on reviewing previews 32
    as a theatre blogging gatekeeper 28, 124
    on *Three Kingdoms* (Lyric Hammersmith) 36, 38, **219–24**, 228, 232, 240–6, 249, 250
Herrera, Brian 74
Hii, Ming-Zhu 21, 44
Hillman, Melissa **196–8**
Histriomatrix (David Cote) 15
'hits' (web visitor stats) 31–2, 68–70, 121 (*see also* search engine optimization)
Holmes, Sean 38, 241
HOME, Manchester 171, 172
Horwitz, Andy 34–5, 34 n.21
Howard, Jane 29
HowlRound 72, 160
Hughes, Tom 73
Hunka, George
    on the decline of theatre blogging 71
    foundations of US blogosphere 15
    on Ming-Zhu Hii and Short + Sweet festival 21 n.7
    on *My Name Is Rachel Corrie* cancellation 19, 205, **209–11**, 211
    responding to Jill Dolan's 'critical generosity' 160
    on writing for theatre 23, 95, 96, *101–4*
Hutton, Dan 38 n.22, **157–9**
Hytner, Nicholas 27, 112, 113, 117, 132

Icke, Robert 38
immersive and interactive theatre 12, 22, 27, *117–20*
The Independent 133
Independent Theater Bloggers Association (ITBA) 41, 41 n.23
Instagram 59
interactive theatre (*see* immersive and interactive theatre)
internet
    early forums, chat rooms, newsgroups 6, 13, 38, 83
    linguistic conventions 60, 60 n.2, 72, 76–7, 83
    mainstreaming/expansion of 3, 4, 6, 28
    memes 38–40, 71, 83
    monetization of 6, 10–11, 66
    and orality 12–13
    as a platform 6–7
internet service providers (ISPs) 75–6
Interval Drinks (Natasha Tripney) 18
In The Depths of Dead Love (The Printroom at the Coronet) 43, *188–96*
IP addresses 21

Isherwood, Charles *122–3*, 160, 162
Israeli–Palestinian conflict 18–20, 202, 203, 206, 213–17
    (*see also My Name Is Rachel Corrie*)

Jacobs, Leonard 40
Jackson, Kevin 45–70
James Hammerstein Productions 20
Jamespeak (James Comtois) 15
Jancovich, Mark 10 n.7
JargonScout 4
Jews and Judaism 18–20, 92, 180–5, 202, 203–4, 213–17
    (*see also* diversity; Israeli–Palestinian conflict)
Jones, Chris 10 n.8
JournalSpace 15
Jubilee (Chris Goode & Company) 34

Kabak, Walter *207–8*
Kavanagh, Katharine 41, 45–70, 74 n.5
Kene, Arinzé 44
Kneehigh Theatre 33
Kressly, Laura 41
Kushner, Tony 19, 199, 205, 208

labour 42, 43, 66, 68, 74, 105, *110–11*
Laera, Margherita 73 n.3
LA Weekly 23, 95
Letts, Quentin 37, 133, 146, 230
Lew, Mike 83, **178–80**
libel 21 n.7, 81 (*see also* defamation)
Lippy (Dead Centre) 164
literacy 12–13
Little Achievements (Tom Hughes) 73
livecasting 3
Lloyd Webber, Andrew 29–30, 30 n.16, *113–15*, 135–8
London Theatre Bloggers initiative 29 n.15
Love, Catherine
    on critical distance 83, **155–7**
    on *Three Kingdoms* (Lyric Hammersmith) 36, 38, **224–9**, 232, 233, **246–51**
Love Never Dies (West End) 29–30, 82, *134–8*
Lovesong (Frantic Assembly) 155–7
Luthra, Manan 33
Lyric Hammersmith, London 24, 35, 38, 82, 156, 219–51

MacArthur, Michelle 12
Macmillan, Duncan 17
magazine-style review sites 9, 17, 49, 71, 72–3, 84
MailChimp 73
Mail on Sunday 24 n.9
mainstream arts journalism
    decline of 9–11, 22, 42–3, 48
    hierarchies within 7, 9, 44
    moving online 10–11, 25 n.12
    practices of 14, 31, 37, *122–3*
Mahfouz, Sabrina 44, 44 n.25, 77
Manthorpe, Rowland 10

Index

Marx, Karl 11
McDonald, Harry 83, **198–201**
McDougall, Ellen 38
McKenna, Aileen 29
McMillan, Joyce 150
Meadwell, Stacey 29, 45–70
Medium 8
Melbourne Festival *115–16*
memes (*see* internet)
mental health (*see* wellbeing)
Merholz, Peter 4
MetaFilter 5, 5 n.2
#MeToo 37 (*see also* women)
Metropolitan Opera, New York 3
'micro-blogging' 7
Miller, Paul 18
Minamore, Bridget 44, 44 n.25, 77
Minetta Lane Theater, New York 20
Mink Tails (Ming-Zhu Hii) 21
misogyny (*see* women)
Misty (Bush Theatre) 44
Mitchell, Katie 22, 24–5, 27, 82, 117, *131–4*, 220, 232, 244
Mono No Aware (Jana Perkovic) 16
The Morning After (Chris Boyd) 16
Morris, Tom 22
Motta, Laura 29
Mr Excitement (Mark Armstrong) 15
Muhammad, Zarina 60 n.2
Munich Kammerspiele 35, 219, 229, 233
musical theatre 29–31, 112–13, 114, 134–8, 180–5
MusicOMH 18
My London Life (Paul Miller) 18
My Name Is Rachel Corrie (Royal Court Theatre) 18–22, 77, 82, 83, *202–18*
My Theatre Mates 40

The Nation 20
National Student Drama Festival (NSDF) 28, 33, 61, 123, 149, 150
National Theatre, London
    2007–2008 season announcement 95
    Attempts On Her Life 24–5, *131–4*
    audiences at 127
    bloggers reviewing previews at 31, 65
    Encore Theatre Magazine coverage of 17
    Kenneth Tynan's departure from 94
    Nicholas Hytner 'dead white men' comments 27
    NT Live livecasting 3
    The History Boys 97
    Trevor Nunn's artistic directorship of *112–13*
    West End Whingers on *Death and the King's Horseman* 38 n.22
National Theatre of Scotland 157
National Theatre Wales 58 n.1
naturalism 24, 36, 38, 104, 221, 236, 239, 242
neoliberalism (*see* capitalism)
Nestruck, Kelly 28

net neutrality 75–6
Network of Independent Critics (NIC) 41, 44
newsletters
    electronic 72, 73–4
    print 16
New Theatre Royal, Portsmouth 44
new writing (*see* playwriting)
New York Stage Review 10 n.6
New York Theatre Workshop (NYTW) 18–20, 82, 175, *202–18*
New York Times
    Ben Brantley reviews 31 n.17, 160, 162
    Charles Isherwood reviews 122–3, 160, 162
    coverage of celebrity casting 176
    coverage of *My Name Is Rachel Corrie* cancellation 18–20, 204, 207
    coverage of women in theatre 90–1, 175
    as an example of mainstream media 3, 53
Nguyen, Mary 45–70, 77
Nicola, James 18, 19, 202–4, 208–9
Nicol, Eve 38–40, 77
Noises Off (*The Guardian*) 28, 29, 150
Noises Off (NSDF) 28
No Plain Jane (Jane Howard) 29
Norman, Molly 45–70, 77
Northcott Theatre, Exeter 22
Notional Theatre 25, 95
Nübling, Sebastian 35–8, *219–51*
Nunn, Trevor 82, *112–13*, 233

'objectivity' 9, 11, 35, 40, 76, 77, 83, 123, 148, 151, *155–7*, 160, 162–3, 247
One Hundred Years of Jason Grote (Jason Grote) 15
One Writer and His Dog (David Eldridge) 18
Ong, Walter 13
On Theatre and Politics (Matthew Freeman) 15
Open Diary 5
Open House (*see* Goode, Chris)
O, Poor Robinson Crusoe! (Stephen Sharkey) 18
orality 12–13
Orange Tree Theatre, London 22, 38
O'Reilly, Tim 6–7
Orr, Jake 34, 144, 147, 150, 243
Osborne, John 17 n.3
Ought To Be Clowns (Ian Foster) 31

Paddock, Terri 41
Pai, Ajit 76
'Paint Never Dries' (*see Love Never Dies*)
Parabasis (Isaac Butler) 15, 206
Parachute of a Playwright (Ben Ellis) 18
participation 141–4
Pataphysical Science (Linda Buchwald) 29
Patel, Vinay 73, **185–8**
Patreon 42, 43, 66–7, 74
payment 31, 41–3, 65–7, 74–5, 105, 110 (*see also* capitalism; funding; labour)
paywalls 11

267

Index

Peard, Anne-Marie 45–70
Pearson, Deborah 82, **92–3**
The Peking Duck (Richard Burger) 116
Performance Space 122, New York 34 n.20
Perkovic, Jana 16, 29, 33
permalinks 6
Phantom of The Opera (West End) 29–31, 114, 134–8
Pinter, Harold 17 n.3, 35, 221
Pitas 5
Playbox Theatre, Melbourne 16
The Playgoer (Garrett Eisler) 15, 19–20, 204, 206
Playhouse Theatre, London 20
The Play's The Thing UK (Laura Kressly) 41
playwriting
 and the body *211–17*
 the playwright's intent *196–8*, 228
 playwrights' relationship with directors *85–92*, 226, 228, 232, 247–8
 as primary creative act in theatremaking 22–4, 25–7, *93–104*
 realities and practices of 14, *105*, 222, 226, 229
 rules for *105–7*
 supporting structures of 22, 22 n.8, 23, 112
podcasting 9, 27, 59
political theatre 18–20, *125–8*, 202, 204–5, 206, 210–11
Poll, Melissa 37
Pomona (Orange Tree Theatre) 38
Postcards From The Gods (Andrew Haydon) 26
Post:Critical (Diana Damian Martin) 243
post-dramatic theatre 35, 38
PR
 bloggers' relationship to 10, 41, 50–1, 61, 63–5, 69, 75, 134
 from New York Theater Workshop regarding *My Name Is Rachel Corrie* 19–20, 210
 press nights 147
 review embargoes 32
 sponsored posts 75
Prescott, Paul 11
preview performances 29, 30–2, 63–5
The Printroom at the Coronet, London 43, 189, 193, 194, 195
The Privileged (Jamal Harewood) 40
profanity 42, 77
professionalism 42–3, 48, 74
programming 24, *115–16*
pseudonyms 17
public relations (*see* PR)
public sphere 26 n.13, 71
publishing 81–2
Punchdrunk 22, 97
Punshon, Sarah 38, **238–9**, 245–6, 249
Pursued By A Bear (podcast) (*see Exeunt Magazine*)
Purves, Libby 10 n.6
Pyra Labs 5

'quality' 76–7
Quill, Erin 43, **188–95**

race (*see also* diversity)
 Critics of Colour Collective 44, 57, 77
 marginalization of POC 15, 28, 126
 political attacks on POC 71
 representation of British Asians *185–8*
 ticket sales for work by POC 126
 work about race by white people *178–80*
 yellowface casting *188–96*
Rachel's Words 20, 77
Radosavljević, Duška 12–13, 77
Ravenhill, Mark 24
Really Useful Group 30 n.16
Rebellato, Dan 16–17, 84, **229–33**, 248 (*see also Encore Theatre Magazine*)
The Reduced Michael Billington 147, 147 n.9
redundancies (*see* criticism)
rehearsal 85–6, 89–90, *107–10*, *138–44*, 151–3
Reid, Kerry 123
Reid, Robert 72 n.2
Revolt. She Said. Revolt Again. (RSC) *168–71*
'RevStan' (*see* Meadwell, Stacey)
Rheingold, Howard 6, 6 n.4
'rhetorical action' 12, 77
Rice, Emma 27
Rickman, Alan 18, 20, 202, 203, 206
rickrolling 15
Riot Act (Chris Goode & Company) 34
Road (Royal Court Theatre) 83, *198–201*
Rogers, Mac 15, **86–8**, 89, 90, 205
Roundhouse, London 44 n.25
Royal Court Theatre, London
 Adler and Gibb 38
 appointment of Vicky Featherstone 243
 Attempts On Her Life 133
 Encore Theatre Magazine coverage of 17
 My Name Is Rachel Corrie 18, 202–11
 Road 198–201
 Teh Internet is Serious Business 40
Royal Exchange Theatre, Manchester 172
Royal Shakespeare Company (RSC) 169, 195, 233
RSS feeds 6, 73

Sadler, Victoria 43–4
Salmon, Shanine 45–70
'Sans Taste' 31
Schimmelpfennig, Roland 33, 145
The Scotsman 150
The Seagull (Belvoir Theatre) 32
search engine optimization (SEO) 7, 32, 69–70
Second Life 98
Secret Theatre (Lyric Hammersmith) 38
selfies 40
Semper, Ene-Liis 35–8, 219–51
Serratore, Nicole 29, 42
sexism (*see* women)
Shakespeare 11, 103, 163, 176, 197
Sharkey, Stephen 18
Shenton, Mark 10, 24 n.9, 40

268

Index

Sherman Theatre, Cardiff 58
Shinn, Christopher 20, 205
Shit On Your Play (Jane Simmons and Manan Luthra) 32–3
Shopping and Fucking (Lyric Hammersmith) 24
Short + Sweet (festival) 21
Shunt 22, 97
Sillitoe, Alan 17 n.3
Silva, Hannah 84
Simmons, Jane 32–3
Simpson, Janice C. 45–70
Slow Learner (Mac Rogers) 15
Smith, Marc 6 n.4
Smith, Molly 180–5
Snapchat 40, 125
social media 7, 14, 29, 35, 37, 59, 71, 73 (*see also* Twitter)
Soyinka, Wole 38 n.22
SOYP: The People's Theatre Advisor (see *Shit On Your Play*)
The Spectator 26 n.13
speech (*see* orality)
spelling 84 (*see also* internet, linguistic conventions)
Spencer, Charles 27, 117
Spiderman: Turn Off The Dark (Broadway) 31, 176
sponsored posts 75
The Stage 10, 17, 33, 53, 71, 117, 123, 124, 145
stage management 167
States of Deliquescence (Maddy Costa) 33–4
Stephens, Simon 35–8, *219–51*
Stevens, Tassos 147, 242, 247
Stone, Simon 32–3
The Strange Undoing of Prudencia Hart (National Theatre of Scotland) 38 n.22, *157–60*
subcultural capital 10 n.7
Summerhall, Edinburgh 44
Sunday Express 10, 24 n.9
Sunday Telegraph 24 n.9
Superfluities (George Hunka) 15, 206, 207
Supple, Augusta 33
swearing (*see* profanity)
Swift, Alex 82, **110–11**
Sydney Theatre Company 32–3
Szymkowicz, Adam **105**, 213

tagging 8, 32, 70
The Tatler 26 n.13
Taylor, Paul 133
Teachout, Terry 15
Teater NO99, Tallinn 35, 219, 233
Teh Internet is Serious Business (Royal Court Theatre) 40
'text-based' theatre (*see* playwriting)
textspeak (*see* internet, linguistic conventions)
Theatre ad Infinitum *155–7*
Theatrecat (Libby Purves) 10 n.6
TheatreClique (Brian Herrera) 74
TheaterTalk (PBS) 30

Theatre and Ideas (Scott Walters) 15
Theatre and Writing (Benjamin Yeoh) 18
Theatre Notes (Alison Croggon) 16, 72 n.2
theatre training 23, 82, *92–3*, 97–8
The Theatrical Board 56, 72
This Last Tempest (Uninvited Guests) *162–4*
Thompson's Bank of Communicable Desire (Chris Goode) 18
Thompson's Live (podcast) (Chris Goode) 27
Thornton, Sarah 10 n.7
Thorpe, Vanessa 32 n.18
Three Kingdoms (Lyric Hammersmith, Munich Kammerspiele, Teater NO99) 35–8, 71, 77, 82, 83, *219–51*
ticket prices 31, 32, 121, 127
ticket sales agencies 67, 75
Time Out Chicago 10 n.8
Time Out New York 15
The Times 10 n.6, 27
Tinder 3
TinyLetter 73
Tompkins, Joanne 8, 11, 12, 21 n.7
Toronto Star 11
Translunar Paradise (Theatre ad Infinitum) *155–7*
The Trial (Young Vic Theatre) 40, *165–8*
Tripney, Natasha 18, 28, 42
True Brits (Vaults festival) *185–8*
Trueman, Matt
    becoming a professional critic 40–1
    on the decline of theatre blogging 71, 123
    on immersive and interactive theatre **117–20**
    on reviewing previews 31–2, *120–2*
    on *Three Kingdoms* (Lyric Hammersmith) 36, **233–7**, 248
    writing the *Guardian*'s 'Noises Off' column 28, 150
Trujillo, Dan 15
Tufekci, Zeynep 13
Tumblr 123
Twine 40
Twitter
    arguments on 64, 160, 168, 169
    launch of 7
    making the theatre blogosphere more inclusive 29, 44
    as a platform for discussion 36, 125, 227, 228, 238, 240, 243, 249
    as a promotional tool for bloggers 50, 74
Tynan, Kenneth 94, 116, 167

The Umbrellas of Cherbourg (Kneehigh) 33
Uncle Vanya (HOME) *171–4*
Uninvited Guests 140, *162–4*

van Hove, Ivo 38, 209
Variety 53
Varney, James 45–70, 83, 125, **171–4**
Vaughan, Megan 36, 40, 82, 163, **165–8**, *237–8*, 246
Venal Scene (Dan Trujillo) 15

269

Index

verbatim theatre 210, 213
Verizon 76
View From the Cheap Seat (Shanine Salmon) 60
Vile, Gareth K. 82, **164**
Viner, Katherine 18, 20
Vire, Kris 10 n.8
'virtual communities' 6, 6 n.4
vlogging 7, 9
volunteer-run review sites (*see* magazine-style review sites)

Walker Rettberg, Jill 5, 5 n.3
Walker, Tim 24 n.9
Wall Street Journal 15
Walters, Scott 15, 205
War Horse (National Theatre) 22
Wastwater (Royal Court Theatre) 220, 222, 235, 236, 244
'Web 2.0' 5–7, 15, 35
'Webcowgirl' 28, 31
Weinert-Kendt, Rob 15
Weiss, Hedy 10 n.8, 123
wellbeing 43, 44
West End Whingers ('Andrew and Phil') 18, 28, 29–30, 38 n.22, 47, 82, **134–8**
Western Society (Gob Squad) *164*
West Yorkshire Playhouse, Leeds 121, 138, 139, 147
Whatsapp 3, 40, 45–70
What's On Stage 24, 25, 30 n.16, 37, 41, 134
The White Pube (Gabrielle de la Puente and Zarina Muhammad) 60, 60 n.2, 61
The Wicked Stage (Rob Weinert-Kendt) 15
Wilkinson, Chris 28

Wired 10
Witness 72
women (*see also* diversity)
   blog criticism by 28–9, 56–7
   directors 24, 27, 83, *175–8*
   feminism 12, 73, 83, 127, 160–2, 168–9, 178, 180, 246, 249
   playwrights 44, *90–2*, 106, 175, 196–7
   sexism and misogyny (other than related to *Three Kingdoms*) 15, 16 n.2, 20–1, 24, 27, *90–2*, 127, 163, *168–71*, 173, 174, *175–8*
   sexual abuse and harassment (other than related to *Three Kingdoms*) *168–71*, 177
   in *Three Kingdoms* (Lyric Hammersmith) 37–8, 83–4, 223–4, 226–8, 230, 233, *238–9*, 242–3, 244–5, 245–6, 249–51
Wong Davies, Ava 45–70, 77, 82, 84, **125–8**
working conditions 14–15, 23, 31–2, 38, 55, 65–8
'World Wide Web' 6
The Writer (Almeida Theatre) *125–8*
Wyver, Kate **168–71**

Xiao Mina, An 13

Yates, Daniel B. 84, 228, 232, 242
yellowface casting (*see* casting)
Yeoh, Benjamin 18
York Loh, Daniel 43, **195–6**
Young Vic Theatre, London 40, 165
YouTube 7, 58

zinemaking 9, 34
Zuckerberg, Mark 15